£10

7/6

FRANCIS JEFFREY
OF
THE EDINBURGH REVIEW

LORD JEFFREY
1773-1850

From the painting by Colvin Smith, R.S.A., in the Scottish National Portrait Gallery

FRANCIS JEFFREY

OF

THE EDINBURGH REVIEW

BY

JAMES A. GREIG

M.A., D.Litt.

OLIVER AND BOYD

EDINBURGH: TWEEDDALE COURT

LONDON: 98 GREAT RUSSELL STREET, W.C.

1948

FIRST PUBLISHED 1948

PRINTED AND PUBLISHED IN GREAT BRITAIN BY
OLIVER AND BOYD LTD., EDINBURGH

TO
H.B.G.

CONTENTS

INTRODUCTION

I FIRST became interested in Francis Jeffrey a goodly number of years ago when, being required to write, as part of my work for an examination, a " dissertation " on a theme selected by myself, I chose for this purpose Jeffrey's critical writings. What impelled me to make that choice I cannot tell now ; but an effect of the investigation it involved was to create in my mind a belief—which subsequent study has deepened, and which, though it has been Jeffrey's fate to be knocked about the mazzard quite considerably on occasion, chiefly on account of his opposition to Wordsworth, I am not alone in holding—that his ideas are worthy of more attention than has sometimes been given to them.

Among the numerous charges that were made against Jeffrey in the later nineteenth century—his critic described it as " perhaps the most damaging accusation that can be brought against Jeffrey "—was one of " inability to read and interpret the age in which he lived." I have, as I hope will shortly be evident, put myself to a certain amount of trouble in an attempt to gain some understanding of Jeffrey's period. I am afraid, however, that I too am with Jeffrey in being unable to submit anything that I should care to think of as even approaching an " interpretation " of it. I am too conscious of belonging to a world in which two witnesses can seldom be found to describe in identical fashion so simple a thing as an ordinary street accident, and in which even the acutest of observers may sometimes be discovered asking that the salt-cellar be passed to him when all the while it lies directly under his nose. Moving through the records of an age appears to me like journeying through a countryside in which one is aware that a single hedge or a single row of cottages may contain enough material to absorb the study of a lifetime, and in which one knows that, even among the things one has done one's best to examine, there cannot but be much that one has missed. I do not know how one determines upon which out of an age's innumerable activities attention ought to be focussed in order to " interpret " it ; or who is to be regarded as qualified to pass final judgment upon the correctness of any interpretation that is offered ; or what length of time should be permitted to elapse before any interpretation can be considered to be final : there may be much in what we call an age the importance of which may not be apparent until long thereafter. These are not expressions of modesty. They are suggestions that, where such matters are concerned, we are all of us in pretty much the same boat.

Another late-nineteenth and early-twentieth-century critic declared that " the very word ' limitation ' suggests the name of Jeffrey, in the sphere of criticism." Again I feel, however, that if there were to be substituted for the name of Jeffrey in that statement the name of any one of us or even of any age it would remain reasonably accurate. Such an assertion indicates as a rule, it appears to me, merely that the limitations of the critic are different from those of the person or the age he is criticising. Catholicity of taste and openness of mind have, it is true, been regarded as important critical virtues in the days that have followed Jeffrey's : and they are, in certain circumstances, undeniably excellent qualities. There may be times, however, in which it may seem that even those who pride themselves on such qualities must decide whether they are for or against certain things. A culture that is obsessed by a fear of narrow-mindedness may end by being mindless.

Jeffrey was certainly not mindless in this sense of the word. His criticisms of certain aspects of his age's doings were not ambiguous. What we have to ask is whether these criticisms were an effect of circumscriptions in his taste or intelligence or if there was reason behind them. It seems to me that Jeffrey's judgment of his age was as able and as significant as was that of most of his successors in criticism, and that he perceived more clearly than did the majority of these the perilous nature of the ground on which his generation were setting their feet.

These are obviously strong statements. How far they are justifiable must be for the following pages to show. They go near to suggesting that everyone was travelling on the wrong road except our Francis. This criticism might be more cogent were it clearly demonstrable that we, Jeffrey's successors, have been travelling on indubitably right roads. I imagine, however, that a number of us must be beginning to think it is time culture wiped its spectacles and looked ruthlessly at the things it has been doing.[1] There is probably no period in human history in which it has had so wide opportunities of contact with the

[1] This MS. was completed before the end of the war of 1939-45.

masses of all nations as it has had in these latter days ; and there is probably no period in history in which its influence has been, in the ultimate, more feeble. I do not think it can remain for ever content to chat amiably to the young—while the technical experts work out increasingly cunning ways of killing them—on the short stages between the cemeteries. Surely, one of these days, there will have to be a re-orientation of its activities. It seems to me that in such a re-orientation the Jeffreyan viewpoint may be worthy of consideration.

The writer who spoke of Jeffrey's limitations described his critical position as " puzzling." One reason for this lies in the fact that Jeffrey's ideas were spread out over reviews written throughout a period of more than a quarter of a century. Before I could arrive at what seemed to me a reasonable comprehension of his position I found it necessary to examine not only his volumes of collected *Contributions to the Edinburgh Review*, but his unreprinted articles as well.

In order to understand Jeffrey it is necessary also, I think, to examine the works with which he dealt—and also others' judgments both of these works and of him—from his particular angle, an angle different from that which later criticism has made orthodox. The following pages contain, accordingly, not only a study of a man, but also an attempt to look from his viewpoint at the literary activities of an era.

I am afraid it follows that these pages will be of little use to any who desire to be presented, in volumes of this kind, with concisely expressed, predigested, and easily assimilable ideas about past authors. It will become increasingly evident as we proceed that to attempt to provide such ideas would be to depart from the viewpoint adopted. But I believe that those who are willing to give a little time to the consideration of such matters will find, in the excerpts that have been made from Jeffrey's criticisms, suggestions about critical standards and methods, about literature, and about life in general, that are provocative of thought. I should like to think that there may be found in these pages something that may help towards a fuller understanding of the selections from Jeffrey's writings that have been made by others. Students, it would give me pleasure to believe, investigating other matters concerning nineteenth-century literature, may find here indications of the exact places in the *Contributions* and in the early numbers of the

Edinburgh Review in which Jeffrey expressed not negligible opinions about the chief authors and the main literary problems of his day. The arrangement of the study has been governed in part by a desire to make this information readily accessible.

Jeffrey, it will be seen, declared in the preface to his *Contributions* that the *Edinburgh* professed to go deeply into the principles upon which its judgments were to be rested. One of his governing principles was implied in that statement. Everything had to be laid before the reader. It will be found that his reasoning made this practice important. His method has been pursued accordingly in this study. It is presented as a case. The reader is asked to judge throughout. The grounds for every assertion have been indicated with particular care in order to make the task of checking all conclusions as easy as possible. It will be found to follow also that complete agreement with Jeffrey's conclusions or with mine is neither expected nor regarded as desirable. His conclusions, and mine in part, are drawn from the reasoning of a party that has been long out of power. All that is asked is that where there is disagreement this be not merely a shouting with the crowd—that it be based upon evidence and not upon what Jeffrey described as the weakest of all arguments, authority.

My thinking, like that of all perpetrators of studies of this kind, has been stimulated from many sources. Frequently too, as is no doubt common, I have imagined I had stumbled upon lines of thought of my own only to discover later that others had had the same thoughts before me. I have done my best to acknowledge all my important debts. If I have failed anywhere in this respect, and if I have been anywhere inaccurate in my facts, these things have occurred in spite of my utmost endeavours to avoid them.

Like all perpetrators of studies of this kind also, I have personal kindnesses to acknowledge. Dr Malcolm of the Solicitors' Supreme Courts Library, Edinburgh, sent me, in the kindliest of letters, information about Jeffrey statues and portraits. A gentleman I have never met searched the booksellers' shops of New York for some months in order to procure for me a copy of Professor Gates's *Three Studies in Literature* which, as it was published in 1899, was difficult to obtain. Some years ago I wrote to the English Department of Berlin University, without having been furnished with any sort of introduction, to ask if they could give me some information about the thesis on Jeffrey which was composed there by Elsner in 1908. A member of the University staff traced a copy of the work to a bookseller in Leipzig and, writing to tell me I could purchase it there, remarked, "We are glad to be able to give you that notice after such a long time." Mr R. Douglas Croall, the present tenant of Craigcrook Castle, Jeffrey's former home near Edinburgh, made me a generous gift of the rare and beautifully-printed *Lord Jeffrey and Craigcrook* by Taylor and Moncreiff. I must acknowledge with gratitude the unfailing patience and courtesy of the staff of Dundee Public Library.

I am deeply indebted to the Carnegie Trust for the Universities of Scotland for a generous guarantee against loss on publication.

Selections from Jeffrey's essays have been edited in later times by Professor Lewis E. Gates (1894) and Professor D. Nichol Smith (1910 and 1928). His essays on Poets and Poetry have been published in Routledge's New Universal Library. The names of numerous other writers—I think I have noted all the most important of them—who have touched upon his criticisms will be found hereafter.

CHIEF DATES IN JEFFREY'S LIFE

1773 (23rd October).   Born in Edinburgh.
1781-7.   Attended High School of Edinburgh.
1787-9.   Attended Glasgow University.
1789-91.   Attended Law Classes in Edinburgh.
1791-2.   At Queen's College, Oxford.
1792.   Joined Speculative Society.
1792-4.   Attended Classes in Edinburgh in Law and History.
1794.   Admitted to the Bar.
1801.   Married Catherine Wilson.   (d. 1805.)
1802.   Foundation of *Edinburgh Review*.
1803.   Became editor of *Edinburgh Review*.
1813.   Married Charlotte Wilkes.
1820.   Lord Rector of Glasgow University.
1829.   Dean of Faculty of Advocates.
1829.   Resigned editorship of *Edinburgh Review*.
1830.   Lord Advocate.
1834.   Raised to the Bench.
1843(4).   Published *Contributions to the Edinburgh Review*.
1850 (26th January).   Death of Jeffrey.

CHAPTER I

CONTEMPORARY WITNESSES

" THE [advocate's] gown," remarked " Dr Peter Morris " in his
description of the Edinburgh of 1819, " is worn at this moment
by two persons, whom all the world must admit to have done
more than all the rest of their contemporaries put together, for
sustaining and extending the honours of the Scottish name—
both at home and abroad. You need scarcely be told, that I
speak of Mr W[alter] S[cott] and Mr J[effrey]." [1]

The words read a trifle oddly to-day. The part played by
Scott in the early years of the nineteenth century in extending
Scotland's reputation is indeed still widely recognised, both in
his own country and elsewhere. The " Scott Monument "
towers over Princes Street ; automobiles converge in multitudes,
in summer-time, upon the " Scott country " ; the poems and
novels of the " Author of *Waverley* " are still read, still have their
influence. But what is to be said of Jeffrey ? There is, it is
true, a " Jeffrey Street " in Edinburgh ; a tablet marks the
outer entrance to the flat at 18 Buccleuch Place where, in 1802,
was founded his once-famous periodical ; a statue and a bust
of him exist in Parliament House ; his portrait hangs in the
Scottish National Portrait Gallery. But how often does anyone
speak to-day of Francis Jeffrey as one who, at one time, played
an important part in sustaining and extending the honours of
the Scottish name ? " Probably Jeffrey," Gates observed, " is
now oftenest remembered for his unluckily haughty reprimand
to Wordsworth, ' This will never do ! '—a sentence which is
popularly taken to be an incontestable proof of critical
incapacity." [2] That was written by an American. I fancy,
however, that few even among Scotsmen nowadays know so
very much more about Jeffrey. " It is hardly possible," Gates
affirmed nevertheless, " to glance through the life of any literary
man of the early part of the century without chancing on evidence

---

[1] *Peter's Letters to his Kinsfolk*, " Second edition," v. 2, p. 8.
[2] *Three Studies in Literature*, Lewis E. Gates, 1899, p. 4. Gates is the only
authority later than Carlyle given for Jeffrey in the fourteenth edition of the
Encyclopædia Britannica.

A

of Jeffrey's popularity and prestige." [1] In his *Selections from the Essays of Francis Jeffrey* Gates quoted, in support of this, from Macaulay's *Life and Letters*, and from the *Reminiscences* of Thomas Carlyle, and remarked that Horner's nickname for Jeffrey, "King Jamfray," was not a misnomer. In his *Three Studies* Gates mentioned, in addition to this, that Jeffrey was "King Jamfray" also to Sydney Smith, quoted a sentence from Allan Cunningham, and added part of another, not entirely laudatory, from Talfourd, the editor of Charles Lamb. Nichol Smith, in speaking of Jeffrey's reputation in his own day, also quoted from Carlyle and Macaulay. As these contemporary opinions indicate, as well as Jeffrey's fame, the way in which he was then regarded, it may be helpful to look for a little, not only at some of the statements to which Gates and Nichol Smith have guided us, but also at some others.

It is evident that "Morris," in speaking thus in the same breath of Jeffrey and of Scott, was not saying anything that would appear to his readers at all out of the ordinary. This coupling of their names seems to have been simply a commonplace in the Edinburgh of the period. A candidate, ultimately successful, for the chair of Oriental languages in Edinburgh University, boasted, in 1812, that he was "so very fortunate as to enjoy the esteem both of Mr Scott and Mr Jeffrey,—one the greatest poet and the other the best critic in the kingdom." [2] "It would be as absurd," Mrs Grant of Laggan asserted in 1817, "for people who, in the most literal sense of the phrase, live by their wits, to enter into rivalry . . . with the great and wealthy, as it would be for these to try to excel Jeffrey in critical acumen, or Scott in poetry." [3] Cockburn writing, about 1830, his reminiscences of early nineteenth-century Edinburgh, spoke of Jeffrey, without dreaming for a moment of pausing to justify the phrase, as Scott's "twin star." [4] Lockhart, writing under his own name in his *Life of Scott*, echoed what he had said as "Dr Morris" by describing Scott and Jeffrey as "the two most distinguished men of letters whom Edinburgh produced in their time." [5] In 1814 Scott had found their reputations linking Jeffrey and himself in another way. It was, he told Morritt

---

[1] *Selections from Essays of Jeffrey*, 1894, p. viii.
[2] *Archibald Constable and his Literary Correspondents*, 1873, v. 1, p. 324.
[3] *Mem. and Corr. of Mrs Grant of Laggan*, v. 2, p. 172.
[4] *Memorials of his Time*, 1874 ed., p. 230.   [5] 1837 ed., v. 1, p. 178.

in that year, the " Edinburgh faith " of the moment that *Waverley*, which had just been published, had come from the pen of the editor of the *Edinburgh Review*. " So you see," he commented, smiling no doubt as he wrote the words, " the unknown infant is like to come to preferment." [1]

The young wife of John Wilson described Jeffrey, in a letter written in the second decade of the century, as a " horrid little man " but—the value of the statement is increased by the remark that preceded it—" held in as high estimation here as the Bible." [2] Even in *Blackwood's*, though one of the magazine's avowed objects was to " baste the Blue-and-Yellow " till it was " black in the back," [3] one discerns every now and then, amid all the babel of " bamming " bullyragging and thwackings light and heavy with which it accompanied its campaigns against its opponents—among whom, naturally, the conductor of the rival periodical was to be numbered [4]—a note of pride in the reputation of the " clever old body," as " North " called him in the number for December 1821,[5] the editor of the *Edinburgh Review*. Jeffrey was the " familiar spirit " of the *Chaldee Manuscript*, to whom Constable the man " crafty in counsel " had sold himself, and who had put " great might " into the " notable horn "—the *Review*—wherewith the Crafty one " ruled the nations." [6] " 'Tis not everybody," ODoherty remarked in the *Noctes* of January 1825, speaking of a change in the editorship of the *Quarterly*, " can play the Jeffrey." [7] The " Shepherd " of the *Noctes* alluded to Jeffrey as a man " proud, and justly proud, o' the rank in literature that his genius has won him." [8] " North," on another Ambrosian night, spoke of Jeffrey as " perhaps, on the whole, the most philosophic critic of his age, and, beyond all comparison, the most eloquent orator of his country." To " much of that eulogium " the " Opium Eater," the " Shepherd " and " Tickler " found it necessary on this occasion to " demur." " Well, gentlemen," replied " North," " demur away ; but such for many years has been my opinion, and 'tis the opinion of all

[1] *Life of Scott*, Lockhart, v. 3, p. 132.
[2] *Memoir of John Wilson*, by Mrs Gordon, 1879 ed., p. 123.
[3] *Noctes Ambrosianæ*, ed. Ferrier, 1864 ed., v. 3, p. 183.
[4] As, for example, in the prophecy that he would " be remembered only by the poring and industrious John Nicholses (honoured be the name) of the next century." V. 14, p. 701.
[5] V. 10, p. 492.
[6] *Noctes*, v. 4, pp. 309, 299.
[7] *Blackwood's*, v. 17, p. 122.
[8] *Noctes*, v. 1, p. 265.

Scotland." [1] "Tickler", in the number for August 1831, ventured the opinion that "Tom Macaulay" put him "more in mind of the Jeffrey of ten years ago, than did the Jeffrey *ipsissimus* of *hodie*." "You pay Mr Macaulay," commented "North," "a high compliment—the highest, I think, he has ever met with." [2] In 1832, three years after Jeffrey's retirement from the editorship of the *Edinburgh*, "Tickler" remarked that now "the weeds of his mind are dead—the flowers are immortal. . . . His is a brilliant name in the literature of Scotland." [3] "It is a service of honour and duty," the *North British Review* remarked in its first number (1844), "as well as of gratification, to introduce our efforts in the cause of sound literature by some notice of this remarkable collection"—Jeffrey's *Contributions to the Edinburgh Review*—"and to consider what instruction we may derive in our self-imposed labours from the writings of the greatest living master of our art." [4] In an article written for the *Witness* for 30th January 1850, four days after Jeffrey's death, Hugh Miller described him as "a man who for nearly half a century has enjoyed European celebrity as first in the realms of criticism." Later in the same essay, speaking of Jeffrey's literary contributions to the *Edinburgh Review*, "In this his peculiar province," Miller continued, "he took his place, we have no hesitation in saying, as the first British critic of the age. He had his prejudices and his deficiencies, and occasionally . . . he committed, as in the case of Wordsworth, grave mistakes ; but, take him all in all, where, we ask, is the critic of the present century who is to be placed in the scale against Francis Jeffrey ? " [5] "We do not much fear," stated *Tait's Edinburgh Magazine* three months later, "the charge of partiality or provincialism in ranking Francis Jeffrey as one of the greatest lights and ornaments of our race." [6] Cockburn, Jeffrey's friend and biographer, does not seem to have been expressing solely his own opinion when he opened his *Life of Lord Jeffrey* with the following resounding sentence—"Francis Jeffrey, the greatest of

---

[1] *Noctes*, v. 2, p. 335.

[2] *Blackwood's*, v. 30, p. 410.

[3] *Noctes*, v. 3, p. 354.

[4] No. 1, p. 252. This article was written by Moncreiff, *Lord Jeffrey and Craigcrook*, p. 42.

[5] *Historical and Critical Essays*, 1873 ed., pp. 66, 73.

[6] V. 17, April 1850, p. 240. It was in this periodical that first appeared De Quincey's *Reminiscences of the Lake Poets*.

British critics, was born in Edinburgh on the 23rd of October 1773."

Much of this, if it stood alone, might be explained away, despite the assertion of *Tait's*, as expressing the naturally hyperbolical pride of a smallish city in the celebrity of one of its sons. It is not, however, difficult to show that high estimates of Jeffrey's importance were not peculiar to men whose mental horizons were bounded by Edinburgh. Lockhart was not merely an Edinburgh man. Lang observed that the thought of Jeffrey appeared constantly to occupy the mind of Lockhart, even against his will, just as the thought of Sir Walter " haunted the mind of Hazlitt," [1]—inspiring sometimes to praise, sometimes to attack. Lockhart spoke of Jeffrey, in the *Life of Scott*, as " the ablest and most influential critic of the time " ; [2] of the *Edinburgh's* review of *Marmion*—which Lang stated eighty-nine years after its publication that he still resented " like a personal affront " [3]—Lockhart wrote that " Jeffrey acquitted himself on this occasion in a manner highly creditable to his courageous sense of duty " ; [4] he described Jeffrey's review of *The Lady of the Lake* as " the best specimen of contemporary criticism on Scott's poetry " ; [5] and in the last article he wrote, or partly wrote and revised for the *Quarterly*, just before he resigned the editorship of that periodical, we read, side by side with a query as to how Jeffrey's writings would fare " 100, 200, 500 years hence," the assertion that Jeffrey's reviews are " remarkable productions, and it is to them that posterity must always refer for much of the ablest contemporary criticism upon the numerous men of genius that arose in his day." [6]

In the first chapter of Carlyle's *Reminiscences* we find a pleasant picture of Carlyle assisting his father to hoe turnips and entertaining him at the same time with an account of the character and manner of existence of the editor of the *Edinburgh Review*. " I would like to hear thee argue with him," was the old man's comment ; Carlyle said that his father " delighted always to hear good argument." [7] Jeffrey and Carlyle did, in fact, " argue " on some occasions ; Mrs Jeffrey, Carlyle tells us,

---

[1] *Life and Letters of Lockhart*, 1897, v. 1, p. 320.   [2] V. 2, p. 26.
[3] *Life and Letters of Lockhart*, v. 1, p. 171.   [4] V. 2, p. 146.   [5] V. 2, p. 296.
[6] *Life and Letters of Lockhart*, v. 2, p. 366. *Quarterly Review*, No. 181, pp. 125, 152.
[7] V. 1, pp. 11, 25.

referred laughingly to their " stormy sittings " together.[1] It is
clear there were many matters on which the two men did not
see eye to eye. At the same time, unresponsive though Carlyle
was to the work of many of his contemporaries, calling Lamb,
as he did, a " pitiful . . . Tomfool," and Shelley " a poor
creature," and describing Jane Austen's novels as " dishwashings,"
he does appear to have been impressed to some considerable
extent by Jeffrey.[2] D. A. Wilson considered that the work and
personality of Jeffrey had a definite influence on Carlyle.
Carlyle, Wilson asserted, " had early read the whole of the
Edinburgh Review from the beginning " ; the relationship between
the two men was, he declared, during the period of Carlyle's
early development, practically that of master and disciple ; it
was to Jeffrey's faithful censorship, he suggested, that Carlyle
owed much of the clearness of his style ; it was Jeffrey who,
perhaps, " as much as Voltaire or Goethe " moulded Carlyle's
opinion upon war ; it was Jeffrey who " by example more than
precept " taught Carlyle " the best of the gospel of silence " ;
Wilson even discerned in Teufelsdröckh something of the
character of Jeffrey.[3] It is possible that Jane Welsh Carlyle's
opinion of Jeffrey may have reflected to some degree that of
her husband. At anyrate we find her in 1845, sixteen years
after Jeffrey's resignation of the editorship of the Edinburgh,
still referring to the ex-reviewer as the " prince of critics." [4]
Carlyle's judgment of Jeffrey's work was, as might have been
expected from their arguments, like Lockhart's, a thing that
varied. We notice him, in 1828, describing the editor of the
Edinburgh Review, in a letter to Goethe, as " our grand ' British
Critic.' " [5] Later, in the Reminiscences, we find him writing of
Jeffrey : " He may be said to have begun the rash reckless
style of criticising everything in heaven and earth by appeal
to Molière's maid ; ' Do you like it ? ' ' Don't you like it ? ' a
style which in hands more and more inferior to that sound-
hearted old lady and him, has since grown gradually to such
immeasurable length among us ; and he himself is one of the

[1] Rem , v. 2, p. 41.
[2] Thomas Carlyle, J. A. Froude, 1882, v. 2, p. 209. Carlyle at his Zenith,
D. A. Wilson, pp. 110, 13.
[3] Carlyle to the French Revolution, Wilson, pp. 64, 115, 84-5, Pref., 112, 182.
[4] Carlyle on Cromwell and others, Wilson, p. 280.
[5] Corr. bet. Goethe and Carlyle, ed. Norton, 1887, p. 121.

first that suffers by it." In the next sentence but one, however, he added that, despite Jeffrey's shortcomings, though he was " by no means the supreme in criticism or in anything else . . . it is certain there has no critic appeared among us since who was worth naming beside him ; and his influence for good and for evil in literature and otherwise has been very great." [1]

Scott was not likely, any more than Lockhart or Carlyle, to be unduly influenced by merely local reputation. Party differences made it impossible for him to be in complete sympathy with Jeffrey. He owed the editor of the *Edinburgh* a " flap with a fox-tail," [2] to quote a phrase of his own, for the manner in which his works had been treated on occasion in the pages of that critical journal. It is plain nevertheless that Scott never regarded Jeffrey's opinions as unimportant. In the " Introductory Epistle " to the *Fortunes of Nigel* (1822), he affirmed that Constable had established in Scotland " a Court of Letters, which must command respect, even from those most inclined to dissent from many of its canons " ; and in his introduction to the *Lay of the Last Minstrel* (1830 edition) he took the trouble to inform his readers that the poem had, before its first appearance in 1805, " received the *imprimatur* of Mr Francis Jeffrey, who had been already for some time distinguished by his critical talent." [3] Brougham was still of opinion in 1867 that if " all Europe " had been searched for an editor for the *Edinburgh Review* a better man " *in every respect* " than Jeffrey " could not have been found." " As a critic," Brougham declared, " he was unequalled." [4] When, in 1825, after the publication in the *Review* of the essay on Milton, the family table of the Macaulays in Bloomsbury was covered with invitations to dinner from every quarter in London, " the compliment," wrote Trevelyan, " that of all others came most nearly home " to Macaulay—" the only commendation of his literary talent which even in the innermost domestic circle he was ever known to repeat,—was the sentence with which Jeffrey acknowledged the receipt of his manuscript : ' The more I think, the less I can conceive where you picked up that style.' " [5] Years later, in 1843, Macaulay asserted that he had read and re-read Jeffrey's

[1] V. 2, pp. 63-4.   [2] *Life of Scott*, Lockhart, v. 2, p. 218.
[3] See also *Life of Scott*, Lockhart, v. 2, p. 26.
[4] *Life and Times*, 1871, v. 1, p. 264.
[5] *Life of Macaulay*, Trevelyan, 1878 ed., v. 1, pp. 121-2.

old articles till he had them by heart, and expressed the opinion
that Jeffrey was " more nearly a universal genius than any man
of our time." [1] Sydney Smith felt as much honoured by
attention from Jeffrey as did Macaulay. His daughter has left
it on record that she had heard her father remark that there
was hardly any event in the whole course of his life that had
gratified him more deeply than the dedication to himself of
Jeffrey's *Contributions to the Edinburgh Review*.[2] He considered it,
he wrote to Murray, the greatest compliment ever paid to him.[3]
Hazlitt, most outspoken of critics, as Birrell has remarked, when
he disapproved, described Jeffrey as " the prince of critics and
the king of men," and spoke of him as " certainly a person in
advance of the age." [4] Thomas Campbell alluded to Jeffrey
as " the critic-king " and " the first critic of the day." " I have
a liking for him," Campbell wrote to Alison, " as I have for
Buonaparte, on account of his great abilities." [5] James Hogg
also seems to have thought of Jeffrey as comparable with
Napoleon. He, we learn from Southey, regarded Jeffrey as
" the greatest man in the world—an intellectual Buonaparte." [6]
Evidence of the respect commanded by the critical judgments
of Jeffrey and the *Edinburgh* may be discerned also in other
directions. Writers whose work was adversely commented upon
in the *Review* were stung, not infrequently, into fury. Moore,
thus adversely criticised in 1806, actually, as is well known,
challenged Jeffrey to a duel. The men met, the duel was
stopped by the police—and Moore lived to be himself an *Edinburgh*
reviewer, and to describe Jeffrey as " the great master of the
art of criticism in our day," as well as his own " now sincerely
regarded and valued friend." [7] The youthful Byron's fury on
account of a similar castigation is equally well-known. The
title of the outburst which that castigation helped to whip out
of him, *English Bards and Scotch Reviewers*, might, as the *North
British Review* pointed out in its article on Cockburn's *Life of*

[1] *Corr. of Macvey Napier*, 1879, pp. 428, 453.
[2] *Memoir of Sydney Smith*, Lady Holland, 1855, v. 1, p. 326.
[3] *Ibid.*, v. 2, pp. 503, 517.
[4] *William Hazlitt*, Augustine Birrell, p. 124. *Liber Amoris*, New Universal
Library, p. 60. *Spirit of the Age*, Everyman, p. 296.
[5] *Life and Letters of Campbell*, W. Beattie, 1849, v. 2, p. 205 ; v. 3, p. 411.
[6] *Life and Corr. of Southey*, ed. C. Southey, 1850, v. 4, p. 93.
[7] *Literary Celebrities*, pub. Chambers, 1887, p. 253. *Memoirs of Moore*,
ed. Russell, 1853, v. 1, p. 199.

Jeffrey, be regarded as significant ; it is as if the poet were taking it for granted that the centre of the world of criticism had shifted, for a moment, to a position north of the Tweed.[1] Noteworthy too were the lines in which Byron alluded to Jeffrey himself. Phrases like " great Jeffrey," " chieftain of the critic clan," " Boast of thy country, and Britannia's guide," though written in irony, were nevertheless testimony to a very considerable reputation. Byron experienced later a revulsion of feeling similar to that felt by Moore. Moore has told how, nine years after the publication of *English Bards and Scotch Reviewers*, Byron scribbled, in his own copy of the poem, after the description of Jeffrey, " Too ferocious—this is mere insanity." [2] By 1814 Jeffrey had become to him " a great soul," " the monarch of existing criticism " ; [3] and in 1823, in the tenth canto of *Don Juan*, he published an expression in verse of his changed attitude to the reviewer. It is plain too that he watched carefully the criticism of his work that appeared in the *Edinburgh* : both Richard Monckton Milnes and Sidney Colvin have drawn attention to the outburst of jealous rage that broke from him on reading Jeffrey's article, published in 1820, on Keats's *Endymion*. " Of the praises of that little dirty blackguard Keats," he wrote, " I shall observe as Johnson did when Sheridan the actor got a *pension*. . . . ' Then it is time that I should give up mine ! ' Nobody could be prouder of the praise of the *Edinburgh* than I was, or more alive to their censure. . . . At present *all the men* they have ever praised are degraded by that insane article." [4]

Colvin has spoken, too, of the impatience with which Keats waited for that notice of his work in the *Edinburgh*, a notice which, unfortunately, did not appear until it was too late to be the comfort to him that it might have been.[5] A glimpse of the influence exercised by the *Edinburgh Review* in the world of readers may be seen, again, in the life of Crabbe. Crabbe's volume of 1807, containing *The Parish Register* and other poems,

[1] *North British Review*, No. 34, p. 316.

[2] *Life of Byron*, Moore (single vol. ed.), 1838, p. 81.

[3] *Life of Byron*, Moore, p. 232. *Lord Byron's Correspondence*, ed. Murray, v. 1, p. 248.

[4] *Life of Keats*, Houghton, New Universal Library, p. 148. *John Keats*, Colvin, 1917, p. 481. *Life of Byron*, Moore, p. 464. *Life of Johnson*, Boswell, Oxford ed., v. 1, p. 257.

[5] *John Keats*, p. 479.

' called forth," the younger Crabbe noted in his biography of his father " the warmest eulogy of the most powerful critical authority of the time . . . and I believe," he added, " that within two days after the appearance of Mr Jeffrey's admirable and generous article, Mr Hatchard sold off the whole of the first edition of these poems." [1] Leigh Hunt remarked wistfully that the *Edinburgh Review* might have noticed his books a little oftener, and added, " I am sure it would have done me a great deal of worldly good by it." [2] Dowden asserted that although at the time of Shelley's first visit to Edinburgh " the most romantic of northern cities could lay no spell upon his spirit," the poet was " drawn back " to that city " by its culture and its recognition of intellect." " The literary reputation of the Scottish capital stood high," said Dowden, " —and justly so— in these palmy days of the *Edinburgh Review*." [3] Evidence of the power possessed by Jeffrey may be discerned in still other and less friendly quarters. Southey was far from being a complete admirer of the *Review* ; but he wrote, nevertheless, to Scott in 1806, asking the Scottish poet to intercede with " Judge Jeffrey " in favour of the book of a friend.[4] There was much in the *Review's* criticisms of which Coleridge disapproved, but he was prepared, at the same time, to go so far as to state that he considered " the commencement of the *Edinburgh Review* an important epoch in periodical criticism." [5] Wordsworth could be stung by the *Review's* criticism into expressions that were possibly as close to the real language of " humble and rustic life " as any he ever employed in his poetry. " If," he burst out to Scott in 1808, " Mr J[effrey] continues to play tricks of this kind, let him take care to arm his breech well, for assuredly he runs desperate risque of having it soundly kicked." [6]

The respect with which the *Review* was regarded by authors was due no doubt, in some degree, to a recognition of the extent of its circulation. Jeffrey, in a letter to Moore in 1814, estimated that each issue of his periodical was read, within a month of publication, by at least fifty thousand people. " No prose

[1] *Life of Crabbe*, by his son, 1855, p. 185.
[2] *Autobiography*, World's Classics, pp. 275-6.
[3] *Life of Shelley*, v. 1, pp. 181, 392.
[4] *Life and Corr. of Southey*, v. 3, p. 19.
[5] *Biographia Literaria*, Bohn, p. 203.
[6] *Private Letter-Books of Sir Walter Scott*, ed. Partington, p. 65.

preachers, I believe," he added, " have so large an audience." [1]
This number of readers seems, indeed, to have been really large
for the period. Gates has pointed out, in commenting on the
circulation of the *Edinburgh*, that in 1813 its subscription list
numbered more than 12,000, and that in those days each copy
of the work was used by a number of readers. The circulation
of the London *Times*, he observed, was, in 1816, only 8000 copies
daily.[2] There is evidence too, that the " audience " to which
Jeffrey referred was not located solely in Britain. We find
Von Gentz, for example, writing from Vienna in 1805 to
Sir James Mackintosh in Bombay expressing agreement with
the views contained in an article in the *Review's* issue of April
1804. On his way home from India in 1812, Mackintosh
picked up in the African Club in Cape Town the 35th number
of the *Review*, and read therein Jeffrey's " most masterly " essay
on Alison's *Nature and Principles of Taste*. Back in Britain later
in the same year he met Jeffrey himself for the first time, and
found him, he declared, " more lively, fertile, and brilliant
than any Scotchman of letters . . . and more sure than any
native of this island " he had met " to have had splendid success
in the literary societies of Paris." [3] In 1828 Goethe wrote to
Carlyle from Weimar enquiring who had written the article
on German literature in the *Review's* 92nd number.[4] In 1813
Washington Irving, in New York, received a letter from an
American friend, Brevoort, who was on a visit to Britain,
expressing gratification at the fact that Irving was to have an
opportunity of meeting " one of the most distinguished literary
ornaments of this country . . . Francis Jeffrey." Jeffrey was
about to visit America. " I really cannot fix," wrote Brevoort,
" upon any man in this country whose acquaintance is better
worth cultivating. . . . It is essential that Jeffrey may imbibe
a just estimate of the United States and its inhabitants . . . the
influence of his good opinion upon his return to this country
would go far to efface the calumnies and absurdities that have
been laid to our charge by ignorant travellers." Irving, remarked

---

[1] *Memoirs of Moore*, 1853, v. 2, p. 40. Gates stated that " in 1809 Jeffrey
boasted that the *Review* was read by 50,000 thinking people within a month
after it was printed." He gave no reference. *Sel.*, p. xxxii.

[2] *Sel.*, p. xxxii.

[3] *Memoirs of Mackintosh*, 1836, v. 1, p. 300 ; v. 2, pp. 192, 256.

[4] *Corr. bet. Goethe and Carlyle*, ed. Norton, 1887, pp. 40, 45. *Carlyle*,
Froude, v. 1, p. 407.

that writer's biographer, "could not be indifferent to the pleasure of a meeting with this celebrated personage . . . and he always spoke of him as one of the celebrities that did not disappoint you, whose conversation was as eloquent as his reviews." [1] More important individuals than Brevoort apparently regarded Jeffrey's good opinion as valuable. Jeffrey landed in America on 7th October 1813. Britain had been at war with the United States since June 1812. James Monroe, then United States Secretary for Foreign Affairs, spent " a long time," Cockburn has informed us, on the 17th November, discussing with Jeffrey the points at issue between Britain and the United States. The "argument" we are told was " renewed " on the following day, and on this day too Jeffrey " had the honour of dining " with Madison, the President, who also took the opportunity of presenting America's case to the Scots editor, in " a discussion which lasted nearly two hours." [2] The influence of the *Edinburgh Review* appears to have remained considerable in the United States, at least during the period of Jeffrey's editorship. " Like most young men at that time," wrote Emerson, for example, referring to the occasion of his first visit to Europe in 1833, " I was much indebted to the men of Edinburgh, and of the *Edinburgh Review*." [3] Compliments as great were heard occasionally in Europe. Moore, for instance, stated that, in 1821, dining in Paris at the Duc de Broglie's, he heard Auguste de Staël affirm that " if there came a being fresh from another planet, to whom he wished to give a clear and noble idea of the arts, literature, philosophy, etc. of this earth, he would present to him the *Edinburgh Review*." [4]

Still further evidence of the manner in which Jeffrey was regarded by his contemporaries may be gleaned from the numerous articles, some of which have been already quoted from, that appeared on him in the periodicals of his own day, especially at the time of the publication of his *Contributions* in 1843, of his death in 1850, and of the publication of his biography by Cockburn in 1852. In 1844, for example, the *Revue des Deux Mondes* spoke of him as the writer whom " Walter Scott et Byron et l'Angleterre avec eux ont proclamé le premier critique

---

[1] *Life and Letters of Washington Irving*, Pierre E. Irving, 1864, v. 1, pp. 173-4.
[2] *Life of Jeffrey*, v. 1, pp. 227-9.
[3] *English Traits, Works*, Routledge, 1905, p. 282.
[4] *Memoirs*, v. 3, pp. 235-6.

de ce siècle " ; " peut-être," it stated also, " ne fut-il jamais plus important qu'aujourd'hui de se bien rendre compte de la solidarité qui unit la prospérité des lettres à la force de l'esprit critique : il serait assurément difficile de trouver pour une étude si opportune des lumières plus précieuses que celles que nous apportent les *essais* de M. Jeffrey." [1] The *Dublin University Magazine*, in its review of Cockburn's *Life*, spoke of Jeffrey as one who would take " his place among the great men of his own and all coming time," and affirmed that he " influenced the opinions of others more than, perhaps, any other writer of his time—certainly, more than any writer, whose organ of communication was the language of England." [2] The *North American Review*, published at Boston, described Jeffrey in 1852 as " one who, both in literature and politics, during the first quarter of the present century, did more than any other man to guide the taste, form the opinions, and direct the conduct of the thinking portion of the English people," and declared him to be " the greatest critic of his age." [3] In 1853 the *Revue Contemporaine* described Jeffrey as " l'homme qui depuis les premières années du présent siècle a donné au sens critique en Europe et à travers le monde civilisé l'impulsion la plus vive "— and his *Review* as " une encyclopédie mobile et progressive des intérêts politiques et littéraires de l'Europe moderne." [4] " Quel que soit," said the *Nouvelle Biographie Générale*, published at Paris in 1858, " le sort réservé au recueil de ses articles, la mémoire de Jeffrey est assurée ; son nom est inséparable du journal périodique qui a été l'expression la plus complète de la critique dans les trente premières années du dix-neuvième siècle." [5]

[1] *Revue des Deux Mondes*, v. 6, Nouvelle Série, 1844, pp. 308, 299.
[2] No. 233, May 1852, p. 625.
[3] No. 157, October 1852, pp. 296, 303.
[4] V. 8, pp. 75, 93.
[5] V. 26, pp. 636-7.

CHAPTER II

LATER WITNESSES—AND THE PROBLEM

WITHOUT stressing unduly the value of the testimonials to the greatness of Jeffrey's contemporary reputation with which the preceding chapter has been filled, this, I think, might be said of them with justice, that they show that Lockhart had grounds for his assertion that Jeffrey, in his own day, accomplished something in the way of sustaining and extending the honours of Scotland. It was not an empty boast that Alexander Smith inserted in an early paragraph of his *Summer in Skye* when he spoke of a time " when the *Edinburgh Review* flourished, when the city was really the Modern Athens, and a seat of criticism giving laws to the empire."

We have noticed signs, at the same time, that the critical dicta of Jeffrey did not, even among his contemporaries, command universal approval. Among his leading opponents were to be found—not unnaturally, considering what he wrote about them— the writers whom he designated the " Lakers," Wordsworth, Coleridge, and Southey. If we turn to the Lakers' observations on Jeffrey we soon become aware that we are in different country. Coleridge's statement that he regarded the establishment of the *Edinburgh Review* as marking an important epoch in the history of periodical criticism preceded a strong attack upon Jeffrey for his treatment of Wordsworth. We have seen how Wordsworth could speak of Jeffrey ; elsewhere we find the Lake poet complaining bitterly of " the conductor of that *Review*, who has taken a perpetual retainer from his own incapacity to plead against my claims to public approbation." [1] " Of Judge Jeffrey of the *Edinburgh Review*," wrote Southey, " I must ever think and speak as of a bad politician, a worse moralist, and a critic, in matters of taste, equally incompetent and unjust." [2]

While the conception of Jeffrey to be found in the last two quotations is obviously, in these instances, not an outcome of disinterested judgment, it represents a view of him which has persisted. In 1929, for example, one of his own country's

[1] *Memoirs of Wordsworth*, Christopher Wordsworth, 1851, v. 2, p. 53.
[2] *Life and Corr. of Southey*, v. 3, p. 125.

periodicals, in a literary article, referred to him flatly, in passing, as " that ass." [1] Sir Leslie Stephen, in one of his *Hours in a Library* volumes, has an essay on " The First Edinburgh Reviewers " which is, in considerable part of it, an expression of much the same idea. Stephen did indeed preface his remarks about Jeffrey with the affirmation that he, and his fellow-reviewer Sydney Smith, deserve " respectful treatment " ; and he asserted later that Jeffrey " was a man of unusual intelligence and quickness of feeling." These statements are, however, considerably discounted by other assertions in the same essay. " Every critic," we read for instance, " has a sacred and inalienable right to blunder at times ; but Jeffrey's blundering is amazingly systematic and comprehensive." " The White Doe of Rylstone," said Stephen again, " may not be Wordsworth's best work, but a man who begins a review of it by proclaiming it to be ' the very worst poem ever imprinted in a quarto volume,' who follows up this remark by unmixed and indiscriminating abuse, and who publishes the review twenty-eight years later as expressing his mature convictions, is certainly proclaiming his own gross incompetence." Another passage in Jeffrey's work, that in which the reviewer mentioned the poets whom he considered, in 1829, to be best maintaining their popularity, contains, in Stephen's opinion, statements of such a kind that it appears " almost incredible " that they should have been made by " any sane critic." [2] A not dissimilar attitude to Jeffrey was taken up by C. E. Vaughan, in his *English Literary Criticism*. Vaughan lumped the *Edinburgh* and *Quarterly Reviews* together as wielders of a " policeman's truncheon " in what was a period of mere critical " anarchy." " The ill-fame of these Reviews, as they were in their pride of youth," he wrote, " is now so great that doubts may sometimes suggest themselves whether it can possibly be deserved." Vaughan, however, appeared to consider that they deserved every bit of it. He did, it is true, like Stephen, throw to Jeffrey a crumb of praise. Some of the *Edinburgh* reviewer's " slashing verdicts," he affirmed —" criticisms they cannot be called "—do at times " fairly hit the mark." But these, he said, were merely " chance strokes." Jeffrey's review of *The Excursion* was, in his opinion, " conceived in the worst style of the professional swashbuckler." [3]

[1] *Scottish Educational Journal.*
[2] *Hours in a Library*, 1899, v. 2, pp. 241-269.   [3] pp. lxx, lxxvii.

The findings of critics of the standing of Sir Leslie Stephen and Professor Vaughan cannot be ignored. Nevertheless simply to write down Jeffrey as a blundering fool, and to regard him as thus completely disposed of, seems, even in the light of what has already been said about him, to be scarcely satisfactory. " It has been fashionable in these later days," an American professor wrote about 1915, " among men who have never read a line of his writings to talk contemptuously of Jeffrey's criticism, as if the supremacy in this particular which he acquired and maintained among the giants of the Georgian era was somehow due to fortuitous circumstances." [1] The present writer is not in a position to estimate how many condemnatory references to Jeffrey's criticism have been based upon knowledge so inadequate. But there does seem to be at least a reasonable possibility that the work of the critic who built up the reputation we have noted contained something more than merely " blunders."

Even " in these later days " one may still find Jeffrey's writings alluded to with a measure of respect. In the *Waverley History of English Literature*, for example (edited 1903 by Thomas Seccombe and W. Robertson Nicoll), one encounters the remark that, if Jeffrey was " unduly exalted in his own day, he has been unduly depreciated ever since." [2] Lord Moncreiff who, as a young man, remembered the reviewer as he was in his later years, would have certainly agreed. " Some critics," he declared, " who constantly assure the world that they are the true æsthetes, while often they have not a ray of the diviner flame, have a fashion of sneering at the magnates of the *Edinburgh Review*, as if they had done nothing. I only know that in their society these cavillers could not have held their place for a moment. Their farthing candles would at once have been extinguished." [3] Professor Saintsbury said in his essay on Jeffrey, first published in 1887, that he did not think that Jeffrey, as an essayist, had been " surpassed among Englishmen in the art of interweaving quotation, abstract, and comment." [4] In his *Nineteenth Century Literature*, published in 1896, Saintsbury asserted that Jeffrey's " faculty of summarising a period of literature has rarely been equalled, and perhaps never surpassed,"

---

[1] *Life and Times of Tennyson*, T. R. Lounsbury, p. 123.
[2] V. 2, p. 454.
[3] *Lord Jeffrey and Craigcrook*, 1892, p. 26.
[4] *Essays in Eng. Lit.*, 1780-1860, p. 124.

and stated that Jeffrey " had, when prejudice of some sort did not blind him, an extraordinary faculty of picking out the best passages in a book." [1] When we recollect that Saintsbury, when writing, was himself engaged upon just such work, the compliments seem all the more valuable. Leslie Stephen again, despite what he said about Jeffrey in the essay on the first *Edinburgh* reviewers, noted, in another part of his book, a " shrewd criticism " of Jeffrey upon Crabbe.[2] Many of the appreciations of Jeffrey's work I have observed, indeed, have occurred in passing, when the writer has been engaged on some task of his own, and has happened upon Jeffrey's dealings with it. J. H. Millar remarked on Jeffrey that if many subsequent critics have imitated his faults, they have been " less solicitous to study his virtues," and have " entirely failed to surprise the secret of his clean-cut and vivacious prose." Millar considered that there was " something invigorating in the freshness and ' gusto ' " that distinguished all Jeffrey's work. Decades of reviewing did not stale him. " He comes to his task," Millar wrote, " as buoyant, as gay, as well primed with ideas, as keenly interested in the game, as if he were a young fellow in the Speculative commencing critic. Of no man," Millar added, " could that be said whose love for literature was not sincere and profound." [3] And we note that the compliment was paid at a moment when the writer had reached the four hundred and ninety-first page of a long and detailed history of Scottish literature. In 1908 a German candidate for his doctorate in philosophy still regarded the critical principles of Jeffrey as of sufficient importance to be " herausgeschält und zusammengefasst " for the benefit of German scholars.[4] " His abstracts," Nichol Smith wrote in 1910, " have still their use to those who are in a hurry, and his choice of quotations, though sometimes made with a purpose, will commonly be found to have anticipated the more deliberate choice of the reading public." [5] That seems evidence in favour of a considerable amount of literary taste. Professor Lounsbury, from whose *Life of Tennyson* (1915) we quoted a moment ago, remarked, in dealing with Joanna Baillie, that that authoress

[1] p. 176.   [2] *Hours in a Library*, v. 2, p. 47.
[3] *Literary History of Scotland*, 1903, pp. 487, 491.
[4] *Francis Jeffrey der Hauptbegründer der Edinburgh Review und seine Kritischen Prinzipien*, Richard Elsner, Berlin, 1908, p. 11.
[5] *Jeffrey's Literary Criticism*, 1928 ed., pp. xii-xiii.

B

had been attacked by minor critics, " but," he wrote, " of the great ones Jeffrey seems to have been the only one who managed to retain his judgment along with his admiration." [1] Professor Waldo H. Dunn of Wooster College, Ohio, writing in 1916 what he claimed to be " the first book in the English language devoted to a careful and somewhat exhaustive study " of Biography, noticed that " as far back as 1835 . . . Francis Jeffrey distinguished three kinds of biographies," and added that " these types are recognised to-day substantially as set forth by Jeffrey." [2] Another American professor, Merritt Y. Hughes, declared in the *Modern Language Review* in 1921 that Jeffrey's " originality " was " only beginning to be appraised." [3] To Donald Carswell, writing his *Sir Walter* (1930), Jeffrey's review of *Marmion* still appeared " a sincere and singularly acute judgment of the poem and of Scott's romanticism generally." [4] Lord Birkenhead included two letters written by Jeffrey in his *Five Hundred Best English Letters* published in 1931.

We remember, too, that Jeffrey was not only a critic ; he was also an editor. By his work in the latter capacity he was able to arouse the enthusiasm even of hard-headed publishers. We notice Alexander Hunter, for instance, writing thus to his partner Constable in 1810 : " The sale of the *Review* in London is indeed most satisfactory. Let us be thankful for that, at least ; and may the Lord long preserve Mr Jeffrey to us and the country. He is indeed a block of pure marble, and the chief pillar of the temple." [5] John Murray boasted to Moore in 1817 that it was a " positive fact " that he printed as many copies of the *Quarterly* as were being printed of the *Edinburgh*, " which," he asserted, " really depends upon *Jeffrey*, in whose department," he added, " we have no match." [6] Millar, noting that Cockburn described Jeffrey as the greatest of British critics, commented that the *Edinburgh* reviewer was at anyrate " certainly among the greatest of British editors." [7]

We remember besides that Jeffrey was not only a critic and an editor ; he was also a barrister who rose to the top of his profession. Jeffrey, Nichol Smith declared, was " first and foremost a lawyer. No advocate at the Parliament House in Edinburgh had a bigger practice. . . . The wealth that gave

---

[1] p. 471.   [2] *English Biography*, pp. 197-8.   [3] V. 16, p. 245.
[4] p. 47.   [5] *Constable and his Lit. Corr.*, v. 1, p. 150.
[6] *Memoirs of Moore*, v. 8, p. 231.   [7] *Lit. Hist. of Scot.*, p. 486.

him Craigcrook, his estate on the slope of Corstorphine Hill
. . . came to him, not from his writings, but from his practice
at the bar." [1] Cockburn, instancing several of Jeffrey's speeches,
remarked, " These, and many others with which our Edinburgh
ears still thrill, were matchless and unalloyed exhibitions—
leaving impressions which no rival effort, by any competitor,
could efface." [2]   " His splendour as an advocate," said Cockburn,
" was exceeded by his eminence as a judge." [3]   " The law,"
Brougham wrote referring to Scotland, " is not so jealous a
mistress there as with us in England : the literary reputation
which would inevitably prove fatal in Westminster Hall, rather
aids than impedes the lawyer's progress in Edinburgh. So at
least it was in Jeffrey's time ; but I am not aware of any other
in which great eminence was attained in both departments.
Sir Walter Scott had no success at the bar : and the works of
Monboddo and Kames were rather the fruit of their leisure,
when they had been raised to the bench." [4]

If, it might be commented, these are the achievements of an
ass, what is to be said of some of the rest of us !

We return, however, to Sir Leslie Stephen. Stephen did
not, in his discussion of Jeffrey, confine himself to general charges
of blundering. " So long," he remarked, " as a man says
sincerely what he thinks, he tells us something worth knowing.
Unluckily," he went on, " this is just where Jeffrey is apt to
fail ; though he affects to be a dictator, he is really a follower
of the fashion. . . . The simple fact is that he accepted whatever
seemed to a hasty observer to be the safest opinion, that which
was current in the most orthodox critical circles, and expressed
it with rather more point than his neighbour. . . . The critic
has been asking himself not ' What do I feel ? ' but ' What is
the correct remark to make ? ' " [5] This is obviously adding
weight to the attack. It is bad enough to be a blundering
fool. It is worse to be a blundering echo. Even at the point
to which we have already travelled, however, there are difficulties
in the way of our acceptance of this as an all-embracing conception

---

[1] *Jeffrey's Lit. Crit.*, p. vii. Jeffrey did not, as Nichol Smith states, buy
Craigcrook. He rented it from the Craigcrook Mortification. The relative
papers are in the hands of Mr Lyndesay G. Langwill, Edinburgh, the present
Clerk and Factor to the Craigcrook Trustees.
[2] *Life of Jeffrey*, v. 1, p. 360.   [3] *Ibid.*, v. 1, p. 412.
[4] *Life and Times*, v. 1, p. 243.   [5] *Hours in a Library*, v. 2, pp. 258-9.

of Jeffrey's work and character. The thing may not be impossible
—strange things have happened in the world—but it is not easy
to understand how the respect of men of the calibre of some of
those that have been mentioned could have been won by a
man who was no more than the fundamentally pusillanimous
person Stephen seems to be describing. Anecdotes told of
Jeffrey in his own day, as well as points in connection with his
work to which attention has been drawn in later times, suggest
a man of a distinctly different quality—a man who, when
seated in the critic's chair, refused to allow himself to be influenced
by any considerations whatsoever external to the merits of the
work before him—either of fashion or of anything else. Mention
has been made of the occasion in 1806 when Southey asked
Scott to exercise his influence with Jeffrey in favour of Duppa's
Michael Angelo : Scott's reply was that he would do what he
could, but that Jeffrey was " not . . . the most tractable of
critics." [1] When, in 1804, Scott's own Lay of the Last Minstrel
was passing through the press, Jeffrey remarked in a letter to
Horner that there was a set in Edinburgh so infatuated with
the poem that " the voice of impartiality " would sound to
Scott " like malignity or envy." " There is no help," Jeffrey
continued however, " —justice must be done, and I, like the
executioner, shall kiss him, and whirl him off, if the sentence be
against him. I rather think though that he will be acquitted." [2]
Horner does not appear to have entirely approved. At anyrate
we find him writing to Jeffrey in January 1805, " You will of
course do it [review the Lay] with a little of the partiality, which
we all feel for the author, and which it would be both disagreeable
to yourself and affected to attempt to avoid." [3] Jeffrey does
not appear to have been thus influenced. His review of the
Lay was, as he had anticipated, not indeed unduly severe. By
1808, however, when Marmion appeared, there was more than
partiality to exercise pressure upon Jeffrey. In the three years
that had elapsed since the publication of the Lay, six editions
of that poem had passed through the press. The seventh
appeared in 1808.[4] It might have seemed " safe " accordingly,

---

[1] Letters (1787-1807), ed. Grierson, p. 292.
[2] Life of Jeffrey, Cockburn, v. 2, pp. 91-2.
[3] Memoirs of Horner, 1843, v. 1, p. 278. The Quarterly article of 1852
tells this story, but makes it appear as if Jeffrey's letter were a reply to Horner's
(Quarterly, No. 181, p. 127). [4] Life of Scott, Lockhart, v. 2, p. 35.

one imagines, for a "hasty observer" to praise the work of Scott ; his poetry was fashionable if ever man's was. So convinced indeed was Constable, the *Edinburgh Review's* own publisher, of the certainty there now was of popularity for anything the Border poet might write that he had offered him for his new work—" very shortly after it had been begun "—a sum which, Thomas Constable wrote later in his biography of his father, " startled the literary world." [1] The situation was further complicated by the fact that Scott was still an *Edinburgh* reviewer, and one of Jeffrey's personal friends. Jeffrey was due, indeed, to dine with Scott on the very evening of the day on which the review of *Marmion* was to appear. It was in these circumstances that Jeffrey wrote the critique which Lang resented like an affront, and which Lockhart praised as vindicating the reviewer's " courageous sense of duty." Jeffrey refused to deviate for a moment from the responsibility he felt to be his of exercising completely independent judgment. Lockhart quotes the letter Jeffrey sent to Scott that day, along with the number of the *Review* containing his article, before putting in his appearance at Scott's house in Castle Street.

" Dear Scott," Jeffrey wrote, " If I did not give you credit for more magnanimity than any other of your irritable tribe, I should scarcely venture to put this into your hands. As it is, I do it with no little solicitude, and earnestly hope that it will make no difference in the friendship which has hitherto subsisted between us. I have spoken of your poem exactly as I think, and though I cannot reasonably suppose that you will be pleased with everything I have said, it would mortify me very severely to believe I had given you pain." [2]

The article was dated April, 1808. Later in that year Scott gave Jeffrey his " flap with a fox-tail," and commenced to assist actively in the foundation of the new periodical that was to challenge the *Edinburgh* on its own ground—the *Quarterly*. The first number of the *Quarterly* appeared in the spring of 1809. In May 1810 Scott published the *Lady of the Lake*. It was reviewed by Jeffrey in the *Review's* August number. Not the minutest reflection of the recent estrangement between the men appeared in the work of Jeffrey the critic. Years later, in his

[1] *Constable and his Lit. Corr.*, v. 3, p. 7. *Life of Scott*, Lockhart, v. 2, p. 114.
[2] *Life of Scott*, v. 2, p. 146.

Life of Scott, Lockhart stated indeed, as has been remarked, that
he had always considered Jeffrey's article on the *Lady of the Lake*
the best specimen of contemporary criticism on Scott's poetry ;
and observed, moreover, that the eulogies of the *Edinburgh,* though
more "discriminative," were not a whit less emphatic than
those of the *Quarterly.*[1]

It is interesting to observe also, in this connection, that the
copyright of the *Lady of the Lake* was not, like that of *Marmion,*[2]
owned by Constable, the *Review's* publisher, but was the property
—three-fourths of it at anyrate—of Constable's new rival,
Ballantyne.[3] But the interests of his publisher, by which a
weakling might have been swayed as much as by fashion,
friendship, or even personal pique, in no wise affected Jeffrey's
criticism. Constable appears to have been taken aback indeed
more than once by the cavalier treatment his own publications
received in his own periodical. One of his successful issues of
1806, for example, was James Montgomery's *The Wanderer of
Switzerland, and other Poems.* The work went into a third edition
within six months. The younger Constable complained, years
later, that this work, despite its success, was particularly singled
out for savage treatment by the *Edinburgh.*[4] The article in
question was written by the *Review's* editor himself. The very
success of the book, Jeffrey held, necessitated complete relent-
lessness. At the time of its first appearance, he wrote, he had
taken "compassion" on the writer, "conceiving him to be
some slender youth of seventeen, intoxicated with weak tea, and
the praises of sentimental Ensigns and other provincial literati,
and tempted, in that situation, to commit a feeble outrage on
the public, of which the recollection would be a sufficient
punishment." A third edition was, he declared however—
Constable's feelings as he read the sentence must have been
mixed—"too alarming to be passed over in silence."[5] On one
occasion, Lockhart tells us, Constable did risk asking Jeffrey
to review a work—Scott's *Life of Swift.* "It was, I think,"

---

[1] V. 2, p. 296. "Nor can we withhold our admiration from the man
who wrote so generously of Scott's poetry when reviewing *The Lady of the
Lake* at the very time when Scott was launching the *Quarterly* on its career
of opposition."—R. C. Bald in *The Nineteenth Century,* v. 97, Feb. 1925, p. 203.
(Art. on "Francis Jeffrey as a Literary Critic," pp. 201-5.)

[2] Constable handed over part of his rights in *Marmion* to Miller and
Murray. Lockhart, *Life of Scott,* v. 2, p. 114.   [3] *Life of Scott,* v. 2, p. 291.

[4] *Constable and his Lit. Corr.,* v. 2, p. 248.   [5] *Ed. Rev.,* No. 18, p. 347.

Constable declared to Lockhart, " the first time I ever asked such a thing of him, and I assure you the result was no encouragement to repeat such petitions." [1] " *The Crafty*," remarked the *Quarterly's* article of 1852, referring to this incident, " . . . had asked a fish and got a serpent." [2]

This same article in the *Quarterly* mentioned, as a further illustration of the independence of Jeffrey's critical outlook, his review of Fox's *History of the early part of the reign of James the Second*. " No subservience to *party*," it remarked, " even in 1808, could make Jeffrey look at purely literary qualities through a buff and blue medium. He managed, to be sure, to discover political reasons why the work was invaluable ; but at once, anticipating the judgment of the world, he pronounced the writing ' unequivocally bad.' " [3] Professor Saintsbury found evidence of a similar refusal to allow political considerations to cloud literary judgment in Jeffrey's article on Scott's *Swift*. The portion of that article to which Constable objected was no doubt the reviewer's attack on Swift's personal character, which Jeffrey considered detestable, and to which he asserted Scott had been much too kind. Jeffrey did not, however, allow his disapproval of Swift's conduct to blind him to the merits of Swift's writings. Of these he wrote, " They are very extraordinary performances : And, considered with a view to the purposes for which they were intended, have probably never been equalled in any period of the world." [4] " They certainly have not ; " commented Saintsbury, " but to find a Whig, and a Whig writing in the very moment of Tory triumph after Waterloo, ready to admit the fact, is not a trivial thing." [5]

Lounsbury noted a refusal to allow himself to be influenced by external considerations in Jeffrey's criticism of the first and second cantos of Byron's *Childe Harold*. Jeffrey, Lounsbury pointed out, could scarcely have failed to remember, when he saw this volume lying on his desk for judgment, the violence

---

[1] *Life of Scott*, v. 3, p. 123. [2] No. 181, p. 127.

[3] *Ibid.*, p. 128. The words " unequivocally bad " do not appear in Jeffrey's article, but in a letter to Horner (Cockburn's *Life*, v. 2, p. 124). For Jeffrey's criticism of Fox's style see *Ed. Rev.*, No. 24, pp. 304-6, and *Cont. to Ed. Rev.*, Jeffrey, 2nd ed., v. 1, pp. 546-7.

[4] *Cont. to Ed. Rev.*, v. 1, p. 209.

[5] *Essays in Eng. Lit.* (1780-1860), 1891 ed., p. 129. Cf. also Saintsbury's reference to Jeffrey's treatment of the Whig " goddess," Madame de Staël, pp. 126-7.

of the attack that had been made upon him by Byron in *English Bards and Scotch Reviewers*. His northern friends had accused him, the poet had stated in the postscript to the second edition of that work, " with justice," of personality towards " their great literary anthropophagus, Jeffrey." " What else," he asked, however, " was to be done with him and his dirty pack ? " The critic had sustained no injury. " What scavenger was ever soiled by being pelted with mud ? " A note to the new work showed that the poet's hostility was undiminished. Jeffrey, however, refused to allow this to affect the impartiality of his criticism. Only in his closing paragraph did he make any reference to Byron's attack. " For our own parts," runs the last sentence of his review, " when we speak in our collective and public capacity, we have neither resentments nor predilections ; and take no merit to ourselves for having spoken of Lord Byron's present publication exactly as we should have done, had we never heard of him before as an author." [1] " Men may take exception," Lounsbury commented, " to Jeffrey's critical views ; but fault can rarely be found with his critical attitude. In that it is easy to see one great reason why he so powerfully impressed his contemporaries as a literary judge." [2]

Byron himself appears to have been thus impressed. It is from the time of the publication of this article that we can date his altered attitude to the reviewer. " I admire him for *this*," he wrote in 1814, " not because he has *praised me* . . . but because he is, perhaps, the *only man* who, under the relations in which he and I stand, or stood, with regard to each other, would have had the liberality to act thus ; none but a great soul dared hazard it." [3] Still later, after he had experienced the bitterness of the social ostracism of the British public, Byron showed himself even more passionately appreciative of the impartiality of Jeffrey as a critical judge. He certainly did not regard Jeffrey's praise of his work as being at that time simply a following of the fashion. " I think," he wrote to Scott in 1822, referring, among other things, to Jeffrey's criticism of the third canto of *Childe Harold*, " that you, and Jeffrey, and Leigh Hunt, were the only literary men, of numbers whom I know (and some of whom I had served), who dared venture even an anonymous word in my favour just then." And of these three,

[1] *Ed. Rev.*, No. 38, p. 477 (1812). [2] *Life and Times of Tennyson*, p. 470.
[3] *Life*, Moore, p. 232.

he continued, Jeffrey, as he was to repeat in his *Don Juan* in the following year, he had never met ; while both Scott and Jeffrey had been attacked by him. " Coals of fire," he affirmed, had been heaped upon him, and these had burned down to his " very heart." [1]

We can trace this same belief, that Jeffrey was a man fearless in the expression of his critical views, whether these were popular or not, in the dedication to the editor of the *Edinburgh Review* of Richard Monckton Milnes's *Life and Letters of Keats*, first published in 1848. " I think," wrote Milnes in that dedication, " that the poetical portion of these volumes, will confirm the opinions you hazarded at the time, when such views were hazardous even to a critical reputation so well-founded as your own." [2] As to the sincerity with which Jeffrey held these opinions, we have the belief of his personal friend Carlyle that " he was a man intrinsically of veracity ; said nothing without meaning it to some considerable degree." [3] And if Jeffrey's own word is worth anything in the matter, we have his statement made in a letter to Mrs Grant, " When I take up my reviewing pen I consider myself as entering the temple of truth, and bound to say what I think." [4]

" S'il est un exemple," maintained the *Revue des Deux Mondes* in 1844, " qui doive fortifier les hommes appelés à juger les œuvres de la poésie, c'est de voir un recueil comme la *Revue d'Edimbourg*, où la critique réunissait tous les élémens d'autorité, le talent, la chaleur des convictions, le désintéressement, la conscience, soulever contre elle la colère des plus grands écrivains de l'Angleterre . . . et cependant, impassible au milieu de ces orages, laisser sur tous ces hommes qui la détestaient, ou du moins la craignaient, des appréciations, presque exemptes de sentimens personnels, dont il n'est personne aujourd'hui qui ne reconnaisse la profondeur, la solidité, la justice." [5]

Stephen does not appear completely consistent in his conception of Jeffrey as a reviewer whose criticisms were to be explained by the " simple fact " that he wrote only what he considered to be " safe." Of Jeffrey's review of *Wilhelm Meister* he stated, for example, that there was " a kind of indecency,

---

[1] *Life*, Moore, p. 547.   [2] p. vi.   [3] *Reminiscences*, v. 2, p. 64.
[4] *Memoirs of Mrs Grant of Laggan*, v. 1, p. 291. Mrs Grant quoted from memory in a letter to a friend. I assume reasonable accuracy.
[5] V. 8, p. 264.

a wanton disregard of the general consensus of opinion, in such treatment of a contemporary classic." [1] And we have observed his drawing attention to the fact that Jeffrey republished his review of Wordsworth's *White Doe*, twenty-eight years after it was first written, " as expressing his mature convictions." The review was republished in 1843. Four years earlier Wordsworth had received the degree of Doctor of Civil Law from Oxford, and the year before he had been granted a civil list pension. In the year of the publication of Jeffrey's volume he was made poet-laureate. These facts do not suggest over-strongly the " follower of the fashion " Stephen conceived Jeffrey to be ; they suggest rather the type of man Nichol Smith was picturing when he wrote of Jeffrey : " To cast doubt on what was accepted, or to find good in what was decried, was an intellectual exercise in which he was always ready to indulge." [2]

While one may fancy, however, that Stephen was possibly unjust to Jeffrey's personal character, there remains untouched his affirmation that Jeffrey in his judgments, whether these were arrived at by independent thinking or not, expressed the opinions of a certain critical circle. One has now to enquire who exactly these critics were. On this point Stephen is explicit. They were, he averred, a group of people whom he regarded as somewhat anachronistic in their outlook in their own period, who carried into the nineteenth century the ideas and standards of the century before. " The truth is," Stephen wrote, " that it is a mistake to suppose that the eighteenth century ended with the year 1800. It lasted in the upper currents of opinion till at least 1832." [3]

This suggestion, that Jeffrey judged from an eighteenth rather than from a nineteenth century viewpoint, is to be found in the writings of other authorities besides Stephen. Professor Hugh Walker, for example, in his *Literature of the Victorian Era*, said practically the same thing. Jeffrey, he affirmed, was " a survival of the eighteenth century school of criticism " ; and again, later in the same work, " To Jeffrey and Gifford," he asserted, " Pope had pronounced the last word, and no progress seemed possible beyond the *Essay on Man* and the *Dunciad* and the *Satires and Epistles*." [4] Professor Herford, again, in his *Age of Wordsworth*, while he stated that Jeffrey was " within the

[1] *Hours in a Library*, v. 2, p. 257. [2] *Jeffrey's Lit. Crit.*, p. xiv.
[3] *Hours in a Library*, v. 2, p. 268. [4] pp. 75, 938.

limits of his discernment, one of the acutest and liveliest [critics] of his time," declared, in discussing Hazlitt, that Hazlitt was " absolute and perverse as Jeffrey in his dealings with his own contemporaries, only that he measured them by the Elizabethans instead of by Pope." [1]   Jeffrey, it is to be inferred, measured them by the latter. " He [Jeffrey] was in the chains of the eighteenth century," we read in another work, " and what he admired was . . . the wit, the verbal felicity, the keen sense, not for beauty, but for the appropriate, that marks the art of Pope." [2]   Sir Edmund Gosse also described Jeffrey as strongly hostile to much that was new in the literature of his own period. " He was a half-hearted supporter," Gosse wrote, " of the Scoto-Teutonic reformers, but a vehement opponent, first of Coleridge and Wordsworth, afterwards of Shelley and "—it is surprising to read—" Keats." [3]

Again one wonders if statements of this kind could have been made by established critics without there being grounds for them.   Nevertheless, when one turns once more to comments on Jeffrey by contemporaries who might be supposed to have been well acquainted with his work, one finds oneself confronted by a curious difference of opinion. It is a little unexpected, for instance, to find in the number of *Blackwood's* for October 1817 the affirmation that " of Mr Wordsworth . . . he [Jeffrey] has uniformly written in terms of far loftier commendation than any other contemporary Critic, and has placed him at all times in the first rank of Genius." [4]   It is still more surprising, in view of the quotations in the previous paragraph, to find a writer in *Tait's Edinburgh Magazine* for April 1850 commenting on Jeffrey's *Contributions* as follows : " As might have been expected, the wits of Queen Anne's time, and their successors, do not rank high in our critic's estimation. Addison is under-rated, and Pope is scarcely less so (considering his extraordinary merit), though he is justly placed at the head of the class." [5] " He contributed largely," the *North American Review* asserted of Jeffrey in 1852, " to overthrow the reputation of the wits of Queen Anne's time, and to a revival of taste for the authors of the Elizabethan age." [6]   Professor William Spalding of

[1] 1897 ed., pp. 52, 51.
[2] *Samuel Rogers and his Circle*, R. Ellis Roberts, p. 268.
[3] *Modern English Literature*, 1898 ed., p. 297.   [4] V. 2, p. 72.
[5] V. 17, p. 244. [6] No. 157, p. 300.   See also *Eclectic Review*, v. 15, p. 438.

St Andrews, who declared in 1861 that Jeffrey was " one of the best writers in the English language," spoke of the " familiarity with which he knew the old masters of English song, whose works indeed he was one of the first to reinstate in public favour." [1] Gosse seems to have varied in his opinion of Jeffrey's writings. At anyrate in *English Literature, an Illustrated Record* (by Richard Garnett and Edmund Gosse, 1903) we read the following : " He was a half-hearted supporter of the Scoto-Teutonic reformers, but a vehement opponent, first of Coleridge, and afterwards of Shelley. It is, however, to be put to his credit that he recognised the genius of both Wordsworth and Keats, in a manner not wholly unsympathetic ; his strictures on *The Excursion* were severe, but there was good sense in them." [2]

One is tempted to wonder for a moment if Vaughan were not right, if a critic who could create in the minds of readers impressions so diverse were not really making statements at random. Here again, however, we find ourselves opposed. All Jeffrey's essays, said the *North British Review*, for example, were " parts of a great and gradually matured system of criticism." [3] " His most extravagant utterances about the Lake School," wrote Professor Gregory Smith, " even his unfortunate gibe at ' dancing daffodils ' for which he is still in the critics' purgatory, are less the expression of mere dislike than the logical outcome of a carefully adopted theory." [4]

Saintsbury also seems to have discerned something systematic in the critical dicta of Jeffrey. " As a literary critic," Saintsbury wrote in 1887, " he is important at this very day, and perhaps more important than he was in his own. For the spirit of merely æsthetic criticism, which was in his day only in its infancy, has long been full grown and rampant ; so that, good work as it has done in its time, it decidedly needs chastening by an admixture of the dogmatic criticism, which at least tries to keep its impressions together and in order, and to connect them into some coherent doctrine and creed. Of this dogmatic criticism Jeffrey, with all his shortcomings, is perhaps the very best example that we have in English." [5]

Saintsbury, it will be noted, not only descried in Jeffrey's

---

[1] *History of Eng. Lit.*, pp. 387-8.   [2] V. 4, p. 97.   [3] No. 1, p. 252.
[4] *Chambers's Cyclopædia of Eng. Lit.*, 1906 ed., v. 3, p. 87.
[5] *Essays in Eng. Lit.* (1780-1860), p. 125. The essay first appeared in *Macmillan's Magazine* for August 1887.

writings something of a " coherent doctrine and creed," but also agreed with certain of Jeffrey's earlier critics in regarding his work as possessing elements of permanent value. Gates stated, in 1894, that there were " of late years . . . causes " that were " tending to gain for Jeffrey a second hearing, and to secure for him a fair recognition." " Jeffrey's frank, comprehensible blunders," he added, " are nearer tolerable to a latter-day, prose-loving public than are the extravagances and cloudy mysticism of much of the poetry he assails." [1]

Saintsbury observed also the apparently puzzling character of Jeffrey's critical position to which it has been the object of the latter part of this chapter to draw attention. " Jeffrey," he wrote, " in the most puzzling way lies between the ancients and the moderns in matter of criticism, and we never quite know where to have him." " My own experience," he said, " is, that a modern reader of Jeffrey, who takes him systematically, and endeavours to trace cause and effect in him, is liable to be constantly thrown out before he finds the secret." [2]

Merritt Hughes was of opinion that he had discovered this " secret." " Really," he wrote of Jeffrey, " a very simple principle inspired his criticism, and for want of a better name, it might as well be called Platonism ; Platonism with the peculiar twist that Jeffrey gave to it." " In that," he remarked, " was his originality as a critic." [3] We have noticed what else he had to say of that originality.

Saintsbury did not travel so far as to ancient Greece to find the key to the *Edinburgh* reviewer's mystery ; it was to be discovered, he considered, somewhat nearer home—to be precise, in France. The explanation of Jeffrey's critical outlook lay, in his opinion, in what he described as the " Gallicanism " of the critic's " mind and character." Jeffrey's " early priggishness," he asserted, " is French ; the effusive domestic affection is French : the antipathy to dogmatic theology, combined with general recognition of the Supreme Being, is French ; the talk (I had almost said the chatter) about virtue and sympathy, and so forth, is French ; the Whig recognition of the rights of man, joined to a kind of bureaucratical distrust and terror of the common people (a combination almost unknown in England), is French." [4]

[1] *Sel.*, p. vii.   [3] *Modern Language Review*, v. 16, pp. 246, 245.
[2] *Essays in Eng. Lit.*, p. 115.   [4] *Essays in Eng. Lit.*, pp. 119-20.

It is interesting to compare with this the opinion of the French scholar, Philarète Chasles, whose article in the *Revue Contemporaine* of 1853 has been previously quoted. Chasles did not consider Jeffrey's viewpoint to be either French or Greek. He regarded it as Scottish !

"Qui l'a créée?" he wrote of the *Edinburgh Review*. "Personne. C'est la fille de l'Écosse elle-même. . . . Le génie de la critique écossaise,—ardent à contrôler l'Angleterre sa rivale et à revendiquer le droit de légitime examen,—a donné pour fruit la *Revue d'Edinbourg*. . . . Son grand mérite et son suprême avantage fut d'être l'expression incisive d'un génie national." [1]

"Though the persons," said Hume, "who cultivate the sciences with . . . astonishing success . . . be always few in all nations and all ages, it is impossible but a share of the same spirit and genius must be antecedently diffused throughout the people among whom they arise." [2] "That there is such a thing as a national character," said Scott, "as well as an individual one, no one can doubt, any more than that there is such a thing as family resemblance." [3] "We conceive," said Jeffrey, in an article in which Gates considered he anticipated "very strikingly" ideas made popular later by Taine, "that his [Shakespeare's] character, and that of other original writers, though no doubt to be considered on the whole as casual, must yet have been modified to a great extent by the circumstances of the countries in which they were bred." [4]

Jeffrey was born in Charles Street, at the north-east corner of George Square in Edinburgh. He learned his letters in a small school "in the abyss of Bailie Fyfe's close" off High Street. Thence he proceeded first to Edinburgh High School, then to Glasgow University, and then to the University of Oxford, in which last place he was unhappy. "I am as much, nay more, a Scotchman," he wrote to a friend, "than I was while an inhabitant of Scotland. My opinions, ideas, prejudices, and systems are all Scotch." [5] Nine months later he was back north of the Tweed. Thereafter, throughout all his writing life, his home was in Scotland. "Indeed," he wrote to Lord Murray in 1813, "I believe I could not live anywhere out of Scotland.

[1] V. 8, p. 87.   [2] *Essays*, World's Classics, pp. 114-5.
[3] *Miscellaneous Works*, 1861, v. 20, p. 360.
[4] *Cont.*, v. 1, p. 260 ; *Sel.* (Gates), p. 210.   [5] *Life*, Cockburn, v. 1, p. 46.

All my recollections are Scottish, and consequently all my imaginations ; and though I thank God that I have as few fixed opinions as any man of my standing, yet all the elements out of which they are made have a certain national cast also." [1] Exiled in London in 1832, " I hunger and thirst," he told Cockburn, " for another view of Loch Lomond and my Highlands " ; and again, " I pine hourly for . . . the Doric sounds of my mother tongue ! " [2]

It is evident that we are still some distance away from comprehension of Jeffrey and his critical position. But his countrymen's and his own statements show a road on which we may travel. We may look at the environment that helped to mould his thinking. And we may try to see his place in the pattern of Scottish history.

[1] *Life*, Cockburn, v. 2, p. 141.
[2] *Ibid.*, v. 1, pp. 335, 348-9.

CHAPTER III

NORTHERN BACKGROUND

Scotland's attractiveness and influence of Scottish traditions perhaps sometimes underestimated. Difference between Scotland and England.
Belief in rules for living. Independence of outlook. " Upon all these
topicks . . . texts at hand." Poverty and its effects. Belief in
advancement through discussion. Delight in poetry. Pressure upon
reality. Sense of inferiority to England. Persistence of Scottish
characteristics. Sound instincts of " common people." Scotland,
hardly realising it, leading in five departments of literature. Place
of *Edinburgh Review* in this development.

HISTORIANS often stress the unattractiveness of eighteenth-century
Scotland. Professor Trevelyan remarked in his *England under
Queen Anne* that there was nothing " in Scotland . . . specially
to attract the seeker after the beautiful as it was understood in
those days." " The Scots," he said, " doubtless loved, in their
innermost hearts, the ' land of brown heath and shaggy wood,'
but they had not yet, through the medium of literature, expressed
that still unconscious passion even to themselves, still less to
their unfriendly neighbours. The Englishman who rode from
Berwick to Edinburgh despised the Lowland scenery as divided
between melancholy wastes and ill-managed fields of oats. . . .
As to the Highland mountains, the very few Englishmen who
ever penetrated into their recesses pronounced them ' horrid,'
' frightful,' and ' most of all disagreeable when the heath is in
bloom.' " [1] In his *Scotland*, Dr George Pryde—the period with
which Pryde dealt commences at 1707—spoke of the visitor to
Scotland as expressing " only contempt and abhorrence for what
met his eye." [2] Seccombe suggested that Gibbon's description
of ancient Caledonia as a land of " gloomy hills . . . lakes
concealed in a blue mist . . . cold and lonely heaths " and
so forth was possibly inspired by the " disgust " aroused in the
mind of Gibbon's friend Johnson during his visit to Scotland
in 1773.[3]

[1] *Ramillies and the Union with Scotland*, p. 176. The quotations in the last
sentence are from Burt, *Letters*, v. 1, pp. 285-6.

[2] *Scotland*, Rait and Pryde, pp. 190-1.

[3] *Age of Johnson*, p. xviii. *Decline and Fall* (*Everyman* ed.) v. 1, p. 5.

While there was certainly much that was unattractive in the Scotland of the period, there seems to me to be sufficient on the other side of the balance-sheet to justify our glancing for a moment at this, I think, less commonly emphasised page. Burt's expression of dislike for the Scottish mountains has been frequently mentioned, I imagine, since Macaulay alluded to it in the thirteenth chapter of his *History*. But I am not sure that it has been so often noted that Burt declared in the first of his *Letters* that the " verbal misrepresentations " that had been made of the Scottish Lowlands were " very extraordinary." " Good part of it," he wrote, was " superior in the quality of the soil to the north of England, and in some parts equal to the best of the south." [1]   Even the Highland mountains appeared to him, when first he viewed them—from a distance—" romantic " and " no bad prospect." The " sufferings " he endured later in traversing their trackless expanses transformed, as was not surprising, this first agreeable impression into one of distaste, so that he came to detest the sight of rocks and heather.[2]   In their recesses, nevertheless, the mountains held surprises for him.   When he came to Strath-Tay he found there a valley " wide, and beautifully adorned with plantations of various sorts of trees," the sight of which gave, he stated, " a greater pleasure than the most romantic description in words, heightened by a lively imagination, can possibly do." [3]   It is interesting to observe too the fascination which, he confessed, the Highlands came gradually to exercise over him.   He never, he said, " by choice, made one retrograde step " when leaving the mountains : " but," he added, " what is pretty strange, though very true (by what charm I know not), I have been well enough pleased to see them again, at my first entrance to them in my returns from England ;   and this has made my wonder cease that a native should be so fond of such a country." [4]   Macky—there is room for only glimpses of other travellers' records—whose *Journey through Scotland* appeared in 1723, spoke of Dunbar as standing " in as delicious a Spot of Country as you can imagine " and asserted that the shire of Moray was " one of the beautifullest Countries " he had seen " in Britain." [5]   " I think," Defoe wrote

[1] V. 1, p. 5.   [2] *Ibid.*, v. 1, p. 25.
[3] *Ibid.*, v. 1, p. 332.   [4] *Ibid.*, v. 2, p. 40.
[5] *Journey through Scotland*, 1732 ed., pp. 26, 122.   Macky was of Scottish birth.   *Dict. Nat. Biog.*

of the meanders of the Forth, "the like is not to be seen in *Britain*, if it is in *Europe*."[1] In the volume of three hundred and fifty pages in which are printed the *Tours in Scotland* (1747, 1750, 1760) of Pococke, the words "beautiful," "fine," "pleasant," "delightful," "charming," "pretty," "romantic," or their corresponding adverbs, used with reference to Scottish scenery, appear at least two hundred and forty times. To Pennant the estate of Faskally appeared "like fairy ground " and the valley of the Leven "unspeakably beautiful."[2] Wesley spoke of the Carse of Gowrie, when he visited it in 1774, as "that lovely valley," and in 1784 as "the fruitfullest valley in the kingdom."[3] Johnson sat near Auchnasheal "on a bank, such as a writer of romance might have delighted to feign " dreamily conceiving the idea of giving to the world an account of his Scottish travels.[4] Journeying on an October day from Oban to Inveraray through a storm of wind and rain—and he was sixty-four—he was roused by his surroundings, not to disgust, but to a mood which afterwards, in his *Journey*, found expression in a passage that was almost Wordsworthian.[5]

Some people may recollect from their schooldays Stopford Brooke's assertion that while the natural description of Chaucer, Shakespeare, or Milton was not distinctively English, in Scotland it was always the scenery of their own land that the poets described, and his finding reflections of Scottish landscapes in the works of Henryson, Dunbar, Douglas, and Lyndsay.[6] Near the beginning of the eighteenth century Scotsmen were to be found singing of "bonny Tweedside," "Sweet Leader Haughs," and the "bonny howms of Yarrow."[7] Defoe declared that Dundee well deserved "the Title of *Bonny Dundee*, so often given it in Discourse, as well as in Song."[8] Ramsay wrote of "Habbie's How, Where a' that's sweet in spring and simmer grow." Fergusson queried if the shores of Tiber were "mair sweet and gay Than Fortha's haughs or banks o' Tay." Burns sang of "sweet Afton " and the "banks and braes o' bonie

[1] *A Tour thro' Great Britain*, ed. G. D. H. Cole, 1927, v. 2, p. 754.
[2] *A Tour in Scotland*, 1769, fourth ed., 1776, pp. 119, 246.
[3] *Journal* (*Everyman* ed.), v. 4, pp. 14, 280.
[4] *Journey to Western Islands* (Gardner, Paisley), p. 67 ; *Tour*, Boswell (*Everyman* ed.), p. 122.
[5] p. 232. *Tour*, pp. 336-7.
[6] *English Literature* (Primer), pp. 62, 63, 64.
[7] *Tea-Table Miscellany*.   [8] *Tour thro' Gt. Britain*, v. 2, p. 805.

Doon." If that is not precisely appreciation of " brown heath and shaggy wood " it is at anyrate appreciation of Scotland.

Two suggestions relevant to our study might be drawn from this brief discussion : first that despite the frequently aggressive patriotism of Scotsmen, the attractiveness of earlier Scotland, and perhaps also, analogously, the quality and power of the influence exercised on the modes of thinking of the Scottish people of those days by their environment in general—we are looking forward here—may have been sometimes underestimated ; and second—this is really contained in the first—that a man reared in a country with those landscapes and these literary traditions did not require to go to the romanticists of the early nineteenth century in order to have his attention directed to natural beauty.

English visitors became aware, the moment they crossed the Border, that they were in a land different from their own. " The first Town we come to," said Defoe, " is as perfectly *Scots*, as if you were 100 Miles North of *Edinburgh* ; nor is there the least Appearance of any Thing *English*, either in Customs, Habits, Usages of the People, or in their Way of Living, Eating, Dress, or Behaviour ; any more than if they had never heard of an *English* Nation." [1] " The Scotch towns," Wesley wrote, " are like none which I ever saw, either in England, Wales or Ireland : there is such an air of antiquity in them all, and such a peculiar oddness in their manner of building." [2]

The Scottish towns, it will be observed from one of our quotations from Defoe, like the Scottish landscapes, were spoken of sometimes with respect. Burt declared that when he first came into the High Street of Edinburgh he thought he " had not seen any thing of the kind more magnificent," and described Glasgow as " the prettiest and most uniform town " he had ever seen.[3] Defoe shared Burt's admiration for both cities.[4] Johnson noted that the town of Montrose was "well built, airy, and clean" and mentioned the " spacious and clean " streets of Aberdeen.[5] Wesley asserted that " as to wood and water, and gently rising hills, etc." Dumfries was, he thought, " the neatest, as well as the most civilized town " he had seen " in the kingdom." [6]

---

[1] *Tour thro' Gt. Britain*, v. 2, p. 692.   [2] *Journal*, v. 2, p. 194.
[3] *Letters*, v. 1, pp. 16-7, 22.
[4] *Tour thro' Gt. Britain*, v. 2, pp. 707 *et seq.* ; 743 *et seq.*
[5] *Journey*, pp. 29, 32.   [6] *Journal*, v. 4, p. 429.

Visitors noticed other tokens of civilisation. If Johnson's and other eighteenth-century English travellers' impressions of Scottish inns were, as Grey Graham has emphasised,[1] frequently unfavourable, Johnson found an inn at Inveraray which he described as " not only commodious, but magnificent." Only twice, Johnson said—he was evidently speaking of his experiences in inns as well as in private houses—did he have " any reason to complain of a Scottish table." Even in the Western Islands, he declared, he found tables " always covered with elegant linen " and silver used " on all occasions where it is common in England." [2] " What miserable accounts," Wesley wrote in his journal for 1753, " pass current in England of the inns in Scotland. Yet here [at Thornhill] as well as wherever we called in our whole journey, we had not only every thing we wanted, but every thing readily, and in good order, and as clean as I ever desire." [3] Speaking of the Scottish " Gentry "—" I must say," Defoe wrote, " without Compliment, none in *Europe*, understand themselves better, or better deserve the Name of *Gentlemen*." [4] Pococke, writing in 1760 from Tongue in Suther- land, described the people as " in general extremely hospitable, charitable, civil, polite, and sensible." [5] " In the *Highlands*," Pennant wrote, " every house gave welcome to the traveller." [6] " Wherever we have come," Johnson declared near the end of his tour, " we have been received like princes in their progress." [7]

There was evidence of advancement also in the country's orderliness. If, said Defoe, travellers in the Highlands had " the Countenance of the Gentlemen, and Chiefs " they would " want neither Guides nor Guards, nor indeed would any Man touch them." [8] Among the clansmen themselves, Burt remarked, " personal robberies " were " seldom heard of." " For my own part," he affirmed, " I have several times, with a single servant, passed the mountain-way from hence to Edinburgh, with four or five hundred guineas in my portmanteau, without any apprehension of robbers by the way, or danger in my lodgings by night ; though, in my sleep, any one, with ease, might have

---

[1] *Social Life of Scotland in Eighteenth Century*, pp. 44-5.
[2] *Journey*, pp. 232, 43, 91.   [3] *Journal*, v. 2, p. 252.
[4] *Tour thro' Gt. Britain*, v. 2, p. 695.
[5] *Tours in Scotland*, p. 128.   [6] *A Tour in Scotland*, p. 246.   [7] *Tour*, p. 308.
[8] *Tour thro' Gt. Britain*, v. 2, p. 828.

thrust a sword, from the outside, through the wall of the hut
and my body together. I wish we could say as much of our
own country, civilised as it is said to be, though one cannot be
safe in going from London to Highgate." Burt discovered that
even the homeless Edinburgh caddies had forms of discipline
of their own, were " often considerably trusted " and " seldom
or never proved unfaithful." [1]   When Johnson arrived in
Edinburgh Boswell discovered that the old man had provided
himself, in preparation for their journey, with " a pair of pistols,
some gunpowder, and a quantity of bullets." Boswell persuaded
his companion to leave the weapons behind, assuring him they
were completely unnecessary.[2]   The sequel showed he was right.
No one in Scotland interfered with them. Burt saw the execution
of a murderer at Inverness. The hangman was " at least eighty
years of age " and mismanaged the business so sorrily that in
the end the poor wretch had to leap from the gallows himself.
A local blacksmith, instructed to fix irons on the corpse, fled
from the task in horror, and the riveting had to be done by one
of the magistrates, " there being none other that would undertake
so shameful a work for any reward whatever." " I thought
it," Burt commented, " a very bungling execution, yet liked the
cause of their unskilfulness." [3]   When Pennant arrived at
Kinross he found that a meeting of magistrates had been
summoned " on a singular occasion " : a vagrant had been
ordered to be whipped, but " such was the point of honor among
the common people, that no one could be persuaded to go to
Perth for the executioner." [4]   Speaking of a field meeting which
lasted nearly seven hours, and to attend which " many of the
poor People had come fifteen or sixteen Miles . . . and had
all the Way to go home again on Foot "—" if," Defoe commented,
" there was an equal Zeal to this in our Part of the World, and
for that Worship which we acknowledge to be true . . . our
Churches would be more throng'd and our Ale-houses and
Fields less throng'd on the Sabbath-day than they are now." [5]
Pococke declared of the worshippers in the Episcopal chapel in
Glasgow, " I think I never saw divine offices performed with
such real edification." [6]   Referring to his visit to Aberdeen in
1776, " I . . . was again delighted," Wesley wrote, " with the

---

[1] *Letters*, v. 2, pp. 133-4 ; v. 1, p. 21.   [2] *Tour*, p. 38.
[3] *Letters*, v. 1, pp. 258-64.   [4] *A Tour in Scotland*, p. 79.
[5] *Tour thro' Gt. Britain*, v. 2, p. 730.   [6] *Tours in Scotland*, p. 51.

exquisite decency, both of the Minister and the whole congregation. The Methodist congregations come the nearest to this.
But even these do not come up to it." " Surely," he exclaimed,
speaking of his visit to Dumfries in 1788, " the Scots are the
best hearers in Europe ! " [1]   They evidently believed, at anyrate,
that life should be conducted according to rules.

This regularity of conduct was not an indication of a cowed
population. To their chiefs, Burt observed, the Highlanders
paid " a blind obedience " though it might be " in opposition
to the government, the laws of the kingdom, or even to the law
of God." [2] If Wesley was delighted by the behaviour of the
Scottish people in church, he did not find them easy to preach
to. " The hearers," he complained after delivering a sermon
at Monymusk, " did not appear to be any more affected than
the stone walls." " There is seldom fear," he remarked, referring
to a visit to Dundee, " of wanting a congregation in Scotland.
But the misfortune is, they know every thing ; so they learn
nothing." " The congregation," he wrote of another Dundee
visit, " was, as usual, very large and deeply attentive ; but
that was all. . . . I admire this people ! So decent ! So
serious ! And so perfectly unconcerned ! " [3] " We were indeed
amazed," wrote Burnet, speaking of a visit to south-western
Scotland in the previous century, " to see a poor commonalty
so capable to argue upon points of government, and on the
bounds to be set to the power of Princes in matters of religion :
upon all these topicks they had texts of scripture at hand ; and
were ready with their answers to any thing that was said to
them." [4] We recall that when the father of Robert Burns felt
in need of a catechism for his children's instruction he went to
no ecclesiastic for advice, but composed one himself.

This stubborn reliance on their own judgment was not, it
is plain from Burnet, an effect solely of ignorance. The Scottish
passion for education was of course notorious. Johnson met
in Col a farmer's son who travelled yearly on foot to Aberdeen
for education and acted in summer as schoolmaster on the

[1] *Journal*, v. 4, pp. 75, 430. The first statement referred to the service
in the English chapel, the second to an open-air meeting.

[2] *Letters*, v. 2, pp. 2-3.

[3] *Journal*, v. 3, pp. 256, 181 ; v. 4, p. 156.

[4] *History of His Own Time*, 1753 ed., v. 1, p. 431. Attention is drawn to
this passage by Lecky, *Eng. in the 18th cent.*, 1892 ed., v. 2, p. 284, and by
Hume Brown, *Hist. of Scotland*, v. 2, p. 453.

island. " There is something noble," the Doctor commented,
" in a young man's walking two hundred miles and back again,
every year, for the sake of learning." In Mull he met a minister
who had had his first lessons in Horace and Virgil in St Kilda.[1]
One wonders if he ever mentioned these things to Gibbon as
well as his " disgust." Had he done so the historian would
not have been surprised. Gibbon stated that he had chosen
as his guides to Caledonian antiquity the works of " two learned
and ingenious Highlanders," one of them a minister in Skye.
" It is," Gibbon commented, " a circumstance honourable for
the present age, that a work replete with erudition and criticism
should have been composed in the most remote of the Hebrides." [2]

No traveller could overlook, at the same time, Scotland's
poverty. Taylor was told in Carlisle that if a Scotsman had
twenty shillings owing him in that town he would come thirty
miles to receive it.[3] Burt observed citizens in Edinburgh giving
a beggar a halfpenny and taking back a " plack " or third
part of a penny in change. At Inverness he saw women
encumbered by heavy loads crossing the river by slippery stepping
stones " almost up to the middle, at the hazard of their lives,"
in order to save the bodle, or sixth part of a penny, it would
have cost them to cross by the bridge.[4] As revealing as any
incident narrated by our travellers, by reason of the abyss of
misery which as by a lightning flash it discloses, is the story
told by a Scotsman of the day, Alexander Carlyle—of an
Edinburgh tailor who sold, about 1738, to some medical students
of the University there, for the sum of six shillings, the body of
his dead child, having been beaten down sixpence in his price
on the ground that the bargain would save him the cost of a
funeral.[5]

This poverty could hardly have failed to exert an influence :
every characteristic we have noted might be regarded as having
been linked in some way with it. The Scotsman's appreciation
of his country's beauty was intensified by the fact that that
beauty shone out to him often from sombre surroundings.
Graham and Trevelyan connected the safety of travel in the
country with its poverty : highwaymen, Graham said, would
have grown weary of waiting, and died from finding so little to

[1] *Tour*, pp. 291, 329.   [2] *Decline and Fall* (*Everyman* ed.), v. 2, p. 496.
[3] *A Journey to Edenborough*, ed. Cowan, 1903, p. 157.
[4] *Letters*, v. 1, pp. 140, 42.   [5] *Autobiography*, 1860 ed., p. 51.

plunder.[1] There are few countries so poor, nevertheless, that
there is nothing whatever in them worth stealing : we have seen
that Burt's guineas were untouched. Poverty may help to
strengthen a moral code in other ways. Poor men may realise
that the prevalence of such a code in society provides for them
the soundest form of protection. Adherence on his own part
to such a code may give a poor man self-respect—that sort of
self-respect to which Burns appealed when he declared that
" the honest man, tho' e'er sae poor " was " king o' men for
a' that." Poverty's denial of opportunities for travel might
well foster opinionativeness. " They were indeed vain of their
knowledge," Burnet remarked of the south-western Scots, " much
conceited of themselves, and were full of a most entangled
scrupulosity ; so that they found, or made difficulties in every
thing that could be laid before them." [2]   Limited intercourse
was bound to stimulate that vanity. Argument was a natural
form of recreation in a country that afforded few other forms
of it. The link between poverty and the Scottish zeal for
education is obvious. Even where, as in the instance of the
landlord of the modest change-house Johnson visited in Glenmoriston,[3] education afforded no outlet for ambition, it too
could help to give a man self-respect. Linked with poverty
also may be the Scottish fondness, noted by Lamb, for keeping
a grip upon facts : nothing is more efficacious than poverty in
forcing a man to see the world as it really is.

Throughout the whole of eighteenth-century Scottish history
there may be discerned the interplay and development of these
characteristics. One of the first activities recorded of Allan
Ramsay, the wigmaker, bookseller, and first original man of
letters the century in Scotland produced, was his joining, at the
age of twenty-six, with five friends to form a " Society " in
which they might " Meet " as their " Journall " put it, " . . . in
order that by a Mutual improvement in Conversation " they
might " become more adapted for fellowship with the politer
part of mankind and Learn also from one anothers happy
observations." [4] We observe the combination of ambition with

[1] *England under Queen Anne, Blenheim,* Trevelyan, p. 91 ; *Social Life of
Scotland in Eighteenth Century,* Grey Graham, p. 48.
   [2] *History of His Own Time,* 1753 ed., v. 1, pp. 431-2.
   [3] *Journey,* pp. 60-1 ; *Tour,* p. 117.
   [4] *New Light on Allan Ramsay,* Gibson, 1927, p. 48.

belief in advancement through discussion. Ramsay's "Easy Club" was one of many similar organisations. We note the "Rankenian Club" set up in Edinburgh in 1716 "by a few young men of good education, belonging probably both to the Church and Bar" the object of which was to encourage among its members "literary conversation, and improvement in composition" ; [1] the association founded in 1718 by Thomas Ruddiman and the Edinburgh High School masters "for improving each other in classical lore" ; [2] the "Robinhood," mentioned by Fergusson ; the "Philosophical" Societies of Edinburgh and Aberdeen ; the "Select Society" ; the "Speculative Society," founded in 1764, among whose members, in later years, were Scott, Jeffrey, Cockburn, Lockhart, and Stevenson ; [3] the "weekly club" founded in Glasgow by Provost Cochrane, the "express design" of which was "to inquire into the nature and principles of trade in all its branches" ; [4] and last, but not least in historical importance, the "Bachelors' Club" of Tarbolton.

Mention of this last reminds us of the other type of gathering described in *The Cotter's Saturday Night*. The characters in that poem spent part of their evening together, it will be remembered, singing. Picture after picture flashes out of the records of Scotland in our period illustrating the fondness of its inhabitants for simple music and the kind of verse that goes naturally with it, and their association of these with scenes of human-kindliness : Patrick Home, for example, writing from exile in Holland in the previous century to ask that his children, one of whom was to be famous later as Lady Grisell Baillie, be kept "laughing, dancing, and singing" ; [5] Gilbert Elliot, himself a song-writer, wagering his sister Jean a pair of gloves or a set of ribbons that she could not make a ballad on Flodden ; [6] Laurence Oliphant writing from Naples to ask that his children, one of whom was Caroline, afterwards Lady Nairne, be kept "in mind of their little song after dinner" ; [7] Lady Anne Lindsay fitting the words of *Auld Robin Gray* to an ancient Scottish melody sung

---

[1] *Life of Kames*, Tytler, v. 1, p. 174.
[2] *Life of Ruddiman*, Chalmers, 1794, p. 83.
[3] *History of the Speculative Society*, 1905, *passim*.
[4] *Autobiography*, Alex. Carlyle, p. 73.
[5] *Songstresses of Scotland*, Tytler and Watson, 1871, v. 1, p. 5.
[6] *Ibid.*, v. 1, p. 206.
[7] *Life of Baroness Nairne*, Rogers, p. 18.

by Sophia Johnston ; [1] Fergusson singing his favourite *Birks of
Invermay* ; [2] Boswell playing on his flute to the natives of Corsica
" some of our beautiful old Scots tunes " ; [3] Burns " southing "
his lyrics to " old Scottish airs." [4] Tytler declared in 1800
that to the country-folk in the Pentlands the *Gentle Shepherd*
was " familiar as their catechism." [5] The recognition of
Fergusson was " by the ' common people ' first of all, and passed
upward, exactly as with Burns." [6] When Burns's poems first
appeared " plough-boys and maid-servants " went without
" necessary clothing " in order to buy them.[7] Pinkerton,
writing in 1786, spoke of the " common people " as " enraptured
with Barbour's History of Bruce, Blind Harry's Life of Wallace,
and the works of Sir David Lindsay, books to be found in modern
spelling at this day in almost every cottage of Scotland." [8]

In the poetry of the period we perceive the Scottish pressure
upon reality. Ramsay's *Gentle Shepherd* may be in some respects
an idealisation ; but it was unusual in the Augustan age to
encounter, in verse intended to be taken seriously, allusions to
such homely things as " haggies," a " mutton-bouk to boil,"
and " gusty ingans with a curn of spice." There is close contact
with reality in certain of Ramsay's other poems, as there is also
in Fergusson's Edinburgh sketches. We observe the same quality
in Burns's " They're no sae wretched's ane wad think " said
of the poor, and in his " Fient haet o' them's ill-hearted fellows "
said of the rich. These last quotations remind us that it is
reality we are speaking of, not the sentimentalised literary thing
that is sometimes called realism.

It was agreed at the commencement of the " Easy Club "
that each member should be " stil'd with a particular name
taken from some eminent person whose Character " might be
before him constantly as a model. All the names chosen were
connected with the literature of England, Ramsay's being " Isaac
Bickerstaff." Later it was further enacted that " one Specktator
be Read at every meeting till all be Read, and Isaac Bickerstaff

---

[1] *Songstresses of Scotland*, v. 2, p. 23.
[2] *Poetical Works*, ed. Ford, 1905, p. xxxvii.
[3] *Account of Corsica*, ed. Birkbeck Hill, 1879, p. 186.
[4] *Life and Works*, Chambers and Wallace, v. 1, p. 142.
[5] *Poems of Ramsay*, 1877, v. 1, p. ci.
[6] *Robert Fergusson*, A. B. Grosart, p. 100.
[7] *Biographical Dict. of Eminent Scotsmen*, v. 1, p. 446.
[8] *Ancient Scotish Poems*, v. 1, p. xvii.

to provide the 1st Volume." [1]   There we perceive the Scottish pressure upon reality in another form.   The northern Parliament had recently followed the Crown to England.   Ambitious Scotsmen were moving in the same direction in ever increasing numbers.   England's literary treasuries were far richer than Scotland's.   It seemed inevitable that English would ultimately supersede Scottish standards.   Home-staying Scots who, seeking culture, looked southward appeared accordingly to be simply facing facts.   " If countries," it was asserted in the preface to the first *Edinburgh Review* (1755)—the " chief conductors " of which were Hugh Blair, Robertson, and Adam Smith—" have their ages with respect to improvement, North-Britain may be considered as in a state of early youth, guided and supported by the more mature strength of her kindred country." [2] Inferiority in culture is generally accompanied by inferiority in language.   A sense of the first tends therefore to involve a sense of the second.   As intercourse with England was " daily . . . increasing," said the regulations of an association formed in Edinburgh in 1761 for the purpose of " promoting the Reading and Speaking of the English Language in Scotland," gentlemen educated in the north had long been " sensible of the dis- advantages " under which they laboured from their " imperfect knowledge " of English.   They were assured, however, that by skilful instructors even persons " well advanced in life " might be taught " to avoid many gross improprieties, in quantity, accent, the manner of sounding the vowels etc.," which rendered " the Scotch dialect so offensive." [3]   Hume strove to purge his writings of Scotticisms and declared to Robertson, intending evidently the highest of compliments, " The town will have it that you was educated at Oxford, thinking it impossible for a mere untravelled Scotsman to produce such language." [4] Boswell took lessons in English pronunciation.[5]   Beattie affirmed in 1776 that it was " now impossible " to write seriously in Scots.[6]   Pinkerton's attitude to the Scots peasants who were enraptured with their old poets was not one of approval. " None," he wrote, " can more sincerely wish a total extinction

---

[1] *New Light on Allan Ramsay*, Gibson, pp. 48, 43, 49.
[2] *A Scottish Man of Feeling*, Thompson, p. 41 ;   *Kames*, Tytler, v. 1, p. 169.
[3] *Works of Allan Ramsay*, 1848 ed., v. 3, pp. 266-7.
[4] *Life of Hume*, Burton, v. 2, p. 49.
[5] *Life of Johnson* (Oxford ed.), v. 1, p. 444.   [6] *Essays*, 1779 ed., pp. 380-3.

of the Scotish *colloquial* dialect than I do." The works of these
poets should, he said, be published only in their original spelling :
the peasants would, in consequence, be "forced to read
English." [1] Mackenzie's well-known article in the *Lounger* on
Burns's Kilmarnock volume, though laudatory, spoke of the
language in which most of the poems were written as a
consequence of the poet's "birth and education" and a "bar
. . . to his fame." [2] "You ought," Moore told Burns in 1787,
". . . to deal more sparingly, for the future, in the provincial
dialect—why should you, by using *that*, limit the number of
your admirers to those who understand the Scottish, when you
can extend it to all persons of taste who understand the English
language ? " In 1789 Moore advised Burns to "abandon the
Scottish stanza and dialect." [3]

In the "Easy Club," however, a small but significant event
happened. Some time after its inauguration one of its number,
not an original member, who had already revealed something
of his feelings by adopting the pseudonym of "George
Buchannan" declared that the others had put an "affront upon
ye Scots Nation" by adopting English names. The protest
awakened no demur. On the contrary, "Scots Blood," runs
the minute,

> "Was fire and flaming fir'd itself
> In other Breasts which kindly took ye Blaze."

It was unanimously resolved "in warm expressions by each"
that Scottish patrons should be substituted for the English.[4]
It was evident that traditions that were the slow growth of
centuries could not be easily obliterated. The Scottish language
was equally stubborn. In certain circumstances Scotsmen found
themselves drifting back irresistibly into the old vocabulary.
"Though our books," said William (later Lord) Craig in 1780,
"be written in English, our conversation is in Scotch. Of our
language it may be said, as we are told of the wit of Sir Hudibras,
that we have a suit for holidays and another for working-days.
The Scottish dialect is our ordinary suit ; the English is used
only on solemn occasions." [5] Even when the words spoken

---

[1] *Ancient Scotish Poems*, v. 1, pp. xvii-xviii.
[2] *Scots Essayists*, ed. Smeaton, p. 52.
[3] *Life and Works*, Chambers and Wallace, v. 2, pp. 94-5 ; v. 3, p. 50.
[4] *New Light on Allan Ramsay*, pp. 55-6.
[5] *Scots Essayists*, ed. Smeaton, pp. 30-1.

were English, Scottish mouths refused to make other than the long-established northern sounds. The " niceties of English pronunciation," Beattie confessed, could not be acquired by a Scot " without an early and long residence among English people." [1]   On those who tried to defy its power the old tongue took impish revenge. " *High English*," Boswell observed, " as we are apt to call what is far removed from the *Scotch*, but which is by no means good English . . . makes ' the fools who use it,' truly ridiculous." [2]   It affected also the written English of Scotsmen. " Our style," said Beattie, " is stately and unwieldy, and clogs the tongue in pronunciation, and smells of the lamp. We are slaves to the language we write . . . and, when an easy, familiar, idiomatical phrase occurs, dare not adopt it, if we recollect no authority, for fear of Scotticisms. In a word, *we* handle English, as a person who cannot fence handles a sword." [3]

The power of the vernacular was not, however, merely negative. To those who accepted its aid it was still able to give rewards. To me it seems hardly true to say that Ramsay, Burns, and Fergusson revived the Scottish vernacular for poetic purposes in the eighteenth century ; it seems far more accurate to say that it vivified them. All three attempted purely English verse with little success. The vernacular, when they turned to it, transformed their expressions into the poetry that warmed the hearts of their countrymen. The old tongue did more than that. The advice of the pundits was wrong, and the instincts of the " common people " who welcomed Scottish poetry were right. Contemned though it might be by the intelligentsia, though to employ it might be to risk incurring reflections upon one's " birth and education," disparaged though it might be as a decrepit patois requiring to be eked out, as has been said of the language of Burns, by archaisms and by " fancy Scotch " made by " Scottifying ordinary English words on an assumed analogy " [4]—which may be only another way of saying that it retained a living language's power of borrowing—it still had strength enough to rise like Banquo's ghost with twenty trenched gashes on its head, to carry works of poets who trusted to it into literature's stateliest chambers, and to give these works a position

---

[1] *Essays*, p. 381.   [2] *Life of Johnson*, v. i, pp. 444-5.
[3] *Life of Beattie*, Forbes, v. i, p. 417.
[4] *Chambers's Cyclopædia of Eng. Lit.*, v. 2, p. 795.

there such as has been commanded by writings in no other dialect, except the standard one, of the whole English speech. When in 1861 Palgrave, Englishman born and bred, assembled in his *Golden Treasury* what he considered to be " the best original Lyrical pieces and Songs in our language, by writers not living," out of the forty-nine works he selected to represent the eighteenth century, twenty were by Scots, and of these, seventeen were in the vernacular. One has only to glance at Palgrave's notes to see how highly he valued some of these vernacular pieces. Quiller-Couch included in his *Oxford Book of Verse* eighty-three poems by authors born between 1665 and 1766. Of these, twenty-six were by Scotsmen, and of these last twenty-one were in Scots. One of the pieces chosen by Couch, *Auld Lang Syne*, reminds us that what is probably the most widely-known song in the entire English-speaking world was written in Scots of the eighteenth century.

The phenomenon makes us wonder what would have happened had the eighteenth-century northern writers of prose laid aside their timidity and dared to write, wherever the subject suited, in the unforced Scoto-English then natural to educated Scottish gentlemen. They might have added a department to English literature.

It appears to me at the same time that when these northern prose writers were most successful they too were being inspired by their Scottish instincts. When a people find themselves in danger of losing their national identity they tend to emphasise the greatness of their country's past. This happened in Scotland after 1707. Abercromby's *Martial Atchievements of the Scots Nation* (1711-16) expressed on its fifth page its author's determination to counter the " emulation and jealousy " of such writers as presumed to deny Scotland's possession, up to that date, of " an uninterrupted series of one hundred and twelve sovereigns,"— " than which," Abercromby exclaimed, " there is nothing so glorious, nothing equal or secondary in its kind ! " [1] Interest in Scotland's past was maintained by the more scientifically historical *Critical Essay* (1729) of Thomas Innes and the *History of the Affairs of Church and State in Scotland* (1734) of Keith. The channel thus dug widened into the historical studies of Hume and Robertson. And in this department Scotland suddenly found herself not " supported by the more mature strength of

[1] 1762 ed., v. 1, p. 5.

her kindred country," but a leader. " I believe," Hume wrote exultantly to Strahan in 1770, " this is the historical Age and this "—the Scots—" the historical Nation." [1] Gibbon called Robertson and Hume his masters.[2] " British historical writing," said the *Cambridge History of Literature*, " . . . was raised by Hume to a foremost place in our prose composition ; its right to that place was maintained by Robertson." [3]

We saw in Cochrane's " weekly club " a combination of the Scottish liking for discussion with the increasing interest in commerce which the opportunities afforded by the Union made natural. Adam Smith was a member of that club and acknowledged his indebtedness, Alexander Carlyle remarked, to Cochrane's information when he was collecting material for his *Wealth of Nations*.[4] Everyone knows what came out of that.

It was natural for Scottish discussion to be extended, as the danger to the Kirk disappeared, to other fields than that of religion. " It is well known," wrote Ramsay of Ochtertyre, " that between 1723 and 1740, nothing was in more request with the Edinburgh *literati* . . . than metaphysical disquisitions. These they regarded as more pleasant themes than either theological or political controversies." [5] Everyone, Hume declared in 1734, who was acquainted with either philosophy or criticism knew there was nothing established in either of these sciences. " Upon examination of these," he wrote, " I found a certain boldness of temper growing in me, which was not inclined to submit to any authority in these subjects, but led me to seek out some new medium, by which truth might be established." [6] There we perceive the Scottish independence of outlook. Hume Brown, while he observed that Hume " only systematised and gave precision to modes of thinking which were current in Scotland in the earlier half of the eighteenth century," remarked that the scepticism which was the logical outcome of Hume's reasoning was " a strange conclusion . . . to have been reached in Scotland, which for nearly two centuries had been the peculiar home of dogmatic assertion on ultimate questions." [7] Here, however, we have Hume himself with us.

---

[1] *Letters of Hume*, ed. Hill, p. 155.   [2] *Autobiography*, 1869 ed., pp. 55, 91.
[3] V. 10, p. 281.   [4] *Autobiography*, pp. 73-4.
[5] *Scotland and Scotsmen*, v. 1, p. 195.
[6] *Life of Hume*, Hill Burton, 1846, v. 1, p. 31.
[7] *Surveys of Scottish History*, p. 111.

The qualities, he observed in one of his essays, " strong spirits, and a presumptuous boldness of character," which helped to bring into being such sects as " the *Anabaptists* in Germany, the *Camisars* in France, the *Levellers*, and other fanatics in England, and the *Covenanters* in Scotland," tended to produce, after the first violence of these forms of religion had died down, a type of people who were prepared to discuss questions of any description. " Our sectaries," Hume affirmed, " who were formerly such dangerous bigots, are now become very free reasoners." [1] Everyone knows also what came out of that. In a fourth department, if we count lyric poetry as one, Scotland had taken the lead.

The fifth eighteenth-century northern triumph in letters, the leadership won by Boswell in biography, is not always regarded as a strictly Scottish achievement. In his *Literary History of Scotland* Millar dismissed Boswell in less than a page, on the ground that his two great works belong, in virtue both of their hero and of their own quality, " to the literature of England rather than to that of Scotland." [2] Professor Raleigh declared that if he had to find a paradox in Boswell he would " find it in this, that he was a Scot." [3] Nevertheless, though Boswell prided himself on being " completely a citizen of the world," he described himself to Rousseau as an " ancient Scots gentleman " and added, " You know the pride of the Scots." [4] He boasted that in his veins there flowed the blood of Bruce, and exclaimed, " Of such ancestry who would not be proud ? " [5] He expressed " warm regret " at the disappearance of Scotland as an independent kingdom.[6] When the landlord at Glenmoriston spoke to him about the Forty-Five he " could not refrain from tears." [7] If in the excitement of his first meeting with Johnson he blurted out that he could not help coming from Scotland he was careful to explain in the *Life* that he meant this as " light pleasantry " and not as " an humiliating abasement " at the expense of his country.[8] When he humoured Englishmen, he remarked in the *Tour*, " in an outrageous contempt of Scotland," he treated them " as children." [9] " Citizen of the world," he asserted in the *Life*, " as I hold

---

[1] *Essays*, World's Classics, pp. 78-9.   [2] p. 368.
[3] *Samuel Johnson*, Leslie Stephen Lecture, p. 5.
[4] *Tour*, p. 9 ; *James Boswell*, C. E. Vulliamy, p. 35.   [5] *Tour*, p. 13.
[6] *Ibid.*, p. 27.   [7] *Ibid.*, p. 122.   [8] V. 1, p. 261.   [9] p. 9.

myself to be, I have that degree of predilection for my *natale solum* . . . that I should have felt a generous indignation at any injustice done to it." [1] To his mention of Johnson's sally about the noblest prospect seen by a Scotsman being the high road to England he appended the obstinate comment : " After all, however, those, who admire the rude grandeur of Nature, cannot deny it to Caledonia." [2] We have noticed his love of Scottish music. He shared other Scottish interests. He dreamed of being a historian, and liked to think of himself as a philosopher.[3] He tried to interest Johnson in Scottish authors, maintaining, for example, that *The Gentle Shepherd* was " the best pastoral that had ever been written," and offering to teach the Doctor to understand it.[4] Should any of his countrymen, he declared, " affect to forget " the " native wood-note wild " of his Scottish speech he would " heartily despise him." [5] He had the Scottish fondness for facts ; he claimed that he had represented Johnson " as he really was," spoke of the " scrupulous authenticity " with which he had tried to compose his narrative, and said he had sometimes " run half over London in order to fix a date correctly." [6] His two great works link themselves immediately with the Scottish love of discussion : it was to a large extent as a debater that he delighted in Johnson ; many passages in the *Tour* and *Life* read like superbly written minutes of a superlative Speculative Society. His attitude to Johnson was exactly that of the preface to the first *Edinburgh Review* to the English literary world. The Johnson circle had for him the charm that comes from distance ; the zest that enlivens the *Tour* and the *Life* springs in part from the fact that they are, in all their best passages, journals of a Scotsman on holiday. The Scottish delight in individuality tended to express itself, at times, in what seems very like a deliberate cultivation of eccentricity. " The country swarmed," Grey Graham wrote of eighteenth-century Scotland, " with ' originals ' in every rank, in town and village." [7] Boswell, with one of his country's eccentrics, Monboddo, in mind, asked the Doctor seriously if he considered

[1] V. 1, p. 555. [2] *Ibid.*, p. 285.
[3] *Tour*, p. 74. *Life*, v. 1, pp. 393, 442 ; v. 2, p. 124. *Boswell the Biographer*, Mallory, p. 187. *Letters to Temple*, ed. Seccombe, 1908, pp. 3-4, 66. *Account of Corsica*, ed. Hill, 1879, p. 193.
[4] *Life*, v. 1, p. 489 ; v. 2, pp. 32, 115-6. [5] *Ibid.*, v. 1, p. 258.
[6] *Ibid.*, v. 1, pp. 20, 4. [7] *Social Life of Scotland*, p. 79.

it wrong to " affect singularity, in order to make people stare."
Johnson replied that he did.[1] This, however, did not prevent
Boswell from making his picture of Johnson one of the most
magnificent studies of a " character " in all literature. It is
plain too that Boswell was not averse from being regarded as
a " character " himself. Boswell's two great works appear to
me to have sprung as naturally from the soil of eighteenth-
century Scotland as did the poetry of Burns.

Cockburn, referring to the opening years of the nineteenth
century, spoke of the age that was receding as " the last purely
Scotch age that Scotland was destined to see." Edinburgh, he
said, was yet far from London in terms of travel, and " still
more distant in its style and habits." [2] Jeffrey, writing in 1809,
described Scotland as " long an independent kingdom, and still
separate in laws, character, and manners." [3] " The generation
that was advancing," said Cockburn, " was still a Scotch
production. Its [Edinburgh's] character," he wrote, " may be
estimated by the names I have mentioned ; and by the fact
that the genius of Scott and of Jeffrey had made it the seat at
once of the most popular poetry, and the most brilliant criticism,
that then existed." [4] To Cockburn, we observe, Jeffrey's
writings appeared Scottish. There is a sense in which these
writings might be regarded as providing a climax to the great
Scottish period at which we have been glancing. Whatever
else may be said of the second *Edinburgh Review*, no one is likely
to question the assertion that its attitude was unlike that of the
first *Edinburgh* in that it was marked by no subservience to,
at anyrate, contemporary English authorship. It is plain that
with Jeffrey a new kind of confidence came to Scotland.
Criticism may not be the highest form of literary activity. But
to be regarded as a centre of criticism does as much, perhaps,
as anything else can do to raise a town to the rank of a literary
capital. Jeffrey, it may be claimed, by the power he instilled
into his *Review*, gave the capital of his country a position of this
kind such as has been occupied by no other town in the British
Empire, except London, either before or since.

There seems a reasonable possibility that where Jeffrey's
criticism was most effective, he also was being true to the Scot
in him.

[1] *Life*, v. 1, p. 383.　　　　　　　[2] *Life of Jeffrey*, v. 1, pp. 157, 159.
[3] *Contributions to the Edinburgh Review*, v. 2, p. 155　[4] *Life of Jeffrey*, v. 1, p. 160.

CHAPTER IV

APPRENTICESHIP—AND SOME QUALITIES

On 23rd October 1773, the day on which Jeffrey was born in Charles Street, Edinburgh, Hume was living in St David Street ; [1] Smith was in London with the manuscript of his *Wealth of Nations* ; [2] Fergusson was seeing his collected works circulate in gift-copies preliminary to general sale ; [3] Burns, aged fourteen, had just finished harvesting at Mount Oliphant ; [4] Boswell and Johnson, on that very Saturday, journeyed from Oban to Inveraray through the rainstorm that has been mentioned.[5] In a letter written to his daughter in February 1840, Jeffrey, then in his sixty-seventh year, spoke of a " long lonely thoughtful walk " he had had in Edinburgh that day, part of which had led him " among the strange narrow gloomy little lanes, running down from the High Street " that he had " used to frequent " in his " boyish days." [6] These must have been among his earliest memories : the first school he attended was situated, we observed, in a close off the High Street. He passed to the High School of Edinburgh at the age of eight, where his first master, Luke Fraser, had the " singular good fortune," Cockburn remarked, to turn out, from three successive classes of four years each, Walter Scott, Francis Jeffrey, and Henry Brougham. His class-mates, Cockburn said, recollected him " as a little, clever, anxious boy, always near the top of the class, and who never lost a place without shedding tears." While we cannot stress too much the behaviour of a child, we shall see, later, evidence of a sensitiveness in Jeffrey that might not have been suspected by people who knew him only by reputation as a savage reviewer. Burns arrived in Edinburgh on 28th November 1786, slightly more than a month after Jeffrey's thirteenth birthday. One day during that winter, Cockburn wrote, Jeffrey " was standing on the High Street, staring at a man whose appearance struck him ; a person standing at a shop door tapped him on the shoulder, and said, ' Aye laddie ! Ye

---

[1] *David Hume*, Calderwood, p. 154.   [2] *Adam Smith*, Hirst, p. 156.
[3] *Fergusson*, Grosart, pp. 101-2.
[4] *Life and Works*, Chambers and Wallace, v. 1, p. 40.
[5] Boswell's *Tour*, pp. 335-7 ; Johnson's *Journey*, pp. 231-2.
[6] *Life*, Cockburn, v. 2, pp. 313-4.

may weel look at that man ! That's Robert Burns.' He never saw Burns again." [1] Some four years afterwards Jeffrey had the privilege of a brief contact with Boswell whom, " in a state of great intoxication," he helped to carry to bed. Next day, we are told, the great man was informed who had been his conveyers, whereupon he clapped Jeffrey on the head, told him he was a very promising lad, and prophesied that if he went on as he had begun he might live to be a " Bozzy " yet.[2]

Before this, Jeffrey had attended the Greek, Logic, and Moral Philosophy classes at Glasgow University. That he did not attend the classes in " Law and Government " conducted by Professor John Millar was accounted for, Cockburn suggested, by the fact that his father, George Jeffrey, was a staunch Tory, by whom " Millar's free doctrines, and his Whig party, were held in abhorrence." [3] His father's political views did not, however, prevent Jeffrey from indulging in the typically Scottish exercise of forming opinions of his own. " His father was a great Tory," said Saintsbury, " and, though it would be uncharitable to say that this was the reason why Jeffrey was a great Liberal, the two facts were probably not unconnected in the line of causation." [4]

We see, in 1787, the beginnings of an independence of character appearing in Jeffrey in another connection. In that year Adam Smith was proposed for the position of Lord Rector of the University. One of Jeffrey's fellow students, later Principal Haldane of the college of St Mary's, St Andrews, related to Cockburn that he recollected seeing Jeffrey, " a little black creature " whom he had not noticed before, holding forth to a number of lads on Glasgow Green against voting for the economist —solely, it appears, on the ground that the candidature of Smith was supported by authority in the shape of the professors. At Glasgow, we learn too, Jeffrey was one of a number of students who formed themselves into an " Elocution Society," and who determined to break into amateur drama with a production of *Tancred and Sigismunda*, in which Jeffrey was to play the role of the heroine. The performance was vetoed by the authorities ; whereupon we find Jeffrey bursting out, on the last page of one of his notebooks, into resentment, and suggesting, among other comments, that it might be profitable

---

[1] *Life*, Cockburn, v. 1, pp. 4-8.   [2] *Ibid*, v. 1, pp. 33-4.
[3] *Ibid.*, v. 1, p. 12.   [4] *Essays in Eng. Lit.* (1780-1860), p. 102

for certain members even of the staff to " pay a little more attention to the Graces " when lecturing and praying.[1]

In Cockburn's account of his stay at Glasgow we catch a glimpse of another trait in his character. Being disturbed at this time by what he regarded as superstitious fears, he set about curing himself by forcing himself to walk alone, at midnight, round the Cathedral and its graveyard.[2] We shall see later that, like others of his countrymen, he liked always to look steadily into the face of reality.

In 1791 he removed to Oxford where, as we noted, he soon began to yearn for his native Scotland. A longer stay might have weakened this feeling ; but it was more than the temporary fancy of a homesick boy : we have noticed that Jeffrey's love of his country remained with him all his life. We observed his telling Cockburn in 1832 that he hungered for a view of Loch Lomond and the Highlands. " He was," Cockburn wrote, " an idolater of Lochlomond." [3]

This last statement brings to mind a letter sent by Jeffrey at the age of eighteen from Oxford to his sister Mary—in which he drew for her a pen picture of the view from his window— " the deep and romantic shades on the sculptured towers—the sparkle of their gilded vanes—their black and pointed shadows upon the smooth green turf of our courts—the strong shades of the statues over the library—the yellow and trembling heads of the trees beyond them ! " [4] We notice the delight in beauty. Cockburn said : " All men pretend to enjoy scenery, and most men do enjoy it, though many of them only passively ; but with Jeffrey it was indispensable for happiness, if not for existence. He lived in it." [5] He could boast on occasion about Scottish scenery as strongly as did Boswell. " Mr Mawman," he remarked in an article published in 1806, " may contrast the cultivated fields, and rich verdure of his country, with our heaths and hollows, as triumphantly as he pleases ; but, for mighty mountains, extensive lakes, and tremendous waterfalls, we boldly challenge all England to produce anything like our Highlands." [6] " The Scotish landscape . . . we must be pardoned for thinking, is better suited for poetical purposes," he wrote in another place, " than the prevailing scenery of

[1] *Life*, Cockburn, v. 1, pp. 12, 14.   [2] *Ibid.*, v. 1, p. 20.
[3] *Ibid.*, v. 1, p. 270.   [4] *Ibid.*, v. 2, p. 5.
[5] *Ibid.*, v. 1, p. 73.   [6] *Ed. Rev.*, No. 16, pp. 290-1.

England." [1] " If Mr Crabbe," he stated in his review of
Crabbe's *Tales*, " had had the good fortune to live among *our*
Highland hills, and lakes, and upland woods . . . what a
delicious picture would his unrivalled powers have enabled him
to give to the world ! " [2] His letters from England—we have
just noticed an illustration—show that he could appreciate, at
the same time, the beauty also of the south. In a letter written
from Southampton in 1806 we encounter an enthusiastic description of the Isle of Wight with its " lofty chalk cliffs, which rise,
in the most dazzling whiteness, out of the blue sea into the blue
sky, and make a composition something like Wedgwood's
enamel." In another written from London sixteen years later
we have a glimpse of an English spring with " all the sloes and
almond trees in blossom, and all the fields alive with lambs,
and the sky echoing with larks." On his way home after this
last visit he stopped at the house of Sir James Mackintosh, and
took the opportunity of writing a letter to his wife's sister in
New York, in which he compared " old England " with America.
Within sight of the house in which he was staying, he said,
were places rich in historical associations, the palace of Hunsdon,
Theobalds, the Rye-house. " Then," he continued, " there are
two gigantic oak stumps, with a few fresh branches still, which
are said to have been planted by Edward the III., and massive
stone bridges over lazy waters ; and churches that look as old
as Christianity ; and beautiful groups of branchy trees ; and a
verdure like nothing else in the universe ; and all the cottages
and lawns fragrant with sweet briar and violets, and glowing
with purple lilacs and white elders ; and antique villages
scattering round wide bright greens ; with old trees and ponds, and
a massive pair of oaken stocks preserved from the days of Alfred . . .
I will not tell you," he added, " about Scotland after this. It
has not these characters of ancient wealth and population, but
beauties of another kind which you must come and see." [3]

In a letter written to Mary from Glasgow in 1789 we find
Jeffrey confessing that he had attended all his classes " very ill,"
and that he was at that moment " under a summons of the
Principal to compear before him and receive condign punishment
for non-appearance in the Common Hall above three times this
Session." [4] " This law," he wrote to Mary from Oxford in

[1] *Ed. Rev.*, No. 31, p. 217.
[2] *Cont.*, v. 2, pp. 334-5.
[3] *Life*, v. 2, pp. 107-8, 201, 207-8.
[4] *Ibid.*, v. 2, p. 1.

1792, " is a vile work. I wish I had been bred a piper." These, however, were merely aberrations. Jeffrey had his share of Scottish perseverance. At Glasgow, we read for instance, he formed the habit of filling notebooks with expansions of the notes of his professors' lectures and " discussions of the doctrines," and he continued this practice throughout all his time as a student. His notes on the lectures on history of Alexander Tytler, whose class he attended at Edinburgh in 1792-3, after his return from Oxford, filled " 436 folio pages," and, according to his biographer, would, in normal handwriting, have occupied at least twice the space ; his account of a course of lectures in chemistry which he attended in 1800 took up " five volumes of notes " ; attendance at a series of lectures on Political Economy delivered by Dugald Stewart added " five small volumes of notes " to his collection. In going through Jeffrey's papers Cockburn found also a great quantity of youthful writing which, he considered, must have been only a fraction of what was originally composed, and which demonstrated that, in his student days, Jeffrey must have worked incessantly upon a course of study of his own devising. There were translations from Greek, Latin, and French, synopses, essays, sermons, speeches, " opinions of . . . authors," a " sketch " of his " own character," verses, and a couple of plays. Further, Jeffrey's " inclination towards analysis and appreciation was so strong," Cockburn wrote, " that almost every one of his compositions closes by a criticism on himself." [1] Jeffrey, Nichol Smith commented on these early studies, " was preparing himself for the *Review* as if he had foreseen it." [2]

Something of Jeffrey's early conception of how a critic should perform his office revealed itself when he was a member of Jardine's logic class at Glasgow. Jardine was accustomed to ask his students to criticise one another's exercises. Haldane, the fellow-student already mentioned, stated that on one of these occasions his own work fell into the hands of Jeffrey. He regretted, he said, that he did not preserve the judgment, as it " gave early promise of that critical acumen which was afterwards fully developed in the pages of the *Edinburgh Review*." It was, at the same time, so caustic that Jardine, having commenced to read it, found, apparently, his heart fail him. He " read some of the remarks at the beginning of the criticism,

[1] *Life*, v. 1, pp. 14-119.　　　　　[2] *Jeffrey's Lit. Crit.*, p. viii.

but the remainder he read in a suppressed tone of voice, muttering something as if he thought it too severe." [1]   Jeffrey was equally unsparing of himself. " The epitome," ran his comment, for example, on a summary of Lucretius, " I have now completed of this beautiful author is, I am sensible, a very disgraceful performance. The poetical beauties of the original are entirely lost." A translation into blank verse of a portion of Racine's *Britannicus* moved him to the following : " This barbarous version of the elegant Racine, I feel myself bound to stigmatize with its genuine character, that as often as the proofs of my stupidity, displayed on the foregoing pages, shall mortify my pride, I may be comforted by the instance of candour set forth on this." One of his plays he summed up as being, upon the whole, " exceedingly flat, slow, and uninteresting." It was " languid, affected, pedantic " ; the fable had " no meaning, and the characters nothing characteristic." There was " too little action " : it was simply " a succession of conversations." Nevertheless, he observed, with a slight recoil from this acerbity, the " simplicity of diction, as well as of soul " which he had tried to exhibit prevented " these defects from being very disgusting," and made it " rather drowsy than abominable." [2]

Another youthful effort, a speech supposed to be addressed to the House of Commons and containing a fierce attack on a member who had agreed with him, but on bad grounds, and who had been moreover " somewhat too abstruse and metaphysical " for his " comprehension," shows, in a different form, a desire to look ruthlessly at truth, whether truth is what one would like it to be or not, and, as well, a suspicion of obscurity. Another shows a love of looking at every side of a question and a consciousness, at the same time, that it is possible to carry this exercise farther than is profitable. Summing up a discourse on the difference between prose and poetry, he remarked that, before he had done asserting the contrary, he had begun to suspect that " the old ground of discrimination " was preferable to his " mode of abrogating it " ; and concluded, " Were I to proceed to unfold this new idea at full length, I would very likely, in the course of my defence of it, discover some new obstacle to my belief, which might return me to my abdicated opinion, or perhaps turn me over to yet another, which might serve me in the same way. I have no mind to

[1] *Life*, v. 1, p. 13.   [2] *Ibid.*, v. 1, pp. 24, 26, 71.

encounter such a hydra." [1] One is reminded of Burnet's " entangled scrupulosity."

We noticed that Jeffrey wrote to a friend that he was even more a Scot when he was at Oxford than when he was at home. " The only part of a Scotchman I mean to abandon," he declared in the same letter, " is the language ; and language is all I expect to learn in England." [2] The vernacular exacted the usual penalty. Lord Holland remarked that though Jeffrey " had lost the broad Scotch at Oxford, he had only gained the narrow English," [3] which feat caused J. H. Millar to describe him as " the ancestor of a numerous progeny, who, in the pulpit, in the law courts, or in private life, talk a mincing and quasi-genteel lingo of their own (the sort of English known in some quarters as ' Princes Street ' or ' Kelvinside ')." [4] Cockburn asserted that " it would have been better if he had merely got some of the grosser matter rubbed off his vernacular tongue, and left himself, unencumbered both by it and by unattainable English, to his own respectable Scotch, refined by literature and good society, and used plainly and naturally, without shame, and without affected exaggeration." [3]

Jeffrey shared the Scottish fondness for discussion. He was remembered as " one of the most acute and fluent speakers " in a debating society at Glasgow.[5] Brougham spoke of his having borne " a most distinguished part " in the Speculative Society, and mentioned having a particular recollection of a speech by him on a subject connected with Russia.[6] Cockburn doubted if he was ever silent throughout a whole meeting of the Speculative. " It has scarcely ever fallen to my lot," Cockburn wrote, " to hear three better speeches than three I heard in that place,—one on National Character by Jeffrey, one on the Immortality of the Soul by Horner, and one on the Power of Russia by Brougham." [7]

Jeffrey was admitted to the Bar in 1794. His already well-practised pen might have been calculated to be of advantage for the written arguments that were then a feature of Scottish court procedure. Against him there were, however, according to

---

[1] *Life*, v. 1, pp. 25-7.　　　　　　　[2] *Ibid.*, v. 1, p. 46.
[3] *Ibid.*, v. 1, pp. 46-7.　Carlyle quoted Braxfield as saying of him : " The laddie has clean tint his Scotch, and found nae English ! " *Rem.*, v. 2, p. 51.
[4] *Lit. Hist. of Scotland*, p. 317.　　　　[5] *Life*, v. 1, p. 13.
[6] *Life and Times*, v. 1, p. 244.　　　　[7] *Life*, v. 1, p. 56.

Cockburn, his Whig opinions, his " English," a tendency to
loquacity, and a something of smart sarcasm in his manner.
Possibly his smallness was also, in those early days, against him :
Southey after meeting him in 1805 spoke of him as " an *homu-
nunculus* of five foot one." [1] Business came slowly. For a
number of years his way of living was uncertain. In 1795 he
told his brother John that he saw little prospect of success in
his profession and was trying to think of some other occupation
in which he might put his " time and application to better
profit " ; in the beginning of the following year he remarked
that " the only kind of work " with which he had employed
himself lately had been " translating old Greek poetry, and
copying the style of all our different poets " ; in January 1798
he confessed to his cousin Morehead that he would like " to be
the rival of Smith and Hume " ; in September 1798 he visited
London with letters of introduction and an ambition of settling
there as a literary " grub," but found the letters useless ; in
July 1800 he told Morehead that he had become " a zealous
chemist " ; in August 1801 he informed his brother that he
was not making £100 a year by his profession ; and in November
1801, with a sudden burst of Scottish recklessness, he married a
dowerless wife, and set up house in his flat on the third floor of
18 Buccleuch Place.[2]

It was in this flat, as we have noted, that the *Edinburgh
Review* was planned. Jeffrey was not hopeful of success. It
required, Brougham said afterwards, " all Smith's overpowering
vivacity to argue and laugh Jeffrey out of his difficulties." [3]
No doubt he was continuing his practice of trying to look squarely
at reality. " My notions of philosophy," he had told his brother
in 1794, " rather lead me to consider a steady contemplation
of the worst as the best preparation for its possible occurrence." [4]
A new *Review*, to be set up far from the centre of the literary
world in London, without a single known man on its staff, did

[1] *Letters*, World's Classics, p. 103.
[2] *Life*, v. 1, pp. 97, 98, 99, 101-2 ; v. 2, pp. 45, 57 ; v. 1, pp. 118-9.
Cockburn stated that Jeffrey was, by 1799, an " occasional contributor "
to the *Monthly Review* (*Life*, v. 1, p. 114). Nichol Smith has pointed out,
however, that the manuscript notes of Griffiths, the editor of the *Monthly*,
now in the Bodleian Library, record June 1802 as the first date of publication
of an article by Jeffrey (*Jeffrey's Lit. Crit.*, p. ix).
[3] *Life and Times*, v. 1, pp. 246, 251. Cf. *Life*, Cockburn, v. 1, p. 124,
et seq.   [4] *Life*, v. 1, p. 62.

not seem, on the face of it, a particularly promising project. " Our Review," Jeffrey wrote to Morehead in May 1802, " has been postponed till September, and I am afraid will not go on with much spirit even then."   " Our review is still at a stand," he wrote to his brother in June of the same year.   " However, I have completely abandoned the idea of taking any permanent share in it, and shall probably desert after fulfilling my engagements, which only extend to a certain contribution for the first four numbers.   I suspect that the work itself will not have a much longer life." [1]

Smith, however, was more hopeful.   He did not regard the fact that the work was being published in Edinburgh as a disadvantage.   " If," he wrote to Constable, " you will give £200 per annum to your editor, and ten guineas a sheet, you will soon have the best review in Europe.   This town, I am convinced, is preferable to all others for such an undertaking, from the abundance of literary men it contains, and from the freedom which at this distance they can exercise towards the wits of the south." [2]   In 1803 the editorship, despite his forebodings, was " pressed upon " Jeffrey.[3]   After, however, writing that sentence to his brother about the best philosophy being a contemplation of the worst, he had added, " But my temper is too sanguine, and my activity, I believe, too great, to render it possible for such occasional anticipation to induce a habit of dejection or remissness." [4]   He had removed in May 1802 from the flat in Buccleuch Place to a house in the upper storey of 62 Queen Street.   Mary D. Steuart, in her *Romance of the Edinburgh Streets*, has remarked, in mentioning Jeffrey's residence at this address, " Anyone who had caught more than a glimpse of the diminutive shabby figure hurrying up the hill to the editorial office in George Street, and noted the stiff black hair which fairly bristled with energy, the determination of the mouth, and the vivid penetration of the eyes, would have seen that here, if ever, was a man destined to force his way ruthlessly through whatever obstacles the Fates chose to put in his way." [5]   " Espérer sans agir," Chasles wrote in his article on Jeffrey, " c'est tout perdre ; agir et ne croire à rien, c'est tout gagner." [6]   It was a philosophy natural to men living in a poor country ; and, as we have just seen, it was undoubtedly Jeffrey's.

[1] *Life*, v. 1, p. 129.   [2] *Ibid.*, v. 1, p. 134   [3] *Ibid.*, v. 1, p. 136.
[4] *Ibid.*, v. 1, p. 62.   [5] p. 191.   [6] *Revue Contemporaine*, v. 8, pp. 81-2.

CHAPTER V

ACHIEVEMENT—CRITICS' FOLLY

THE first number of the second *Edinburgh Review* appeared on 10th October 1802. " The success," Brougham wrote, " was far beyond any of our expectations. It was so great that Jeffrey was utterly dumbfounded." [1] To Cockburn the memory was equally thrilling. The effect of the new publication was, he declared, " electrical." " It is impossible," he wrote, " for those who did not live at the time, and in the heart of the scene, to feel, or almost to understand, the impression made by the new luminary, or the anxieties with which its motions were observed. It was an entire and instant change of every thing that the public had been accustomed to in that sort of composition. The old periodical opiates were extinguished at once." [2]

Hugh Miller pointed out in his article of 1850 that men of literary merit had written for periodicals before 1802, and mentioned Goldsmith, Smollett, Burke, and Johnson, as well as the main conductors, already noted, of the *Edinburgh Review* of 1755-6. (The fact that that periodical had lasted for only two numbers was another reason for Jeffrey's pessimism.) [1] But the English review-writers, Miller observed, were associated in their labours, " with dull amateurs, or the scribblers of Grub Street "; and even when, as in the *Edinburgh* instance, " all the writers were superior," they spared for their articles " merely the odds and ends of their cogitations." Jeffrey and Sydney Smith, Miller stated on the other hand, gave to their review-writing " all they were capable of." [3] The *Quarterly* article of 1852 characterised it as a " mere delusion " that the critical press of London had, immediately before the appearance of the *Edinburgh*, been " unsupported by able and learned writing," and remarked that Southey, William Taylor, Parr, and Mackintosh had all contributed to it. " The mischief was," it added, however, " that the whole concern had fallen under the sway of booksellers, who dictated subjects, paid good hands shabbily, and gave most of their space to articles for which they

[1] *Life and Times*, v. 1, pp. 252-3. [2] *Life*, v. 1, p. 131.
[3] *Historical and Critical Essays*, 1873, pp. 68-9.

could not have paid too little, so that the wheat was lost among the chaff." [1]   Scott, writing to Gifford in 1808, described " most of the other Reviews " as merely booksellers' " advertising sheets to puff off their own publications." [2]   Gates drew attention, in this connection, to the way in which Griffiths, the editor of the *Monthly Review*, dictated to Goldsmith and William Taylor, and remarked that a " final result of this whole system of review-managing and hack-writing was unwillingness on the part of men of position to have anything to do with review-writing." [3]

Confirmation of this may be found in the qualms with which the reviewers of the second *Edinburgh* entered upon their task. Jeffrey complained to Horner in April 1802, for example, that Brougham, though he had approved of their plan at first, had changed his mind, and " rather thought now that he should decline to have any connection with it." [4] Brougham, in his *Life and Times*, explained his reasons. It had not, he said, at that time been made clear to him " that the booksellers were to be *mere instruments*, entirely in subservience to us, and exercising not only no control, but no influence of any kind ; for this was the fundamental object of the *Review*." He thought it possible also " that Jeffrey's control might be interfered with by certain of our body, in whom the same confidence could not be reposed, either as regarded their opinions or their discretion." [5] For the first two or three numbers, Cockburn tells us, the *Review's* founders had the idea that the work could be carried on without any remuneration at all. " It was," Cockburn put it, " to be all gentlemen, and no pay." That suggests a nervousness lest the contributors should be regarded as hacks. It was " during this state of matters," Cockburn said, that Jeffrey feared that the *Review* would not succeed.[6] We notice a hesitation similar to that of his colleagues in Jeffrey himself. The money he would make by the *Review* was, he confessed to Horner, a " monstrous bribe " to a man in his position. On the other side, however, were to be placed " vexation and trouble, interference with professional employment and character, and risk of general degradation." " The publication," he told his

---

[1] No. 181, p. 125.   [2] *Life of Scott*, Lockhart, v. 2, p. 207.
[3] *Three Studies*, pp. 46-51. (Forster's *Goldsmith*, 1848, p. 170 ; *Life of William Taylor*, Robberds, I, 130-132, 139, 122—Gates's references.)
[4] *Memoirs of Horner*, v. 1, p. 186.
[5] V. 1, pp. 249-50.   [6] *Life*, v. 1, p. 133.

brother, " is in the highest degree respectable as yet, as there are none but gentlemen connected with it. If it ever sink into the state of an ordinary bookseller's journal I have done with it." " But," he wrote to Horner, " what influences me the most is, that I engaged in it at first gratuitously, along with a set of men whose character and situation in life must command the respect of the multitude, and that I hope to go on with it as a matter of emolument along with the same associates. All the men here will take their ten guineas I find, and, under the sanction of that example, I think I may take my editor's salary also without being supposed to have suffered any degradation." [1]

The strangeness, as it seems to us now, of all this heart-searching about entering upon a connection with a highly respectable periodical is a measure of the change that has taken place since in the public attitude to work of this kind. J. H. Millar, we noticed, referred to Jeffrey as among the greatest of British editors. Not the least of his achievements as an editor is the improvement he assisted in bringing about in the status of an important branch of the writing profession.

Once again, we observe, Scotland had taken the lead.

That status was helped by the rates which the Review's success, itself the result of course, to a large extent, of Jeffrey's efficiency, made it possible for its managers to pay. The first payment was made, we note from Jeffrey's letter, at the rate of ten guineas a sheet : not long after, Jeffrey recorded, the minimum was raised to sixteen guineas, at which it remained during the period of his editorship, though two-thirds of the articles were paid much higher, averaging, he reckoned, from twenty to twenty-five guineas a sheet on the whole number.[2] " Jeffrey," Horner wrote in his journal in 1802, after the appearance of the Review's first number, " is the person who will derive most honour from this publication, as his articles in this number are generally known, and are incomparably the best : I have received the greater pleasure from this circumstance, because the genius of that little man has remained almost unknown to all but his most intimate acquaintances. His manner is not at first pleasing ; what is worse, it is of that cast, which almost irresistibly impresses upon strangers the idea of levity and superficial talents. Yet there is not any man, whose real character is so much the reverse ; he has indeed a very

[1] *Life*, v. 2, pp. 71, 72, 74.　　　　[2] *Ibid.*, v. 1, p. 136.

sportive and playful fancy, but it is accompanied with very extensive and varied information, with a readiness of apprehension almost intuitive, with judicious and calm discernment, with a profound and penetrating understanding." [1] The last two sentences are worth observing.

The *Review's* independence involved danger. To find themselves able, behind a screen of anonymity, to say to a large extent what they pleased about their contemporaries, and to discover, as time passed, that they were being regarded on that very account as reformers and powerful protectors of the world of readers was, to a group of men still in their twenties or early thirties, hitherto completely obscure, a draught that was distinctly heady. The effect on them was such as might have been anticipated. " Upon the whole," Horner declared of the first number, " I do not think we have gained much character by it ; it is considered as respectable enough in point of talents, but the severity, in some of the papers it may be called scurrility, has given general dissatisfaction." [2] Moore related in his *Memoirs* how, thirty-one years after the foundation of the *Edinburgh*, he had heard Sydney Smith speak of the " fun " he had had in composing his early reviews for it. Smith mentioned an article that Brougham and he had written together, and gave the following instance of their collaboration : " We take for granted (wrote Brougham) that Mr Ritson supposes Providence to have had some share in producing him—though for what inscrutable purposes (added Sydney) we profess ourselves unable to conjecture." [3] Harriet Martineau told in her *Autobiography* how she, years afterwards, taxed Smith with the mischief he and his fellows had done at the outset. " It is all very well," she declared, " to talk sensibly now of the actual importance of reviews, and the real value of reviewers' judgments : but the fact remains that spirits were broken, hearts were sickened, and authorship was cruelly discouraged by the savage and

[1] *Memoirs of Horner*, v. 1, pp. 205-6 ; *Life*, v. 1, p. 135. Horner added : " Indeed, both in point of candour and of vigour in the reasoning powers, I have never personally known a finer intellect than Jeffrey's, unless I were to except Allen's."

[2] *Ibid.*, v. 1, p. 205.

[3] V. 7, p. 13. The exact sentence in the *Review* appears to be : " Hear how this puny worm raises its cry, to arraign the order of nature, and scoff at the Omniscience, which, for wise purposes, though quite unknown to us, suffers it to crawl upon the earth." *Ed. Rev.*, No. 3, p. 135.

reckless condemnations passed by the *Edinburgh Review* in its early days. 'We *were* savage,' replied Sydney Smith, 'I remember' (and it was plain that he could not help enjoying the remembrance) ' how Brougham and I sat trying one night how we could exasperate our cruelty to the utmost. We had got hold of a poor nervous little vegetarian,' "—the reference was to Ritson again— " ' who had put out a poor silly little book ; and when we had done our review of it, we sat trying,' —(and here he joined his finger and thumb as if dropping from a phial) ' to find one more chink, one more crevice, through which we might drop in one more drop of verjuice, to eat into his bones.' " [1]

This sort of thing may have been " fun " to the reviewers. It may also have been " fun " to the readers, and have helped, therefore, to sell the *Review* : it is an odd trait of human nature that, in such cases, the reader tends to identify himself with the attacker rather than with the attacked. That does not, however, prevent the whole thing from being pitiful enough. Jeffrey was not always easy in his mind about it. Among Sydney Smith's letters there is one dated June 1802—before, we observe, the appearance of the first number of the *Review*— written evidently in reply to a remonstrance of Jeffrey against the severity of Smith's manner of criticism.[2] " We must," Jeffrey remarked in a letter to Horner dated October 1803, " abate something of our general asperity." [3] We find him again in August 1804 apparently attempting tactfully to soften the critical asperities of Brougham, to whom he wrote asking the latter's " indulgence," as he put it, " for the liberty I took in suppressing and altering a few sentences in the beginning of your Lauderdale. They did not bear at all upon the argument, and I was really anxious that there should be no pretext for complaining of anything personal or contemptuous in the manner. . . . It will give me great pleasure to find that the confutation, which must, I think, be the most masterly and convincing, is also the most temperate and polite." [4] Years later, in 1822, in an article on Byron, reprinted in the *Contributions*, we find him expressing himself as follows : " There is nothing so certain, we take it, as that those who are the most alert in discovering the faults of a work of genius, are the least touched

[1] V. 1, pp. 321-2.   [2] *Memoir of Smith*, Holland, 1855, v. 2, pp. 4-5.
[3] *Life*, v. 2, p. 86.   [4] *Life and Times*, Brougham, v. 1, p. 266.

with its beauties. Those who admire and enjoy fine poetry, in short, are quite a different class of persons from those who find out its flaws and defects. . . . It is in vain to expect the praises of such people ; for they never praise ;—and it is truly very little worth while to disarm their censure." [1] In the *Contributions* also we find him expressing regret for some of his own critical severities. " I have, in my time," he remarked in one footnote, " said petulant and provoking things of Mr Southey :—and such as I would not say now " ; [2] and, in another, " I have spoken in many places rather too bitterly and confidently of the faults of Mr Wordsworth's poetry : And forgetting that, even on my own view of them, they were but faults of taste, or venial self-partiality, have sometimes visited them, I fear, with an asperity which should be reserved for objects of moral reprobation." [3]

These quotations show that Jeffrey was not free from the faults he deprecated. A fuller quotation from the letter to Horner of October 1803 suggests at the same time that he was unwilling to renounce entirely this kind of criticism. " Walter Scott," the full passage runs, " has, in a manner, offered to do Godwin's *Life of Chaucer* ; and as he understands the subject, and hates the author, I have a notion he will make a good article of it. We must abate something of our general asperity ; but I think we should make one or two examples of great delinquents in every number." [4] The extracts we quoted in an earlier chapter from his review of Montgomery's *Wanderer of Switzerland* show how, on occasion, he himself was prepared to wield the lash. " I should not hesitate," Montgomery remarked on his reviewer and on that review, " even in his presence, to say that it *was* unmerited, not because I did not deserve the chastisement due to imbecility and presumption, but because I was visited with the punishment due only to turpitude." [5] Whatever may be said of the worth of Montgomery's poetry, or of the right of the reviewer to protest against the public's buying so many editions of his work, the quiet modesty and dignity of that reply make one wonder if the reviewer comes the better out of the incident.

Jeffrey was no believer, we know, in letting weaknesses pass unchallenged : we noticed his mercilessness towards his own

[1] *Cont.*, v. 2, p. 92.　　[2] *Ibid.*, v. 2, p. 404.　　[3] *Ibid.*, v. 2, p. 504.
[4] *Life*, v. 2, p. 86.　　[5] *Constable and his Lit. Corr.*, v. 2, p. 252.

E

youthful efforts. It is clear, too, that he was not in sympathy with writers who were afraid of criticism. " There is," he wrote in the article on Byron from which we quoted a moment ago, " a great want of magnanimity, we think, as well as of wisdom, in this sensitiveness to blame ; and we are convinced that no modern author will ever write with the grace and vigour of the older ones, who does not write with some portion of their fearlessness and indifference to censure. *Courage*, in short, is at least as necessary as genius to the success of a work of imagination." [1]

No doubt there is something in this. It is the important office of criticism to preserve at the highest possible level the standard of general taste—to force under its microscope every claim that is made to admiration, as well as all admiration itself—to strive constantly against what is false being mistaken for what is true. The writer cannot and should not desire to escape it. But it was not criticism that Martineau objected to ; it was the method by which criticism was sometimes conducted. When Jeffrey gave way to severity, Cockburn asserted, " it was generally from mere lightness of spirit. Totally devoid of ill nature . . . he handled the book as a thing to be played with ; without duly considering that the gay and moral pleasantry of Horace might produce as much distress as the declamatory weight of Juvenal." [2] Haydon, when he visited Edinburgh, noted that " whatever you praise to Jeffrey, he directly chuckles out some error that you did not perceive." [3] The word " chuckles " suggests, like Cockburn's passage, a man who had learned not to take the world—or criticism—too seriously. That might be regarded as sensible enough. But when the matter comes to what Martineau described as spirits being broken, hearts being sickened, and authorship being discouraged, mere lightness of spirit on the part of the reviewer seems scarcely a adequate defence. It is regarded as sportsmanship in most games to show respect for a gallant loser. In the game of book-writing, defeat, with its accompanying realisation of much time and effort utterly wasted, might be looked upon as itself a fairly complete punishment. " There is not," as poor Keats expressed it, " a fiercer hell than the failure in a great object." Literature may surely be regarded as being, in all its branches,

[1] *Cont.*, v. 2, p. 93. [2] *Life*, v. 1, p. 289.
[3] *B. R. Haydon and his Friends*, Paston, p. 111.

criticism included, a part of man's quest for truth, and happiness, and sweetness, and beauty, in a world in which these things are all too rare and all too easily destroyed—an endeavour to keep the lamp of civilisation from going out, and, if possible, to make it burn more brightly. It seems an odd tradition that this quest should be carried on in an atmosphere of backbiting, and that failure in it should be accompanied by jeers.

The tradition springs partly, no doubt, from a delusion that tends to be inspired by the critic's chair—a delusion that contact with the seat of it dissociates the occupant from fallible humanity, so that it appears to him that while there may be blindnesses and weaknesses in all writing that is placed before him, there is none in what he himself writes by way of judgment. Judgments must, however, either sink into oblivion because of their unimportance, or remain to be judged themselves. When the day of fuller judgment comes, and the critic's own blindnesses, as is inevitable, become apparent, the more unsparingly he has derided the weaknesses of others, the fiercer may be expected to be the attacks upon his own. What seemed at the time to the critic, therefore, to be his strongest writing, may easily turn out to be his weakest, the parts of his work that are most vulnerable. So it has come about with Jeffrey. He belonged, it is true, to an age of hard hitting in criticism, but his own hard hitting need not be defended to any extent on that account. We have seen that he himself, in older and wiser days, made no attempt to defend it. His hard hitting has been an obstacle in the way of readers' finding elements of value in his criticisms. Were there nothing more than hard hitting in his writings, these would not be worth considering further.

CHAPTER VI

SYSTEM—CONTRIBUTIONS—THE AUGUSTAN FALLACY

IT seems as unlikely, however, that the reputation acquired by Jeffrey among the giants of the Georgian era was gained by writings containing merely critical severities as that it was gained by writings containing merely critical blunders. We saw that the *North British Review* found in Jeffrey's essays " a great . . . system of criticism," and that Gregory Smith perceived in them evidence of " a carefully adopted theory." " He was," Cockburn asserted, " the founder of a new system of criticism, and this a higher one than had ever existed." [1] There is nothing anomalous in the idea that orderliness may be discoverable in the thinking of a man reared in eighteenth-century Edinburgh : we noticed that Jeffrey dreamed, in his ambitious early twenties, of rivalling Adam Smith and Hume. Horner, after he had removed to England, told a friend that he had found, in literary conversation, the necessity of unlearning something of the manners one imbibed " in the metaphysical climate of Edinburgh : such as the inclination to theorize, and to present general principles . . . in a scholastic dress." [2] " They are," Sydney Smith declared, in characteristic fashion, of the Scots, " so imbued with metaphysics that they even make love metaphysically ; I overheard a young lady of my acquaintance, at a dance in Edinburgh, exclaim in a sudden pause of the music, ' What you say, my Lord, is very true of love in the *aibstract*, but '—here the fiddlers began fiddling furiously, and the rest was lost." [3] Jeffrey remarked to Horner, discussing one of his own articles, " There is a good part of that article which I thought in considerable danger of being attacked and ridiculed, as a caricature of our Scotch manner of running everything up to elements, and explaining all sorts of occurrences by a theoretical history of society." [4] He claimed definitely also that there was

---

[1] *Life*, v. 1, p. 412. Cf. Saintsbury : " He arranged his critical judgments on something like a regular and co-ordinated system. Even his prejudices and injustices were systematic." *Hist. of Nineteenth Cent. Lit.*, p. 176.

[2] *Memoirs*, v. 1, p. 238.   [3] *Memoir of Smith*, Holland, v. 1, p. 15.

[4] *Life*, v. 2, p. 139.

system in the *Edinburgh's* criticism. "The *Edinburgh Review*, it is well known," he stated in the preface to his *Contributions*, "aimed high from the beginning :—And, refusing to confine itself to the humble task of pronouncing on the mere literary merits of the works that came before it, professed to go deeply into *the Principles* on which its judgments were to be rested ; as well as to take large and Original views of all the important questions to which those works might relate." [1]

Jeffrey's *Contributions to the Edinburgh Review* were published in four volumes in 1843, in three volumes in 1846, and in a single-volume edition in 1853.[2] Saintsbury remarked of this selection that it was made by Jeffrey with great care, at a time when his faculties were in perfect order, and that it includes specimens of every kind of his work.[3] Accordingly, in his essay on Jeffrey, he confined his consideration of Jeffrey's writings to the *Contributions*. Nichol Smith observed that the *Contributions* contain the work " by which, on full deliberation," Jeffrey " was willing to be judged." [4] It is obvious that in articles written throughout a period of many years there were bound to be, as Jeffrey himself said, " discrepancies and small inconsistencies." [5] " I beg you to judge it," he wrote to Horner, referring to another article, " as I fear you must judge all that I say or write, by the whole *broad effect and honest meaning*." [6] It is only fair to him that, in looking for that broad effect and honest meaning, one should lay greatest stress on the articles he chose for republication. It has seemed to me helpful, at the same time, as was remarked in the Introduction, in an attempt to understand his " system," to take into some if not so emphatic consideration his unprinted articles as well. I have found there amplification of his ideas, but no serious inconsistency.

His articles for the *Review* were identified by Jeffrey himself.

---

[1] *Cont.*, v. 1, p. xi. In *The Spirit of the Age* Hazlitt stated that the " style of philosophical criticism " which had been " the boast of the *Edinburgh Review* " was first introduced into the *Monthly* about 1796 by Taylor of Norwich (*Everyman* ed., p. 293). I imagine that Jeffrey's main inspiration came from nearer home.

[2] *Jeffrey's Lit. Crit.*, Nichol Smith, p. 210. The date on the title-page of the first edition is 1844. It appears from Cockburn (v. 1, p. 391) that the work was actually published in 1843. References in this study are to the three-volume edition of 1846. Only in the case of unreprinted passages are references given to the *Ed. Rev.* [3] *Ess. in Eng. Lit.* (1780-1860), p. 115.

[4] *Jeffrey's Lit. Crit.*, p. v. [5] *Cont.*, v. 1, p. xv. [6] *Life*, v. 1, p. 198.

A list of them, numbering two hundred, was printed as an appendix to the first volume of Cockburn's *Life*. One day in 1840, Cockburn said, Jeffrey and he commenced the task of identification. " In the course of a week or two " they went through the whole work, authenticating Jeffrey's papers.[1] Nichol Smith pointed out that there are passages in Jeffrey's letters which indicate that the list is not complete.[2] Cockburn informs us that Jeffrey was in the habit of revising his contributors' articles—" so aiding the original by lively or graceful touches, that reasonable authors were surprised and charmed on seeing how much better they looked than they thought they would." [3] Cockburn's list, Nichol Smith observed, was meant to include only the articles of which Jeffrey was sole author ; and he drew attention to the fact that, even of these, one, the famous *Don Cevallos* article which helped to bring about the establishment of the *Quarterly*, was claimed by Brougham—though Smith considered, on viewing the evidence, that it was mainly, though not wholly, the work of Jeffrey—and that another, that on Coleridge's *Biographia Literaria*, was in part at least by Hazlitt. Of another article, accepted by Nichol Smith, it was stated in a later number of the *Review* that it was by two authors.[4] On the whole, however, no doubt Jeffrey's list may be accepted as correct.[5]

There are obvious dangers in trying to extract a viewpoint from so great a mass of writing. There might be a tendency to stress, albeit perhaps unconsciously, passages fitting favourite theories, and to pass more lightly over passages running counter to them. Many of Jeffrey's discussions must be summarised here very cursorily and therefore imperfectly. One can, however, endeavour to perform the business fairly, letting one's picture of his mind shape itself with as little as may be of forcing. In order to help in this, and to provide a check upon all conclusions, Jeffrey's own words will be quoted frequently hereafter, and, where they are condensed or paraphrased, the original will be adhered to as closely as is possible. To any who may not

[1] *Life*, v. 1, p. 285.   [2] *Jeffrey's Lit. Crit.*, pp. 209-16.
[3] *Life*, v. 1, pp. 302-3. Cf. *Life of Scott*, Lockhart, v. 2, pp. 208-9.
[4] On French Poetry, *Ed. Rev.*, No. 74, Art. 6. See *Ed. Rev.*, No. 75, p. 269.
[5] In 1895 there was privately printed in Manchester a small book entitled *Authorship of the First Hundred Numbers of the Edinburgh Review*, by W. A. Copinger, Professor of Law and President of the Bibliographical Society. Copinger did not give his authorities.

chance to be familiar with his work this will provide also illustrations of his ways of thinking and writing.

Perhaps as good a way as any other of commencing this portion of our study may be to return for a little to the easy explanation of Jeffrey indicated by certain quotations in our second chapter—that he was simply a man who carried into the nineteenth century the critical ideas of the eighteenth.

" You know," he wrote in another letter to Horner, " I always profess to write for babes and sucklings, and take no merit but for making things level to the meanest capacities." [1] It is evident from this that Jeffrey endeavoured to maintain in his thinking what is, I imagine, by no means always unnecessary— a grip of the obvious. If we are to move over to his viewpoint we must begin, therefore, by trying to do the same.

The moment we regard the matter from this elementary standpoint it becomes plain that the statement that Jeffrey was an eighteenth-century survival is simply literally true. Before the dawn of 1801 he had reached his twenty-eighth year. Unless, therefore, he were to erase from his mind all he had learned before reaching that fairly mature age he was bound to carry into the nineteenth century much of the thought that was current in the eighteenth. We have seen that in eighteenth-century Scotland there was widespread veneration for the literary masters of contemporary England. Jeffrey made it clear that this attitude was still common in the Scotland of his youth. " When we were at our studies, some twenty-five years ago," he wrote in 1816, " we can perfectly remember that every young man was set to read Pope, Swift, and Addison, as regularly as Virgil, Cicero, and Horace. All who had any tincture of letters were familiar with their writings and their history ; allusions to them abounded in all popular discourses and all ambitious conversation ; and they and their contemporaries were universally acknowledged as our great models of excellence, and placed without challenge at the head of our national literature." [2] Jeffrey, in other words, stood in a relationship to the writers of the Age of Pope similar to that in which people educated in Scotland in the closing years of the nineteenth century and the earlier years of the twentieth stand to the writers of the Age of Wordsworth. It is clear that he never lost respect for those eighteenth-century authors. He described

[1] *Life*, v. 2, p. 139. [2] *Cont.*, v. 1, p. 158.

a passage in Crabbe, for instance, as written " in the good old taste of Pope and Dryden " ; [1] he praised " the delicacy, the modest gaiety, and ingenious purity " of Addison's prose ; [2] he said he admired the " diction and versification " of the *Deserted Village* and the *Vanity of Human Wishes*.[3] Speaking of the influence of the writers of Pope's period on the " new style " that was introduced into English literature at the time of the Restoration, " They corrected," he wrote, " its gross indecency —increased its precision and correctness—made its pleasantry and sarcasm more polished and elegant—and spread through the whole of its irony, its narration, and its reflection, a tone of clear and condensed good sense, which recommended itself to all who had, and all who had not any relish for higher beauties. This," he added, " is the praise of Queen Anne's wits—and to this praise they are justly entitled." [4]

These statements, however, taken alone, hardly give us grounds for thinking of Jeffrey as no more than a walking anachronism ; there is nothing in them with which a critic of the twentieth century might not still agree. On the other hand, there are considerations already evident to us which militate against this conception of him. One is the analytical and argumentative disposition common among his race, a quality of which, it is becoming increasingly apparent, he possessed his full share. The *Edinburgh*, the *Quarterly* remarked, was " a child of the Speculative." [5] It seems unlikely on the face of it that Jeffrey, a prominent speaker in those strenuous debating societies, who was prepared when in his teens to challenge the views of his own professors, and who, from a time very early in his career, made a habit of criticising everything he read, including his own compositions, would be willing to abandon, in favour of the thought of a literary school situated in a distant city, the greatest members of which were dead before he was born, what he described, in words characteristic of the outlook of his nation, as " that scrupulous estimate of the grounds of decision, and that jealous questioning of first impressions, which necessarily precede the formation of all firm and wise opinions." [6] The reference, quoted a moment ago, to those who had no relish for " higher beauties " suggests that he was not uncritical of those authors.

[1] *Cont.*, v. 2, p. 290.   [2] *Ibid.*, v. 2, pp. 45-6.   [3] *Ibid.*, v. 2, p. 276.
[4] *Ibid.*, v. 1, p. 164.   [5] No. 181, p. 125.   [6] *Cont.*, v. 3, p. 650.

We need not labour the point. Critics like Gates, Saintsbury, and Nichol Smith, who have investigated the matter, have had no difficulty in pointing to statements in Jeffrey's articles which show that his attitude to the writers of the Augustan school was certainly not one of unquestioning discipleship. He declared of Dryden that that poet had " not written one line that is pathetic, and very few that can be considered as sublime." [1] Of Addison, he asserted, " The extreme caution, timidity, and flatness of this author in his poetical compositions—the narrowness of his range in poetical sentiment and diction, and the utter want either of passion or of brilliancy, render it difficult to believe that he was born under the same sun with Shakespeare, and wrote but a century after him." [1] He spoke of the " solemn mawkishness " of Addison's *Cato*.[2] Even Addison's prose, despite what we have observed him say of it a moment ago, did not win from him undivided praise. " Junius and Johnson," he stated, were " the first who again familiarized us with more glowing and sonorous diction—and made us feel the tameness and poorness of the serious style of Addison and Swift." [3] " Gray," he wrote, " with the talents, rather of a critic than a poet—with learning, fastidiousness, and scrupulous delicacy of taste, instead of fire, tenderness, or invention—began and ended a small school, which we could scarcely have wished to become permanent, admirable in many respects as some of its productions are—being far too elaborate and artificial, either for grace or for fluency, and fitter to excite the admiration of scholars, than the delight of ordinary men." [4] He described Johnson's *Irene* as " nothing better than a tissue of wearisome and unimpassioned declamations." [5] " Pope," he wrote, " is a satirist, and a moralist, and a wit, and a critic, and a fine writer, much more than he is a poet. He has all the delicacies and proprieties and felicities of diction—but he has not a great deal of fancy, and scarcely ever touches any of the greater passions. He is much the best, we think, of the classical continental school ; but he is not to be compared with the masters—nor with the pupils—of that Old English one from which there had been so lamentable an apostasy." [6] He referred in one review to " the paltry flippancy and disgusting affectation of Sterne " [7] and in

[1] *Cont.*, v. 2, p. 45.   [2] *Ibid.*, v. 2, p. 88.   [3] *Ibid.*, v. 1, p. 167.
[4] *Ibid.*, v. 1, pp. 165-6.   [5] *Ibid.*, v. 2, pp. 88-9.   [6] *Ibid.*, v. 2, p. 46.
[7] *Ibid.*, v. 1, p. 131.

another to the " mawkish morality " and " dawdling details "
of Richardson.[1]   The style of Goldsmith he described as one
of " mellow tenderness and elaborate simplicity." [2]

It is evident from the allusion to Pope that Jeffrey regarded
the typical English poetry of the eighteenth century as alien in
essence to the English mind, and handicapped—as it was
suggested in our third chapter that much Scottish eighteenth-
century writing also was for a similar reason—on that account.
One observes how, as he moved away from the Augustans,
either forward or backward in time, his enthusiasm became
warmer.   He described Thomson as " the first writer of any
eminence " who seceded from the " foreign school " and " made
some steps back to the force and animation of our original
poetry."   He remarked that " Thomson, however, was educated
in Scotland, where the new style," he believed, ". . . had not
yet become familiar."   (But Allan Ramsay was familiar with
the work of Pope.)   Thomson, he affirmed, had " always been
popular with a much wider circle of readers " than Pope or
Addison, and " in spite of considerable vulgarity and signal
cumbrousness of diction " had drawn " even from the fastidious
. . . more heartfelt admiration." [3]   In another place he spoke
of Thomson's " beautiful fancy . . . gorgeous diction, and
generous affections." [4]   " At last," he said, " Cowper threw off
the whole trammels of French criticism and artificial refinement ;
and . . . ventured to write again with the force and the freedom
which had characterised the old school of English literature. . . .
Cowper had . . . some radical deficiencies ;—but this atoned
for all.   There was something so delightfully refreshing, in seeing
natural phrases and natural images again displaying their
unforced graces, and waving their unpruned heads in the
enchanted gardens of poetry, that no one complained of the
taste displayed in the selection ;—and Cowper is, and is likely
to continue, the most popular of all who have written for the
present or the last generation." [5]   In an earlier article he
referred to Cowper's " shaking off the tawdry incumbrance of
that poetical diction which had nearly reduced the art to the
skilful collocation of a set of conventional phrases."   " It is . . .
true," he wrote of Cowper's work at the same time, " that we
can scarcely read a single page with attention, without being

[1] *Cont.*, v. 1, p. 266.   [2] *Ibid.*, v. 1, p. 166.   [3] *Ibid.*, v. 2, pp. 46-7.
[4] *Ibid.*, v. 2, p. 88.   [5] *Ibid.*, v. 2, pp. 47-8.

offended at some coarseness or lowness of expression, or disappointed by some ' most lame and impotent conclusion.' " [1] Speaking, in the same essay—it appeared in the third number of the *Review*—of the " variety " and " truth " of Cowper's descriptions, of the " sterling weight and sense of most of his observations " of the " great appearance of facility," with which everything in his work is executed, and of " the happy use he has so often made of the most common and ordinary language," —he declared that all these things " concur to stamp upon his poems the character of original genius, and remind us of the merits that have secured immortality to Shakespeare." [2]   " We are of opinion," he wrote in 1816, " . . . that the writers who adorned the beginning of the last century have been eclipsed by those of our own time ; and that they have no chance of ever regaining the supremacy in which they have thus been supplanted." [3]   " The present age, we think," he wrote in 1828, contrasting it this time with the later part of the eighteenth century, " has an hundred times more poetry, and more true taste for poetry, than that which immediately preceded it,— and of which, reckoning its duration from the extinction of the last of Queen Anne's wits down to about thirty-odd years ago, we take leave to say that it was, beyond all dispute, the most unpoetical age in the annals of this or any other considerable nation." [4]

Jeffrey's admiration for sixteenth and seventeenth century poetry, of which there are hints in the last paragraph, is as easily illustrated as any of the other facts mentioned in this chapter. There was nothing, he remarked in 1803, discussing Joanna Baillie's *Plays on the Passions*, by which the writings of Shakespeare and Beaumont and Fletcher were so remarkably distinguished from those of later dramatists as by the truth and completeness of their representations of character : their dramatis personæ were " all drawn with the full lineaments and just proportions of real men." [5]   In an article published later in the same year, on *Le Malheur et La Pitié* by Jacques de Lille, he remarked that, though most of that author's writing recalled to him " the manner of English poetry," he was seldom reminded " of the loftier flights of Milton, the luxuriant tenderness of Thomson, or the fairy fancy and magical facility of

[1] *Cont.*, v. 1, pp. 412, 415 (1803).   [2] *Ibid.*, v. 1, p. 416.
[3] *Ibid.*, v. 1, p. 160.   [4] *Ed. Rev.*, No. 95, pp. 48-9.   [5] *Ibid.*, No. 4, p. 274.

Shakespeare." [1] In 1810, reviewing the autobiography of Alfieri, he expressed a belief that " those who are duly sensible of the merit of Shakespeare, will never be much struck with any other dramatical compositions." [2] " All true lovers of English poetry," he wrote in 1811, " have been long in love with the dramatists of the time of Elizabeth and James ; and must have been sensibly comforted by their late restoration to some degree of favour and notoriety." There was never " any where, any thing," he asserted, like the period from the middle of Elizabeth's reign to the Restoration. " In point," he declared, " of real force and originality of genius, neither the age of Pericles, nor the age of Augustus, nor the times of Leo X., nor of Louis XIV., can come at all into comparison." The writings produced in that period he pronounced the work of " Giants. . . . Giants of one nation and family " whose characteristics were " great force, boldness, and originality ; together with a certain raciness of English peculiarity, which distinguishes them from all those performances that have since been produced among ourselves, upon a more vague and general idea of European excellence." No one, he asserted, could have even " a tolerably adequate idea " of the riches of the English language and of the English genius who had not made himself acquainted with the prose writers as well as with the poets of that " memorable period." [3] Of the " old English dramatists "—he mentioned here, besides Shakespeare, Beaumont and Fletcher, Massinger, Jonson, Ford, Shirley, Webster, Dekker, Field, and Rowley— he maintained that in poetry, originality of diction, variety of images, excursions of fancy, and illustrations and figures borrowed from rural life and from mankind's " simple occupations or universal feelings," they excelled " the dramatists of any other age or country." [4] In this essay he defended his countrymen against the Continental accusation that the literary taste of Britain had been corrupted by Shakespeare-idolatry. In an article on Madame de Staël, published in 1813, he repeated this defence in a passage of which Saintsbury declared that " hardly anything in English criticism is better." [5] In a review of

---

[1] *Ed. Rev.*, No. 5, p. 29.   [2] *Cont.*, v. 1, p. 392.   [3] *Ibid.*, v. 2, pp. 38-42.
[4] *Ibid.*, v. 2, p. 51.
[5] *Ibid.*, v. 1, p. 126 *et seq.* In the *Contributions* this article is dated in error Nov. 1812. See *Ed. Rev.*, No. 41, p. 1. *Essays in Eng. Lit.* (1780-1860), Saintsbury, p. 127.

Campbell's *Specimens*, printed in 1819, he affirmed that the nation was " yet but very imperfectly recovered from that strange and ungrateful forgetfulness of our older poets, which began with the Restoration, and continued almost unbroken till after the middle of the last century " [1]—which certainly supports Stephen's assertion that there were people who carried into the nineteenth century the tastes of the century before, but hardly supports his inclusion of Jeffrey in their number. In an article written in 1835—six years, that is, after his resignation from the editorship of the *Review*—Jeffrey objected to a suggestion by Mackintosh that " soft, graceful, and idiomatic English " was not to be found before the Restoration. " It is," he maintained, " at least as old as Chaucer. The English Bible is full of it ; and it is among the most common, as well as the most beautiful, of the many languages spoken by Shakespeare. Laying his verse aside, there are in his longer passages of prose—and in the serious as well as the humorous parts . . . a staple of sweet, mellow and natural English, altogether as free and elegant as that of Addison, and for the most part more vigorous and more richly coloured." [2]

" We are not," Jeffrey wrote in one of his legal articles, " partial to idols " [3]—another evidently characteristic remark. He kept his admiration even of the Elizabethans on this side idolatry. " There is," he said, answering De Staël's criticism of Shakespeare, " a primitive fertility of soil that naturally throws out weeds along with the matchless crops which it alone can bear ; and we might reasonably grudge to reduce its vigour for the sake of purifying its produce." [4] But he did not suggest that imperfections, however defensible or even inevitable, should ever be regarded as anything else than faults. The " unsteadiness and irregularity of dialogue," he remarked, " which gives such an air of nature to our older plays . . . is frequently carried to a most blamable excess " ; he spoke of their writers' " passion for verbal quibbles," and stated that there was " an inequality and a capricious uncertainty in the taste and judgment of these good old writers, which excites at once our amazement and our compassion." [5] Alluding to the French complaint that the English persist in admiring Shakespeare " in spite of his buffooneries, extravagances, and bombast "—" We admit," he

[1] *Cont.*, v. 2, p. 9.   [2] *Ibid.*, v. 3, pp. 656-7.   [3] *Ed. Rev.*, No. 18, p. 481.
[4] *Cont.*, v. 1, p. 127.   [5] *Ibid.*, v. 2, p. 53.

wrote, " that he has those faults ; and, as they are faults, that he would be better without them "—though he insisted at the same time that there were " many more things which the French call faults, but which we deliberately consider as beauties." [1] He spoke of Shakespeare's " daring improprieties, his trespasses on the borders of absurdity," [2] and stated that he could not " sympathise with all the conceits and puerilities " in *Romeo and Juliet*. [3] " If it be true," he asserted bluntly in the essay of 1811, " that no other man has ever written so finely as Shakespeare has done in his happier passages, it is no less true that there is not a scribbler now alive who could possibly write worse than he has sometimes written,—who could, on occasion, devise more contemptible ideas, or misplace them so abominably, by the side of such incomparable excellence." [4]

This quotation indicates, nevertheless, that Jeffrey considered Shakespeare to be the greatest of poets. A portion of his article on Hazlitt's *Characters* is almost a rhapsody on Shakespeare. Shakespeare's loveliest passages, Jeffrey claimed, are not digressions. They are part of the proper business of the scene. " HE ALONE," Jeffrey wrote " . . . when the object requires it, is always keen and wordly and practical—and . . . yet, without changing his hand, or stopping his course, scatters around him, as he goes, all sounds and shapes of sweetness. . . . More full of wisdom and ridicule and sagacity, than all the moralists and satirists that ever existed—he is more wild, airy, and inventive, and more pathetic and fantastic, than all the poets of all regions and ages of the world :—and has all those elements so happily mixed up in him, and bears his high faculties so temperately, that the most severe reader cannot complain of him for want of strength or of reason—nor the most sensitive for defect of ornament or ingenuity. . . . Although his sails are purple and perfumed, and his prow of beaten gold, they waft him on his voyage, not less, but more rapidly and directly than if they had been composed of baser materials. All his excellences, like those of Nature herself, are thrown out together ; and instead of interfering with, support and recommend each other. His flowers are not tied up in garlands, nor his fruits crushed into baskets—but spring living from the soil, in all the dew and freshness of youth ; while the graceful foliage in which they lurk, and the ample branches,

---

[1] *Cont.*, v. 1, p. 127.   [2] *Ibid.*, v. 1, p. 266.   [3] *Ibid.*, v. 2, p. 84.
[4] *Ibid.*, v. 2, p. 53.

the rough and vigorous stem, and the wide-spreading roots on which they depend, are present along with them, and share, in their places, the equal care of their Creator." Jeffrey instanced in illustration, among other passages, the " sweet South " in *Twelfth Night,* that " breathes upon a bank of violets," Caliban's speech on the music of his island, the picture of the castle of Macbeth, Lady Macbeth's " Look like the innocent flower, But be the serpent under it," and Tyrrell's " Their lips were four red roses on a stalk, And in their summer beauty kissed each other." [1]   In a footnote to the reprint of this article he spoke of the " vow of allegiance " he had " so often taken anonymously, to the only true and lawful King of our English Poetry," and said that he now ventured " fondly to replace this slight and perishable wreath "—his essay—on Shakespeare's " august and undecaying shrine." [2]

It is plain, in the light of all this, that before it could be maintained that Jeffrey was simply a belated Augustan, much would have to be explained away.   It seems unprofitable to attempt to reach his viewpoint by travelling along that road.

Our discoveries in this chapter have not, at the same time, been solely negative.   We have caught some glimpses of Jeffrey's tastes.   The stressing of the facts that the characters of Shakespeare and Beaumont and Fletcher were " real men," the mention of Thomson's " generous affections," and the preference of poetry that pleases " ordinary men " to that which excites the admiration of scholars [3]—we remember the Scottish common people's delight in poetry—may be illustrative of the Scot in him.   We note the liking for clear and condensed good sense, for width of range, for writing with colour, fire, and naturalness in it, for the " fairy fancy and magical facility of Shakespeare," and the appreciation of Shakespeare's power of remaining, when the object required it, " keen . . . worldly and practical."   We observe the distaste for timidity in writing, for affectation, and for " mawkish morality."   The dislike of " vulgarity " of language in poetry might be regarded as an eighteenth-century touch.   This question is complicated for later generations by the way in which word-associations change : the now respectable word " pluck " had once, for instance,

---

[1] *Cont.,* v. 2, pp. 71-5.   [2] *Ibid.,* v. 2, p. 69.
[3] Cf. " The beauties of Shakespeare are not of so dim or equivocal a nature as to be visible only to learned eyes."   *Cont.,* v. 2, p. 70.

associations similar to those possessed by the modern " guts." [1]
But there may be implicit here an idea which is not yet obsolete
—an idea of which the now long-discredited Augustan poetic
diction, discredited we have seen even in Jeffrey's eyes, was an
expression—that the language of poetry should be of finer
quality than that of everyday life, that there should be something
in all art which, as Grattan I believe once put it, takes our
minds " out of the dirt."

We observe that we are beginning, too, to see Jeffrey not
merely as a specimen to which it is our business to attach a
dated museum index-card, but as a complex human being.

[1] *The Romance of Words*, Weekley, pp. 83-4.

CHAPTER VII

FUNDAMENTAL PRINCIPLES

Scholarship. Politics. Jeffreyan philosophy. Essay on Beauty. Ethical outlook. Evidence and reasoning, or *coups d'œil* and entertainment.

I

STEPHEN asserted that a large part of the writing in the early numbers of the *Edinburgh* was the work simply of amateurs.[1] This statement, looked at in the obvious Jeffreyan sense, is not of course precisely accurate. By accepting payment for their articles, and that at a rate considerably above what was then normal, the first *Edinburgh* reviewers quite definitely infringed their amateur status. They earned their fees, moreover, so efficiently that the *Edinburgh* was spoken of, by Lockhart, as the " great primary source of the wealth and authority of the house of Constable." [2] It is true at the same time that all these men had other employments in life besides writing : their reviews were composed in hours of leisure.

In this respect, however, they conformed to the Scottish tradition of their time. Professor Masson remarked that, of the writers who lived in Scotland in the eighteenth century, hardly one was by profession a man of letters. Scots who wished in those days to make authorship their sole vocation tended, he pointed out, to drift to London. He quoted in this connection a passage in which Henry Mackenzie contrasted the " natural play of good humour " which then prevailed among Scottish authors with what Mackenzie described as the " prize-fighting of wit, which distinguished a literary circle of our sister country." " The literary circle of London," Mackenzie wrote, " was a sort of sect, a *caste* separate from the ordinary professions and habits of common life. They were traders in talent and learning, and brought, like other traders, samples of their goods into company, with a jealousy of competition which prevented their enjoying, as much as otherwise they might, any excellence in their competitors." [3]

[1] *Hours in a Library*, v. 2, p. 248.   [2] *Life of Scott*, v. 2, p. 200.
[3] *Edinburgh Sketches and Memories*, pp. 182-5.

This suggests that Mackenzie did not regard undivided attention to their trade as of unmixed advantage to authors. It is obvious, nevertheless, that the man who has thousands of hours to devote to the study of books is likely to have a fuller and more exact knowledge of books than can be possessed by the man who can spare only hundreds. And it is obvious, when we look at Jeffrey the human being, that, whatever his industry, he must, in comparison with many scholars, be placed in the latter class ; his reading of books and his writing about them were part-time occupations of a very busy person. Cockburn, speaking of the period between 1815 and 1820, remarked that during these years Jeffrey " was in the full career of a professional practice that occupied the greatest portion of his whole time, and during about eight months yearly could not be got through without the exclusive use of ten or even twelve hours a day ; besides which, those who only saw him in society, and knew not how the fragments of a diligent man's time may be gathered up, might suppose that he had nothing to do but to dine and to talk." Yet Cockburn computed that in those six years Jeffrey wrote some thirty-nine articles—and review articles were then, we remember, lengthy essays—on subjects connected with politics, literature, biography, and general history.[1] And he was, of course, performing simultaneously his duties as editor. Horner, referring in 1808 to Jeffrey's review of Fox's *History*, observed that the inconsistencies discoverable in that article were very intelligible to anyone who knew " with what carelessness in general " Jeffrey set himself to do what all the world imagined he undertook with an overwhelming sense of its importance.[2] Jeffrey himself, in the preface of his *Contributions*, spoke of his articles as " written hastily, in the intervals of graver occupations." [3] We need not look to Jeffrey, then, for great weight of scholarship. " Jeffrey wrote about Mrs Hutchinson's ' Memoirs ' and Pepys's ' Diary,' " Stephen declared, " as though the books had for the first time revealed to him the existence of Puritans or of courtiers under the Restoration." [4] Saintsbury discussing, in his *History of Criticism*, some of Jeffrey's sayings regarding the Greek and Roman classics,

[1] *Life*, v. 1, pp. 247-8.
[2] *Memoirs*, v. 1, p. 431.   The date is misprinted in the *Memoirs* as 1806.
[3] p. ix.
[4] *Hours in a Library*, v. 2, p. 249.

remarked that the reviewer had " apparently never so much as heard of Apollonius Rhodius." [1]

It is easy, at the same time, to be over-patronising towards Jeffrey's learning. We have seen that he imposed on himself a strenuous apprenticeship ; his work as a reviewer prevented his ever ceasing to read. Stephen's affirmation seems to me, on re-examining the articles he mentioned, decidedly sweeping. Macaulay had a considerable knowledge of history ; yet he described Jeffrey, as we have seen, as more nearly a universal genius than any other man of the period, and asserted that he had read Jeffrey's articles till he knew them by heart. Saintsbury's criticism seems to me to illustrate the remark made in the introduction to this study that even the acutest of observers may fail sometimes to notice the salt-cellar under his nose. In the number of *Blackwood's* for May 1824 there appears the following statement, in a letter addressed by " Timothy Tickler " to Francis Jeffrey : " I know that in the days of your youth you were very fond of doing into English bits of Apollonius Rhodius, and other classics." [2] Saintsbury might not, of course, be expected to have read that. But in the second volume of Cockburn's *Life* we read the following, in a letter written by Jeffrey to Morehead in 1795, " I have also written 600 lines in a translation of the Argos of old Apollonius, which I am attempting in the style of Cowper's Homer." [3] And in the first volume Cockburn stated that there was found, among Jeffrey's papers, " a translation into blank verse of the third book of the Argonauticon of Apollonius Rhodius." The other books, Cockburn said, were lost, " but he translated the whole poem, extending to about six thousand lines." [4]

" Tested for range alone," Saintsbury wrote in his essay on Jeffrey, " or for subtlety alone, he will frequently be found wanting ; but he almost invariably catches up those who have thus outstripped him, when the subject of the trial is shifted to soundness of estimate, intelligent connection of view, and absence of eccentricity." [5]

That suggests that there may be qualities of service in criticism procurable outside the walls of libraries as well as qualities procurable only within them—that the qualities which, as a literary judge, Jeffrey lost on the swings of erudition may

[1] Revised edition, 1911, p. 402. [2] V. 15, p. 564. [3] V. 2, p. 20.
[4] V. 1, p. 70. [5] *Essays in Eng. Lit.* (1780-1860), p. 133.

have been compensated for by qualities gained on the round-abouts of practical living. It is natural, of course, for a man to estimate highly the worth of the qualities he has, and to tend to depreciate the worth of those he lacks. And, as the criticism of our great writers has fallen largely into the hands of men of academic outlook, it is natural that the point of view of such men should, in connection with that criticism, have come to be regarded as most important. Jeffrey was not, at the same time, always over-respectful in his attitude to men of this type, or to the system that produces them. He was inclined to imagine, for example, that undue preoccupation with what is sometimes regarded as strictly academic scholarship tended to hinder the development of a completely adult mind. " Our Scotish prejudices lead us irresistibly to believe," he wrote of Sir William Jones, " that he was a little spoiled by the classical and metrical discipline of English schools and universities ; and we cannot help fancying, that his understanding would have been more vigorous, and his judgment more decisive, if he had not imbibed so deeply that affection for Greek and prosody, and classical and mythological allusions, which characterises so decidedly the seminaries in which he was bred. These things are the proper boast and ornament of a schoolboy, but will not long go far in procuring glory to a man." [1] Much of what is called scholarship he looked upon as a waste of precious time and brains. " How many powerful understandings," he exclaimed, " have been lost in the Dialectics of Aristotle ! And of how much good philosophy are we daily defrauded, by the preposterous error of taking a knowledge of prosody for useful learning ! " [2] Over-devotion to matters of this sort was apt, in his opinion, to destroy a man's power of thinking for himself. " Our scholars," he alleged, " are now little else than pedants, and antiquaries, and grammarians,—who have never exercised any faculty but memory." [3] " The mind of a man, who has escaped this training," he declared, speaking of what he called " regular education," " will at least have fair play. . . . His prejudices will be those of a man, and not of a schoolboy ; and his speculations and conclusions will be independent of the maxims of tutors, and the oracles of literary patrons." [2] We notice the Scottish attitude of challenge, the refusal to be brow-beaten, the insistence on the right of individual judgment.

[1] *Ed. Rev.*, No. 10, p. 331. [2] *Cont.*, v. 1, p. 139. [3] *Ibid.*, v. 3, p. 479.

" Argument from authority," he asserted, " is, in general, the weakest and the most tedious of all arguments ; and learning, we are inclined to believe, has more frequently played the part of a bully than of a fair auxiliary ; and been oftener used to frighten people than to convince them,—to dazzle and overawe, rather than to guide and enlighten." [1] He had no respect for mere displays of erudition ; they were, he considered, signs frequently both of weak intelligence and of vanity. " Scholars," he wrote, " who are capable of reasoning, have ceased to make a parade of their scholarship ; while those who have nothing else must continue to set it forward—just as gentlemen now-a-days keep their gold in their pockets, instead of wearing it on their clothes—while the fashion of laced suits still prevails among their domestics." [2] He protested against directions in which he saw learning developing in his own day, and in which it has developed still more strongly since. " The age of original genius, and of comprehensive and independent reasoning " appeared to him " to be over." Works such as those of " Bacon, and Shakespeare, and Taylor, and Hooker " seemed no longer to be written. Instead, he saw produced " Encyclopædias, and geographical compilations, and county histories, and new editions of black-letter authors "- -and so forth. " One man," he wrote, " spends his life in improving a method of dyeing cotton red ;—another in adding a few insects to a catalogue which nobody reads ;—a third in settling the metres of a few Greek choruses ;—a fourth in decyphering illegible romances, or old grants of farms ;—a fifth in picking rotten bones out of the earth ;—a sixth in describing all the old walls and hillocks in his parish ;—and five hundred others in occupations equally liberal and important : each of them being, for the most part, profoundly ignorant of everything out of his own narrow department, and very generally and deservedly despised by his competitors for the favour of that public—which despises and supports them all." [3] The treatment accorded by men of this order to the work of his favourite, Shakespeare, aroused him to particular wrath. " A short glossary," he declared, " a few explanations of old usages, and a few suggestions for the restoration of a corrupted text, would be gratefully accepted, and generally consulted. But these helps become hindrances,—and nuisances indeed of the first magnitude, when they swell to six times the

[1] *Cont.*, v. 3, p. 479. [2] *Ibid.*, v. 3, pp. 479-80. [3] *Ibid.*, v. 1, pp. 100-1.

bulk of the original author, and engage us, at every tenth line, in the paltry polemics of purblind annotators, and grovelling transcribers of black letter." Shakespeare's popularity held out such temptations to these beings that there was now an edition of the plays in twenty-one volumes, in which the text bore so slender a proportion to the commentary that one wishing to read only Shakespeare had to turn the leaves continually and often earned no more by the labour than a single line in a page. " We are not only disturbed," Jeffrey wrote, " . . . with the perpetual intrusion of the commentator ; but can scarcely ever recall to our memory any of our favourite passages, without finding them defiled by the adherence of some of his filth and tatters." [1] " It strengthens and assists the feeble," he declared of " regular education "—" but it deprives the strong of his triumph, and casts down the hopes of the aspiring. It accomplishes this, not only by training up the mind in an habitual veneration for authorities, but, by leading us to bestow a disproportionate degree of attention upon studies that are only valuable as keys or instruments for the understanding, they come at last to be regarded as ultimate objects of pursuit ; and the means of education are absurdly mistaken for its end." [2] " We would not be understood," he stated, speaking of the achievements of Benjamin Franklin, " to say any thing in disparagement of scholarship and science ; but the value of these instruments is apt to be overrated by their possessors ; and it is a wholesome mortification, to show them that the work may be done without them." [3]

It becomes increasingly difficult, we observe, as we proceed, to keep Jeffrey quietly fastened down to the index-card : his gauntlet is here thrown down to the indexers. It might be said that these passages express what was spoken of a moment ago as the natural depreciation of qualities one lacks. This, however, is hardly a complete answer. Nor can Jeffrey be completely answered by a superior and unsupported " Absurd ! " That is simply the resort to authority which he insisted was evidence of inability to make a reasoned reply. The last sentence quoted from him shows he was not so lunatic as to suppose that there was no case for " scholarship and science." He does force us, however, to ask if there is no grain of truth

---

[1] *Ed. Rev.*, No. 24, pp. 449-50.   [2] *Cont.*, v. 1, pp. 138-9.
[3] *Ibid.*, v. 1, p. 157.

in his suggestions that a proportion of " scholarly " investigation comes short of being an adult exercise ; that there is a danger of a scholar's losing a sound sense of values ; that concentration upon the means of learning may lead to forgetfulness of its ends. What, he drives us to enquire, is the real end of learning ? That, we shall see, is one of the obvious and elementary questions that Jeffrey keeps asking, in connection with all kinds of activities, continually.

It was, we note, " Scotish prejudices " that set him upon this line of thought.

II

Jeffrey's refusal to shut himself up in academic cloisters, his desire to move freely in the world of men, helped to make him a politician. The *Review* he edited was not only, we remember, a literary journal. The " Right leg " of the *Review*, Jeffrey said himself, was " Politics." [1] Its party attachment was attested to by the very colours of its covers. " Blue and buff " were the colours of the followers of Fox : they had been the colours also of the uniform of George Washington.[2]

That Jeffrey, J. H. Millar remarked, was ever unconsciously influenced by party passion in his literary criticism it might be rash to deny ; but it did not appear to him that the editor of the *Edinburgh* had ever been consciously so influenced.[3] We observed Saintsbury's tribute to Jeffrey's freedom from party prejudice in his dealings with Swift and de Staël, and the *Quarterly's* acknowledgment of the impartiality with which he reviewed Fox's *History*. " I do not think," Jeffrey wrote, " that I was ever a violent or (consciously) uncandid partisan." [4] " In the *Edinburgh*," Hazlitt declared, " nothing is ever adverted to but . . . literary merits. Or if there is a bias of any kind, it arises from an affectation of magnanimity and candour in giving heaped measure to those on the aristocratic side in politics, and in being critically severe on others." [5]

---

[1] *Cont.*, v. 1, p. xix.

[2] *History of England in Eighteenth Century*, Lecky, v. 6, pp. 139-40. The *Edinburgh Review* pointed out in its centenary number that " as a matter of fact Washington's uniform was that worn by Virginian officers in the King's service before the Rebellion." *Ed. Rev.*, No. 402, p. 280.

[3] *Lit. Hist. of Scotland*, pp. 487-8.

[4] *Cont.*, v. 3, p. 144.   [5] *Spirit of the Age*, p. 294.

Jeffrey said also, however, that his party principles did not
" sit . . . loosely " upon him ; and spoke of years spent " as
their uncompromising advocate—at the hazard at least, if not
to the injury " of his " personal and professional interests." [1]
Cockburn, referring to the time of his own youth and Jeffrey's,
remarked that " even in private society a Whig was viewed
somewhat as a Papist was in the days of Titus Oates." Against
the junior members of the Bar who, in those days, embraced
Whiggism, every official gate, Cockburn asserted, was closed ;
judges were unkind to them ; and agents kept their fees for
men of the safer faith.[2] While, therefore, Jeffrey may have
striven against allowing party partisanship to influence him
unfairly in his literary judgments, it seems evident that principles adopted in such circumstances must have formed part
of the warp and woof of his thinking, and must, accordingly,
be taken into account in any serious attempt to understand
him.

We noticed that the elder Jeffrey refused to allow his son
to attend, when at Glasgow, the lectures of the Whig professor
John Millar. Cockburn said that after Jeffrey's political opinions
became apparent George Jeffrey " used to blame himself for
having allowed the mere vicinity of Millar's influence to corrupt
and ruin his son." [3] There is a description of Millar, written
by Jeffrey, in the fifth number of the *Review*. " To form a
sound judgment upon all points of substantial importance,"
Jeffrey wrote, " appeared to him to require little more than the
free and independent use of that vulgar sense on which no man
is entitled to value himself ; and he was apt to look with
sufficient contempt upon the elaborate and ingenious errors
into which philosophers are so liable to reason themselves. To
bring down the dignity of such false science, and to expose the
emptiness of ostentatious and pedantic reasoners, was therefore
one of his favourite employments. He . . . was apt to regard
those minute enquiries in which many great scholars have
consumed their days, as a species of most unprofitable trifling.
Mere learning did not appear to him to deserve any extraordinary
respect ; and his veneration was reserved for those who had
either made discoveries of practical utility, or combined into a
system the scattered truths of speculation. To some of our
readers, perhaps, it may afford a clearer conception of his

[1] *Cont.*, v. i, p. xvii.   [2] *Memorials*, pp. 79-80.   [3] *Life*, v. i, p. 12.

intellectual character, to say, that it corresponded pretty nearly with the abstract idea that the learned of England entertain of a *Scotish philosopher* ; a personage, that is, with little or no deference to the authority of great names, and not very apt to be startled at conclusions that seem to run counter to received opinions or existing institutions ; acute, sagacious, and systematical ; irreverent towards classical literature ; rather indefatigable in argument, than patient in investigation ; vigilant in the observation of facts, but not so strong in their number, as skilful in their application." [1]

The resemblance between this and the character of Jeffrey we are building up makes one feel that Millar may indeed have influenced him. We note too that it is a " Scotish philosopher " that is described.

Of Millar's political views, " There never was any mind, perhaps," Jeffrey wrote, " less accessible to the illusions of that sentimental and ridiculous philanthropy which has led so many to the adoption of popular principles. He took a very cool and practical view of the condition of society ; and neither wept over the imaginary miseries of the lower orders, nor shuddered at the imputed vices of the higher." [2] We are back, we observe, at the Scottish emphasis upon actuality : the words are almost an exact paraphrase of the lines extracted in an earlier chapter from *The Twa Dogs*. " He laughed at the dreams of perfectibility," Jeffrey continued, " and looked with profound contempt upon all these puerile schemes of equality that threatened to subvert the distinctions of property, or to degrade the natural aristocracy of virtues and of talents. At the same time, he was certainly jealous, to an excess, of the encroachments of the regal power ; and fancied that, in this country, the liberty of the subject was exposed to perpetual danger, from that patronising influence which seemed likely to increase with the riches and importance of the nation." [2]

We learn, from a passage quoted by Jeffrey in another article from an account of Millar's life and works, that Millar " refused the offer of a lucrative place, which might have introduced him to higher honours, because he feared that his acceptance might be construed into an engagement to support an adminis-tration whose measures he condemned." [3] Perhaps it was in part from Millar that Jeffrey learned that it was possible to

---

[1] *Ed. Rev.*, No. 5, p. 156.   [2] *Ibid.*, p. 158   [3] *Ibid.*, No. 17, p. 91.

take " a very cool and practical view of the condition of society,"
and to make sacrifices, nevertheless, for one's beliefs.

From Jeffrey's political writings we have room for only a
few brief citations. These may, however, give an idea of some
of the lines of his thinking.

The phrase we have just noticed—" cool and practical view
of the condition of society "—hits one of the fundamental notes
of it. One of the first things that struck Jeffrey, in looking
coolly and practically at society, was its complexity. " Human
society," he declared, ". . . is not like a piece of mechanism
which may be safely taken to pieces, and put together by the
hands of an ordinary artist. It is the work of Nature, and not
of man." [1] " In the elastic frame of artificial society," he wrote
in another place, " it is hard to say what vibrations may be
excited, or to what extent they may be propagated, by a mere
local impulse. It is a great living body, animated by sympathetic
nerves, of which no anatomist has yet demonstrated the course
or the connexion ; and we may paralyse the hand or the tongue,
while we are seeking to remove a blemish from the eye." [2]
Sincerity alone, and an ardent desire to make things better, are,
it follows, of no more practical service to the statesman than
they are to the physician. " They have probably learned, by
this time," Jeffrey declared of the French in 1814, " that for a
nation to be free, something more is necessary than that it
should will it." [3] " Liberty," he said, " like love, is as hard to
keep as to win." [4]

Jeffrey saw danger, accordingly, in writers who, in the
political realm, substituted emotionalism for careful and
responsible thinking—who " intruded upon the public with . . .
extravagance and absurdity " instead of " sober reasoning, and
practical observation." Of Rousseau he asserted, " Whatever
influence he had . . . was unquestionably pernicious ; and
though some apology may be found for him in the enthusiasm
of his disordered imagination, he is chargeable with the highest
presumption, and the most blamable imprudence." [5] If we
grant with certain historians that Rousseau's writings helped
to bring about the French Revolution, and if we regard revolutions
of that kind as pernicious, then Jeffrey's reasoning is complete.

Jeffrey certainly did not care for revolution. " We have

[1] *Cont.*, v. 1, p. 555.   [2] *Ed. Rev.*, No. 18, p. 464.   [3] *Cont.*, v. 3, p. 205.
[4] *Ibid.*, v. 1, p. 518.   [5] *Ed. Rev.*, No. 1, p. 11.

almost as little love for revolutions," he remarked in his review
of Southey's *Wat Tyler*, " as the Laureate has." [1] Nearly half
a century before the French Revolution, he remarked, it had
been pointed out by Hume that " illegal violence, with whatever
pretences it may be covered, and whatever object it may pursue,
must inevitably end . . . in the arbitrary and despotic government of a single person." [2] The most deplorable evil inflicted
on mankind by the French Revolution was, he wrote in 1805,
the injury which, by producing an " undiscriminating dread of
all . . . reform," it did to the cause of " rational freedom." [3]
He declared of Cobbett in 1807 : " He looks forward to a
revolution, not only without sadness or dismay, but with a kind
of vindictive eagerness and delight." [4] He answered Cobbett
by asking him to look at the facts, to consider how much there
was of good as well as bad in the country's constitution, and
how much, accordingly, in a general upheaval, the nation was
in danger of losing.[5] We perceive the same desire to look
squarely at truth in his attitude to Parliamentary Reform.
" We are," he wrote in 1809, " rather partial to this medicine
upon the whole ; but it requires no ordinary skill and caution
in the preparation and dosing ; and, at all events, we are
perfectly certain, is not capable of effecting half the wonders
that are expected from it." [6] The first volume of the *Westminster
Review* accused the *Edinburgh* of perpetual trimming.[7] Jeffrey
alluded to the *Westminster's* attacks in 1826. He acknowledged
that the *Edinburgh* was " fairly chargeable with a fear of opposite
excesses—a desire to compromise and reconcile the claims of
all the great parties in the State—an anxiety to temper and
qualify whatever may be said in favour of one, with a steady
reservation of whatever may be justly due to the rest." [8] He
maintained at the same time that in holding itself aloof from
extremism the *Review* was identifying itself with a class of people
very numerous in the country. " It should always be
recollected," he asserted, " that a middle party like this is
invariably much stronger, as well as more determined and
formidable, than it appears." [9] We perceive once more his
desire to speak for " ordinary men."

Parties, Jeffrey considered, were necessary in all free govern-

---

[1] *Ed. Rev.*, No. 55, p. 167. [2] *Cont.*, v. 1, p. 554. [3] *Ibid.*, v. 1, p. 548.
[4] *Ed. Rev.*, No. 20, p. 399. [5] *Ibid.*, p. 406. [6] *Ibid.*, No. 28, p. 279.
[7] V. 1, pp. 206-49. [8] *Cont.*, v. 3, p. 295. [9] *Ibid.*, v. 3, p. 301.

ments. To be effective they had to be disciplined. As to the lengths to which upright men might go in sinking their individual views in the party's general policy it did not appear to him, though " purists " might " startle at shadows," that anyone need be often at a loss for a rule of conduct. The " leading principle " was that a man should satisfy himself that the party he joined meant well to the country, and that more good would accrue from its success than from that of any other likely to come into power. On this principle, he would support his party in all things he approved, in all things that were " indifferent," and even in some things he partly disapproved, provided these neither touched the country's honour and vital interests, nor broke " the ordinary rules of morality." Similarly he would attack in his adversary not only what he disapproved, but things that might to a neutral spectator appear tolerable, if this afforded an opportunity of weakening the adversary in public opinion, and increased the chance of bringing into power the party from which he sincerely believed most good was to be expected.[1] " This," the *Westminster* commented, " is the Whig morality." [2] It does not appear indeed, at first glance, consistent with what we have seen in Jeffrey—with his love of truth, for instance, and his refusal to bend the knee to " authority." And yet, regarded in another way, it may be simply a further example of his recognition of reality. He had, we have seen, read the attacks in the *Westminster*. He reprinted this passage, nevertheless, in the *Contributions*. In a footnote in that volume he remarked that his essay might " suggest cautions and grounds of distrust, to rash discontent and thoughtless presumption." [3] It seems like a challenge. It is as if he were seizing us by the scruff of the neck and compelling us to look at things as they are. This, he seems to be saying, is how the system works out in practice ; and there is no use pretending that it can be carried on otherwise. One is made to feel at the same time— and this may apply to Jeffrey's policy in literary as well as in political matters—that he may have considered it legitimate on occasion to try deliberately to discredit an opponent he imagined to be gravely in the wrong, and likely to lead others seriously astray.

We see the same desire to look squarely at truth in Jeffrey's attitude to the French war. This desire made him more

[1] *Cont.*, v. 3, pp. 175-6.   [2] No. 2, p. 528.   [3] *Cont.*, v. 3, p. 145.

pessimistic at times regarding the outcome of that struggle than, fortunately, were large numbers of his countrymen : he forgot that reality includes the future, part of which must be unexpected, and that part of this may be unexpectedly good. He asserted in 1807 that Napoleon was no worse than " the common run of conquerors " and remarked that he would " place him, as to general character, not far from the level of the great Frederick, or the illustrious Catharine," of whom people still talked " not only with patience, but with admiration " ; [1] but he indicated clearly at the same time that he was no idolater of the breed. " We do not think," he wrote at the time of Buonaparte's downfall in 1814, " that an ambitious despot and sanguinary conqueror can be too much execrated, or too little respected by mankind " ; [2] and again, " Undoubtedly there is no other single source of wretchedness so prolific as that strange fascination by which atrocious guilt is converted into an object of admiration, and the honours due to the benefactors of the human race lavished most profusely on their destroyers." [3] But he still tried to maintain his balance. " History, we think," he wrote, " will not class him [Napoleon] quite so low as the English newspapers of the present day. He is a creature to be dreaded and con- demned, but not, assuredly, to be despised by men of ordinary dimensions." [4]

His antipathy to war was equally clear. " What are victories to rejoice at," he wrote to Morehead in 1801, referring to the cessation of hostilities in that year, " compared with an event like this ? Your bonfires and illuminations are dimmed with blood and with tears. . . . The victors are only the least unfortunate, and suffering and death have in general brought us no nearer to tranquillity and happiness." [5] In 1803, telling his brother that he was joining a " corps of riflemen,"—" I hate the business of war," he exclaimed, " and despise the parade of it." [6] " In one part of the striking letter you read to me," he wrote to Macvey Napier in 1837, " I cordially and entirely concur, and that is in the utter reprobation of all avoidable war." [7]

It did not appear to Jeffrey, at the same time, that simple recognition of and talk about evils went far towards curing

[1] *Ed. Rev.*, No. 19, pp. 9-10.   [2] *Cont.*, v. 3, p. 183.   [3] *Ibid.*, v. 3, p. 188.
[4] *Ibid.*, v. 3, p. 184.   [5] *Life*, v. 2, pp. 60-1.   [6] *Ibid*, v. 2, p. 75.
[7] *Corr. of Macvey Napier*, pp. 222-3.

them. Young men, he remarked in one of his articles on
de Staël, were continually warned against the consequences of
youthful imprudence. But young men knew that excesses did
not bring invariable punishment, and they persuaded themselves
accordingly that their particular luck and judgment would
class them among the exceptions to the rule. He remained
convinced therefore that the young would be as incapable of
profiting by their elders' experience ten thousand years thereafter as they were at that moment. Increase of wealth in the
world had brought with it, he said, increase of vices and follies.
It was not for want of being told that these were wrong that
men persisted in them : moralists and divines had been occupied
with little else for the best part of a century. Looking to the
future, he perceived no Utopian prospects. The effect, he said,
of the way in which industry was developing—this was written
in 1813—was to turn peasants into artisans and artisans into
paupers. The natural tendency of the system was to crush
out " moderate dealers " and to throw all business " into the
hands of great capitalists." There appeared to him a likelihood
that the artisans would be reduced to a " fixed and degraded
caste " out of which no person could hope to escape who had
once been enrolled among its members. He saw no sign that
war would be brought to an end by the progress of intelligence
and civilisation. Instead, he said, of becoming less frequent
or destructive in proportion to the rapidity of that progress in
Europe, wars had become more constant and more sanguinary,
and had been most obstinate and most popular in its most
civilised countries. The lovers and conductors of war were by
no means the most ferocious or stupid of their species. " Men
delight in war," Jeffrey wrote, " in spite of the pains and miseries
which they know it entails upon them and their fellows, because
it exercises all the talents, and calls out all the energies of their
nature—because it holds them out conspicuously as objects of
public sentiment and general sympathy—because it gratifies
their pride of art, and gives them a lofty sentiment of their own
power, worth, and courage,—but principally because its sets
the game of existence upon a higher stake, and dispels, by its
powerful interest, those feelings of *ennui* which steal upon every
condition from which hazard and anxiety are excluded, and
drive us into danger and suffering as a relief." While human
nature continued to be distinguished by these attributes he saw

no chance of war's being superseded by the increase of wisdom and morality. " We should be pretty well advanced in the career of perfectibility," he wrote, " if all the inhabitants of Europe were as intelligent, and upright, and considerate, as Sir John Moore, or Lord Nelson, or Lord Collingwood, or Lord Wellington,—but we should not have the less war, we take it, with all its attendant miseries." [1]   The French Revolution, he remarked to Charles Wilkes in 1818, had laid the foundations of a struggle between democracy and tyranny that might involve the world in sanguinary conflicts for fifty years, and might end in the establishment of a brutal and military despotism for a hundred more.[2] " Looking," he wrote to Wilkes in 1822, " at the improved intelligence of despotic governments, and the facilities which the structure of society affords to the policy of keeping nations in awe by armies, I confess I do not think it unlikely that we shall go [on] with our old tyrannies and corruptions for 4000 or 5000 years longer." [3] We have seen that he perceived little defence against these evils in the way in which culture was developing. " Men learn," he wrote, " instead of reasoning. Instead of meditating, they remember ; and, in place of the glow of inventive genius, or the warmth of a generous admiration, nothing is to be met with, in society, but timidity on the one hand, and fastidiousness on the other—a paltry accuracy, and a more paltry derision—a sensibility to small faults, and an incapacity of great merits— a disposition to exaggerate the value of knowledge that is not to be used, and to underrate the importance of powers which have ceased to exist." [4]

The *Westminster* commented on the main discussion here referred to that it threw some light upon the logic as well as upon the morality of the *Edinburgh Review*.[5] *Blackwood's*, dealing with the same passage, suggested that while intelligence among men like Wellington and Collingwood had nothing in it inconsistent with ambition and the love of command, increase of intelligence among the lower orders would make them less willing to obey. " Universal intelligence," it declared, " would not take the general from the army, but it would take the army from the general." [6] Stephen granted to the discussion an " originality and sincerity " which he failed to find in most of

[1] *Cont.*, v. 1, pp. 93-105.   [2] *Life*, v. 2, pp. 183-4.   [3] *Ibid.*, v. 2, p. 197.
[4] *Cont.*, v. 1, p. 101.   [5] V. 1, p. 531.   [6] V. 72, p. 278.

Jeffrey's work. " Still," he added, " one cannot help observing that if the *Edinburgh Review* was an efficient organ of progress, it was not from any ardent faith in progress entertained by its chief conductor." [1]

Jeffrey remarked in that same article that it would be " very agreeable " to believe in the doctrine of perfectibility.[2] It is plain, however, that he refused to permit himself to be convinced of the truth of theories simply on the score of their agreeableness. It may appear to some that it will be time to convict him of false reasoning, weak morality, and lack of faith in progress, when we are able to demonstrate that he was, in all those anticipations, indisputably in the wrong.

Jeffrey, Carlyle affirmed, was, " on the whole exceedingly pleasant in light talk. Yet alas," Carlyle continued, " light, light, too light ! He will talk of nothing *earnestly*, tho' his look sometimes betrays an earnest feeling. He starts contradiction in such cases, and argues, argues. Neither is his arguing like that of a Thinker, but an Advocate ; Victory not Truth." [3]

The fact that the discussions between the two men were, as we have seen, frequently " stormy " suggests that Carlyle may also have argued to some extent for victory ; no doubt it appeared fortunate to him that in his case " Victory " and " Truth " were generally identical. Whatever else may be said of the views just quoted from Jeffrey, " light " seems hardly the most appropriate adjective to apply to them. It does not follow, however, that Carlyle was an imperfect observer : the lightness he noted appears to have been a product of Jeffrey's philosophy. Face the truth unflinchingly seems to have been Jeffrey's doctrine, even where it is bleakest, and then refuse to allow that bleakness to subdue you. An undistorted view of reality could help here as well as chasten. Human beings, it appeared to him, tended to exaggerate considerably their importance in the scheme of things—" poor little bits of rattling timber " he called them in a letter to Horner, " —to be jostled in a bag as soon as the curtain drops." [4] They forgot often how small a proportion of the world's troubles actually rested on their individual shoulders. Even in the midst of the most tumultuous and disastrous periods in history, Jeffrey pointed out, men go on making money, searching for personal distinction,

[1] *Hours in a Library*, v. 2, p. 261. [2] *Cont.*, v. 1, p. 88.
[3] *Carlyle to French Rev.*, Wilson, p. 181. [4] *Life*, v. 2, pp. 120-1.

dancing, courting, marrying, prattling with their children—
continuing, in short, a multitude of everyday human pursuits.[1]
" I really cannot console myself," he wrote to Horner in 1815,
" for the certainty of being vexed and anxious ; and the chance
of being very unhappy all my life, by the belief that some fifty
or a hundred years after I am dead, there will be somewhat
less of folly or wretchedness among the bigots of Spain, or the
boors of Russia. One reads and thinks so much of past ages,
and extends the scale of our combinations so far beyond the
rational measure of our actual interest in events, that it is
difficult not to give way now and then to that illusion. But I
laugh at myself ten times a day for yielding to it." [2] Having
long set his standard of human happiness at a moderate pitch,
he told Wilkes, and persuaded himself that men were considerably
lower than the angels, he was not greatly given to discontent,
and was sensible that much that was vexatious was necessary
to help life along.[3] We glimpse his philosophy in action in
Cockburn's description of his days of early struggle. He was
then not only professionally insignificant, Cockburn remarked,
but also conscious of adequate ability, and aware that " very
inferior rivals " on the opposite political side were " flaming
over his head like rockets." " Notwithstanding all this,
however," Cockburn wrote, " his prevailing state, as at every
period of his life, when not in actual distress, was that of gaiety." [4]
Some of the statements just quoted from him become less un-
relievedly pessimistic when we add a little more from the
context. A " palliative," he suggested, to the situation of the
working classes might spring from the effects of increasing
intelligence among the lower orders themselves, " and," he
added, " we are far from undervaluing this influence." (He
did not, at the same time, see anything at that moment beyond
" the universal adoption of a good system of education," the
development of habits of foresight, self-control, and rigid economy,
to replace " the improvidence and profligacy which too commonly
characterize the larger assemblages of our manufacturing
population," and the general institution of friendly societies
and savings banks.) [5] The passage in the letter to Wilkes
which speaks of the struggle between tyranny and democracy
which might end in the establishment of a military despotism

---

[1] *Cont.*, v. 3, pp. 59-60.   [2] *Life*, v. 2, p. 159.   [3] *Ibid.*, v. 2, pp. 177-8.
[4] *Ibid.*, v. 1, p. 106.   [5] *Cont.*, v. 1, p. 105.

for a century, continues, " but *must* end, I think, in the triumph
of reason over prejudice, and the infinite amelioration of all
politics, and the elevation of all national character. Now I
cannot help thinking," it is interesting to observe him add,
" that the example of America . . . will have a most potent
. . . effect, both in shortening this conflict . . . and in insuring
. . . its happy termination." [1]   " The true hope of the world,"
he repeated to Wilkes in 1822, " is with you in America ; in
your example now, and in fifty years more I hope, your influence
and actual power." [2]

We catch another glimpse of his philosophy in a letter written
to Carlyle. " You will never persuade anybody," he told
Carlyle, " that the regulation of life is such a mighty laborious
business as you would make it, or that it is not better to go
lightly through it, with the first creed that comes to hand, than
to spend the better part of it in an anxious verification of its
articles.   If you were only amusing yourself with these paradoxes,
I should have no objection, but you take them so dreadfully
in earnest that it vexes me—for it will neutralise half the fame
and all the use of your talents—and keep aloof from you most
of the men who are fittest for your society." " You have no
mission upon earth," he said to Carlyle, " . . . half so important
as to be innocently happy." [3]

This doctrine—that a man should not allow himself to be
too " dreadfully in earnest," that his first duty is to solve, not
the problems of the universe, but simply the problem of finding
happiness for himself in an always imperfect world—might, if
regarded alone, seem to indicate indolence and egotism. We
recall, however, Horner's affirmation that if the first impression
created by Jeffrey was one of levity there was no man whose
character was in reality so much the opposite. We recollect
that if he refused to indulge a hopefulness, that might be
disappointed, of the success of the *Review* at its commencement,
no man worked harder than he did to bring that success about.
We remember Sydney Smith's list of the reforms that, in the
early years of the nineteenth century, were " not a little assisted
by the honest boldness of the *Edinburgh Review* "—repeal of the
Corporation and Test Acts ; emancipation of Roman Catholics ;
abolition of the slave trade ; abolition of steel traps and spring

---

[1] *Life*, v. 2, p. 184.   [2] *Ibid.*, v. 2, p. 197.
[3] *Carlyle to French Rev.*, Wilson, pp. 63, 62.

guns ; provision of counsel for prisoners ; improvements of the
Court of Chancery, of the Game Laws, of the Laws of Libel,
Debt, and Conspiracy.[1] If Jeffrey refused to consume his spirit
with anxiety, he evidently believed in doing whatever practicable
lay to his hand. The *North British Review* spoke of his toil " year
by year . . . to undermine that fabric of corrupt and autocratic
principle "—of his being " content to introduce his lever one
day, and waiting for the next to make its power felt—until by
degrees, not startling but sure, in thirty years he saw the temple
of the idol crumbling at his feet, and the altar of popular right
raised upon its ruins." [2]

" It should never be forgotten," Jeffrey declared, " that
good political institutions, the sole end and object of all our
party contentions, are only valuable as means of promoting the
general happiness and virtue of individuals ;—and that,
important as they are, there are other means, still more direct
and indispensable for the attainment of that great end. The
cultivation of the kind affections, we humbly conceive, to be of
still more importance to private happiness, than the good
balance of the constitution under which we live. . . . A man
must love his fellows before he loves their liberty." [3] We
observe the direction of attention once again to ends, the
association of happiness with virtue—Carlyle's duty was, we
remember, to be " innocently happy "—and the linking of both
with " kind affections." " The great art," he wrote in another
place, " is the art of living ; and the chief science the science
of being happy." [4] In an article on Wilson's poems he spoke
of the author's being " habitually familiar with thoughts and
affections, far more to be envied than the fading renown that
genius has ever won for her votaries." [5] Reviewing a selection
from the correspondence of Collingwood, " We do not know,"
he asserted, " when we have met with so delightful a book as
this,—or one with which we are so well pleased with ourselves
for being delighted. Its attraction consists almost entirely in
its moral beauty." [6] Of a work by Bishop Heber he wrote :
" This is another book for Englishmen to be proud of—almost
as delightful as the Memoirs of Lord Collingwood, and indebted
for its attractions mainly to the same cause—the singularly

[1] Preface to *Works*.
[2] No. 25 (May 1850), p. 278.
[3] *Cont.*, v. 3, pp. 361-2.
[4] *Ibid.*, v. 3, p. 3.
[5] *Ed. Rev.*, No. 38, p. 385.
[6] *Cont.*, v. 3, p. 415.

amiable and exalted character of the person to whom it relates." [1]
" We cannot *Envy*," he wrote in an article on prisons, " the
happiness "—we note the word—" which Mrs Fry must enjoy
from the consciousness of her own great achievements ;—but
there is no happiness or honour of which we should be so proud
to be partakers : And we seem to relieve our own hearts of
their share of national gratitude, in thus placing on her simple
and modest brow, that truly Civic Crown, which far outshines
the laurels of conquest, or the coronals of power—and can only
be outshone itself, by those wreaths of imperishable glory which
await the champions of Faith and Charity in a higher state
of existence." [2]   We perceive there standards and a scale of
values that are by no means narrowly literary.

" I cannot always get time now," Jeffrey wrote to Carlyle
in 1828, " to walk out before going to sleep in the dewy dawn,
or even to read for half-an-hour in some sweet and soothing
poem, after my dull task is over, washing its earthy stains from
my brain in these waters of healing." [3]   " If it were not for
my love of beautiful nature and poetry," he burst out in a letter
written to Cockburn from London in 1833, " my heart would
have died within me long ago.   I never felt before what
immeasurable benefactors these same poets are to their kind,
and how large a measure, both of actual happiness and prevention
of misery, they have imparted to the race.   I would willingly
give up half my fortune, and some little of the fragments of
health and bodily enjoyment that remain to me, rather than
that Shakespeare should not have lived before me." [4]   That
indicates what poetry meant to Jeffrey : its function was to
help towards mastery of the greatest of arts.   " The only use
of the faculty of taste," he wrote, " is to afford an innocent
delight, and to assist in the cultivation of a finer morality " [5]
—still the same combination.

A critic of Jeffrey's experience may be presumed to have
noticed the elementary point that there is no necessary connection
between ethics and technical artistic skill.   " Moral qualities
alone," he remarked, " will not make a good writer ; nor are
they even of the first importance on such an occasion." [6]   We
have noticed also his dislike of " mawkish morality."   Moral

---

[1] *Cont.*, v. 3, p. 436.   [2] *Ibid.*, v. 3, p. 543.
[3] *Carlyle to French Rev.*, Wilson, p. 59. [4] *Life*, v. 1, p. 350.
[5] *Cont.*, v. 1, p. 76.   [6] *Ibid.*, v. 3, p. 394.

qualities become important, nevertheless, when a work is judged
as a contribution to the art of living. Jeffrey did so regard them :
he thought them so important indeed that he placed his concentration upon these qualities in the forefront of his claim as
a critic. "If I might be permitted," he wrote in the preface
to his *Contributions*, ". . . to state, in what particular department,
and generally, on account of what, I should most wish to claim
a share of those merits"—the merits, that is, that could be
attributed to the *Edinburgh Review*—"I should certainly say,
that it was by having constantly endeavoured to combine Ethical
precepts with Literary Criticism, and earnestly sought to impress
my readers with a sense, both of the close connection between
sound Intellectual attainments"—the operative word there is
surely "sound"—"and the higher elements of Duty and
Enjoyment"—we note still again the combination—"and of the
just and ultimate subordination of the former to the latter.
The praise in short to which I aspire, and to merit which I am
conscious that my efforts were most constantly directed, is,
that I have, more uniformly and earnestly than any preceding
critic, made the Moral tendencies of the works under consideration
a leading subject of discussion." [1]

In thus constantly linking happiness with goodness, and in
teaching that the preservation and furtherance of these should
be the supreme aim of every human activity—the writing and
criticism of books being included—Jeffrey was not moving out
of the sphere of Scottish thought. It was proclaimed on the
opening page of a book long familiar in Scotland that man's
chief end was "to glorify God, and to enjoy Him for ever."

All men, it might be said, search for happiness in one form or
another. But there is a profound difference between the very
common "Happiness tomorrow, but never happiness today !"
and the art of distilling the best, in the best possible manner,
from every passing contaminated moment.

III

Jeffrey placed first in his collected *Contributions* his article on
Alison's *Nature and Principles of Taste*.[2] This essay, after its
appearance in the *Edinburgh* in 1811, was enlarged and printed
in the supplement to the *Encyclopædia Britannica* in 1824, was

[1] *Cont.*, v. 1, p. xii.   [2] *Ibid*, v. 1, pp. 3-78.

incorporated into that work in 1841, and remained there, Gates noted, till 1875.[1] As philosophy the article may now be expected to be as out of date as most similar productions published to-day may be expected to be an equal period hereafter. As, however, the position Jeffrey gave the essay suggests that he regarded it as important, and as it seems to me to indicate further fundamental principles, we may glance at it here very briefly.

Beauty, according to the theory of Alison and Jeffrey, is not an intrinsic quality of objects, but an effect of the associations that objects arouse in our minds. Blue, for example, is beautiful in a spring sky ; green is beautiful in summer meadows ; pink may be beautiful on the cheeks of a woman. If, however, we change the associations, the beauty disappears. The blue of the sky would not be beautiful on a woman's face, or the green of the meadows in the sky, or the colour of beautiful skin on the grass. Contemporary fashions, to take another of Jeffrey's illustrations, appear beautiful to us because we associate them with the young and the elegant ; yesterday's fashions, though once thought beautiful, now appear ugly because we associate them with the dowdy and decayed ; fashions of a remoter past have re-assumed attractiveness because they are associated with what has now become romantic. A cancerous ulcer may display the finest effects of colour and shade, but the associations are such that no normal person can see beauty there.

This theory creates, it will be observed, a problem for critics. If beauty depends upon associations, and if, as must follow from the fact that no two men have had the same experiences, objects must awaken different associations in different minds, how can there be any objective æsthetic standard ? " The principal conclusion," Stephen remarked of Jeffrey's essay, " is the rather unsatisfactory one for a professional critic, that there are no particular rules about beauty, and consequently that one taste is about as good as another." [2] One might answer to this, of course, that the object of a philosophical enquiry is not to arrive at a conclusion satisfactory to a professional critic. But the question remains. Jeffrey did not overlook it. Associations, he said, are of two kinds. There are, in the first place, what he called " personal and accidental associations "— associations, that is, peculiar to the individual. A man may

---

[1] *Cont.*, v. 1, p. 3 ; *Three Studies*, Gates, p. 1.
[2] *Hours in a Library*, v. 2, p. 254.

see beauty—in a song for example, to take one of Alison's illustrations, heard in his infancy—where it is perceptible to no one else. If he tells another, who cannot perceive it, that he finds beauty there, then he says something about which there can be no argument. But besides these accidental associations there exist, Jeffrey held, " associations that are universal and indestructible . . . emotions of which the greater part of mankind are susceptible." It is, he said, this type of associations that an artist must endeavour to arouse ; and, it follows, it is by his success in doing so that a critic must judge him. " Jeffrey, however," Gates commented, " suggests no means of determining abstractly what associations are universal and indestructible, and hence no means of discriminating in thought between a man's own peculiar objects of beauty and those objects which may be regarded as universally or absolutely beautiful. Jeffrey's standard of beauty therefore becomes purely arbitrary." [1] " Good judges," Jeffrey wrote in his article on *The Lady of the Lake*, " . . . are persons eminently qualified, by natural sensibility, and long experience and reflection, to perceive all beauties that really exist, as well as to settle the relative value and importance of all the different sorts of beauty." [2] " How these judges," Gates commented, " are to be recognized or chosen,—whether, for example, Gifford of the *Quarterly Review* is one of these judges, and how they are to settle their disputes among themselves,—these are questions that Jeffrey leaves unanswered. In other words, Jeffrey can discover no objective standard of beauty, and the only escape from absolute lawlessness, that he suggests, consists in his offer of himself as ' self-constituted judge of poesy.' " [3]

I think that we are now sufficiently acquainted with Jeffrey to guess how he would have replied to these objections. I do not think he would have admitted that he had been driven to the wall. " A great deal of labour," he remarked on one occasion to Horner, " is bestowed in making useless distinctions, and imperfect catalogues of things that never were either overlooked or mistaken by reasonable men." [4] I imagine that he would have agreed immediately that he had discovered no particular rules about beauty, that he had indicated no way of discriminating abstractly between personal and universal

---

[1] *Selections*, p. 208. [2] *Cont.*, v. 2, p. 239. [3] *Sel.*, p. 208.
[4] *Life*, v. 2, p. 88.

associations, and that he had found no formula by means of
which sound judges could be distinguished infallibly from the
unsound. I fancy, however, that he might have added that
neither had anyone else. I imagine he would have pointed
out that in speaking of personal and universal associations he
was using words in a way in which words must very often be
employed—as representing approximations ; that between the
extremes of purely-personal associations, which are purely
theoretical, and equally theoretical purely-universal associations
there must be an infinite number of gradations, and that no
clear boundary-line can therefore be drawn between them ;
that every man who has written a letter that has interested a
friend has taken a step from the purely-personal in the direction
of the purely-universal ; and that artists, by appealing to a
greater or less degree—no artist has ever reached the purely-
universal—to audiences widely dispersed in space and time
have solved the problem approximately in practice over and
over again. I think he would have pointed out that it is equally
impossible to draw any exact line of demarcation between good
judges and bad, and that they too can be distinguished from
one another only by the extent to which they have been found
capable of appealing to universal associations. It follows that
no properly accredited critic has ever been really a " self-
constituted judge " : Jeffrey's right to be regarded as a critic
in his own day rested, not on any claims of his own, but on the
simple fact that large numbers of educated people were willing
to view his opinions with respect. His right to be still so regarded
depends upon the extent to which we find ourselves prepared
to do the same.

Jeffrey's ethical outlook might be similarly criticised : if
beauty is not precisely the same to any two men neither is
morality. Jeffrey's answer was on this subject explicit. " The
truth is," he stated, " . . . that this uncertainty is in all cases
of a very limited nature ; and that the common impressions of
morality, the vulgar distinctions of right and wrong, virtue
and vice, are perfectly sufficient to direct the conduct of the
individual . . . for all useful purposes." " Moral maxims and
impressions," he wrote, " . . . may be compared . . . to those
acquired perceptions of sight by which the eye is enabled to judge
of distances ; of the process of acquiring which we are equally
unconscious, and yet by which it is certain that we are much

more safely and commodiously guided, within the range of our ordinary occupations, than we ever could be by any formal scientific calculations, founded on the faintness of the colouring, and the magnitude of the angle of vision, compared with the average tangible bulk of the kind of object in question. . . . The established rules and impressions of morality . . . we consider as the grand recorded result of an infinite multitude of experiments upon human feeling and fortune, under every variety of circumstances ; and as affording, therefore, by far the nearest approximation to a just standard of the good and the evil that human conduct is concerned with, which the nature of our faculties will allow. In endeavouring to correct or amend this general verdict of mankind, in any particular instance, we not only substitute our own individual feelings for that large average which is implied in those moral impressions, which are universally prevalent, but obviously run the risk of omitting or mistaking some of the most important elements of the calculation." When the way was obscure, therefore, it was on these general impressions that it was safest to rely. " They are," Jeffrey asserted, " observations taken in the calm, by which we must be guided in the darkness and the terror of the tempest ; they are beacons and strongholds erected in the day of peace, round which we must rally, and to which we must betake ourselves, in the hour of contest and alarm." [1]

This theory was bound to mould Jeffrey's thinking. The assertion, for example, noted earlier in this chapter, that argument from authority—the authority, that is, of an individual—was the weakest of all arguments follows from it as the night the day. The critic, however highly trained, remained, like every other man, in constant danger of mistaking his personal for general associations. He had to keep in mind, therefore, that his judgments had always to be ratified by the court of common sense. And if a sound verdict was to be reached, his case had always to be presented fairly. The effect of this mode of thinking has been perceived in Jeffrey's critical method. " A too restless display of talent," Hazlitt wrote of him for example, " a too undisguised statement of all that can be said for and against a question, is perhaps the great fault that is to be attributed to him." [2] *Blackwood's* found in him what it regarded as a tendency to evade accurate decision. " If one observation,"

[1] *Cont.*, v. 2, pp. 578-83. [2] *Spirit of the Age*, p. 296.

it averred, " is erroneous, or extravagantly expressed, it is neutralised by some other observation ;—there is black and white thrown before you on the palette, mix them to your own pleasure ; you cannot complain that there is withheld from you any one reasonable view of the case." [1] " When he is dull or commonplace," said Gregory Smith, " as he is on occasion, it is nearly always because he has looked at the subject too carefully and from both sides, and has declined to give a bias to the indolent reader." [2] " I found," Carlyle declared even of his conversation, " that essentially he was always as if speaking to a jury." [3] " He addresses," said Nichol Smith, " the grand jury of public opinion." And again—" Jeffrey's inexhaustible vivacity," Nichol Smith wrote, " made him too fond of argument. . . . It helped him at the bar, but it has not helped his reputation as a judge of literature." [4]

This last sentence sends us to other passages in Jeffrey. He remarked in one of his essays that if men continued to write and rhyme as they were doing for a further two hundred years there would have to be " some new art of *short-hand reading* invented " or all reading would be given up in despair.[5] It was inevitable that this vast expansion of literature should cause men to look more and more for ready-made opinions. Jeffrey, as we have seen, saw this process at work in his own day. " So many easy and pleasant elementary books," ran another of his pictures of his time, " —such tempting summaries, abstracts, and tables,—such beautiful engravings, and ingenious charts, and *coups-d'œil* of information,—so many museums, exhibitions, and collections, meet us at every corner,—and so much amusing and provoking talk in every party, that a taste for miscellaneous and imperfect information is formed, almost before we are aware ; and our time and curiosity irrevocably devoted to a sort of Encyclopedical trifling." [6] The Jeffreyan procedure by which every statement is submitted with full evidence and reasonings annexed cannot but appear clumsy in comparison with the encyclopedical method by which information is passed swiftly and painlessly from unquestioned teacher to unquestioning taught. Jeffrey did not deny, we observe, that the latter method could be neat, entertaining, and effective. What he suggested

[1] V. 72, p. 468. [2] *Chambers's Cyclopædia of Eng. Lit.*, v. 3, p. 87.
[3] *Rem.*, v. 2, p. 41. [4] *Jeffrey's Lit. Crit.*, pp. xiii-xiv.
[5] *Cont.*, v. 2, p. 15. [6] *Ibid.*, v. 2, p. 646.

was that it was dangerous. There may be some to whom it may appear that his fears have been justified ; that the multiplicity of information in modern times has caused large numbers of educated people to become, even where matters of the highest importance to themselves are concerned, to a larger extent than they themselves have perhaps sometimes realised, mere learners ; that where doctrine has been based upon simple authority charlatanry has shown itself at least the equal, in impressiveness, of scholarship ; that great masses of mankind, scholars among them, have found themselves lured in consequence far outside the channels of safety marked by the ancient buoys ; and that scholarship must, for its life's sake, labour consciously to maintain in the world a widespread independence of judgment.

The Jeffreyan theory must, of course, govern the method adopted in this study.

CHAPTER VIII

JEFFREY AT WORK

Impartiality. Glimpse of the Lakers. A metrical discussion. Antiquarianism. Artificiality of poetry. Appreciation. The Two-fold standard. Critical attitude.

I

ON entering a stage set for film purposes one may sometimes see, I believe, erections which on one side appear façades of buildings, and, on the other, intricacies of supporting joiner-work. These may be of widely different sizes, varying from the normal to that of dolls' houses. In a corner may be some irregularly-shaped heaps of plasticine, perhaps a foot or so in height. Then suddenly, as one moves through this jumble, one finds oneself at the camera-angle. And the whole is abruptly transformed. The joiner-work intricacies have disappeared. The buildings have become orderly rows of streets, diminished in size apparently only by distance. The heaps of plasticine have become a mountain range, its peaks towering into a far-off sky. The landscape has moved into perspective. But to an observer a few yards away it still appears unreal and absurd.

Perhaps the facts are inaccurate : the description has been built up merely from some dim recollections of reading. But there may be here at anyrate an analogy. It may be said that we all of us view the world from such camera-angles—angles from which our own ways of thinking appear perfectly proportioned while we see, often with such clarity that it seems ridiculous that our neighbours should be unable to perceive them for themselves, the absurdities on the stages, ranged alongside ours, that represent the thinking of our fellows. It may be difficult for us to realise at times that our neighbours can see the disproportions in our thinking with equal plainness, and that it may be only courtesy, or indifference, or, in some instances, fear of our power that keeps them from telling us so. This may suggest at least one " end " for such a study as this. If from our angle we can see plainly the weaknesses in the thinking and methods of a man belonging to a different generation from ours, it may be that, in endeavouring to look from his viewpoint, we may catch a glimpse of some of the weaknesses in our own.

In turning now for a spell, in search of further insight into his mind, to watch Jeffrey at work upon the writings of particular authors, it may be well to glance first at his dealings with men who, being of his own nationality, may be presumed to have been to some degree in tune psychologically with himself. We have seen that he had his full share of the Scottish love of country. If he tried, with indifferent success, to rid himself of his Scottish accent, he could "speak Scotch," Cockburn declared, "when he chose, as correctly as when the Doric of the Lawnmarket of Edinburgh had only been improved by that of Rottenrow of Glasgow; and had a most familiar acquaintance with the vocabulary of his country." [1] "I used to find in him," Carlyle wrote, "a finer talent than any he has evidenced in writing. This was chiefly when he got to speak Scotch" [2]—an interesting comment in view of the suggestion in our third chapter. Cockburn said that he was "familiar with the writers in . . . classic Scotch . . . from Gavin Douglas to Burns." [3] "Scotch," Jeffrey wrote himself, "is not to be considered as a provincial dialect—the vehicle only of rustic vulgarity and rude local humour. . . . It is by no means peculiar to the vulgar; but it is the common speech of the whole nation in early life—and, with many of its most exalted and accomplished individuals, throughout their whole existence; and, though it be true that, in later times, it has been, in some measure, laid aside by the more ambitious and aspiring of the present generation"— perhaps he was thinking here of himself—"it is still recollected, even by them, as the familiar language of their childhood, and of those who were the earliest objects of their love and veneration. . . . Add to all this, that it is the language of a great body of poetry, with which almost all Scotchmen are familiar; and, in particular, of a great multitude of songs, written with more tenderness, nature, and feeling, than any other lyric compositions that are extant—and we may perhaps be allowed to say, that the Scotch is, in reality, a highly poetical language; and that it is an ignorant, as well as an illiberal prejudice, which would seek to confound it with the barbarous dialects of Yorkshire or Devon." [4] Cockburn did not say whence he had the anecdote

---

[1] *Life*, v. 1, pp. 47-8. [2] *Rem.*, v. 2, p. 65.
[3] *Life*, v. 1, p. 48. [4] *Cont.*, v. 2, pp. 155-6.

of Jeffrey's meeting with Burns, but it is probable it was from
Jeffrey himself : we are told elsewhere that Jeffrey used to dwell
with pleasure on the incident.[1] The eagerness of the " person "
in the doorway to point out Burns on that occasion demonstrates
the enthusiasm of the Scots for their new poet ; Jeffrey's frequent
telling of the story shows he shared it. In 1800, having been
looking at Currie's newly-published edition, " Some of the songs,"
he wrote to Morehead, " are enchantingly beautiful, and affect
one more than any other species of poetry whatsoever." [2] " I
can never read anything about Burns," he told Carlyle in 1828,
" without a melting and a burning in my blood." [3] It would
not have been surprising, in the light of all this, had Jeffrey
employed part of his influence, after he discovered that the
Edinburgh had gained the attention of the English-speaking
world, in helping to spread the fame of the great poet Scotland
had produced in his day. His opportunity came in 1808, with
the publication of Cromek's *Reliques*.

Part of his review [4] was on the lines that might have been
expected. The defence of Scots just noticed was contained in
it. It was a derogation from Burns's merits, Jeffrey argued,
to regard him as a rustic prodigy. Before Burns had composed
a stanza he was not only familiar with many prose-writers but
was more intimately acquainted with Shakespeare, Pope, and
Thomson than were nine-tenths of the youths that in those days
entered the universities. He had " about as much scholarship,
in short . . . as Shakespeare." It might have been a disadvantage to Burns, Jeffrey suggested indeed, had he read
more widely. When a man's head was filled with splendid
passages from ancient and modern authors he was " perpetually
haunted and depressed by the ideal presence of those great
masters, and their exacting critics." If his reading supplied
him with an abundant store of images, he would tend to feed
his mind contentedly on these. On the other hand, a youth
of quick parts, living in an environment in which he had no
reputation to lose and in which he could easily excel all around
him, was in a situation exceedingly favourable for the composition
of poetry. Jeffrey saw " no propriety " accordingly, in admiring
Burns's poetry " much in the same way as if it had been written
with his toes." Much of the praise in Jeffrey's article is now

[1] *Literary Celebrities*, Chambers, 1887, p. 222.   [2] *Life*, v. 2, p. 45.
[3] *Carlyle to French Rev.*, Wilson, p. 54.   [4] *Cont.*, v. 2, pp. 143-175.

scarcely worth recording : it is simply part of the general stock of criticism. Jeffrey found in Burns " traits of a delicate and tender feeling, indicating that unaffected softness of heart which is always so enchanting " : we are prepared for that emphasis. The " felicity and delicacy of imitation " with which Burns improved upon the old Scottish ballads he took as his models for his songs were, Jeffrey claimed, " altogether unrivalled in the history of literature." The " whole beauty " of *The Cotter's Saturday Night* could not " be discerned but by those whom experience " had " enabled to judge of the admirable fidelity and completeness of the picture." There we have the emphasis upon actuality. Whatever may be said of the accuracy of the picture, Jeffrey, it must be agreed, had opportunities of acquiring a more intimate knowledge of the eighteenth-century Scottish peasantry than has any modern critic. So also had John Murdoch—who described William Burnes, the prototype of the cotter, as " by far the best of the human race " he had " ever . . . had the pleasure of being acquainted with." [1] It was impossible, Jeffrey declared, " to read the productions of Burns, along with his history, without forming a higher idea of the intelligence, taste, and accomplishments of our peasantry, than most of those in the higher ranks are disposed to entertain."

The whole essay was not, however, so encomiastic. Jeffrey found in Burns's poetry certain " peculiarities " which reminded him of the lowness of the writer's origin, and " faults " for which the defects of the poet's education afforded " an obvious cause if not a legitimate apology." Among these was the " undisciplined harshness " of Burns's invective. The great boast of polished life, Jeffrey remarked, was the delicacy and even generosity of its hostility, a principle which " enjoins us, in forging the shafts of satire, to increase the polish exactly as we add to their keenness or their weight." This kind of delicacy was absent in Burns. His raillery consisted in railing, and his satire displayed itself " chiefly in calling names and in swearing." He meant this, the reviewer asserted, to apply mainly to Burns's personalities : in the more general representations there was undoubtedly much that was genuinely satirical.

Jeffrey found a similar want of polish, " or at least of respectfulness," in the poet's " gallantry." Burns had expressed admirably the feelings of " an enamoured peasant," but had

[1] *Life and Works of Burns*, Chambers and Wallace, v. 1, p. 41.

never caught the tone of chivalry in courtship. " Accordingly,"
Jeffrey wrote, " instead of suing for a smile, or melting in a tear,
his muse deals in nothing but locked embraces and midnight
rencontres ; and, even in his complimentary effusions to ladies
of the highest rank, is for straining them to the bosom of her
impetuous votary." The allusion is evidently to Burns's

> " And nightly to my bosom strain
> The bonny lass o' Ballochmyle."

These verses were inspired, it may be remembered, by Wilhelmina
Alexander, sister of the Laird of Ballochmyle—to whom Burns
had not so much as even spoken, but who had merely passed
him one evening in the dusk, as she was walking in the grounds
of her brother's estate. Even in these freer modern days the
aspiration might, in such circumstances, still appear a trifle
startling.[1]

Another blemish in Burns was the poet's perpetual boast of
independence. The sentiment, Jeffrey granted, was noble, and
often finely expressed. " But a gentleman," he wrote, " would
only have expressed it when he was insulted or provoked ; and
would never have made it a spontaneous theme to those friends
in whose estimation he felt that his honour stood clear." Still
another fault was a frequent mistake of violence for force and
sublimity. Burns had evidently a very false notion of what
constituted strength of writing.

Jeffrey's main criticism of Burns, however, went deeper than
this. " The leading vice in Burns's character," he said, " and
the cardinal deformity, indeed, of all his productions, was his
contempt, or affectation of contempt, for prudence, decency,
and regularity ; and his admiration of thoughtlessness, oddity,
and vehement sensibility ;—his belief, in short, in *the dispensing
power* of genius and social feeling, in all matters of morality and
common sense." We are in contact, we note, with Jeffrey's
central principles. It was true, Jeffrey went on, that men of
genius had been often hurried by their passions into violations
of prudence and duty. There was something generous in
apologies made for them by admirers on the ground of their
keener feelings. But this apology, unsatisfactory even in an
admirer, became " an insult and an absurdity " when advanced
by a man for himself. It simply marked him as a determined

---

[1] *Life and Works of Burns*, Chambers and Wallace, v. 1, p. 380.

profligate seeking to disguise his selfishness under a name less
revolting. It required no deep thought to perceive the baseness
of spending in superfluities what belonged rightfully to hard-
working tradesmen and their families. To talk of the goodness
and generosity of a man who raved about philanthropy in a
tavern while his wife and children sat in solitary poverty at
home was " the heroics only of the hulks and the house of
correction " : the style had " no chance . . . of being greatly
admired, except in the farewell speech of a young gentleman
preparing for Botany Bay." It was " humiliating " to think
how deeply Burns had fallen into this error. He was perpetually
parading his " thoughtlessness, inflammability, and imprudence,"
and talking with " complacency and exultation " of the offence
he had occasioned to " the sober and correct part of mankind."
" He could not," the reviewer declared, " have seen *much* of
the beings who echoed this raving "—we have here, we may
fancy, a reflection of Jeffrey's legal experience—" without feeling
for them that distrust and contempt which would have made
him blush to think he had ever stretched over them the protecting
shield of his genius."

" These points," Nichol Smith commented, " are all valid,
as valid as the devil's advocate can make them." [1] It was
this review Smith was discussing when he drew attention to
Jeffrey's readiness to point out what might be said on the other
side. I do not imagine that Jeffrey found much pleasure in
the exercise on this occasion. " Peter Morris " characterised
" the whole spirit and tone " of the reviewer's attack as " radically
and essentially abominable." Jeffrey, " Morris " declared,
" displayed . . . a very lamentable defect, not merely of
nationality of feeling, but of humanity of feeling." [2] Jeffrey
could not but be aware that this would be an effect of his article
in Scotland. In a letter to Empson (later his son-in-law) dated
1837, " In the last week," he wrote, " I have read all *Burns'*
life and works—not without many tears, for the life especially.
What touches me most is the pitiable poverty in which that
gifted being (and his noble-minded father) passed his early
days—the painful frugality to which their innocence was doomed,
and the thought, how small a share of the useless luxuries in
which *we* (such comparatively poor creatures) indulge, would
have sufficed to shed joy and cheerfulness in their dwellings,

---

[1] *Jeffrey's Lit. Crit.*, pp. xiii-xiv.   [2] *Peter's Letters*, v. 1, pp. 113-4.

and perhaps to have saved that glorious spirit from the trials and temptations under which he fell so prematurely. Oh my dear Empson, there must be something *terribly* wrong in the present arrangements of the universe, when those things can happen, and be thought natural. I could lie down in the dirt, and cry and grovel there, I think, for a century, to save such a soul as Burns from the suffering and the contamination and the *degradation* which these same arrangements imposed upon him ; and I fancy, that, if I could but have known him, in my present state of wealth and influence, I might have saved, and reclaimed, and preserved him, even to the present day." [1] That, like the letters to Morehead and Carlyle, shows how he thought of Burns privately. In a review of Campbell's *Specimens* published in 1819 he professed himself " most willing to acknowledge " that Campbell's defence of Burns against " some " of his severities was " substantially successful." He was sensible, he said, that he had made the words of his censure " far more comprehensive " than his meaning.   " We gladly make," he wrote, " this expiation to the shade of our illustrious countryman." [2] But he did not take back all he had said.   And in the *Contributions* he reprinted both this passage and the original article.

The reason seems obvious. Burns, it appeared to him, was an imperfect guide to the greatest of arts. And by a critic who believed that when taking up his reviewing-pen he must enter the temple of truth, this, at whatever cost to Burns's reputation, or his own, or to Scottish national vanity, had to be said.

The essay on Burns closed with a reference to the school of writers Jeffrey's dealings with whom must be studied in detail later.   " Those gentlemen," Jeffrey wrote, " are outrageous for simplicity ; and we beg leave to recommend to them the simplicity of Burns. He has copied the spoken language of passion and affection, with infinitely more fidelity than they have ever done, on all occasions which properly admitted of such adaptation : But he has not rejected the helps of elevated language and habitual associations ; nor debased his composition by an affectation of babyish interjections, and all the puling expletives of an old nursery-maid's vocabulary. They may look long enough among his nervous and manly lines, before they find any ' Good lacks ! '—' Dear hearts ! '—or ' As a body may

[1] *Life*, v. 2, p. 292.   [2] *Cont.*, v. 2, p. 33.

says,' in them ; or any stuff about dancing daffodils and sister Emmelines." (Gregory Smith, we have noticed, spoke of the " unfortunate gibe at ' dancing daffodils ' " as one for which the reviewer was still in the critics' purgatory ; Saintsbury referred to " such almost unforgivable phrases as ' stuff about dancing daffodils.' ") [1] " Let them think," Jeffrey went on, " with what infinite contempt the powerful mind of Burns would have perused the story of Alice Fell and her duffle cloak,—of Andrew Jones and the half-crown,—or of Little Dan without breeches, and his thievish grandfather." They should " contrast their own fantastical personages of hysterical schoolmasters and sententious leechgatherers " with the " authentic rustics " of *The Cotter's Saturday Night* and Burns's songs, and reflect upon the way in which these latter had been received by the public. " Though," Jeffrey wrote, " they will not be reclaimed from their puny affectations by the example of their learned predecessors, they may, perhaps, submit to be admonished by a self-taught and illiterate poet, who drew from Nature far more directly than they can do, and produced something so much liker the admired copies of the masters whom they have abjured." The standard of judgment employed is, it will be observed, that of actuality. The use in the last sentence of the word " illiterate " suggests that Jeffrey's warmth had made him, in the latter part of his argument, forget to some extent its beginning.

II

In dealing with Burns, Jeffrey was criticising a body of writing that was complete. In dealing with the other great Scottish writer of his time, Sir Walter Scott, he was criticising works as they were published.[2] " It may not be altogether without interest," he remarked in introducing the section of his

---

[1] *Essays in Eng. Lit.* (1780-1860), p. 118. Coleridge found in *Daffodils* " an approximation to what might be called mental bombast." *Biog. Lit.* (Bohn), p. 221.

[2] Jeffrey wrote the following articles on Scott : *Lay of the Last Minstrel* (*Ed. Rev.*, No. 11, Art. 1 ; *Cont.*, v. 2, p. 214) ; *Marmion* (*Ed. Rev.*, No. 23, Art. 1) ; *Lady of the Lake* (*Ed. Rev.*, No. 32, Art 1. ; *Cont.*, v. 2, p. 237) ; *Roderick* (*Ed. Rev.*, No. 36, Art. 6) ; *Waverley* (*Ed. Rev.*, No. 47, Art. 11 ; *Cont.*, v. 3, p. 32) ; *Lord of the Isles* (*Ed. Rev.*, No. 48, Art. 1) ; *Tales of my Landlord* (*Ed. Rev.*, No. 55, Art. 9 ; *Cont.*, v. 3, p. 45) ; *Rob Roy* (*Ed. Rev.*, No. 58, Art. 7 ; *Cont.*, v. 3, p. 66) ; *Ivanhoe* (*Ed. Rev.*, No. 65, Art. 1 ; *Cont.*, v. 3, p. 72) ; *Fortunes of Nigel* (*Ed. Rev.*, No. 73, Art. 8 ; *Cont.*, v. 3, p. 88).

Contributions containing his articles on Scott's novels, " to see, from a contemporary record, what were the first impressions produced by the appearance of this new luminary on our horizon." [1]   Most of the criticisms to be noticed from this point onwards have this kind of interest.

Jeffrey's article on the *Lay*, the first of Scott's compositions he reviewed, gives us an opportunity of glancing at a more technical discussion.   The poem's versification he described as " in the highest degree irregular and capricious."   While the nature of the work entitled Scott to some licence in metre, and while the poet had often employed this irregularity with a very pleasing effect, he had frequently exceeded its just limits, and presented his readers with such combinations as would put their " teeth . . . into some jeopardy."   Many lines could be put into verse only by running the words together in a way that was very unusual ; some appeared to have " no pretension to the name of verses at all." [2]   Saintsbury remarked that Jeffrey criticised the metre of the *Lay* " in a way which shows that he had not in the least grasped its scheme." [3]   The statement appears to me venturesome.   We saw that Scott passed the manuscript of this, his first important poetical work, to Jeffrey. Jeffrey stated, years later, that he had heard Scott say that he was indebted to *Christabel* " for the first idea of that romantic narrative in irregular verse, which he afterwards exemplified in his *Lay of the Last Minstrel*, and other works." [4]   It seems to me reasonable to assume that something of this sort was said at the time when Scott gave Jeffrey his manuscript, that Scott was able to make clear what he was trying to do, and that the man whom Scott described as " already for some time distinguished by his critical talent " was capable of understanding the explanation.   Jeffrey quoted in illustration of his point the following verses :

> " St Kentigern's hall,"

and

> " How the brave boy, in future war
> Should tame the unicorn's pride."

The first of these is evidently intended, from the context, to be an iambic trimeter and the third to be an iambic tetrameter.

---

[1] *Cont.*, v. 3, p. 32.   [2] *Ibid.*, v. 2, pp. 235-6.
[3] *Essays in Eng. Lit.* (1780-1860), p. 117.   [4] *Ed. Rev.*, No. 56, p. 510.

Both verses must be pronounced, accordingly, to make them metrical, with a strongly-trilled Scottish " r "—which may not, to other ears as well as Jeffrey's, appear to add to their sweetness. Scott seems to have taken some notice of the criticism : in modern editions " St Kentigern's hall " has become " St Andrew's cloistered hall." [1]

One observes, in the articles on Scott's poetry, criticisms of the poet's narrative construction, of his liberal use of coincidence, of his minuteness, and of his antiquarianism. The notes appended to the *Lay* were " too long," Jeffrey declared, ". . . for the general reader " : [2] he was speaking, as usual, for " ordinary men." Poetry, he remarked in the article on *Marmion*, with no other recommendation than that the substance of it had been derived from obscure books had, in his estimation, the least of all possible recommendations. It was reasonable, he said, when a great personage was introduced, to assist the imagination by giving some account of the character's appearance and surroundings ; but it was " seldom . . . advisable to present the reader with a full inventory of the hero's dress . . . or to enumerate all the drawbridges, portcullises, and diamond cut stones in the castle." He was glad enough, he said, to encounter detailed descriptions in genuinely ancient compositions because there, even if they were valueless as poetry, they had the merit of authenticity. This indulgence could not be extended, however, to " elaborate pictures extracted by a modern imitator from black-letter books, and coloured, not from the life, but from learned theories, or at best from mouldy, monkish illuminations, and mutilated fragments of painted glass." He was sensible that many of his contemporaries were finding such things attractive. " Fine ladies and gentlemen," he wrote, " now talk . . . of donjons, keeps, tabards, scutcheons, tressures, caps of maintenance, portcullises, wimples, and we know not what besides." He did not think, however, that the world would be " long pleased " with what it did not " readily understand." [3] " To write a modern romance of chivalry," he asserted, " seems to be much such a fantasy as to build a modern abbey, or an English pagoda." [4] He had criticised *Marmion* at length, he said, not only because he regarded it as a " misapplication, in some degree, of very extraordinary talents," but

---

[1] Canto 1, Stanzas xi, xix.　　　　　　　　[2] *Cont.*, v. 2, p. 236.
[3] *Ed. Rev.*, No. 23, pp. 28-32.　　　　　　　[4] *Ibid.*, p. 3.

because he could not help considering it as the foundation of a new school which might occasion " no little annoyance " both to himself and to the public. He felt it his " duty," he wrote, to " stop the insurrection " before it became " desperate and senseless." " We admire Mr Scott's genius," he declared, " as much as any of those who may be misled by its perversion ; and, like the curate and the barber in Don Quixote, lament the day when a gentleman of such endowments was corrupted by the wicked tales of knight-errantry and enchantment." [1] " Desperate," " senseless," " misled," " perversion," " corrupted " —these are strong words. I think Jeffrey meant them strongly.

He could not help regretting, Jeffrey said of the *Lay*, that the feuds of border chieftains should have monopolised so much poetry. He liked " very well," he remarked, to hear of " ' the Gallant Chief of Otterburne ' or ' the Dark Knight of Liddisdale ' " and he felt " the elevating power of great names." " But," he wrote, " we really cannot so far sympathise with the local partialities of the author, as to feel any glow of patriotism or ancient virtue in hearing of the *Todrig* or *Johnston* clans, or of *Elliots*, *Armstrongs*, and *Tinlinns* ; still less can we relish the introduction of *Black John of Athelstane*, *Whitslade the Hawk*, *Arthur-fire-the-braes*, *Red Roland Forster*, or any other of those worthies who

      ' Sought the beeves that made their broth,
        In Scotland and in England both,'

into a poem which has any pretensions to seriousness or dignity. The ancient metrical romance might have admitted those homely personalities ; but the present age will not endure them : And Mr Scott must either sacrifice his Border prejudices, or offend all his readers in the other parts of the empire." [2]

Mr John Buchan characterised this last statement as " one of the inspired follies in the history of criticism." [3] Stephen noted the lines here quoted by Jeffrey and remarked, with an evident touch of amusement, that the critic thought them " terribly undignified." [4] Jeffrey certainly did not foresee, in 1808, the swarms of motor-cars mentioned on the first page of this study. I imagine too that he made insufficient allowance for the ordinary reader's willingness to " skip," and to find in

[1] *Ed. Rev.*, No. 23, pp. 34-5.   [2] *Cont.*, v. 2, p. 234.
[3] *Sir Walter Scott*, p. 72.   [4] *Hours in a Library*, v. 2, p. 258.

such names simply a flavour. One may wonder, at the same time, if many even of the closest students of Scott have been sufficiently interested in the characters the reviewer mentioned to be able to tell offhand whether or not he cited all their names quite correctly.[1] Stephen's remark carries us back to Jeffrey's insistence upon reality. Neither Scott nor Stephen had had the experience of seeing cattle they had reared with much care and patience driven off by freebooters. Had they seen manuscripts of their own, fruits of long years of labour, wantonly destroyed by burglars, they might have come to feel that it was beneath the dignity of poetry to romanticise exploits of this character.

Connected also with Jeffrey's sense of reality was, it seems to me, another portion of his criticism of Scott's poetry that has been sometimes thought astonishing. " Scott," Lockhart remarked of the review of *Marmion*, " . . . must, I think, have wondered, to say the least, when he found himself accused of having ' throughout neglected Scottish feelings and Scottish characters ! ' " [2] Saintsbury, observing that *The Lord of the Isles* was not particularly popular in Scotland because the work was regarded as not sufficiently bitter against England, commented that this could be mentioned only " with all but silent amazement." [3] Jeffrey knew very well how Scott regarded his country. He was, as Lockhart pointed out in making his criticism, one of the two men who had been with Scott on the night, about two years before the publication of *Marmion*, when the poet, fearing that certain schemes of innovation would undermine all that remained of ancient Scotland, burst into tears, and had to rest his head on the wall of the Mound till he recovered himself.[4] He quoted in the review of *Marmion* the passage containing the outburst " Mine own romantic town ! " in which Scott gave expression to his love of his country's capital. It seems to me, however, that if we read Jeffrey's words with his general viewpoint in mind his criticism becomes explicable. " *Marmion*," he wrote, " is no more a tale of Flodden Field, than of Bosworth Field, or any other field in history.

[1] " Liddesdale," " Johnstone," and " Black John of Akeshaw."
[2] *Life of Scott*, v. 2, p. 148.
[3] *Sir Walter Scott*, p. 64.   Saintsbury had Jeffrey in mind.   He mentioned in the same paragraph, among the best passages in the poem, " Bannockburn, which even Jeffrey admired, though its want of ' animosity ' shocked him."
[4] *Life of Scott*, Lockhart, v. 2, pp. 110-1, 149.

The story is quite independent of the national feuds of the
sister kingdoms ; and the battle of Flodden has no other
connection with it, than from being the conflict in which the
hero loses his life. . . . We nowhere find any adequate expressions
of those melancholy and patriotic sentiments which are still
all over Scotland the accompaniment of those allusions and
recollections.   No picture is drawn of the national feelings before
or after that fatal encounter. . . . There is scarcely one trait
of true Scotish nationality or patriotism introduced into the
whole poem ; and Mr Scott's only expression of admiration or
love for the beautiful country to which he belongs, is put, if we
rightly remember "—Scott's references to Edinburgh surely
constitute an exception—" into the mouth of one of his Southern
favourites." [1]   He failed, Jeffrey said, to descry in *The Lord of
the Isles* " that animosity towards England, or that exultation
over her defeat which must have animated all Scotland " at the
time of the wars of independence, and which, accordingly,
ought to have been " the ruling passion " of the poem.   Scott,
he asserted, had not only dwelt fondly on the valour and the
generosity of the invaders, but had actually made " an elaborate
apology to the English for having ventured to select for his
theme a story which records their disasters."   " It is not natural,"
he argued, " and we are sure it is not poetical, to represent the
agents in such tremendous scenes, as calm and indulgent judges
of the motives or merits of their opponents ;—and by lending
such a character to the leaders of his host, the author has actually
lessened the interest of the mighty fight of Bannockburn, to
that which might be supposed to belong to a well-regulated
tournament among friendly rivals." [2]   Jeffrey wanted to see
in Scott's poetry, in other words, a realisation that there is
more in love of country than love of its picturesqueness, and
more in history than the flash of ancient weapons and the
colourfulness of antique costume.   We remember how he spoke
of war.   Battles in which a country fought desperately for its
right to existence, that swept the minds of its inhabitants with
agonies of desolation, ought not, he felt, to be dealt with mainly
as stirring pieces of pageantry.   We are reminded of two strong
statements made about Scott by Mr Donald Carswell : " He
never really understood anything, for though he had solid
reasoning powers, he had little insight. . . . He was . . . an

[1] *Ed. Rev.*, No. 23, pp. 12-13.   [2] *Ibid.*, No. 48, p. 276.

historian who knew everything about history except its meaning." [1]

To a critic who held that the greatest poetry appealed to universal associations the enormous contemporary popularity won by Scott raised an obvious problem. Might it not be said that the court had clearly decided in this case, and that there was nothing left, accordingly, for an individual critic to do? We have seen part of his answer. So far as literary merit was concerned, the verdict was pronounced by " good judges." This is not necessarily inconsistent with the other doctrine. Good judges, we have noted, were not men of a different order from their fellows : they were separated from the rest of the world in precisely the same way as are craftsmen skilled in any other trade—by possession, that is, of a certain natural aptitude that had been developed by training. They were, as Jeffrey put it, " in that very state, in short, to which all who are in any degree capable of tasting those refined pleasures would certainly arrive, if their sensibility were increased, and their experience and reflection enlarged." Poetry which pleased the multitude, he considered also, rested its appeal on the same qualities, in essence, as that which pleased the most instructed. The most popular passages in popular poetry were, he maintained, generally beautiful. When a novice found more attractiveness than did the expert, the difference between them lay in the fact that the novice judged absolutely, with reference only to what was before him, while the expert judged relatively to all that he knew. " To the ignorant and the careless," Jeffrey wrote, " the twentieth imitation has all the charm of an original." The expert, however, could perceive at once when he was in contact with what was merely hackneyed, and, moreover, being aware of the extent to which the ancients might be said " to have got possession of all the choice materials of their art," he could appreciate the skill that produced something that was new.[2]

Gates discerned in this discussion an utter failure on the part of Jeffrey to realise the conditions under which the earliest poetry was produced. Jeffrey, he declared in another place, regarded poetry as " something *artificial*, to be consciously wrought out in harmony with laws and precedents and conventions." [3] It is certainly true that we need not look to Jeffrey for a specialist's

[1] *Sir Walter*, p. 161. [2] *Cont.*, v. 2, pp. 238-45. [3] *Selections*, pp. 193, 196.

account of the origins of poetry.   It seems to me that he took
insufficiently into reckoning in this discussion the kind of
originality that springs naturally out of the thought of different
environments and eras and out of the workings of individual
minds.   I think at the same time that Gates, while he regarded
the argument unsympathetically, indicated here an essential
feature of Jeffrey's thinking.   One recalls Lamb's reference to
the " evil hour " in which he saw some of the manuscripts of
Milton, " interlined, corrected ! as if their words were mortal,
alterable, displaceable at pleasure ! " and Lamb's resolve that
he would " never go into the workshop of any great artist again." [1]
This experience would not have dismayed Jeffrey.   He did not
romanticise the making of poetry.   He did see poetry as something artificial, in the sense that it was a product of human brains
employing human processes.[2]   He regarded poets as separated
no more than critics by an impassable gulf from their fellow-
men ;   as obliged, like their fellows, to labour in their vocation
—to interline, correct, and expunge the hackneyed ;   and as
liable, like all their fellow-mortals, to fall at times into grave
human error.

Scott, Jeffrey felt, had made his way to popularity frequently
by easy roads.   He availed himself of commonplaces of diction ;
he took the assistance of a story ;   his characters were selected
from the most common dramatis personæ of poetry ;   he raised
all the most familiar poetical emotions ;   writing " for the world
at large," he " wisely abstained from attempting to raise any
passion to a height to which worldly people could not be trans-
ported ;   and contented himself with giving his reader the chance
of feeling, as a brave, kind, and affectionate gentleman must
often feel in the ordinary course of his existence." [3]

One is inevitably tempted, in considering Jeffrey's dealings
with now established writers, to lay most stress upon his passages
of adverse criticism :   it is there that he tends to differ most
from others.   We cannot do him justice, however, if we do not
glance also at the other side—of which our last quotation has
already afforded us a glimpse.   If Scott indulged in the
hackneyed, Jeffrey said, " the rapidity of his transitions, the

---

[1] *Essays of Elia and Eliana*, 1879, pp. 485-6.
[2] He considered at the same time that the poet should conceal the
machinery by which he produced his effects.   See *Post*, p. 190.
[3] *Cont.*, v. 2, pp. 245-7.

novelty of his combinations, and the spirit and variety of his own thoughts and inventions" showed that he was not a borrower from poverty, but "*took* only what he would have *given*, if he had been born in an earlier generation." [1] If he disclosed at times too much "brave neglect," he compensated for this by the fire and animation of his composition, and by the brilliant colouring of his figures.[2] "There is nothing cold, creeping, or feeble," Jeffrey declared, "in all Mr Scott's poetry ; —no laborious littleness, or puling classical affectation." "There is certainly no living poet," he wrote again, "whose works seem to come from him with so much ease." [3] If Jeffrey did not care much for the antiquarianism in the *Lay*, he was "inclined to place" the picture of the Minstrel himself which was "of modern workmanship," in the "very first rank of poetical excellence." If he perceived defects in the construction of Scott's narratives he had "no hesitation in conceding to the author" that the fable was a secondary consideration in performances of this nature.[4] If Scott dealt too much in conventional aristocratic characters there was something "very striking" in the "air of freedom" he had contrived to impart to these. No poet, Jeffrey asserted, later than Shakespeare, had ventured so to represent personages of such dignity. He did not allude "merely to the genuine familiarity and homeliness" of many of Scott's scenes and dialogues, "but to that air of gaiety and playfulness in which persons of high rank seem, from time immemorial, to have thought it necessary to array, not their courtesy only, but their generosity and their hostility." [5] Jeffrey welcomed, as might have been expected, the human touch whenever he found it in Scott. On a passage he quoted from the *Lay* describing the feelings aroused by the death of Lord Walter he commented that there were "not many passages in English poetry more impressive than some parts of this extract." [6] Alluding, in the review of *The Lady of the Lake*, to Scott's "singular talent for description, and especially for the description of scenes abounding in *motion* or *action* of any kind,"—"In this department," Jeffrey declared, ". . . we conceive him to be almost without a rival, either among modern or ancient poets ; and the character and process of his descriptions are as extraordinary as their effect

[1] *Cont.*, v. 2, p. 246.   [2] *Ibid.*, v. 2, pp. 221-2.
[3] *Ibid.*, v. 2, p. 248.   [4] *Ibid.*, v. 2, pp. 222, 221.
[5] *Ibid.*, v. 2, p. 250.   [6] *Ibid.*, v. 2, p. 227.

is astonishing." [1]   If he felt that Scott had not, in *Marmion*,
given adequate expression to the emotions that were associated
in Scotland with the battle of Flodden, Scott's description of
the battle itself aroused him to warm enthusiasm. " Of all the
poetical battles which have been fought," he burst out, " from
the days of Homer to those of Mr Southey, there is none . . .
at all comparable, for interest and animation,—for breadth of
drawing, and magnificence of effect,—with this of Mr Scott's." [2]
" He will always be a poet, we fear," ran the last two sentences
of the article on *The Lady of the Lake*, " to whom the fastidious
will make great objections ; but he may easily find, in his
popularity, a compensation for their scruples. He has *the jury*
hollow in his favour ; and though *the court* may think that its
directions have not been sufficiently attended to, it will not
quarrel with the verdict." [3]   " The Novels of Sir Walter Scott,"
Jeffrey wrote in the *Contributions*, " have, no doubt, cast his
Poetry into the shade. . . . Yet, when I recollect the vehement
admiration it once excited, I cannot part with the belief that
there is much in his poetry also, which our age should not allow
to be forgotten." [4]

III

Scott's novels, Jeffrey declared on another page of the
Contributions, were " beyond all question, the most remarkable
productions " of his age. They had produced an effect all
over Europe to which there had been nothing parallel " since
the days of Rousseau and Voltaire." In Britain, they had
attained a place " inferior only to that which must be filled
for ever by the unapproachable glory of Shakespeare." [5]

It was, of course, easy to write that in 1843. Jeffrey had,
however, recognised Scott's greatness in this department the
moment the first of the novels appeared. *Waverley* was published
in July 1814.[6]   Jeffrey's review of it was published in the
following November. The work, Jeffrey asserted, was " obviously
very hastily, and, in many places, very unskilfully written."
Half of it was composed in a dialect unintelligible to four-fifths
of the reading public. It related to a period too recent to be
romantic and too far gone to be familiar. (It is interesting to
notice how Jeffrey, in 1814, regarded the now highly-romanticised

[1] *Cont.*, v. 2, p. 249.   [2] *Ed. Rev.*, No. 23, p. 22.   [3] *Cont.*, v. 2, p. 273.
[4] V. 2, p. 214.   [5] V. 3, p. 2.   [6] *Life of Scott*, Lockhart, v. 3, p. 296.

period of the Forty-Five.) It had appeared in a part of the island where materials and talents for novel-writing had been supposed to be equally wanting. And yet it was already casting the whole tribe of works of the kind into the shade. " The secret of this success, we take it," Jeffrey wrote—he had by now reached the fourteenth line of the original review—" is merely that the author is a person of genius." [1]

Though, he stated in the *Contributions*, he had been at that time living in familiar intercourse with Scott, the identity of the author had not been revealed to him. He had had, indeed, no assurance of this till the fact was made public. He would venture to say, he had remarked at the same time in closing the *Waverley* article, that if this was really the work of a new writer, Scott would do well to look to his laurels.[2] " Mr Jeffrey," Lockhart commented, " had known Scott from his youth—and, in reviewing *Waverley*, he was at no pains to conceal his conviction of its authorship." [3]

The faults found by Jeffrey in Scott's novels are such as we are now ready to anticipate. Scott was again criticised for writing too much. Even his most striking characters, Jeffrey asserted, appeared rather too often and went on rather too long : it was reserved for Shakespeare alone to leave his characters as unworn as when he found them. " It is no light praise to the author before us," Jeffrey wrote nevertheless, " that he has sometimes reminded us of this, as well as other inimitable excellences in that most gifted of all inventors." [4] Jeffrey was not, we are prepared to find, greatly attracted either by the characters in *Nigel*—" borrowed from the written memorials " of their time—or by the character of the Antiquary ; but he admitted that the Antiquary turned out to be more interesting than he had expected.[5] He had declared of " poor lady Clare " in *Marmion* that she appeared to be formed on " Mr Pope's maxim, that women have no characters at all." [6] He listed first among Scott's failures as a novelist his pictures of virtuous young ladies and of courtship in society's upper ranks. A girl possessed, at eighteen, of the qualities that were Diana Vernon's

[1] *Ed. Rev.*, No. 47, p. 208. In the *Contributions* Jeffrey altered " very unskilfully " to " somewhat unskilfully," and " person of genius " to " man of Genius," *Cont.*, v. 3, pp. 32-3.
[2] *Cont.*, v. 3, pp. 33, 44.   [3] *Life of Scott*, v. 3, p. 302.   [4] *Cont.*, v. 3, p. 51.
[5] *Ibid.*, v. 3, pp. 100, 53.   [6] *Ed. Rev.*, No. 23, p. 12.

seemed to him " a more violent fiction . . . than a king with
marble legs." Yet, he said of Diana nevertheless, so many
features of truth were blended with the fiction that one forgot
the impossibility, and was " at least as much interested as by a
more conceivable personage." [1] The Wizard of the North
wielded a potent wand. A passage in *Kenilworth* overcame
even Jeffrey's distaste for antiquarianism. " The most surprising
piece of mere description " he had " ever seen " was that of
Amy's apartments at Cumnor Place. " We had no idea before,"
he confessed, " that upholstery and millinery could be made
so engaging." [2] In *Ivanhoe* he encountered once more the stock
figures he had met in the poetry. Yet Scott, he remarked,
had invested those " traditional and theatrical persons " here
with so much of actual feelings that one was often brought to
regard them as alive. Jeffrey continued to make it plain, at
the same time, where his own taste lay. *Ivanhoe*, he said, was
" more akin to the most splendid of modern poems, than the
most interesting of modern novels " : it savoured " more of
Marmion, or *The Lady of the Lake*, than of *Waverley*, or *Old
Mortality*." " For our part," he declared, " we prefer, and we
care not who knows it, the prose to the poetry—whether in
metre or out of it." [3]

Jeffrey found attractiveness, in the prose as in the poetry,
in Scott's pictures of the " chivalrous character." But he
counted these " only in the third rank " of Scott's excellences
as a writer of fiction. Such pictures, he remarked, had long
been common in novels, though they had never been drawn
before " with such an air of truth, and so much ease and happiness
of execution." He placed above these Scott's " delineation of
the grand and gloomy aspects of nature, and of the dark and
fierce passions of the heart." Scott's " natural gaiety of . . .
temper " did not allow him to dwell long on such themes, but
the sketches of this kind the novelist occasionally introduced
were very impressive.[4] The account of the adventure under
the cliffs in *The Antiquary* Jeffrey pronounced " the very best
description we ever met with,—in verse or in prose, in ancient
or in modern writing." [5] He ranked " by far " the highest,
however, of Scott's achievements as a novelist his success in
portraying " rustic and homely characters "—success " not in

---

[1] *Cont.*, v. 3, pp. 50, 69-70.   [2] *Ibid.*, v. 3, p. 93.   [3] *Ibid.*, v. 3, pp. 80-1.
[4] *Ibid.*, v. 3, p. 50.   [5] *Ibid.*, v. 3, p. 53.

the ludicrous or contemptuous representation of them—but by
making them at once more natural and more interesting than
they had ever been made before in any work of fiction ; by
showing them, not as clowns to be laughed at—or wretches to
be pitied and despised—but as human creatures, with as many
pleasures and fewer cares than their superiors—with affections
not only as strong, but often as delicate as those whose language
is smoother—and with a vein of humour, a force of sagacity,
and very frequently an elevation of fancy, as high and as natural
as can be met with among more cultivated beings." [1]   " Dandie
Dinmont," Jeffrey asserted in reviewing *Guy Mannering*, " is,
beyond all question, we think, the best rustic portrait that has
ever yet been exhibited to the public—the most honourable to
rustics, and the most creditable to the heart, as well as the
genius of the artist—the truest to nature—the most interesting
and the most complete in all its lineaments." [2]   The family of
the Mucklebackits in *The Antiquary* was " an exquisite group
throughout." [3]   " But," Jeffrey affirmed when he came to *The
Heart of Midlothian*, " the great boast of the piece, and the great
exploit of the author—perhaps the greatest of all his exploits—
is the character and history of Jeanie Deans. . . . The singular
talent with which he has engrafted on the humble and somewhat
coarse stock of a quiet unassuming peasant girl, the heroic
affection, the strong sense, and lofty purposes, which distinguish
this heroine—or rather, the art with which he has so tempered
and modified those great qualities, as to make them appear
noways unsuitable to the station or ordinary bearing of such a
person, and so ordered and disposed the incidents by which
they are called out, that they seem throughout adapted, and
native as it were, to her condition—is superior to any thing we
can recollect in the history of invention." [4]   There is no sign
there of a critic with pseudo-classical leanings. Dinmont, the
Mucklebackits, Jeanie Deans—they are all Scottish. This fact
supports the thesis suggested in our third chapter. Jeffrey
would certainly have agreed with it so far as Scott was concerned.
" He is," Jeffrey declared of the Great Unknown, " above all
things national and Scottish,—and never seems to feel the powers
of a Giant, except when he touches his native soil." [5]

" We are unwilling," Jeffrey remarked in closing his article

[1] *Cont.*, v. 3, p. 49.   [2] *Ibid.*, v. 3, p. 52.   [3] *Ibid.*, v. 3, p. 54.
[4] *Ibid.*, v. 3, pp. 75-6.   [5] *Ibid.*, v. 3, p. 51.

on *Marmion*, " to quarrel with a poet on the score of politics."
He did have a small political brush there with Scott, nevertheless
—he confined it to a single paragraph—mainly in connection
with the poet's attitude, in the introduction to the first canto
of the work, to Fox.[1] We perceive traces of the difference in
political outlook between the two men in Jeffrey's criticism also
of the novels. It was " sufficiently manifest," he said in the
article on *Tales of my Landlord*, that the Unknown was " a
decided Tory " ; and, Jeffrey imagined too, " something of a
latitudinarian both in morals and religion." He was very apt
at least to make a mock of enthusiasm for liberty or faith, and
not only gave a decided preference to the social over austerer
virtues, but seldom expressed any hearty admiration " except
for those graceful and gentleman-like principles, which can
generally be acted upon with a gay countenance—and do not
imply any great effort of self-denial, or any deep sense of the
rights of others, or the helplessness and humility of our common
nature." Unless, Jeffrey continued, he was much mistaken, the
novelist thought no times so happy as those in which an indulgent
monarch awarded a reasonable portion of liberty to grateful
subjects who did not question his right either to give or to
withhold it, in which a dignified hierarchy received the homage
of submissive flocks, and in which a gallant nobility redeemed
" the venial immoralities of their gayer hours " by acting bravely
and honourably towards one another, and by showing spontaneous
kindness to vassals in whom they recognised " no independent
rights, and not many features of a common nature." [2] We
notice the repetition of the last phrase. Jeffrey was prepared
to defend Scott, nevertheless, upon occasion, even where politics
were concerned. To those who objected to the representations
of the Covenanters in *Old Mortality* he replied that in his opinion
the author had " dealt pretty fairly with both sides." The
Covenanters could not but be always remembered in Scotland
with gratitude and with veneration. But it could not be denied
that there were many absurd persons among them. For a Tory
novelist to bring such characters prominently forward was not
only natural, but was almost the least blamable way in which
party feelings could be shown. Scott had even made his hero
a Covenanter. A zealous Presbyterian might have said more
in favour of the sect ; but while zealous Presbyterians would

[1] *Ed. Rev.*, No. 23, p. 35.   [2] *Cont.*, v. 3, pp. 48-9.

not write entertaining novels they could not expect to be treated in the fictions of those who were not zealous Presbyterians with the indulgence they would have granted to themselves. For the other side, except for Claverhouse, for whom was shown " a foolish fondness," the novelist had manifested no signs of undue partiality. If, said Jeffrey, anyone could read Scott's pictures of military insolence without feeling his blood boil within him, the fault was in his own apathy. He knew no Whig author who had exhibited the baseness of the government that persecuted the Covenanters more powerfully than Scott had done in the scene of torture before the Privy Council.[1]

It is evident from more than one passage we have quoted that Jeffrey felt that Scott could give us lessons in the art of living. He did not fail to perceive the personality which, like a kindly sun, irradiates page after page of the *Waverley* novels. " It is," he wrote in his article on *Tales of my Landlord*, " very honourable indeed, we think, both to the author, and to the readers among whom he is so extremely popular, that the great interest of his pieces is for the most part a Moral interest—that the concern we take in his favourite characters is less on account of their adventures than of their amiableness—and that the great charm of his works is derived from the kindness of heart, the capacity of generous emotions, and the lights of native taste which he ascribes, so lavishly . . . even to the humblest of these favourites. With all his relish for the ridiculous, accordingly, there is no tone of misanthropy, or even of sarcasm, in his representations ; but, on the contrary, a great indulgence and relenting even towards those who are to be the objects of our disapprobation. . . . He is evidently . . . one who has . . . learned indulgence for human faults and follies, not only from finding kindred faults in their most intolerant censors, but also for the sake of the virtues by which they are often redeemed, and the sufferings by which they have still oftener been chastised." [2]

Jeffrey expressed wonder, in this same review—it was written in 1817—that the works were remaining so long unclaimed. There was no name in our literature, he declared, to which they would not " add lustre—and lustre, too, of a very enviable kind." In the ease, brilliancy of colouring, and profusion of

[1] *Cont.*, v. 3, pp. 63-4.　　　　　　[2] *Ibid.*, v. 3, pp. 47-8.

his delineations the novelist reminded him " of Shakespeare
himself." [1]   He compared the novelist with Shakespeare again
in 1820. He did not mean, he said, that the Unknown was
to be put on a level with Shakespeare. " On that level," he
wrote, " no other writer has ever stood—or will ever stand—
though we do think that there is fancy and poetry enough in
these contemporary pages, if not to justify the comparison we
have ventured to suggest, at least to save it, for the first time for
two hundred years, from being altogether ridiculous." [2] We
have noted that he compared Scott with Shakespeare still again
in the *Contributions*.

If the conclusions arrived at here are to be submitted fairly
to the jury, there must be placed beside them at least a reasonable
number of findings arrived at by others. It has been suggested
that Jeffrey's praise of Scott was reluctant. Stephen, supporting
his conception of Jeffrey as a follower of fashion, wrote : " He
could endorse, though rather coldly, the general verdict in
Scott's favour, only guarding his dignity by some not too judicious
criticism ; preferring, for example, the sham romantic business
of the ' Lay ' to the incomparable vigour of the rough moss-
troopers." [3]   Though Saintsbury, as we have seen, gave considerable credit to Jeffrey—he said on the page containing the
words we are about to quote that Jeffrey's criticism had been
" distinctly undervalued "—he stated that Jeffrey " pooh-poohed
and belittled his own contributor and personal friend Scott." [4]
While, too, Saintsbury found Jeffrey free at times from party
prejudice, he spoke of the admiration which *Marmion* " extorted
. . . from the partisan rancour and the literary prudishness of
Jeffrey." [5]

Another view of the rough moss-troopers' vigour has been
suggested here. So far as " sham romantic business " is
concerned, we have noticed what Jeffrey said about the " modern
romance of chivalry," about pictures coloured from " mutilated
fragments of painted glass," and about Scott's being " corrupted "
by tales of knight-errantry. We have observed too, in the
preceding pages, that a passage in the *Lay* was described by
Jeffrey as in the very first rank of poetical excellence, and that
it was said of another that there were not many passages in
English poetry more impressive ; that Scott's Flodden was

[1] *Cont.*, v. 3, p. 46.   [2] *Ibid.*, v. 3, p. 73.   [3] *Hours in a Library*, v. 2, p. 258.
[4] *Nineteenth Cent. Lit.*, p. 175.   [5] *Sir Walter Scott*, p. 54.

pronounced to be, in certain respects, the best battle-piece since Homer ; that—if the criticism of the prose may be also admitted —Jeffrey declared a passage in the *Antiquary* to be the very best description he had ever met with ; that he spoke of the delineation of Jeanie Deans as superior to anything of the kind he could recollect in the history of invention ; that he asserted that Scott was the first writer that had appeared in two hundred years who could be compared with Shakespeare. The jury must judge whether, if these statements appeared in a modern review, written of contemporary work, it would seem to them that the author under consideration was being pooh-poohed or coldly eulogized. It is true, as we have seen, that Jeffrey, in a paragraph of the *Marmion* review, protested against Scott's treatment of a Whig leader. Against that, however, may be placed the tribute to the moral beauty of Scott's works extracted a page or so back. The jury must judge if that suggests praise yielded grudgingly by party rancour.[1]

Jeffrey, speaking of Scott's wide charitableness, asserted that the " temper of his writings " was " precisely the reverse of those of our Laureates and Lakers, who . . . make it a conscience to loathe and abhor all with whom they happen to disagree ; and labour to promote mutual animosity . . . among mankind ; by referring every supposed error of taste, or peculiarity of opinion, to some hateful corruption of the heart and understanding." [2] We catch there another glimpse of the Lake School as he saw them. In an article on John Wilson's *Isle of Palms* he developed this point.[3] He spoke there of the " offensive assumption of exclusive taste, judgment and morality which pervades most of the writings of this tuneful brotherhood." They could scarcely differ from anyone " upon a point of criticism, politics or meta-physics, without wondering what a heart he must have." They thought it barely possible for anyone to have " any just notion of poetry . . . genuine warmth of affection . . . or . . . large views as to the true principles of happiness and virtue "—we note once more the combination—who did not agree with them in most of their vagaries, and live a life nearly akin to that

---

[1] There is also the point that Jeffrey wrote ten articles on Scott for the *Review*—excluding the article on Scott's edition of Swift—and that of these he republished seven in the *Contributions*.   [2] *Cont.*, v. 3, p. 48.

[3] Jeffrey wrote two articles on Wilson : *Isle of Palms* (*Ed. Rev.*, No. 38, Art. 6), and *City of the Plague* (*Ed. Rev.*, No. 52, Art 10).

they had elected for themselves. " The inhabitants of towns, therefore," Jeffrey wrote, " and most of those who are engaged in the ordinary business or pleasures of society, are cast off without ceremony as *demoralized* and *denaturalized* beings." [1] There were, Jeffrey declared in his second article on Wilson, some faults in poetry to which he found it " impossible to show any mercy." The first was " self-admiration, when united with ordinary talents." The second was " affectation." The third was " the visible indication of any great moral defect in those highly gifted spirits, whose natural office it seems to be, to purify and exalt the conceptions of ordinary men, by images more lofty and refined than can be suggested by the coarse realities of existence." Again we perceive Jeffrey's conception of the part poetry should play in the world. He did not allude, he said, " so much to the loose and luxurious descriptions of love and pleasure which may be found in the works of some great masters, as to . . . meaner and more malignant vices . . . paltry jealousy and envy of rival genius . . . adulation to power or riches . . . party profligacy or personal spite or rancour." [2] We see here his twofold standard of judgment. Though, he remarked in closing the first article, Wilson's volume had many faults, it had a redeeming spirit of fancy and kindness about it which would not let these be numbered. While he could not undertake to defend it from " the scorn of the learned," he said he would be much mistaken if it did not " afford a great deal of pleasure to many persons almost as well worth pleasing." [3] " We are conscious," he wrote in the second review, " of being more pleased with the volume before us than we feel any assurance that our readers will be." [4] We perceive the twofold standard again in a letter written to Wilson himself after the publication of the second article. " It is," Jeffrey wrote, " impossible, I think, to read your writings without feeling affection for the writer ; and under the influence of such a feeling, I doubt whether it is *possible* to deal with them with the same severe impartiality with which works of equal literary merit, but without that attraction, might probably be treated. Nor do I think that this is desirable or would even be fair ; for part, and not the least part, of the merit of poetry consists in its moral effects, and the power of exciting kind and generous

[1] *Ed. Rev.*, No. 38, p. 375.   [2] *Ibid.*, No. 52, pp. 459-60.
[3] *Ibid.*, No. 38, p. 388.   [4] *Ibid.*, No. 52, p. 460.

affections seems entitled to as much admiration as that of presenting pleasing images to the fancy." [1]

While criticism, Jeffrey remarked in an article on Hogg's *Queen's Wake*, might help to confer distinction upon writers, it could not take it away. His reasoning is now plain. A critic might draw attention to what appeared to him merit that had been overlooked ; but the final verdict did not rest with him. It did not follow, however, that when even the court of general educated opinion had pronounced a favourable verdict the work of criticism was over. On the contrary, the critic's office was in such instances, Jeffrey believed, more important than ever. It was of greater consequence, he maintained, to point out the defects than the merits of writers who had risen to distinction, because the two were so intermingled that, unless clearly dis-criminated, the faults were extremely apt to be praised along with the beauties, and " sometimes even imitated in their stead." [2]

There remained, however, criticism's more agreeable task of " bringing into view . . . such ill-starred talents as have presented themselves to us, rather than to the more powerful dispensers of glory." Jeffrey felt—this is obviously consistent with his general position—that " more circumspection " was necessary in this branch of his trade than in any other. " We should," he wrote, " in general be a little shy of informing the public that they have long had a prodigy of genius before their eyes without being at all aware of it." But he ventured in this and in the following article to draw the public's attention to two works which, he suspected, had been little known so far outside a narrow circle. One was *The Queen's Wake*. He picked out as his " especial favourite " in this volume *Bonny Kilmeny*. This poem belonged " altogether," he remarked, " to what Warton has rather affectedly denominated ' pure poetry ' . . . a very dangerous species of poetry—requiring . . . a certain caution . . . in the management, without which it is apt to run into mere mysticism and extravagance." We perceive once again the belief that it is safer for poetry to keep in touch with reality. Hogg, Jeffrey asserted however, had attained " no ordinary degree of excellence " in this kind of writing. On the strength of *Kilmeny* " alone," the reviewer wrote indeed, " we should feel ourselves completely justified, in assuring the author, that no doubt can be entertained that he is a poet—in

[1] *Memoir of John Wilson*, p. 150. [2] *Ed. Rev.*, No. 47, p. 157.

the highest acceptation of the name." [1] We were prepared
for this by the appreciation of the " fairy fancy " of Shakespeare.
This has to be reconciled at the same time, if Jeffrey is to be
shown to be consistent, with the strong criticism of the romanticism
of Scott.

The second work was *Anster Fair*—a poem which,
while Jeffrey was " very far from thinking " that its success
was " perfect," seemed to him " bold . . . vigorous " and
" eminently original." " We leave them now," Jeffrey wrote
in concluding his articles on Hogg and Tennant, " to their
fate ; and if they do not turn out well, we engage to be more
cautious in giving out words of good augury for the future." [2]
Again we note the attitude.

[1] *Ed. Rev.*, No. 47, pp. 158, 163, 164, 168.   [2] *Ibid.*, pp. 174, 182.

CHAPTER IX

THRILL OR TRUTH

Welcome to Byron. Technical faults. Some features of the age and a radical incongruity. Jeffrey's charges against Byron. Alleged blindness of Jeffrey. Doctrine of the thrill. Insidious verses. Criticism and appreciation of Moore.

IN passing to Jeffrey's criticism of Byron [1] we are not moving wholly away from Scotland. Byron described himself as " half a Scot by birth, and bred a whole one," and declared, with his early encounter with the *Edinburgh* in mind, that he " *scotch'd* not kill'd " the Scotchman in his blood.[2] Moore said that Byron never forgot Scotland, remarked that on the occasion of the early visit to Greece the appearance of the country and the dress and build of the Albanese carried the poet " back to Morven," and observed that the dress Byron chiefly wore during his last fatal expedition was a tartan jacket.[3] It is interesting to recollect also, in view of the Scottish delight in " characters," that Byron succeeded in persuading a large part of contemporary Europe to regard his as one of the most colourful personalities of his time.

It is plain that Jeffrey, like the rest of his generation, was impressed by Byron. " Lord Byron," ran the first words he ever wrote on the poet—he was reviewing the first two cantos of *Childe Harold*—" has improved marvellously since his last appearance at our tribunal ;—and this, though it bear a very affected title, is really a volume of very considerable power, spirit and originality—which not only atones for the evil works of his nonage, but gives promise of a further excellence hereafter ; to which it is quite comfortable to look forward." He

---

[1] Jeffrey wrote the following articles on Byron : *Childe Harold*, Cantos 1 and 2 (*Ed. Rev.*, No. 38, Art. 10) ; *Giaour* (*Ed. Rev.*, No. 42, Art. 2) ; *Corsair* and *Bride of Abydos* (*Ed. Rev.*, No. 45, Art. 9) ; *Childe Harold*, Canto 3 (*Ed. Rev.*, No. 54, Art. 1 ; *Cont.*, v. 2, p. 435) ; *Manfred* (*Ed. Rev.*, No. 56, Art. 7 ; *Cont.*, v. 2, p. 128) ; *Beppo* (*Ed. Rev.*, No. 58, Art. 2) ; *Marino Faliero* (*Ed. Rev.*, No. 70, Art. 1—part reprinted in *Cont.*, v. 2, pp. 110-6) ; *Sardanapalus*, etc. (*Ed. Rev.*, No. 72, Art. 5 ; *Cont.*, v. 2, p. 87) ; *Heaven and Earth* (*Ed. Rev.*, No. 75, Art. 2—with Moore's *Loves of the Angels*).

[2] *Don Juan*, Canto x, Stanzas xvi-xix.   [3] *Life of Byron*, Moore, p. 12.

had " little doubt," Jeffrey said, that the poem would " find favour." There was " something *piquant* " in the novelty of its " cast of . . . universal scorn." He found in it a " plain manliness " that was " infinitely refreshing after the sickly affectations " of many contemporary writers. Byron's " nervous simplicity " reminded his critic of Dryden. Byron's " occasional force and compression " made him think of Crabbe.[1] In the second of his articles on Byron, on *The Giaour*, referring to the passage commencing " He who hath bent him o'er the dead," Jeffrey asserted that Byron had illustrated the beautiful but melancholy aspect of the once glorious shores of Greece " by an image more true, more mournful, and more exquisitely finished " than any he could at that moment recollect " in the whole compass of poetry." [2] " While other poets," he wrote in his third review of Byron, on *The Corsair* and *The Bride of Abydos*, " delight by their vivacity, or enchant by their sweetness, he alone has been able to *command* the sympathy, even of reluctant readers, by the natural magic of his moral sublimity, and the terrors and attractions of those overpowering feelings, the depths and the heights of which he seems to have so successfully explored." [3] He was convinced that the third canto of *Childe Harold* would not be pronounced inferior to either of the former, and thought it would probably be ranked above them by those who had been most delighted with the whole. Byron, he affirmed in this article, was " the most concise " of living writers, and might go far by his example to redeem the great reproach of contemporary literature, its " intolerable prolixity." Poets, he remarked, were generally unsuccessful in the representation of great but recent events. Speaking of the battle of Waterloo, he pointed out that all the bards of the day, from Scott and Southey down to hundreds that were nameless, had attempted this theme and failed in its management. It required courage accordingly to venture anew on such a subject. " See, however," Jeffrey wrote, in introducing the passage commencing " There was a sound of revelry by night "—" with what easy strength he enters upon it." [4]

Jeffrey was not blind, at the same time, to the technical faults that later criticism has found in Byron. In the first two cantos of *Childe Harold* he discovered " considerable marks

---

[1] *Ed. Rev.*, No. 38, pp. 466-8.
[2] *Ibid*, No. 42, p. 307.
[3] *Ibid.*, No. 45, p. 199.
[4] *Cont.*, v. 2, pp. 451, 436-7, 454.

of haste and carelessness " ; the language of *The Giaour* was " abrupt and disorderly " ; in *The Corsair* and *The Bride of Abydos* there was " a sort of emphatic obscurity . . . every now and then " that was " always distressing, and sometimes absurd " ; the poet's construction was " often ungrammatical or imperfect " ; Byron, Jeffrey declared in the article on the third canto of *Childe Harold*, had " still something to learn, and a good deal to correct " ; the tragedies " considered as Poems " were " rather heavy, verbose, and inelegant." [1]

Jeffrey felt that the immense popularity of Byron, like that of Scott, had to be accounted for. Poetry, his theory ran on this occasion, was " destined to complete a certain cycle." In rude ages, men's passions were vehement, and their sensibilities dull. The poetry of such periods dealt in consequence with strong passions and with the actions to which they gave birth— not only because these were familiar, but because only these could impress. The first triumph of regulated society was to protect its members from violence. The first trait of refinement in manners was, correspondingly, to exclude unrestrained emotions. When, however, restraint continued beyond a certain point, the effect was not merely to banish vehemence but also to eradicate in part humanity's warmer affections. Further, as the dangers of intemperance ceased to be thought of in the upper ranks of society, the utility of the precautions that had been taken against it came to be questioned, and their severity relaxed. There was in the human breast an avidity for strong sensations that was ultimately irrepressible. Accordingly, when hearts became cold, and control so common that it ceased to be a distinction, the more powerful spirits were awakened to a sense of degradation. " This," Jeffrey wrote, " is the stage of society in which fanaticism has its second birth, and political enthusiasm its first true development—when plans of visionary reform, and schemes of boundless ambition are conceived, and almost realised by the energy with which they are pursued—the era of revolutions and projects—of vast performances, and infinite expectations." To this stage, he considered, his own generation had arrived. If, he said, he had " rightly seized " the principle by which its peculiarities were to be accounted for, it would not be difficult to show that the poet who had

[1] *Ed. Rev.*, No. 38, p. 475 ; No. 42, p. 301 ; No. 45, p. 228 ; *Cont.*, v. 2, pp. 437, 95.

devoted himself most successfully to the delineation of the
stronger passions was likely to be the period's reigning favourite.
It was " at least . . . a fact, independent of all theory " that
the successful poets of the previous twenty years had dealt more
in powerful sensations than had those of the century before,
and had employed themselves on subjects their predecessors
would have rejected as vulgar.   It was natural that in such a
period writers should turn back in imagination to times when
strong passions had been displayed without control by people
in society's upper levels.   There were, it was true, barbarians
still in the world.   But it was safer, at least for moderate genius,
to work upon the past.   Not only was there a charm in antiquity,
but there was an advantage in treating of what had been already
the subject of successful art.   Thus Southey, who had searched
for strong passions among the savages of America and among
the gods and enchantments of India, had been less successful
than Scott, who had used the more familiar scenes of European
chivalry.   Byron had turned to the desperadoes of the
Mediterranean.   These were not very amiable.   But they also
had an advantage—that of being placed within the circle of
ancient Greece and Rome.

Jeffrey found in these delineations of action and character,
at the same time, as we have seen he found also in Scott's
reconstructions of the background of the past, an essential
artificiality.   The personages who had been resurrected were
not made to act and to feel exactly as they did in their first
natural presentation.   While in primitive poetry the character
of the agent was unavoidably revealed in glimpses, attention
was always directed to what he did, not to what he felt.   In
the later poetry there was added to the old legends a new analysis
of emotions, and feelings were often imputed to the characters
of which persons in their condition were incapable, and which
no description could have made intelligible to their contemporaries.   The nineteenth-century poets had, in brief,
borrowed situations and passions from primitive states of society,
and had conjoined with these a sensibility and a delicacy that
belonged to their own time and to themselves.   This combination
appeared to Jeffrey " radically incongruous."   The most outrageous instance of it he remembered was that of Southey,
who had represented a wild Welsh twelfth-century chieftain
abuccaneering in America " with all the softness, decorum, and

pretty behaviour of Sir Charles Grandison. But the incongruity itself," Jeffrey wrote, " is universal—from Campbell, who invests a Pennsylvanian farmer with the wisdom and mildness of Socrates, and the dignified manners of an old Croix de St Louis —to Scott, who makes an old, bloody-minded and mercenary ruffian talk like a sentimental hero and poet, in his latter days— or the author before us, who has adorned a merciless corsair on a rock in the Mediterranean, with every virtue under heaven —except "—we note the dryness of the comment—" common honesty." [1]

Both this last phrase and what we have already learned of Jeffrey's outlook make it not unexpected to discover that the typical Byronic " character," though he admitted that he found a piquancy in it, did not move him to admiration. The author, he remarked in reviewing the first two cantos of *Childe Harold*, had taken the trouble to caution his readers against supposing that he meant to shadow out his own character under the " dark and repulsive traits " of his hero : the caution, the reviewer added, was " surely unnecessary." [2] " We own," Jeffrey wrote in reviewing *The Giaour*, " we should like now and then to meet in his pages with something more cheerful, more amiable, and more tender." Energy of character and intensity of emotion were, he said, sublime in themselves, but the admiration they excited, when presented in combination with worthlessness and guilt, was " one of the most powerful corrupters . . . of our moral nature," and was the more to be lamented as it was apt to exert its influence upon the noblest characters. [3] Referring to the passage in the third canto of *Childe Harold* containing Byron's asseveration that he had " not loved the world " nor the world him—" The reckoning," Jeffrey commented, " . . . is steadily and sternly made ; and though he does not spare himself, we must say that the world comes off much the worst in the comparison." Jeffrey's sympathies, it is evident, were, as always, with the rest of us. Quoting, on an earlier page, the portion of the poem containing the lines

> " He who ascends to mountain-tops, shall find
> The loftiest peaks most wrapt in clouds and snow ;
> He who surpasses or subdues mankind,
> Must look down on the hate of those below "—

---

[1] *Ed. Rev.*, No. 45, pp. 199-204. [2]*Ibid.*, No. 38, p. 466.
[3] *Ibid.*, No. 42, p. 309.

and so forth—" This," he remarked, " is splendidly written, no doubt. . . . With regard to conquerors," came however another of his dry comments, " we wish with all our hearts that the case were as noble as the author represents it." But he was afraid that conquerors were " very commonly idolised and admired " even by those on whom they trampled. He suspected that in general conquerors passed their time " rather agreeably " and derived " considerable satisfaction " from the desolation of the world. " From Macedonia's madman," he burst out, " to the Swede—from Nimrod to Bonaparte, the hunters of men have pursued their sport with as much gaiety, and as little remorse, as the hunters of other animals." As always we are being asked to look at actuality. It would be strange, he went on, if men who were great and more innocent were less friended than those " splendid curses of mankind " ; and it would be " *passing strange*, and pitiful " if the Almighty's most precious gifts produced only wretchedness, and humanity regarded with hostility its greatest benefactors. Misery of the kind to which Byron referred was, he insisted, evidence not of greatness but merely of vanity : it was not, in short, those who actually surpassed mankind who were unhappy, but those who strove in vain to surpass them. The master spirits of every age had always escaped the unhappiness of which Byron spoke. In the whole list of English poets, Jeffrey said, he recollected only two, and these " of the lowest " who were discontented. " These," he wrote, " it appears to us, are not merely errors in taste, but perversions of morality ; and, as a great poet is necessarily a moral teacher, and gives forth his ethical lessons, in general, with far more effect and authority than any of his graver brethren, he is peculiarly liable to the censures reserved for those who turn the means of improvement to purposes of corruption." [1]

The jury may, in connection with part of this argument, feel inclined to echo Jeffrey's own wish that the case were as noble as the author represents it. If the gifts that make men masters of the art of expression made them simultaneously masters of the art of living the problem of reconciling æsthetic and ethical standards would be easier than it is. Byron's own case raises, of course, the whole question.

Jeffrey observed the monotony of character-delineation in

[1] *Cont.*, v. 2, pp. 464, 457-8, 459, 440.

Byron that later criticism has stressed. "It is really too much," he wrote in the review of the third canto of *Childe Harold*, "to find the scene perpetually filled by one character." "The world," he wrote in the article on the tragedies, "will weary at last of the most energetic pictures of misanthropes and madmen—outlaws and their mistresses!" Byron's heroes, he declared in the *Childe Harold* article, were "as monstrous . . . as . . . hippogriffs." [1]

Jeffrey returned, in his review of the tragedies, to Byron's defects as a guide to the art of living. Byron, he said, had certainly not been patient of criticism. This, he feared, did not indicate superiority to censure but merely aversion to it : a critic who wished to hurt could have desired no better proof that he had succeeded.[2] It did not appear to Jeffrey that Byron had much reason for protest. He declared indeed that he could recollect in the whole course of his experience no writer to whose genius the public had been so early and so constantly just, and to whose faults they had been so long indulgent. It was true that this enthusiasm had diminished. Byron had tried to persuade himself that this was an effect of jealousy, of party rancour, and of his being "a *Nobleman*." Jeffrey admitted that there might be some who had assailed Byron from unworthy motives. But the dissatisfaction was not confined to them. "*We*," he wrote, "are not bigots or rival poets. We have not been detractors from Lord Byron's fame, nor the friends of his detractors ; and *we* tell him—far more in sorrow than in anger—that we verily believe the great body of the English nation—the religious, the moral, and the candid part of it—consider the tendency of his writings to be immoral and pernicious." He was not, Jeffrey insisted, indulging in "priestlike cant." He did not accuse Byron of being an apostle of Satan. He was "inclined to believe" that the poet wished well to mankind's happiness. He was "glad to testify" that Byron's works abounded with sentiments of dignity and tenderness as well as passages of sublimity and beauty. He made it clear, as we have seen him do before in another connection, that he had not in mind ordinary indelicacies. (It is an illustration of the departmentalising tendency in modern thought that the moment immorality in writing is spoken of many people think at once only of the seventh commandment.) There were

---

[1] *Cont.*, v. 2, pp. 438, 96, 440.   [2] *Ibid.*, v. 2, p. 94.

" indecencies " in Byron's work that Jeffrey considered repre-
hensible. But Byron was " not more obscene, perhaps, than
. . . other classical and pardoned writers." No doubt it was
" a wretched apology " for a man of genius that equal indecencies
had been forgiven to his predecessors. But the precedent might
have been followed. The dangers inherent in Byron's writings
were more subtle than those to be apprehended from unabashed
bawdry : the effect of his writings was, Jeffrey declared, to
confound " our notions of right and wrong," and to shake
" our confidence in virtue . . . to the foundation." " *This*,"
he wrote, " is the charge which we bring against Lord Byron.
We say that, under some strange misapprehension as to the
truth, and the duty of proclaiming it, he has exerted all the
powers of his powerful mind to convince his readers, both directly
and indirectly, that all ennobling pursuits, and disinterested
virtues, are mere deceits or illusions—hollow and despicable
mockeries for the most part, and, at best, but laborious follies.
Religion, love, patriotism, valour, devotion, constancy, ambition
—all are to be laughed at, disbelieved in, and despised !—and
nothing is really good, so far as we can gather, but a succession
of dangers to stir the blood, and of banquets and intrigues to
soothe it again ! " The method adopted was to personate
these " lofty illusions " with such grace and force that it was
impossible not to suppose, for the moment, that the writer was
one of the most devoted of their votaries, and then to cast off
the character with a jerk and let his readers " down at once
on some coarse joke, hard-hearted sarcasm, or fierce and relentless
personality—as if on purpose to show

' Whoe'er was edified, himself was not '—

or to demonstrate practically as it were, and by example, how
possible it is to have all fine and noble feelings, or their
appearance, for a moment, and yet retain no particle of respect
for them—or of belief in their intrinsic worth or permanent
reality." [1]

(We recall Lady Byron's story of her husband's coming home
one evening from a dinner, drunk, calling himself a monster,
and throwing himself at her feet. " Astonished," her narrative
ran, " at the return of virtue, my tears, I believe, flowed over
my face, and I said, ' Byron, all is forgotten ; never, never shall

[1] *Cont.*, v. 2, pp. 119-24.

you hear of it more.' He started up, and folding his arms while
he looked at me, burst into laughter. 'What do you mean?'
said I. 'Only a philosophical experiment ; that's all,' said he,
'I wished to ascertain the value of your resolutions.' ") [1]

Thus, Jeffrey continued, after the "indelicate but very
clever scene" of Juan's concealment in the bed of an amorous
matron, the poet chose to make this "shameless and abandoned
woman" address to her gallant a letter "breathing the very
spirit of warm, devoted, pure, and unalterable love—thus
profaning the holiest language of the heart." The "sublime
and terrific description" of the shipwreck in the same poem
was "strangely and disgustingly broken by traits of low humour
and buffoonery" ; and we passed immediately from the moans
of a father over his famished son to "facetious stories of Juan's
begging a paw of his father's dog—and refusing a slice of his
tutor !—as if it were a fine thing to be hard-hearted—and pity
and compassion were fit only to be laughed at." In the same
spirit the glorious ode on Greece's aspirations for liberty was
instantly followed by "a strain of dull and cold-blooded ribaldry,"
and readers were hurried on from the death of Haidée to merry
scenes of masquerading in the seraglio. "How opposite to
this," exclaimed Jeffrey, "is the system, or the temper, of the
great author of *Waverley*—the only living individual to whom
Lord Byron must submit to be ranked as inferior in genius—
and still more deplorably inferior in all that makes genius either
amiable in itself, or useful to society !" [2]

"The adverse critics," Professor Nichol wrote of the critics
of *Don Juan*—he mentioned Jeffrey among them—"missed their
mark. They had not learned to say of a book of which they
disapproved that it was weak or dull : in pronouncing it to be
vicious, they helped to promote its sale." [3] The present writer
is not in a position to say how widely the method here alluded
to has been practised. It will be plain, however, that, from the
Jeffreyan angle, from which criticism appears as an entry into
the temple of truth, it is an impossible method. In that temple,
ability, whether one approves or disapproves of its activities,
must be recognised. Further, the Jeffreyan critic is not a

---

[1] *Byron*, Ethel C. Mayne, v. 2, p. 31.
[2] *Cont.*, v. 2, pp. 124-6. Actually the reference to the paw and the
tutor comes before the episode of the father and son, but the point, of course,
remains (Canto 2).   [3] *Byron*, pp. 172-3.

censor. He has no right to impede independent judgment.
He can only submit his opinions. Jeffrey would have held,
besides, that the method was impracticable where Byron was
concerned. " Lord Byron's poetry," he wrote in the article
on the third canto of *Childe Harold*, " . . . is too attractive and
too famous to lie dormant or inoperative." [1] " It is impossible,"
he declared at the same time, " not to mourn over such a
catastrophe of such a mind ; or to see the prodigal gifts of
Nature, Fortune, and Fame thus turned to bitterness, without
an oppressive feeling of impatience, mortification and surprise.
Where there are such elements, however, it is equally impossible
to despair that they may yet enter into happier combinations,—
or not to hope that ' this puissant spirit '

> ' yet shall re-ascend
> Self-raised, and repossess its native seat.' " [2]

In his article on the third canto of *Childe Harold* Jeffrey
remarked that in Byron's dealing only with the greater passions,
and in his general notion of the means and ends of poetry, he
had sometimes thought that the poet's views " fell more in with
those of the Lake poets, than of any other existing party in the
poetical commonwealth." [3] Gates in his *Selections* added a note
to this assertion. " Jeffrey," part of it ran, " has an inkling
here of an important truth that he never thoroughly grasped.
Byron's madly egoistic revolt and Wordsworth's high spiritual
conservatism were alike attempts to give life greater richness
of coloring and wealth of emotion than it had had in the
eighteenth century." [4] Later in the same review Jeffrey said
that the great success of *Childe Harold* had always appeared to
him an extraordinary proof of its merits. The work had no
action, little variety of character, and much reasoning and
reflection of no very attractive tenor. It required therefore
" great force of writing, and a decided tone of originality " to
recommend a performance of this kind so powerfully to the
public.[5] Again Gates appended a note. " In such passages
as this," he commented, " Jeffrey fails to appreciate the organic
relation between literature and life. He regards Byron as
catching the popular taste by clever devices of style ; he does
not see that Byron was the product of his time and that he

---

[1] *Cont.*, v. 2, p. 439.   [2] *Ibid.*, v. 2, p. 469. *Paradise Lost*, Bk. 1, ll. 633-4.
[3] *Ibid.*, v. 2, p. 436.   [4] p. 198.   [5] *Cont.*, v. 2, p. 451.

received so eager a welcome because he was giving utterance to
ideas and feelings that had long been fermenting in the minds
and hearts of many people." [1]   There is a similar observation
in Gates's *Three Studies*.   " He missed entirely," we read there
of Jeffrey, " the meaning of Byron's savage revolt against the
conventionalism of eighteenth-century moral ideals, and he was
equally unable to understand Wordsworth's high conservatism.
Perhaps the most damaging accusation that can be brought
against Jeffrey, as a critic, is inability to read and interpret
the age in which he lived." [2]

Gates's criticisms may suggest some considerations to the
jury.   The early part of the eighteenth century saw the bursting
of the Bubble.   The century was marked by war after war.
Canada and India were won.   The American colonies were
lost.   There were two civil wars in Britain.   Large numbers
of travellers were held up by highwaymen on the English roads.
Large numbers of citizens were assaulted by footpads in the
streets of English towns.   Executions were a frequent public
spectacle.   In the latter half of the century there was a series
of No-Popery riots during which Newgate and the house of the
Chief Justice were burned.   The close of it saw the French
Revolution, and two mutinies in the British navy.   It may
appear odd to some of the jury to find " life " in such a century
regarded as outstandingly deficient in " coloring and wealth of
emotion."   Surely these things stirred some pulses.   Did the
life of Byron's own predecessor in the peerage, to descend to
smaller matters, require much injection of colour when he
killed his kinsman, Chaworth, or even when, lying on the kitchen
floor at Newstead, he amused himself by " staging races of
cockroaches up and down his own body " ? [3]   One may wonder,
in the second place, if human conduct is susceptible of such
succinct explanation as that by which Gates accounted for
" Byron's madly egoistic revolt."   Byron, when a child at
Aberdeen, bit " a large piece, in a fit of passion " out of a china
saucer.[4]   It would surely be stretching matters somewhat to
explain this as a precocious outburst of protest against the moral
conventionalism of the century in which the incident took place.
Byron's " revolt " may have been connected with the fact that
his grand-uncle was " the wicked Lord " and his father " mad

[1] *Sel.*, p. 201.   [2] p. 38.
[3] *Byron*, Maurois, p. 24.   [4] *Life of Byron*, Moore, p. 12.

Jack " ; that his maternal ancestors " kept the north country in terror " ; [1] and that his mother " without judgment or self-command, alternately spoiled him by indulgence, and irritated, or—what was still worse—amused him by her violence." [2] His turbulence of spirit may have been due in part to indigestion, " that inward fate," to quote his own words, " which makes all Styx through one small liver flow." [3] Augusta Leigh thought that this was the cause of her half-brother's passionateness. Maurois suggested that this explanation arose from " the nature of her mind, which made her always bring the most tragic events down to her own level." [4] An insult to Augusta does not, however, necessarily dispose of the idea : indigestion has had similar effects upon less important people. Byron's passionateness may have been connected with his lameness. It may have sprung in part from a desire to see himself as a " character." It might be said that not much of the emotional excitement which, it has been suggested, characterised the eighteenth century found its way into the most characteristic literature of the period. But if this be so, it suggests that some qualification is necessary to the assertion of Gates, in the second of our quotations from him, that there is an " organic relation between literature and life." If we take our stand on the much more modest ground that the men—belonging to a particular stratum of society—who chanced to be the outstanding authors of the eighteenth century disliked exhibitions of emotion, and that the reading public of the next period had grown tired of this attitude and were craving for writing with more vigour in it, Jeffrey, we have seen, was there long before us. I think, at the same time, that Jeffrey would have continued to maintain that more was required to win success in literature than merely to give utterance to what was in the minds of many people, and that his references to force and originality of writing remained accordingly relevant. Were this not so, *Childe Harolds* might be commoner than they are. We have seen too how Jeffrey spoke of his own time—as one marked by a re-birth of fanaticism, plans of visionary reform, and so forth. If this was not an interpretation of the age it was at least an attempt to describe some of its features. We saw how Jeffrey submitted that description—not as an interpretation, but merely as a tentative

---

[1] *Byron*, Maurois, pp. 22-7. [2] *Life of Byron*, Moore, p. 13.
[3] *Don Juan*, Canto 9, St. xv. [4] *Byron*, p. 233.

and very possibly imperfect theory by which a particular literary
phenomenon might become intelligible. I do not think that
Jeffrey would ever have claimed to be able to submit anything
so all-embracing as an interpretation. Might it not be said
that the very succinctness of Gates's statements makes them
necessarily imperfect as interpretations? If Byron expressed
what was in the minds of many of his contemporaries so also,
surely, did the editor of so widely-read a work as the *Edinburgh
Review*. Jeffrey's mode of thinking, it would follow—and it
was with Jeffrey, not with Byron, that Gates was dealing primarily
—was as characteristic of the age's thought as was Byron's,
and must also be taken into reckoning before anything even
approximating to an interpretation can be arrived at. I think
that Jeffrey would have admitted at once that in encyclopedical
writing concise statements of the kind Gates supplied are
inevitable, and that they can be exceedingly useful as starting-
places for thought. But I think he would have said that when
an academic teacher elevates his particular formulæ to the
status of important truths, and suggests that the men of the past
are to be regarded as defective in mental grasp if they failed
to anticipate these, we are catching a glimpse of the process by
which—though this may not be at all the effect that was intended
—ordinary men may be dazzled into supposing that " life " is
far more nearly explicable by those in the know than is actually
the case, and dazzled in consequence out of the habit of thinking
for themselves.

Jeffrey's criticisms of Byron appeared to Saintsbury " not
. . . very satisfactory." " He is so completely overcome,"
Saintsbury wrote, " by what he calls the ' dreadful tone of
sincerity ' of this ' puissant spirit,' that he never seems to have
had leisure or courage to apply the critical tests and solvents
of which few men have had a greater command. Had he done
so, it is impossible not to believe that, whether he did or did
not pronounce Byron's sentiment to be as theatrical, as vulgar,
and as false as it seems to some later critics, he would at any
rate have substituted for his edifying but rather irrelevant moral
denunciations some exposures of those gross faults in style and
metre, in phrase and form, which now disgust us." [1] Arnold
and Swinburne, it may be remembered, as well as Jeffrey,
credited Byron with sincerity. " Whoever stops," Arnold wrote,

[1] *Essays in Eng. Lit.* (1780-1860), pp. 131-2.

" at the theatrical preludings does not know him." [1] Byron,
at the time when Jeffrey's reviews were being written, was
influencing powerfully the thinking of multitudes of people.
To Jeffrey, therefore, he was a " puissant spirit " simply by
definition. We have seen that Jeffrey discerned a radical
incongruity between the actions of Byron's characters and their
sentiments, and that he likened Byron's heroes to hippogriffs.
We have seen too that he did not ignore Byron's faults of style.
It may appear to some that the critic who asserted roundly
that the tendency of Byron's writings was " immoral and
pernicious " was some distance from being overawed by the
author he was reviewing. More important, however, for our
present study than these questions of detail is the evidence we
have, in the description of Jeffrey's " moral denunciations "
as " rather irrelevant," of the wide difference there was in
critical position between Jeffrey and his successor in criticism.
Saintsbury made his viewpoint, in these matters, completely
clear. Speaking of the valuation of the poetry of Wordsworth,
" There is only one principle," he wrote, " on which that
valuation can properly proceed, and this is the question, ' Is
the poet rich in essentially poetical moments of the highest
power and kind ? ' And by poetical moments I mean those
instances of expression which, no matter what their subject,
their intention, or their context may be, cause instantaneously
in the fit reader a poetical impression of the intensest and most
moving quality." [2] Saintsbury was not, of course, by any
means expressing here solely his own opinion. " That poetry,"
Mr Greening Lamborn wrote for example in his *Rudiments of
Criticism* (1917) " is not a means of . . . improving the morals
. . . or serving any practical purpose, let us with joy admit
and declare. It is the charm and the glory of poetry that its
high and single purpose is ' to make glad the heart of man.' . . .
Art has really no more to do with morality than with the intellect.
. . . Art criticism is concerned not with the matter but with
the manner of expression." [3] This way of regarding criticism
is obviously in harmony with what we spoke of a moment ago
as the departmentalising tendency of modern thought. This,
we have seen at the same time, was not a tendency that Jeffrey
regarded with favour so far as literature was concerned. " That

---

[1] *Essays in Criticism*, Second series, " Byron."
[2] *Nineteenth Cent. Lit.*, p. 52.   [3] pp. 8, 127, 128.

minute subdivision of labour," he wrote, "which is the great
secret of the mechanical arts . . . can never be introduced
into literature without depriving its higher branches of all force,
dignity, or importance." [1] Subdivision of labour in this instance
of course, as in all others, simplifies the work in hand. The
problem, for example, towards which we have found ourselves
drawn more than once, of reconciling æsthetic and ethical
standards, is simply set aside as the business of another section
of the factory. The new position makes for safety. The critic
who occupies himself solely with questions of style, metre, phrase,
and form is in no danger of being charged with the " priggishness " that Saintsbury found in Jeffrey. It seems neat and
logical to argue that art criticism should deal only with artistic
questions—that the only principle on which the valuation of an
engraving, for instance, can "properly proceed" is by a
consideration of its artistic effectiveness.

What, however, if the engraving in question were a forged
banknote, a result of the excellence of which, and of a multitude
of duplicates, were to reduce one's children to destitution?
Could an adult criticism continue to hold that its only proper
concern was estimation of the engraver's skill? The question,
I imagine Jeffrey would have argued, is not what we say or
think poetry should do, but what it actually does. One can
readily understand Lamborn's protest against regarding it as
a collection of edifying maxims. Can we be sure, however,
that the sole effect of this, one of the most powerful forms of
human expression, is to provide humanity with thrills? We
have seen that Jeffrey held that a great poet was "necessarily
a moral teacher." I think he would have argued that if there
was a possibility that certain ways of thinking and writing were
undermining morality's foundations this was something that, in
the long run, no adult could afford to ignore.

"He began," Saintsbury wrote of Jeffrey, "by snubbing
Byron, and did not change his tone till politics and circumstances
combined made the change obligatory." [2] The first sentence
Jeffrey wrote upon Byron has been quoted. I do not think
anyone could describe it as a snub. Saintsbury appears to
have regarded Jeffrey as in some way responsible for Brougham's
article on *Hours of Idleness*. Cockburn had stated definitely

[1] *Cont.*, v. 1, p. 101.
[2] *Nineteenth Cent. Lit.*, p. 175.

that this article was not written by Jeffrey.[1]   It is anachronistic
to describe the article as a snubbing of the Byron we know.
It was a review of a work—in which Saintsbury himself discerned
no merit [2]—by an entirely obscure young author who had
irritated his critic to no doubt unnecessary savagery by an
exhibition of snobbishness.   There is a distinct possibility that
the editor of the *Edinburgh* had done no more than glance at the
book, if he had done even that.   There is no sign of political
bias in the contrast we have noticed, written in 1822, between
the " temper " of Byron and that of " the great author of
Waverley."   Looking at the matter from the Jeffreyan angle
I can perceive no circumstance, political or other, that might
have caused the editor of the *Edinburgh* to desire to curry favour
with Byron, and no cause for the altered attitude of the *Edinburgh*
between 1808, when the article on *Hours of Idleness* appeared,
and 1812, when Jeffrey opened his first review of Byron, despite
the poet's continued antagonism, in the way we have observed,
beyond the fact that, in the interval, there had been published
the first two cantos of *Childe Harold*.

It is well known that Jeffrey's severe criticism of the early
poems of Byron's friend and biographer, Moore, was inspired
by immorality of writing in the more departmental modern
sense of the word.[3]   Jeffrey made it plain, at the same time,
that it was not against the kind of coarseness to be found in a
Rochester or a Dryden that he felt it most necessary to protest.
There was, he said, an antidote to the poison contained in the
works of these authors in the undisguised profligacy with which
it was presented.   If these writers were wicked, they had the
honesty at least to profess wickedness.   If they had the boldness
to recommend vice, they had not the effrontery to make it pass
for virtue.   Moreover, they scarcely ever seemed to be perfectly
in earnest, and appeared neither to wish nor to hope to make
proselytes.   Moore's immorality, Jeffrey considered however,
was " infinitely more insidious."   It seemed to be Moore's aim
" to impose corruption upon his readers, by concealing it under

[1] *Life*, v. 1, p. 198.   See *Byron*, Nichol, p. 49, and *Byron*, Mayne, v. 1,
p. 118.

[2] *Essays in Eng. Lit.* (1780-1860), p. 131.

[3] Jeffrey wrote the following articles on Moore's poetry :   *Epistles*, *Odes*
(*Ed. Rev.*, No. 16, Art. 18) ;   *Lalla Rookh* (*Ed. Rev.*, No. 57, Art. 1 ;   *Cont.*,
v. 2, p. 470) ;   *Loves of the Angels*—with Byron's *Heaven and Earth* (*Ed. Rev.*,
No. 75, Art. 2).

the mask of refinement ; to reconcile them imperceptibly to the most vile and vulgar sensuality, by blending its language with that of exalted feeling and tender emotion ; and to steal impurity into their hearts, by gently perverting the most simple and generous of their affections." [1] What Jeffrey feared, it is obvious, was, as always, a confounding of standards. Sculdudry seemed to him to be most dangerous when it disguised itself in the garb of uplift.

By the time, eleven years later, that Jeffrey came to write his second review of Moore's poems, on *Lalla Rookh*, his attitude to the Irish poet had entirely changed. " This," he declared, " is the finest Orientalism we have had yet." He explained, at the same time, that he confined this observation to what he called the " *materiel* " of the poem. The characters, so far as they had geographical affinities, were European. Jeffrey, in other words, found in Moore also that radical incongruity which appeared to him to be one of the prominent features of the poetry of his day. He felt, too, that Moore had travelled too far out of the actual world. All Moore's personages were so " beautiful . . . brave, and agonizing," so lofty in rank and so sumptuously surrounded that the " herd of ordinary mortals " had difficulty in conceiving of their proceedings and in sympathising with their fortunes. " There is nothing," Jeffrey declared, " . . . that we ever truly care for, but the feelings of creatures like ourselves : —and we are obliged to lend them to the flowers and the brooks of the valley, and the stars and airs of heaven, before we can take any delight in them." [2] " Mr Moore," he asserted in his third review, " hardly ever describes entire objects, but abstract qualities of objects. It is not a picture that he gives us, but an inventory of beauty. He takes a blush, or a smile, and runs on whole stanzas in extatic praise of it, and then diverges to the sound of a voice, and ' discourses eloquent music ' on the subject ; but it might as well be the light of Heaven that he is describing, or the voice of Echo—we have no human figure before us, no palpable reality, answering to any substantive form in nature." [3] This last appears to me a shrewd description of Moore's method.

Stephen included among the things Jeffrey " put up with . . . because admiration was respectable "—" Moore's most

[1] *Ed. Rev.*, No. 16, p. 457.   [2] *Cont.*, v. 2, pp. 470, 471, 474, 477.
[3] *Ed. Rev.*, No. 75, p. 30.

intolerable tinsel." [1]   Jeffrey's criticism of Moore seems, however, hardly to bear out this statement.   In his first article on Moore he spoke of the poet's " tawdry, affected, and finical style." After quoting some lines—" This," he commented, " is in the right millinery taste." [2]   " No-one," he wrote in the article on *Lalla Rookh*, " would like to make an entire meal on *sauce piquante* ; or to appear in a dress crusted over with diamonds ; or to pass a day in a steam of rich distilled perfumes.   It is the same with the glittering ornaments of poetry—with splendid metaphors and ingenious allusions, and all the figures of speech and of thought that constitute its outward pomp and glory.   Now, Mr Moore, it appears to us, is decidedly too lavish of his gems and sweets." [3]   " Poetry, in his hands," he declared in reviewing the *Loves of the Angels*, " becomes a kind of *cosmetic* art—it is the poetry of the toilette.   His Muse must be as fine as the Lady of Loretto.   The naked Venus to some eyes would seem a dowdy to her ! "   After quoting a snatch from the first Angel's story, " This," he wrote, " we pronounce to be tinsel." [4]

Jeffrey found much in Moore, nevertheless, that he could " put up with."   The faults of *Lalla Rookh* were, he asserted, " beyond all doubt less conspicuous than its beauties."   The richness and brilliance of diction spread over the work indicated " the greatest activity and elegance of fancy in the author." It is not now surprising to find him speaking of the " strain of tender and noble feeling " that " everywhere pervaded " the poem.   There were in it, he said, " passages . . . and these neither few nor brief, over which the very Genius of Poetry " seemed " to have breathed his richest enchantment." [5]

Jeffrey wrote no review of Moore's lyrics.   It is evident from a remark by Moore that Jeffrey and his family loved to hear the poet sing his own songs.[6]   I feel that such a piece as *Oft in the Stilly Night* must have moved Jeffrey greatly.

---

[1] *Hours in a Library*, v. 2, p. 258.

[2] *Ed. Rev.*, No. 16, p. 462.

[3] *Cont.*, v. 2, p. 473.

[4] *Ed. Rev.*, No. 75, pp. 29, 34.

[5] *Cont.*, v. 2, pp. 478-9.

[6] *Life*, Cockburn, v. 1, p. 174.

CHAPTER X

THE WORLD AS IT IS

Merits and defects of Crabbe. Satire. Limits to realism. Lowly simplicity.
Useless distinctions. Learning that dazzles. Problem of the two-fold
standard. Early appreciation of Keats. Keats's use of classical
mythology. Was Jeffrey's appreciation tardy?

I

IN a footnote to the *Contributions* [1] Jeffrey said that in his reprint
he had given more space to Crabbe than to any other contemporary poet—not only because he thought more highly of
Crabbe than he did of most of the others, but also because he
fancied that Crabbe had had less justice done to him. This
obviously makes his dealings with Crabbe important to us here.
A first impression might be that we have now caught sight of
the Augustan in him. The remainder of the footnote does not,
however, bear out this idea. The nature of Crabbe's subjects,
Jeffrey remarked, was not such as to set him at the head of a
school. Crabbe's claims to distinction depended " fully as
much on his great powers of observation, his skill in touching
the deeper sympathies of our nature, and his power of inculcating,
by their means, the most impressive lessons of humanity, as
on any fine play of fancy, or grace and beauty in his delineations." [2]
Those qualities are not peculiarly Augustan. Towards the
formal characteristics in Crabbe, in respect of which the poet
is most obviously eighteenth-century, Jeffrey's attitude was
distinctly critical. He found " some degree of unsteadiness
and inconsistency " in Crabbe's " expression and versification " ;
he noted, without commendation, Crabbe's habit of copying
" antithetical and half-punning lines " from Pope ; Crabbe,
he said, was " frequently misled by Darwin into a sort of mock-
heroic magnificence, upon ordinary occasions " ; Crabbe's

---

[1] V. 2, p. 274. Jeffrey wrote the following articles on Crabbe : *Poems*
(*Ed. Rev.*, No. 23, Art. 8 ; *Cont.*, v. 2, p. 274) ; *Borough* (*Ed. Rev.*, No. 31,
Art. 2 ; *Cont.*, v. 2, p. 295) ; *Tales* (*Ed. Rev.*, No. 40, Art. 2 ; *Cont.*, v. 2,
p. 322) ; *Tales of the Hall* (*Ed. Rev.*, No. 63, Art. 7 ; *Cont.*, v. 2, p. 348).

[2] *Cont.*, v. 2, p. 274.

" many imitations of . . . Goldsmith and Campbell " did not
" always make a very harmonious combination " ; some of
Crabbe's verses were marked by a " tame heaviness and
vulgarity." [1] He complained too of a " want of habitual fire,
and of a tone of enthusiasm in the general tenor " of Crabbe's
writings.[2] Crabbe, he said, was so unequal a writer, and
sometimes so unattractive, that he required " more than any
other of his degree, some explanation of his system, and some
specimens of his powers, from those experienced and intrepid
readers whose business it is to pioneer for the lazier sort." [3]
(Gates remarked that Jeffrey's various descriptions of his duties
as critic are worth careful comparison : [4] this description may
be noted.)   " Considering Mr Crabbe," Jeffrey stated in another
place, " as, upon the whole, the most original writer who has
ever come before us . . . we have directed our remarks rather
to the moral than the literary qualities of his works ;—to his
genius at least, rather than his taste—and to his thoughts rather
than his figures of speech."   " In such an author," he said,
" the attributes of style and versification may fairly be considered
as secondary." [5]

The description, noticed in an earlier chapter, of a passage
in *The Parish Register* as being " in the good old taste of Pope
and Dryden " makes it clear, at the same time, that there were
qualities common to Crabbe and to the Augustans that Jeffrey
found it possible to admire.   Among these qualities was " compression . . . a sort of sententious brevity, once thought essential
to poetical composition " of which Crabbe's work afforded
" now the only living example." [6] From the " childish and
absurd affectations " of certain of the authors of his day, Jeffrey
declared also, he turned " with pleasure to the manly sense
and correct picturing of Mr Crabbe."   After being " dazzled
and made giddy with the elaborate raptures and obscure
originalities of these new artists " he found it " refreshing,"
he said, " to meet again with the spirit and nature of our old
masters "—not necessarily, however, only the Augustans—in
Crabbe's " nervous pages." [7] " We trust," Jeffrey wrote in
the concluding sentence of his first review of Crabbe, " . . . that
he will soon appear again among the worthy supporters of the

[1] *Cont.*, v. 2, pp. 318-20.   [2] *Ibid.*, v. 2, p. 346.   [3] *Ibid.*, v. 2, p. 372.
[4] *Selections*, p. 200.   [5] *Cont.*, v. 2, p. 346.   [6] *Ibid.*, v. 2, p. 318.
[7] *Ibid.*, v. 2, p. 282.

old poetical establishment, and come in time to surpass the revolutionists in fast firing, as well as in weight of metal." [1]

The reference to " correct picturing " indicates one reason why Jeffrey felt thus drawn to Crabbe. A brief consideration of Crabbe himself reveals further affinities in taste between the two men. In his *Library* Crabbe spoke of youthful days in which he was thrilled by works teeming with " moats . . . castles . . . ghosts . . . demons . . . black suits of armour . . . foaming steeds," and similar paraphernalia. The younger Crabbe told how, as a child, he used to delight in the fairy tales related to him by his father, " all sparkling with gold and diamonds, magic fountains and enchanted princesses." [2] Opening, in *The Borough*, his tale of Ellen Orford, Crabbe recalled his boyhood reading : in his *Tales of the Hall* he made his Squire George one who, in his early days, mused " on tragic tales of lovers dead," and who dreamed of rescuing some lady " none on earth Of higher rank or nobler in her birth," falling in love with her, and extolling her " in glorious rhyme." [3] Proceeding, however, with his tale of Ellen, Crabbe remarked that he soon learned there was no need to suffer any real apprehension for the heroines of romance : however dire their perils or heartrending their difficulties, they were all destined to be delivered, before the tale was fully told, unimpaired in wind, limb, virtue, and beauty, into the arms of their adorers. " These," Crabbe continued, " let us leave, and at her sorrows look. Too often seen, but seldom in a book." Few who have read Squire George's story are likely to forget the way in which that character was wrenched out of his intellectual playroom and made to see the world as it could be in reality—" a way," Jeffrey commented, " that no one but Mr Crabbe would either have thought of—or thought of describing in verse." [4] In *The Library* Crabbe spoke of the pleasures of romance as " joys, Which Reason scatters, and which Time destroys." He thought of indulgence in romanticism, in other words, in much the same way as that in which Jeffrey thought of indulgence in certain forms of scholarship—as natural to a schoolboy but no credit to a man. Jeffrey's reference to the " childish . . . affectations " of some contemporary writers indicates that this was his attitude also to certain aspects of the romantic movement of his day.

[1] *Cont.*, v. 2, p. 294.
[2] *Life of Crabbe*, p. 140.
[3] Book 7.
[4] *Cont.*, v. 2, p. 359.

A discussion of Crabbe's "talent for observation" throws further light on Jeffrey's conception of authenticity. The first fruit of this talent, he remarked, was generally satire—"the unmasking the vain pretenders to wisdom, and worth, and happiness, with whom society is infested." But he did not think this its "just or natural termination." The satirist's "uncharitable application" of his powers of observation he was "inclined . . . to ascribe" to love of popularity—which was well known to be best secured by successful invective—and also to "the narrowness and insufficiency of the observations themselves." The satirist made use, Jeffrey said, of only half, and the worse half, of the lessons that might be deduced from his occupation. The "true and proper effect" of a habit of observation was not to extinguish sympathy but to extend it, "to turn, no doubt, many a throb of admiration . . . into a smile . . . but at the same time to reveal much that commands our homage and excites our affection, in those humble and unexplored regions of the heart and understanding, which never engage the attention of the incurious,—and to bring the whole family of mankind nearer to a level"—we note the phrase— "by finding out latent merits as well as latent defects in all its members, and compensating the flaws that are detected in the boasted ornaments of life, by bringing to light the richness and the lustre that sleep in the mines beneath its surface." [1] The attitude both to satire and to the obscure among mankind surely indicates that we have travelled some distance away from the typical Augustan viewpoint.

"Mr Crabbe," Jeffrey wrote, "exhibits the common people of England pretty much as they are, and as they must appear to every one who will take the trouble of examining into their condition." [2] Crabbe, he said, never sentimentalised his humbler characters. On the contrary, he represented certain of these "as altogether as dissipated, and more dishonest and discontented, than the profligates of higher life" ; and, instead of conducting us through groves and meadows, had "led us along filthy lanes and crowded wharfs, to hospitals, alms-houses, and gin-shops." "Many ingenious writers," Jeffrey commented, "who make a very good figure with battles, nymphs, and moonlight land-scapes," would find themselves helpless if set down among surroundings of that description.[3]

[1] *Cont.*, v. 2, pp. 349-53.   [2] *Ibid.*, v. 2, p. 277.   [3] *Ibid.*, v. 2, pp. 295-6.

Crabbe, Jeffrey felt at the same time, tended often to indulge too much in this kind of detail. His "chief fault" was to excite frequently "disgust, instead of pity or indignation, in the breasts of his readers." It was needless, Jeffrey supposed, to explain what were "the objects of disgust in physical or external existences." "These," he said, "are sufficiently plain and unequivocal ; and it is universally admitted, that all mention of them must be carefully excluded from every poetical description." So far as human character was concerned, he regarded that as disgusting which represented misery without making any appeal to the reader's love, respect, or admiration. If a sufferer were amiable, the pain aroused by his suffering was enhanced into pity. Respect was awakened when to guilt there was added power. Even mean and atrocious guilt could, if efficient, arouse in the spectator sympathy for the victim and a desire for vengeance on the oppressor—which made a compound that was pleasurable on the whole. The case was different, however, when one encountered characters that were too vicious to arouse affection, and too insignificant to be a cause of misery to others. Such were "the depraved, abject, diseased, and neglected poor—creatures in whom every thing amiable or respectable has been extinguished by sordid passions or brutal debauchery ;—who have no means of doing the mischief of which they are capable—whom every one despises, and no one can either love or fear." It might perhaps serve some moral purpose to set such spectacles occasionally before us, but they could never awaken either pity or horror. He knew no writer, Jeffrey said, who had sinned so deeply as Crabbe had done in portraying such pictures. It was strange that a writer of his quick observation should have failed to notice that even Shakespeare, who had "ventured every thing," had never shocked our feelings "with the crimes or the sufferings of beings absolutely without power or principle." [1]

It would have been uncharacteristic of the Jeffrey we have come to know had this argument sprung from any desire to shut his eyes to the world's ugliness. If, he declared of *The Parish Register*, several of the groups were composed of disagreeable subjects, allowance had to be made for the author's purpose of giving an exact view of village life. "He aims," Jeffrey wrote, "at an important moral effect by this exhibition ; and must

[1] *Cont.*, v. 2, pp. 301-6.

not be defrauded either of that, or of the praise which is due to the coarser efforts of his pen, out of deference to the sickly delicacy of his more fastidious readers." [1] " By the mere force of his art," he wrote of Crabbe in the review of *The Borough*, " and the novelty of his style, he forces us to attend to objects that are usually neglected, and to enter into feelings from which we are in general but too eager to escape." [2] But Jeffrey was equally appreciative of Crabbe's more sympathetic pictures of the poor. Nothing, he said, could be more touching than the quiet suffering of Phoebe Dawson in *The Parish Register* ; and he pointed out to his readers that the passage containing her story was the last piece of poetry that had been read to Fox.[3] (It may be remembered that this tale was read also, in his last days, to Scott, who, Lockhart said, when his mind was in its full strength, could have repeated every line of it.) [4] The felon's dream in *The Borough* appeared to Jeffrey " to derive an unspeakable charm from the lowly simplicity and humble content of the characters—at least," he added, " we cannot conceive any walk of *ladies and gentlemen* that should furnish out so sweet a picture as terminates the following extract." [5] The *Tales*, he declared, contained a greater number of instances than did Crabbe's previous work in which the poet had " combined the natural language and manners of humble life with the energy of true passion, and the beauty of generous affection "—we notice the now very familiar last phrase—and had " unfolded, in the middling orders of the people, the workings of those finer feelings, and the stirrings of those loftier emotions which the partiality of other poets had attributed, almost exclusively, to actors on a higher scene." [6] " If," he wrote in the article on *The Borough*, " the most admirable painting of external objects —the most minute and thorough knowledge of human character— and that warm glow of active and rational benevolence which lends a guiding light to observation, and an enchanting colour to eloquence, can entitle a poet to praise, as they do entitle him to more substantial rewards, we are persuaded that the following passage will not be speedily forgotten." [7] A few lines from the extract he quoted show how Crabbe could, like an artist highly

[1] *Cont.*, v. 2, pp. 285-6.
[2] *Ibid.*, v. 2, p. 296.
[3] *Ibid.*, v. 2, pp. 289-90.
[4] *Life of Scott*, v. 7, p. 388.
[5] *Cont.*, v. 2, p. 309.
[6] *Ibid.*, v. 2, p. 323.
[7] *Ibid.*, v. 2, p. 311.

skilled with pen or brush, with a few easy strokes make his picture leap to the mind.

> " There, in one house, throughout their lives to be,
> The pauper-palace which they hate to see :
> That giant-building, that high-bounding wall,
> Those bare-worn walks, that lofty thund'ring hall,
> That large loud clock, which tolls each dreaded hour,
> Those gates and locks, and all those signs of power ;
> It is a prison, with a milder name,
> Which few inhabit without dread or shame." [1]

" The Lover's Journey " in Crabbe's *Tales* awakened in Jeffrey the wish, already noticed, that Crabbe had lived among Scottish scenery so that he might have had that excellent material on which to exercise his " unrivalled powers." [2] Of the felon's dream in *The Borough* Jeffrey declared that the " exquisite accuracy and beauty of the landscape painting are such as must have recommended it to notice in poetry of any order." [3] " We should have liked," Jeffrey wrote in the opening paragraph of his article on the *Tales*, " a little more of the deep and tragical passions ; of those passions which exalt and overwhelm the soul—to whose stormy seat the modern muses can so rarely raise their flight—and which he has wielded with such terrific force in his Sir Eustace Grey, and the Gipsy Woman." [4] " Last, though not least," he enumerated among Crabbe's qualities in the review of *The Tales of the Hall*, " that sweet and seldom sounded chord of Lyrical inspiration, the lightest touch of which instantly charms away all harshness from his numbers, and all lowness from his themes—and at once exalts him to a level with the most energetic and inventive poets of his age." [5] Of these criticisms also, whether or not we agree with Saintsbury that Jeffrey's praise of Crabbe is extravagant [6]—some of us may think that this may be said of the praise in the last quotation —it cannot be held that they are appreciations of peculiarly Augustan qualities. Nor is Jeffrey's mention of Crabbe's " minute and thorough knowledge of human character " appreciation of a peculiarly Augustan quality. Such an " admirable sketch," as Jeffrey called it,[7] as that of the completely ineffective and yet highly successful Vicar in *The Borough* appears

[1] *The Borough*, Letter xviii.   [2] *Ante*, p. 54.   [3] *Cont.*, v. 2, p. 309.
[4] *Ibid.*, v. 2, p. 322.   [5] *Ibid.*, v. 2, p. 349.   [6] See *post*, p. 161.
[7] *Cont.*, v. 2, p. 312.

to me, style and versification apart, as fresh to-day as when it
was written. The Curate in the same poem, who " weigh'd
the Greek page, and added note on note. . . . And dream'd
what his Euripides would be," [1] is, I think, still alive. The
subtle psychological effects to be found in such a story as *The
Patron*, the fifth of Crabbe's *Tales* are, it seems to me, as modern
as those of the novel published yesterday.

It might be argued by some that in part of his criticism of
Crabbe, Jeffrey was according high praise to what was not, in
the highest sense of the word, poetry at all—that he was showing
himself insensitive to the difference there is between writing
of the Crabbe type and poetry with enchantment in it, that
kind of poetry of which Shakespeare was thinking when he
wrote of " the poet's eye, in a fine frenzy rolling," glancing
" from heaven to earth, from earth to heaven." This is, of
course, a relic of an ancient controversy. Crabbe discussed
it himself in the preface to his *Tales*, quoting the passage in the
Midsummer Night's Dream just referred to, and making the obvious
comment that the question is one simply of definition. While
Crabbe was prepared to concede that the work of the writer
who was " of imagination all compact " was a " more dignified
kind of composition " than was that of the versifier who addressed
his productions to his readers' " plain sense and sober judgment,"
he was unwilling to grant that the former should monopolise
the title of poet—remarking that this idea of poetry would
exclude much of Chaucer, Dryden, and Pope, and recalling
Johnson's observation that it would be difficult to frame a
definition of a poet in which Pope should not be admitted.
Jeffrey, we recollect, spoke of Pope as more of a satirist, moralist,
wit, and critic than a poet. I do not think, however, that with
his unwillingness to waste time on useless distinctions Jeffrey
would have cared to pursue this discussion very far. I imagine
he might have pointed out that it does not require much
intelligence to perceive that Keats's famous " magic casements "
passage, for instance, belongs to a different order of writing
from, say, the passage in *The Newspaper* in which Crabbe,
describing the conversation of comfortable people in taverns
who indict

> " roads, and rates that still increase ;
> The murmuring poor, who will not fast in peace "

[1] Letter iii.

mirrored a whole social attitude in a single brilliant and biting
line. If we desire to mark that difference by refusing to accept
the ordinary usage of language that includes both as poetry,
then we have to find a new name for the second type. To call
it simply verse is surely unsatisfactory. That is to confuse it
with writing which has aimed at being poetry and missed its
mark. Crabbe's line has hit the dead centre of its target. It
seems even more unsatisfactory to describe it as prose measured
out in even syllables. We have only to try expressing the idea
contained in it in another way to realise how much of its
effectiveness is inseparable from its rhythm.

"In poetry," Stephen wrote of the first *Edinburgh* reviewers,
"they clung, as long as they could, to the safe old principles
represented by Crabbe." [1] This figure—of a man clinging
desperately until swept from his hold by the tide of the next
generation's wisdom—is inaccurate so far as Jeffrey is concerned :
Jeffrey, we have seen, never abandoned his admiration of Crabbe.
The remainder of Stephen's statement seems to me, however,
to be completely correct : Jeffrey always clung to principles
which appeared to him to be, ultimately at least, safe. He
conceived it to be criticism's high office, it is becoming more
and more evident, to act as a guardian of civilisation.

"Even his praise of Crabbe," Saintsbury wrote of Jeffrey
in a passage that has just been alluded to, "excessive as it may
now appear, is diversified by curious patches of blame which
seem to me at any rate, singularly uncritical. There are, for
instance, a very great many worse jests in poetry than—'Oh,
had he learnt to make the wig he wears !'—which Jeffrey
pronounces a misplaced piece of buffoonery." [2] We have here,
it seems to me, another example of the possibly unintended
process by which ordinary readers may be dazzled out of
judgment. Neither the jest nor the criticism can, it is clear, be
appreciated without a knowledge of the context. To the
whereabouts of this Saintsbury gave no clue. The effect upon
the ordinary reader of this airy allusion is, I imagine, to induce
him to believe that there exists a body of experts by whom
the line quoted is as immediately recognisable as is " Friends,
Romans, countrymen " ; and that it would be well for him,
accordingly, in such formidable company, to hold his peace,

---

[1] *Hours in a Library*, v. 2, p. 268.
[2] *Essays in Eng. Lit.* (1780-1860), pp. 117-8.

L

even about so elementary a matter as a joke. Whether or not
that assumption would be justified in every instance must be
left to the conscience of any expert who may chance to read this
paragraph. Perhaps our ordinary reader might be a little
surprised to learn that that line is not to be found within the
body of a poem in any modern edition of Crabbe's collected
works—as Crabbe, being apparently less confident of the success
of his jest than Saintsbury was, struck the line out of the poem
in which it originally appeared.[1]

II

Contact with the poetry of Barry Cornwall,[2]—of whom it
has been written that he " will be remembered as the man
whom everyone loved—that company including a hundred of
the greatest of the century " [3]—moved Jeffrey to criticism which
gives us some additional glimpses of his conception of the " end "
of poetry, and of his dual standard of judgment. Jeffrey asserted
of Cornwall that he seemed to be " altogether free from any
tincture of bitterness, rancour or jealousy." [4] It was " delightful," he said " to turn . . . to the unalloyed sweets of such
poetry as Mr Cornwall's ; and to refresh our fancies, and
strengthen and compose our good affection, among the images
of love and beauty, and gentle sympathy and sorrow, with
which it everywhere presents us." [5] The outlook in these
passages is not very different from that of the man of an earlier
period who declared that " he who would not be frustrate of
his hope to write well hereafter in laudable things, ought himself
to be a true poem," and who said that the abilities of poets
" are of power . . . to imbreed and cherish in a great people
the seeds of virtue and public civility, to allay the perturbations
of the mind, and set the affections in right tune." [6] " Why
this," Jeffrey wrote in the second of his articles on Cornwall,
" should not be thought the highest kind of poetry, we profess
ourselves rather at a loss to explain ;—and certainly are ourselves
often in a mood to think that it is so." " In spite of his neglect

---

[1] *Poetical Works of Crabbe*, 8 vol. ed., 1834, v. 3, p. 56, footnote.

[2] Jeffrey wrote two articles on Bryan W. Procter (" Barry Cornwall ") :
A Sicilian Story (*Ed. Rev.*, No. 65, Art. 8) ; *Marcian Colonna* (*Ed. Rev.*, No. 68,
Art. 11).

[3] *Chambers's Cyclopædia of Eng. Lit.*, v. 3, pp. 227-8.

[4] *Ed. Rev.*, No. 68, p. 449.   [5] *Ibid.*, No. 65, pp. 146-7.

[6] Milton, *Apology for Smectymnuus, Reason of Church Government.*

of the terrible passions," he wrote also of Cornwall, " he *does*
rank very high in our estimation." [1] He enumerated, as
Cornwall's models, Shakespeare in his tender, sweet, and fanciful
passages, some of the other sixteenth and seventeenth century
dramatists, the earlier Milton, Byron, Coleridge, Wordsworth,
and Leigh Hunt.   The materials, Jeffrey said, " really harmonize
very tolerably." [2]   Some of this may appear extravagant praise
of a poet who is now remembered, so far as he is remembered
at all, mainly in connection with one not entirely fortunate lyric.
One may not wish to question over-strongly the verdict of later
criticism.   Nevertheless it might be wise for one unacquainted
with Cornwall's poetry, before springing to the conclusion that
Jeffrey had in this instance jettisoned his critical taste, to glance
at the two narrative poems, *A Sicilian Story* and *Marcian Colonna*,
with which he chiefly dealt, or even merely at the passages he
quoted from them.   There will be found there in particular a
passage, extracted from the latter poem, describing an ocean-
voyage, that has a rhythm in its lines that is very different from
the jingle of " The Sea ! the Sea ! the open Sea ! "—though
that poem too is not, to my ears, in its penultimate stanza,
entirely devoid of music.

Jeffrey's criticism of Cornwall has occasioned another of
those incidental tributes to him that we have noticed.   " It is
not often," Coventry Patmore wrote, " that the first public
criticism of a poet's work is the best ; and such an early judgment
is especially liable to error when it includes a comparison with
other and contemporary poetry.   But Lord Jeffrey's estimate
of ' Mr Cornwall's ' writing is probably fuller and juster than
anything which has been printed on the subject during the
fifty-six years that have since gone by.   The following extract
from the *Edinburgh* notice of a *Sicilian Story* could scarcely be
improved upon." [3]

Jeffrey said of Cornwall that he had " less affectation, and
far less conceit " than had Leigh Hunt, but expressed doubt
whether Cornwall " could have written any thing so good, on
the whole, as the beautiful story of *Rimini*." [4]   " It is very
sweet," he wrote to Moore, speaking of *Rimini*, " and very lively
in many places, and is altogether piquant, as being by far the

---

[1] *Ed. Rev.*, No. 68, pp. 450, 449.   [2] *Ibid.*, No. 65, pp. 144-5.
[3] *Bryan Waller Procter, an Autobiographical Fragment*, 1877, pp. 44-5.
[4] *Ed. Rev.*, No. 65, p. 146.

best imitation of Chaucer and some of his Italian contemporaries that modern times have produced." [1] In the *Review*, while he noted the negligence of Hunt's style, he declared that there was " a great deal of genuine poetry in this little volume ; and poetry, too, of a very peculiar and original character." [2]

Jeffrey's appreciation of the Elizabethans, of Hogg, of Cornwall, and of Hunt, prepares us for appreciation of Keats. " Jeffrey's natural taste in poetry," Sir Sidney Colvin wrote in his *John Keats* " was conservative, and favoured the correct, the classical and traditional : but in this case, whether from genuine and personal opinion, or to please influential wellwishers of Keats on his own side in politics and criticism like Sir James Mackintosh, he on the appearance of the new volume took occasion to print, now when Keats was far past caring about it, an article on his work which was mainly in eulogy of *Endymion* : eulogy not unmixed with reasonable criticism, but in a strain, on the whole, gushing almost to excess." [3] Colvin, it is evident, was inclined to believe that Jeffrey's personal taste alone was insufficient to account for his eulogy of Keats. *Endymion* was published in 1818. Jeffrey's review of the poem did not appear until 1820. " We had never happened," Jeffrey stated in the opening sentence of his article, " to see either of these volumes till very lately." [4] It is possible, therefore, that in the interim someone drew his attention to the work of the new young poet. But to say this is different from suggesting that Jeffrey was prepared to tamper with his critical conscience in order to please some " influential " person or persons unknown. It is not easy to see why the editor of the most powerful literary organ of the day, a critic of British, European, and American renown —whose intractability was commented upon by his publisher Constable and by his personal friend Scott—should be supposed to have felt himself under any necessity of pleasing such persons. It is interesting, in the light of Colvin's statement, to notice

[1] *Memoirs*, Moore, v. 2, p. 100.

[2] *Ed. Rev.*, No. 52, pp. 491, 476.   Jeffrey wrote only this article on Leigh Hunt. A writer in the *Westminster* for 1852 (New Series, v. 2, p. 105) stated that this review was by Hazlitt. Both the style of the article and the letter from Jeffrey in Moore's *Memoirs* (v. 2, p. 100) seem to me conclusive in favour of Jeffrey's authorship.   [3] p. 479.

[4] *Cont.*, v. 2, p. 373. (*Ed. Rev.*, No. 67, Art. 10.) Jeffrey reviewed *Endymion* along with the volume containing *Lamia*, etc. which was published in 1820.

how closely Jeffrey's taste and ideas, as revealed by this review, anticipated Colvin's own. " That imitation of our old writers," Jeffrey wrote, " and especially of our older dramatists, to which we cannot help flattering ourselves that we have somewhat contributed, has brought on, as it were, a second spring in our poetry ;—and few of its blossoms are either more profuse of sweetness, or richer in promise, than this which is now before us." [1] We observe that he linked Keats immediately with the Elizabethans. " Not merely," Colvin asserted, " by delight in particular poets and familiarity with favourite passages, but by rooted instinct and by his entire self-training, Keats was beyond all his contemporaries,—and it is the cardinal fact to be borne in mind about him,—the lineal descendant and direct heir of the Elizabethans." [2] Jeffrey remarked that Keats's models for *Endymion* were " obviously " Fletcher's *Faithful Shepherdess* and Jonson's *Sad Shepherd*, and he found traces of imitation also of Milton's *Comus* and *Arcades* : [3] Colvin mentioned the first three of these among the works that influenced Keats when he was writing the poem.[4] Of the choral hymn to Pan in the first book of *Endymion* Jeffrey wrote that it appeared to him " to be full of beauty " and that it reminded him " in many places, of the finest strains of Sicilian—or of English poetry " : [5] Colvin numbered this hymn, along with the song of the Indian Maiden in Book IV, " among Keats's very finest achievements." [6] Jeffrey quoted the eleven lines in the second book that give a picture of Cybele in her chariot, and spoke of them as " another, and more classical sketch . . . with a picture of lions that might excite the envy of Rubens, or Edwin Landseer ! " [7] Colvin quoted the same eleven lines and described the passage as " a vision of intense imaginative life expressed in verse of a noble solemnity and sonority." [8] Jeffrey quoted the eighteen lines in the third book that describe the debris on the sea-floor and remarked that the passage " comes of no ignoble lineage— nor shames its high descent " : [9] Colvin quoted the same eighteen lines and placed beside them Shakespeare's description of the dream of Clarence in Richard III. He quoted also Jeffrey's comment, describing it as " a fine phrase." [10]

---

[1] *Cont.* v. 2, p. 373.
[2] *Keats*, p. 171.   [3] *Cont.*, v. 2, p. 374.   [4] *Keats*, pp. 206, 195.
[5] *Cont.*, v. 2, p. 378.   [6] *Keats*, p. 225.   [7] *Cont.*, v. 2, p. 382.
[8] *Keats*, p. 224.   [9] *Cont.*, v. 2, p. 383.   [10] *Keats*, p. 239.

Keats, Jeffrey remarked, was, he understood, "still a very young man." His whole works, indeed, bore evidence of that. They were "full of extravagance and irregularity, rash attempts at originality, interminable wanderings, and excessive obscurity." They required therefore indulgence. Jeffrey considered, however, that they deserved it. He knew no book, he declared indeed, that he would "sooner employ as a test to ascertain whether any one had in him a native relish for poetry, and a genuine sensibility to its intrinsic charm." The "greater and more distinguished poets" had, he said, so much in them to gratify other tastes—the interest of their stories, their delineations of character, the weight and force of their maxims and sentiments, their pathos, wit, and humour—that they could captivate readers to whom their poetry was only a hindrance, as well as those to whom it constituted their chief attraction. It was only when those other recommendations were wanting, or existed in a weaker degree, that the true force of the attraction exercised by "pure poetry" could be fairly appreciated.[1]

It is plain, nevertheless, that Jeffrey did not regard this narrow if bright stream as constituting the highest kind of poetry : we observed him describe "pure poetry," in the article on Hogg, as a "very dangerous species" of the art. Keats, Jeffrey said, dealt "too much with shadowy and incomprehensible beings" : he was "too constantly rapt into an extramundane Elysium, to command a lasting interest with ordinary mortals" ; and he would require to "employ the agency of more varied and coarser emotions" if he desired to take rank with "the enduring poets." He found in Keats the same pseudo-re-creation of the past that he had found elsewhere in contemporary poetry. Keats had not, in his opinion, really dealt with classical mythology ; instead, "sheltering the violence of the fiction under the ancient traditionary fable," the poet had fashioned an entirely new set of characters to whom he had attached the ancient names. Jeffrey had "more than doubts of the fitness of such personages to maintain a permanent interest with the modern public" ; though he remarked that this method certainly gave them the best chance that remained for them. We perceive here the reasoning that led Jeffrey to say that he could not "advise the completion" of *Hyperion*. While, he said, there were passages in the poem "of some force and grandeur," the subject was

[1] *Cont.*, v. 2, pp. 373-6.

" too far removed from all the sources of human interest, to be successfully treated by any modern author." Quoting from the *Ode to a Nightingale*, he italicised in the *Contributions*, for special notice, the snatch, with human feeling in it,

> " sick for home,
> She stood in tears amid the alien corn,"

but not the later so celebrated " magic casements." Keats, he remarked in concluding his article, had " unquestionably a very beautiful imagination, a perfect ear for harmony, and a great familiarity with the finest diction of English poetry," but the poet would have to learn " neither to waste the good gifts of nature and study on intractable themes, nor to luxuriate too recklessly on such as are more suitable." [1]

In *Sleep and Poetry*, after asking for " ten years " in which to " overwhelm " himself in poesy—" First," Keats wrote, " the realm I'll pass Of Flora, and old Pan," and added,

> " And can I ever bid these joys farewell ?
> Yes, I must pass them for a nobler life,
> Where I may find the agonies, the strife
> Of human hearts."

That, we observe, was precisely the road along which Jeffrey wanted him to travel. " Strength alone," Keats wrote,

> " though of the Muses born
> Is like a fallen angel : trees uptorn,
> Darkness, and worms, and shrouds, and sepulchres
> Delight it ; for it feeds upon the burrs
> And thorns of life ; forgetting the great end
> Of poesy, that it should be a friend
> To soothe the cares, and lift the thoughts of man."

There we have precisely Jeffrey's conception of poetry's " great end "—and the justification of ethical criticism. " So I believe," Keats wrote in one of his letters, " . . . that works of genius are the first things in this world. No ! for that sort of probity . . . which such men as Bailey possess does hold . . . the tip-top of any spiritual honours that can be paid to anything

---

[1] *Cont.*, v. 2, pp. 376-90. The words " a perfect ear for harmony " were added in the *Contributions*. Cf. *Ed. Rev.*, No. 67, p. 213.

in this world." [1]   There we have precisely the Jeffreyan scale
of values.   " I find," Keats wrote, " there is no worthy pursuit
but the idea of doing some good to the world. . . . There is
but one way for me.   The road lies through application, study,
and thought." [2]   There we have the Jeffreyan conception of
man's chief end.   He had " honestly endeavoured," Jeffrey said
in the preface to his *Contributions*, to select from the large mass
of his articles not those which he thought most likely still to
attract notice by boldness of view or vivacity of expression, but
those which by enforcing what appeared to him " just principles
and useful opinions " he " really thought had a tendency to
make men happier and better."   Once more the familiar
combination !   He was quite aware, Jeffrey added, of the
ridicule that might be attached to this statement ; but it was
" the only apology " he wished to make for his re-publication.[3]
Crossing the Bay of Biscay in 1820, Keats ran into rough weather.
" After the tempest had subsided," Milnes wrote, " Keats was
reading the description of the storm in *Don Juan*, and cast the
book on the floor in a transport of indignation.   ' How horrible
an example of human nature,' he cried, ' is this man, who has
no pleasure left him but to gloat over and jeer at the most
awful incidents of life.   Oh ! this is a paltry originality, which
consists in making solemn things gay, and gay things solemn,
and yet it will fascinate thousands, by the very diabolical outrage
of their sympathies.   Byron's perverted education makes him
assume to feel, and try to impart to others, those depraved
sensations which the want of any education excites in many.' " [4]
That, we have seen, was precisely Jeffrey's criticism.   It may
be that part of the attractiveness he found in Keats sprang
from a subconscious perception of the fundamental harmony
there was between much of his thinking and that of the younger
man.

   " So late as 1844," Colvin wrote on a later page than that
on which appeared the first passage we extracted from him in
this chapter, " Jeffrey, who in spite of the justice he had been
induced to do to Keats in his lifetime, had no real belief in the
new poetry and was an instinctive partisan of the conventional
eighteenth-century style, could write that the ' rich melodies '
of Keats and Shelley were passing out of public memory, and

---

[1] *Life and Letters of Keats*, Houghton, p. 76.   [2] *Ibid.*, pp. 93-4.
[3] V. I, p. x.   [4] *Life and Letters of Keats*, Houghton, p. 259.

that the poets of their age destined to enduring fame were
Campbell and Rogers." [1]   Colvin's use of the word " induced "
suggests, we observe, that the purely hypothetical influence
spoken of some fifty pages earlier had now become an established
fact.   Consideration of what has been alluded to as one of
Jeffrey's "unlucky blunders" in prediction may be postponed
yet awhile.   So far as Keats is concerned, however, we may
look, at this point, at a few other dates besides 1844.   In 1818
Blackwood's advised "Mr John" to go "back to the shop" and
the *Quarterly* reviewer of *Endymion* declared that he had been
able to struggle through only the first book of the poem. [2]
Jeffrey's assertion, in opposition to these statements, that he knew
no book he would sooner employ than *Endymion* as a test to
ascertain whether anyone had in him a native relish for poetry
seems hardly, on the face of it, evidence of unbelief in at anyrate
Keats's poetry.   The warmth of Jeffrey's eulogy, to which Colvin
drew attention, may have been due in part to a feeling that
Keats had been treated with undue harshness in the other
periodicals.   It must be evident by now, at the same time,
that Jeffrey tended, when he was pleased with what he had
been reading, to express himself hyperbolically.   It was a
tendency he perceived in himself.   "We . . . believe we have,
upon the whole," he wrote in one of his reviews of Wilson,
"incurred the displeasure of the judicious much oftener by an
excessive lenity, than by any undue measure of severity—for
our rash and unqualified praises, than for our intemperate or
embittered censures." [3]   "My natural foible," he said in a
letter to Moore, " is to admire and be pleased too easily, and
I am never severe except from effort and reflection." [4]   " I
think it nearly impossible," Keats's first biographer wrote,
nevertheless, of an extract he quoted from Jeffrey's criticism
of *Endymion*, " to express, in fewer or better words, the impression
usually left by this poem on those minds which, from their
constitution, can claim to possess an opinion on the question." [5]
Jeffrey was not the only reviewer who criticised Keats's poetry
favourably in 1820. [6]   But neither the verdicts of the other
journals nor that of Jeffrey appears to have exercised much

[1] *Keats*, p. 528.   [2] *Blackwood's*, v. 3, p. 524.   *Quarterly*, No. 37, p. 204.
[3] *Ed. Rev.*, No. 52, p. 460.   [4] *Memoirs*, Moore, v. 2, p. 101.
[5] *Life and Letters of Keats*, Houghton, p. 145.
[6] *Adonais, A Life of John Keats*, Dorothy Hewlett, pp. 366-84.

influence on the public mind on this occasion. What Keats thought of his literary position in 1821 is evident from the inscription which, " in the bitterness of his heart," he caused to be inscribed on his tombstone.[1] In 1824 Hazlitt, writing in the *Edinburgh*, referred to " the shaft . . . venal, vulgar, venomous " that followed Keats to his grave.[2] In the same year, however, a writer in *Blackwood's*, referring both to Hazlitt's article and to Shelley's having been drowned with a volume of Keats in his possession, delivered himself as follows : " But what a rash man Shelley was, to put to sea in a frail boat with Jack's poetry on board ! Why, man, it would sink a trireme." [3] *Blackwood's* in 1828 made " North " speak of Keats's " genius " being seen " to the best advantage " in *Lamia* and *Isabella*, but did so, Colvin remarked, " we feel, less for the sake of praising Keats than of getting in a dig at Jeffrey for having praised him tardily and indiscriminately "—surely an odd charge coming from *Blackwood's*.[4] (" North," Colvin, and Monckton Milnes— who also spoke of Jeffrey's appreciation of Keats's genius as " somewhat tardy " [5]—had all of course one advantage over Jeffrey. All three knew that Keats had died in 1821. It is evident from Jeffrey's review that he supposed that the " very young man " with whom he was dealing would have many years of writing life still in front of him. To gain, at barely twenty-five, from the " chieftain of the critic clan " the kind of commendation Jeffrey gave Keats might not appear, to a modern writer, to be receiving recognition too " tardily.") " Our readers," the *Quarterly* said in 1828, " have probably forgotten all about ' *Endymion*, a poem,' and the other works of this young man, the all but universal roar of laughter with which they

[1] *Keats*, Colvin, p. 524.

[2] *Ed. Rev.*, No. 80, p. 499. *Keats*, Colvin, pp. 521-2.

[3] V. 16, p. 288. The writer thought the article was by Procter.

[4] *Keats*, Colvin, p. 527. *Noctes Ambrosianæ*, v. 2, p. 144. It may have been from this number of the *Noctes* that Colvin derived unconsciously the idea that outside influence might have been exerted on Jeffrey. " North " remarked on the same page that it was " not unjust or unfair to suspect the insertion of the article on *Endymion* was brought about by a Cockney job of Hunt or Hazlitt's." *Blackwood's* is, however, hardly a trustworthy witness on such a matter. Cf. *Memoir of John Wilson*, p. 195, where we learn that Hunt was accused by the *Magazine*, evidently quite falsely, of having pestered Hazlitt to review him in the *Edinburgh*. We have here, perhaps, the origin of the error alluded to on p. 164, footnote.

[5] *Life and Letters of Keats*, Houghton, p. 145.

were received some ten or twelve years ago, and the ridiculous story . . . of the author's death being caused by the reviewers." [1] " I fear," Fanny Brawne wrote of Keats in December 1829, " the kindest act would be to let him rest for ever in the obscurity to which unhappy circumstances have condemned him." [2] Two months before that, Jeffrey had declared in the *Edinburgh*, as Colvin noted, that the " rich melodies " of Keats were fading from public memory.[3] Does not this seem to have been simply a statement of fact ? There had been up to this time no reprint of Keats's poems in Britain. There was a reprint in 1829, but only for a Paris firm, which printed for the continental market, in a collective edition of the poems of Shelley, Coleridge, and Keats.[4] Not until 1840 did there appear the first separate British republication of Keats's collected poems. This sold badly, and before long was " remaindered." [5] In 1843 Jeffrey returned to the charge. " I still think," he wrote in a footnote in his *Contributions*, " that a poet of great power and promise was lost to us by the premature death of Keats . . . and regret that I did not go more largely into the exposition of his merits, in the slight notice of them, which I now venture to reprint. But though I cannot . . . without departing from the principle which must govern this republication, now supply this omission, I hope to be forgiven for having added a page or two to *the citations*,—by which my opinion of those merits was then illustrated, and is again left to the judgment of the reader." [6] We note once more the customary attitude. This passage, read in its " honest meaning," seems hardly evidence of a lack of faith in the poetry of Keats. Not until five years after that did the first biography of the poet appear—written by Milnes, who had been one of a " Cambridge group of Shelley-Keats enthusiasts

[1] No. 74, p. 416.

[2] *Letters of John Keats*, ed. M. Buxton Forman, p. lxiii.

[3] *Cont.*, v. 2, p. 567. This was not, of course, written in 1844. It was reprinted in that year (or 1843). Jeffrey stated in the preface to his *Contributions* that in a " professed Reprint " he did not think himself entitled to make " any change in the substance of what was originally published," or " even in the expression," except for slight verbal corrections to clear the meaning or remedy slips of the pen. *Cont.*, v. 1, p. xiv.

[4] *Keats*, Colvin, p. 527.

[5] *Ibid.*, p. 528. " America," Colvin remarked, " had in this matter been in advance of England, an edition of the poet's works having appeared at Buffalo in 1834."

[6] *Cont.*, v. 2, p. 373.

of 1830." [1] It was, we have noted, to the reviewer who had, twenty-eight years before the publication of that first biography, expressed his appreciation of Keats's poetry that Milnes considered it most appropriate to dedicate his memoir—with the remark that the appreciation was, when written, hazardous to even such a reputation in criticism as then was Jeffrey's. Doubtless it was not until after the publication of Milnes's work that the encyclopedical writers began to include Keats confidently among the poets. It may appear to some of the jury that it is, in these circumstances, a trifle hasty for us who live in later days to describe Jeffrey's review of 1820 as imperfect, and to speak of his recognition of Keats as slow.

[1] *Keats*, Colvin, p. 530. Colvin pointed to a sentence, appreciative of Keats, written for the *Athenæum* in 1828 by a Cambridge man, John Sterling, p. 527.

CHAPTER XI

THE BATTLE JOINED

Criticism of Jeffrey. Origins of new poetry. Talent of Lakers. Lakers'
simplicity. Jeffrey's early attitude to poor. Idle discontent. Criticism
of Southey.

I

It appears to me a sound instinct that has caused such general
interest as has remained in Jeffrey to focus upon his dealings
with the Lakers. Until we see plainly that his lifelong contest
with these poets was an inevitable consequence of his whole
philosophy we have not, it seems to me, properly comprehended
what he has to say to us.

We are now, I think, in a position to commence examination
of that contest. It began in the first number of the *Review*,
in an article on Southey's *Thalaba*.[1]

" Poetry," ran the opening paragraph of the article, " has
this much, at least, in common with religion, that its standards
were fixed long ago, by certain inspired writers, whose authority
it is no longer lawful to call in question ; and that many profess
to be entirely devoted to it, who have no *good works* to produce
in support of their pretensions. The catholic poetical church,
too, has worked but few miracles since the first ages of its
establishment ; and has been more prolific, for a long time, of
Doctors, than of Saints : it has had its corruptions and reforma-
tion also, and has given birth to an infinite variety of heresies
and errors, the followers of which have hated and persecuted
each other as cordially as other bigots." [2]

Criticisms passed upon Jeffrey by writers looking from
different angles may be employed, not merely as a means of
testing the accuracy of our attempt here to interpret him, but
also, so far as the soundness of that interpretation is being
accepted, as a means of measuring how far we are able to travel,

[1] Jeffrey wrote the following articles on Southey : *Thalaba* (*Ed. Rev.*,
No. 1, Art. 8) ; *Madoc* (*Ed. Rev.*, No. 13, Art. 1) ; *Kehama* (*Ed. Rev.*, No. 34,
Art. 11) ; *Roderick* (*Ed. Rev.*, No. 49, Art. 1 ; *Cont.*, v. 2, p. 404) ; *Lay of the
Laureate* (*Ed. Rev.*, No. 52, Art. 8) ; *Wat Tyler* (*Ed. Rev.*, No. 55, Art. 7) ;
Vision of Judgment (*Ed. Rev.*, No. 70, Art. 9).   [2] *Ed. Rev.*, No. 1, p. 63.

momentarily at anyrate, over to Jeffrey's viewpoint. It will be evident that they have been employed to some extent in this way already. We may notice two criticisms of the passage just quoted, one by Professor C. E. Vaughan in his *English Literary Criticism*, and the other by Professor George McL. Harper in his *William Wordsworth*. Vaughan described the passage—he paraphrased the major part of it—as containing " a laboured parallel between poetry and religion." " With an alteration of names," he wrote, " it might have been written by a member of the English Church Union, or of the Holy Inquisition." [1] Harper, quoting the first sentence as far as the word " question," commented, " It is startling to find that the first words of his [Jeffrey's] review of *Thalaba* stamp him at once as an enemy of the living light." And again—" False," he asserted, " as this statement is in both of the propositions involved, it has a doctrinal not an æsthetic basis." [2]

We have to remember, in considering Vaughan's criticism of the style of the passage, that these are the first words of the first review of a poetical work that Jeffrey wrote for the *Edinburgh*. We have here, accordingly, an effort of his prentice pen. A man is generally granted a little time in which to learn his trade. The parallel between poetry and religion, we can now perceive at the same time, was consistent with all his teaching : we have observed that, throughout his whole career, he stressed the close connection that existed, in his view, between morality and proper enjoyment. We perceive that he was holding here that the fundamental standards of art had been arrived at by the same process as that by which he considered those of ethics had come into being—by age-old experimentation. " The elements of poetical interest," he declared in his second article on Southey, " . . . are within and about all men ; and the topics by which they are suggested are proved to have been the same in every age, and every country of the world. Poetry, as we have formerly hinted, is in this respect . . . nearly upon a footing with morality." The emotions that established writers continued to excite under every variation of circumstances, to command among every class of readers, and to impress upon every successive generation, constituted, Jeffrey said, " the sole and ultimate criterion " of their merit.[3] It followed, as we have seen, that single men, or even small groups of men, hampered

---

[1] pp. lxxi, lxxii.   [2] V. 2, p. 135.   [3] *Ed. Rev.*, No. 13, pp. 2, 3.

by their restricted fields of vision and by their particular associations, could not, whatever their individual feelings, challenge
that establishment.   But it did not follow, as we have also seen,
that established authors could not be criticised.   We observe
that it was only the " authority " of inspired writers—" authority "
I take to mean here establishment in their position as exemplifiers
of the standards—that Jeffrey said it was no longer lawful to
call in question.   Inspired writers remained, in his view, human
beings : we recollect, not only his contention that genius had
no " dispensing power . . . in . . . matters of morality and
common sense " [1] but his argument also that it was in dealing
with the works of the greatest men that the exercise of critical
discrimination was most greatly necessary, lest the weaknesses
of these men should be confused with their strength.[2]   We note,
in the second place, that this theory did not preclude originality.
It is plain from what has gone before that Jeffrey regarded
originality as an essential quality of the highest art.   But
originality had, in his opinion, to be attained within the standards.
It was only a mock-originality that was reached by the easy
road of eccentricity.   " We should certainly look with compassion," he wrote, continuing his analogy, " . . . on any man
who should pretend to have discovered a new way to be virtuous ;
and who, in pursuit of supreme moral excellence, should affect
to put no value upon the vulgar elements of justice, generosity,
or benevolence." [3]   " Originality . . . we are persuaded," he
wrote in the article on *Thalaba*, " is rarer than mere alteration." [4]

It seems to me that, whatever they said, Vaughan and
Harper were in essential agreement with Jeffrey.   Criticism,
we read on the first page of Vaughan's introduction, " is a
derivative art, and could scarcely have come into being without
a large body of literature to suggest canons of judgment, and
to furnish instances of their application." [5]   Are not the creators
of that body of literature from which the canons are derivable
simply Jeffrey's " inspired writers " ?   Vaughan selected, as
" typical writers " from whose works the development of English
criticism might be illustrated, Sidney, Dryden, Johnson, Coleridge,
Hazlitt, Lamb, Shelley, Carlyle, and Pater.   I do not imagine
that he anticipated that any educated man would regard it as
lawful to call into serious question the authority of any one

[1] *Ante*, p. 112.   [2] *Ante*, p. 133.   [3] *Ed. Rev.*, No. 13, p. 3.
[4] *Ibid.*, No. 1, p. 64.   [5] *Eng. Lit. Crit.*, p. ix.

of these authors.   In turning over Vaughan's pages one notices
the following words used to describe literary qualities—" discrimination," " tact," " extravagance," " vagueness."   It is
unlikely that anyone would argue that the first and second
should be regarded as literary vices and the third and fourth as
literary virtues.   In other words, these nouns represent standards
that have been " fixed."   By " the living light " Harper
apparently meant something to be found in the works of
Wordsworth.   One may feel that he anticipated easy agreement
from his readers on the ground that Wordsworth's authority
was so completely established that Jeffrey's opposition to the
great Laker tended to carry with it its own condemnation.   In
opening thus his first article on a poetical work for the *Edinburgh*,
Jeffrey, it may be submitted, was simply laying down, in
methodical Scottish fashion, the foundations of all literary
criticism.

   " This," Vaughan wrote in introducing his summary of the
paragraph, " is the unpardonable sin of both Reviews [the
Edinburgh and the *Quarterly*] : that mediocrity was applauded,
but that, whenever a man of genius came before them, the
chances were ten to one that he would be held up to ridicule
and contempt.   The very first number of the *Edinburgh* lays
this down as an article of faith." [1]   There is a tendency in
nineteenth and early twentieth century encyclopedical writing
to assume that the increase in mechanical efficiency that resulted
from division of labour was accompanied by a corresponding
increase in general intellectual power.   Jeffrey's view, we have
seen, however, was that increase of the first tended to diminish
the second.   To suggest that the English-speaking world of the
first half of the nineteenth century accepted as the leading
critical organs of the day works conducted in the manner
described by Vaughan is surely to regard the upward slope of
evolution as having been very steep.   It would be a large task
to test Vaughan's statement by the whole of the *Edinburgh* and
Quarterly.   But we are now in a position to test it by, at anyrate,
the work of Jeffrey.   We have seen, in the articles examined
so far, Scott compared on several occasions with Shakespeare ;
Hogg spoken of as a poet in the highest sense of the word ;
Byron as a puissant spirit ; Moore as a writer over whose work
the Genius of poetry seemed to have breathed its richest

[1] p. lxxi.

enchantment ; Crabbe as the most original author of the day ; Keats as a poet whose writings afford a true test of taste. If these six can be called men of genius, and if these phrases are accepted as evidence of respectful treatment, it would appear that, to substantiate Vaughan's arithmetic, there would require to be found sixty other contemporary geniuses whom the *Edinburgh* treated with complete ridicule and contempt.

Jeffrey's other statements, stripped of metaphor—that masterpieces are rare, that more people teach from and talk about literature than create it, and that these latter incline to be magisterial in their attitude towards those who express views different from their own—do not appear to me to be greatly extraordinary. I wonder if it occurred to Jeffrey that in commencing business, as he was at that moment, as a reviewer, he was enrolling himself among the teachers and talkers.

Harper amplified his assertion that Jeffrey's pronouncement had a doctrinal not an æsthetic basis by remarking that Jeffrey's prejudice might " be termed religious ; for it originated in a fundamental unwillingness to acknowledge the divinity in man." [1] In his use of the word " religious " Harper indicated precisely, it seems to me—though the full significance of this statement has yet to be developed—the essential nature of the difference between the outlook of Wordsworth and that of Jeffrey.

" There can be little doubt," Jeffrey stated in the review of *Thalaba*, " that their [the Lakers'] doctrines are of *German* origin." The italics are his own. The greater part of their material, he affirmed, would be " found to be composed of the following elements : 1. The antisocial principles, and distempered sensibility of Rousseau—his discontent with the present constitution of society—his paradoxical morality, and his perpetual hankerings after some unattainable state of voluptuous virtue and perfection. 2. The simplicity and energy (*horresco referens*) of Kotzebue and Schiller. 3. The homeliness and harshness of some of Cowper's language and versification, interchanged occasionally with the *innocence* of Ambrose Philips, or the quaintness of Quarles and Dr Donne." [2] Vaughan described this as " perhaps the most motley crew that was ever brought together for excommunication." [3] Jeffrey, as I read the passage however, was not excommunicating these men. He was referring only

---

[1] *Wordsworth*, v. 2, p. 135. [2] *Ed. Rev.*, No. 1, pp. 63-4.
[3] *Eng. Lit. Crit.*, p. lxxii.

M

to certain of their qualities. We have noticed him praise Cowper highly : he emphasised, when he felt this necessary, the merit of Rousseau.[1] Harper regarded the passage differently. After drawing attention to Jeffrey's account of the first part of the Lakers' material—" If," he wrote, " the venturesome word ' unattainable ' and the slanderous word ' voluptuous ' were omitted from this charge, it would be just in every particular. The critic has discovered the real origin of what was most dynamic in the new poetry." [2] Harper was bound, from his viewpoint, to disagree with Jeffrey. Writing as he was in 1916 he had abundant material for his study ; and he had, he tells us, spent many years in preparation for his work. This tribute to Jeffrey's acumen, from a scholar thus circumstanced to a critic writing one of his first reviews, on a group of poets whose work was still new, seems to me not unimportant.

Unestablished in reputation though the Lakers might be, Jeffrey recognised immediately that these were by no means writers to be despised. " The authors, of whom we are now speaking," he asserted on the second page of his article, " have, among them, unquestionably, a very considerable portion of poetical talent, and have, consequently, been enabled to seduce many into an admiration of the false taste (as it appears to us) in which most of their productions are composed. They constitute, at present, the most formidable conspiracy that has lately been formed against sound judgment in matters poetical ; and are entitled to a larger share of our censorial notice, than could be spared for an individual delinquent." [3] " He is aware," Harper commented, " of what the new movement involves." [4]

The first symptom of a breakdown of standards Jeffrey perceived in the Lakers' work was in their use of language. They disdained, he said, to make use of " the common poetical phraseology, or to ennoble their diction by a selection of fine or dignified expressions." He admitted that there were times when technique was not of the first importance in writing. The language of strong emotion could scarcely, he said, be deficient in elevation : if an author were wanting on such an occasion he might be presumed to have failed in the truth as well as in the dignity of his expression. There were in poetry, however,

[1] *Cont.*, v. 1, pp. 390-1.
[2] *Wordsworth*, v. 2, p. 136.
[3] *Ed. Rev.*, No. 1, p. 64.
[4] *Wordsworth*, v. 2, p. 136.

subordinate passages that were necessary for connection. In these all the requisite ideas could be conveyed in mean and negligent diction. But where an effect of sublimity was desired, dignity had nowhere to be lost sight of. " A poet," Jeffrey declared, " who aims at all at sublimity or pathos, is like an actor in a high tragic character, and must sustain his dignity throughout, or become altogether ridiculous. We are apt enough to laugh at the mock-majesty of those whom we know to be but common mortals in private ; and cannot permit Hamlet to make use of a single provincial intonation, although it should only be in his conversation with the grave-diggers." The question, we observe, is not one of simplicity versus decoration ; it is one of technique versus none. " *Their* simplicity," Jeffrey declared of the Lakers, " does not consist, by any means, in the rejection of glaring or superfluous ornament . . . or in that refinement of art which seeks concealment in its own perfection. It consists, on the contrary, in a very great degree, in the positive and *bona fide* rejection of art altogether." He perceived no advantage in Wordsworth's project of adapting for poetic purposes " the language of conversation in the middle and lower classes of society." The language of cultivated people might, he said, be presumed to be better than that of their inferiors. It had in its favour the associations of long use for poetry. The speech of the vulgar had all the opposite associations. A great genius might, Jeffrey conceded, overcome these disadvantages. But it seemed scarcely conceivable that he should court them. To an author of education such a style of writing would always be assumed and unnatural, and one from which he would be perpetually tempted to deviate. His composition would, in short, be " like that of a person who is attempting to speak in an obsolete or provincial dialect." [1] We are back, we observe, at the charge levelled, in one form or another, over and over again by Jeffrey against the poetry of what has been called the age of the " Return to Nature "— that it was permeated with artificiality.

This innovation did not appear to Jeffrey to be merely a harmless experiment : a breakdown in standards of diction involved inevitably, in his opinion, a breakdown of other standards besides. " The mischief of this new system," he wrote, " is not confined to the depravation of language only ; it extends

[1] *Ed. Rev.*, No. 1, pp. 64-6, 68.

to the sentiments and emotions, and leads to the debasement
of all those feelings which poetry is designed to communicate."
The different classes of society had each, he held, a distinct
character as well as a separate idiom. The emotions of a
cultivated person were not only differently expressed, but were
actually different emotions from those of a " market-wench."
The question then resolved itself into simply this—which was
the more proper object for poetical imitation ? It was needless,
Jeffrey asserted, to answer a question which the practice of the
world had " long ago decided irrevocably." The " poor and
vulgar " might interest us by their situation, but never by
sentiments and language peculiar to their condition. It was
impossible to copy faithfully in serious composition the expressions
and sentiments of the poor and vulgar " not merely," Jeffrey
asserted, " because poverty makes men ridiculous "—but because
just taste and language fitted for its expression were rarely to
be met with among the uncultivated part of mankind. The
low-bred heroes and interesting rustics of poetry had " no sort
of affinity to the real vulgar of this world." In serious poetry
a man of this type had to lay aside grammatical errors and a
considerable part of his vocabulary, and had, moreover, to
speak in good verse and observe the graces of collocation.
" After all this," Jeffrey declared, " it may not be very easy
to say how we are to find him out to be a low man, or what
marks can remain of the ordinary language of conversation in
the inferior orders of society." [1] This last passage contains, it
will be observed, precisely the argument Coleridge was to use
fifteen years later in the seventeenth chapter of *Biographia
Literaria*.[2] " The sculptor," Jeffrey continued, " employs his
art in delineating the graces of Antinous or Apollo, and not in
the representation of those ordinary forms that belong to the
crowd of his admirers. When a chieftain perishes in battle,
his followers mourn more for him, than for thousands of their
equals that may have fallen around him." [3]

There may be perceived here, it seems to me, an effect of
the instruction of Jeffrey's eighteenth-century preceptors. In
this first review, if anywhere in his criticism, he might have
been expected to reflect their ideas. It does not follow, however,
that because an idea was characteristic of eighteenth-century

---

[1] *Ed. Rev.*, No. 1, pp. 66-7.   [2] 1876 ed. (Bohn), p. 168.
[3] *Ed. Rev.*, No. 1, p. 67.

teaching it is in consequence absurd. There is much in that passage that Jeffrey might have verified by his own observation. The suggestion that poetry concerns itself more with the world's chieftains than with its rankers was true to a considerable extent of the English poetry that existed before 1802. Other parts of Jeffrey's argument may have sprung from his firm refusal to sentimentalise. It may appear a hard saying that poverty makes men ridiculous. Jeffrey, we remember at the same time, when he wrote these words, was himself a very poor man. While he would certainly not have numbered himself among the " poor and vulgar " of whom he was speaking, it is possible that he had discovered from personal experience that a man's social position and the size of his bank account are not uncommonly regarded by the world as having a bearing upon the assessment of his dignity and the importance of his feelings and opinions. We can still see reflections of this idea in jokes in periodicals and certain stage-plays. As for his other statements, Jeffrey had only to walk through some of the streets of his native Edinburgh at a time, say, when the taverns were emptying, to hear emotions expressed freely around him in language that might reasonably be regarded as unsuitable for imitation in serious poetry.

It is plain, nevertheless, that much of this is inconsistent with what we have found in the later Jeffrey. I imagine that Jeffrey, had he been able to discuss the matter with us, might have remarked that the faultiness of his conclusions here sprang not so much from the inaccuracy of his observations as, to repeat a phrase we have observed him use, from their " narrowness and insufficiency." He had still much to learn both from life and from literature. The assertion that no one could read the works and history of Burns without forming a higher idea of the intelligence, taste, and accomplishments of the peasantry than those in the upper ranks of society were disposed to entertain, and the warm appreciation of Scott's and Crabbe's representations of poor people, came afterwards. The articles on Burns, Scott, and Crabbe were reprinted. This one on *Thalaba* was not. " Make him," Jeffrey wrote to Jane Welsh Carlyle about her husband in 1830 " . . . more indulgent to ordinary people. If God endures them, and cares for them, and has made them, such as they are, he has no right either to despise or to draw back from them. It is all sheer vanity and presumption, and he should be chidden out of it." [1] Jeffrey was, I think, passing on a lesson he had learned himself.

This modification of his views did not, however, reconcile Jeffrey to Wordsworth. We may observe in this connection that Burns, Scott, and Crabbe, however sympathetically they delineated their humbler characters, portrayed these characters from the standpoint of the highest culture that they knew. They did not, as it seemed to Jeffrey that Wordsworth in his linguistic experiments was trying to do, throw away humanity's whole cultural heritage.

Another standard which it seemed to Jeffrey in 1802 that the Lakers were abandoning was that of restraint. Their works, he said, were characterized by "perpetual exaggeration of thought." "There must," he declared, " be nothing moderate, natural, or easy, about their sentiments. There must be a ' qu'il mourut,' and a ' let there be light,' in every line ; and all their characters must be in agonies and ecstasies, from their entrance to their exit." It would be untrue to say that they never succeeded in their attempts at elevation ; but their failures were far more numerous than their successes. After having been promised a sublime allusion the reader had often to be content with a miserable substitute. "Of the many con- trivances they employ," Jeffrey wrote, " to give the appearance of uncommon force and animation to a very ordinary conception, the most usual is, to wrap it up in a veil of mysterious and unintelligible language, which flows past with so much solemnity, that it is difficult to believe it conveys nothing of any value." Other methods were to embody cold ideas in unusually harsh verses, to use portentous compound words, and to versify lines of scripture.[2]

Jeffrey turned next to what he called the " moral character " of the new school. Vaughan spoke of this portion of the review as containing " the true root of bitterness between the critic and his victims." [3] Harper described it as " the passage which

---

[1] *Carlyle to French Rev.*, Wilson, p. 153.

[2] *Ed. Rev.*, No. 1, pp. 69-70. Elsner remarked that the mention of " qu'il mourut " and " let there be light " in juxtaposition reminds one of Home's *Elements of Criticism* in which, within three pages, Home quoted the " Qu'il mourut " of Corneille as an example of a sentiment of indignation, and referred to Longinus's quotation of " Let there be light " as an example of the sublime. Elsner, p. 46 ; *Elements of Criticism*, 1774 ed., v. 1, pp. 240, 242.

[3] *Eng. Lit. Crit.*, p. lxxii.

indicates Jeffrey's real animus—which, moreover, he takes no pains to conceal." [1] Both writers have, I think, drawn attention to an important passage.

" A splenetic and idle discontent with the existing institutions of society," Jeffrey wrote, " seems to be at the bottom of all their serious and peculiar sentiments. Instead of contemplating the wonders and the pleasures which civilization has created for mankind, they are perpetually brooding over the disorders by which its progress has been attended. They are filled with horror and compassion at the sight of poor men spending their blood in the quarrels of princes, and brutifying their sublime capabilities in the drudgery of unremitting labour. For all sorts of vice and profligacy in the lower orders of society, they have the same virtuous horror, and the same tender compassion. While the existence of these offences overpowers them with grief and confusion, they never permit themselves to feel the smallest indignation or dislike towards the offenders." [2] " Except," Harper commented, " for the gratuitous term ' splenetic and idle,' could the most enthusiastic eulogist have penned loftier praise ? Could a clearer title to the name of Christian patriot have been bestowed upon the two poets ? But Jeffrey thought he was condemning." [3] " The Edinburgh," Vaughan commented, " takes up the work of the Anti-Jacobin ; with no very good grace Jeffrey affects to sit in the seat of Canning and of Frere." [4]

" The present vicious constitution of society," Jeffrey continued, " alone is responsible for all these enormities : the poor sinners are but the helpless victims or instruments of its disorders, and could not possibly have avoided the errors into which they have been betrayed. Though they can bear with crimes, therefore, they cannot reconcile themselves to punishments ; and have an unconquerable antipathy to prisons, gibbets, and houses of correction, as engines of oppression, and instruments of atrocious injustice. While the plea of moral necessity is thus artfully brought forward to convert all the excesses of the poor into innocent misfortunes, no sort of indulgence is shown to the offences of the powerful and rich. Their oppressions, and seductions, and debaucheries, are the theme of many an angry verse ; and the indignation and

[1] *Wordsworth*, v. 2, p. 137.
[2] *Ed. Rev.*, No. 1, p. 71.
[3] *Wordsworth*, v. 2, p. 138.
[4] *Eng. Lit. Crit.*, pp. lxxii-lxxiii.

abhorrence of the reader is relentlessly conjured up against those perturbators of society, and scourges of mankind." [1]

" It is worth while," Harper commented, " to remind ourselves that in 1802 poor men were still liable to be savagely punished for poaching and other venial offences, and that embezzlement, bribery, and the purchase of promotion, were practised with comparative immunity by the powerful and rich." [2]

By one looking from the Jeffrey-angle some additional points may be discerned. When Jeffrey wrote this passage he was himself, we have just recalled, very far from rich. It was just the year before that he had told his brother he was not making £100 a year by his profession. He had written five articles in addition to this one for the first number of the *Edinburgh*. The copy he had furnished occupied between eighty and ninety pages. As it was all reviewing, it had involved a considerable amount of preliminary study. This indicates how small a portion of his time was being taken up by legal business. For all this literary work he was receiving no remuneration whatever. He had, as we have seen, little expectation that the *Review* would succeed. His poverty was due in part to his political principles. Inferior Tory rivals were, we remember, " flaming over his head like rockets." He was hazarding for these principles his whole professional future. He recalled years later, when he was Lord Advocate, in a letter to his niece, his father's " sad predictions " of the " ruin " he was bringing on his prospects by his Whig politics, and of the " bitter repentance " he would one day feel for not having followed his parent's " Tory directions." [3] And he had now a wife to keep, and the rent of a flat to pay, and only his own exertions to depend upon.

Wordsworth was not, in 1802, very rich either. On the whole, however, the then existing organisation of society had been kinder to him than it had been to his critic. It had provided the income of the brothers Calvert, men of " considerable independent means," one of whom had been paying the expenses of a holiday for him about the time he was condemning that organisation in lines then being composed for *Guilt and Sorrow*. It had provided for him Raisley Calvert's legacy, which had

[1] *Ed. Rev.*, No. 1, p. 71.   [2] *Wordsworth*, v. 2, p. 138.
[3] *Life*, Cockburn, v. 1, p. 307.

" released him from the fear of want." It had provided the
nine per cent. of interest which that legacy had been able to
gain for him, thus giving him all the leisure he required for the
free development of his genius.[1] It begins to appear odd, as
one considers these facts, that it was Jeffrey who, in 1802, was
defending the existing state of society, and Wordsworth who
was attacking it.

Harper seems to be implying that while Wordsworth's soul
was stirred to its depths by the injustices that were then to be
found in society Jeffrey was callously unmoved by them. Jeffrey,
I imagine, might have suggested that there was being maintained
here the Lakish tradition of countering disagreement with one's
opinions by " wondering what a heart " the opponent must
have. Jeffrey's joining, at considerable personal sacrifice, the
party of the opposition indicates plainly, however, that he was
not indifferent to these evils. But we are reminded at this
point also of Jeffrey's insistence that it is necessary, if one is to
maintain a sane view of the world, to look always steadily at
reality. We begin to perceive that he was asking Wordsworth,
as he was later to ask Cobbett, to look at all the facts, good as
well as bad. We have seen how intensely he hated war ; but
he asked here if all wars were as easily to be accounted for and
as plainly unjustifiable as Wordsworth was suggesting. He
asked if all felons, even among the poorest classes, were sinners
by necessity and never by choice ; if there was really no
justification for the infliction of punishment by law ; if there
was not dramatisation in the suggestion that most rich men
were scoundrels. There is, of course, an obvious case for the
exposure of wrong by great writers. This is evidently what
Harper considered that Wordsworth was trying to achieve.
But when one looks, in Jeffreyan fashion, squarely at the facts,
may one not discern danger here ? Is there not a possibility
that the practice of powerfully representing humanity's miseries
and dwelling with emotional appreciation upon such representations may degenerate into a sort of sentimental self-indulgence,
like that of the countess in the Russian story who wept in her
carriage over an account of the sufferings of the poor while her
coachman froze to death on the box ?[2] Jeffrey may have had

[1] *Wordsworth*, Harper, v. 1, pp. 248, 201-6, 249, 274.
[2] *A Book of Verse*, ed. J. C. Smith, Pref. to Part III. Dr Smith states that
it is in Tourguenieff.

some such thought in mind when he used the phrase " voluptuous virtue." Is there not a possibility that one may acquire a sentimental illusion that because one sorrows violently over such matters one becomes, on this account alone, superior morally to one's fellows ? A pose of moral superiority was, we recollect, one of Jeffrey's charges against the Lakers.

Jeffrey was sceptical, we remember too, of the value of simply telling the world that certain things were wrong. He preferred, it is evident, to see individuals doing what they could in their own particular environments in order to bring about specific and attainable improvements. His refusal to follow his father's prudent instructions was, it might be said, such a step. A few years later Jeffrey had to choose between modifying his literary principles—and he and his associates to choose between modifying their political principles—and risking losing the friendship and certainly losing the assistance of Scott. We know the choice that was made. We have seen that as Jeffrey's experience of life grew and his observation widened he became steadily more sympathetic to the less privileged classes. We have noticed Sydney Smith's account of the reforms that the *Edinburgh* supported. Among the good things in the state to which Jeffrey drew Cobbett's attention were " freedom of speech and of publication." [1] His *Review* advocated strongly the education of the poor.[2] We have observed the warmth with which he praised the work of Mrs Fry in the amelioration of prison conditions. He introduced in the House of Commons, after he had resigned his editorship, the Scottish section of the Reform Bill.[3]

What, it seems fair to ask, is there corresponding to these fruits of Jeffrey's dissatisfaction with the existing state of society in the career of Wordsworth ? It would, I think, be difficult to show that Wordsworth was making any serious personal sacrifice for his beliefs when he wrote the *Lyrical Ballads*. For the remainder of his career we may, in order to avoid bias, use the words of Harper, selecting from him passages embodying facts as closely parallel as may be to those just enumerated. " No man," Harper wrote, " . . . can resist altogether the influence of respected friends. The conservatism of Walter

---

[1] *Ed. Rev.*, No. 20, p. 406.
[2] *Ibid.*, No. 21, Art. 4 ; No. 33, Art. 3 ; No. 37, Art. 1 ; No. 41, Art. 9.
[3] *Life*, Cockburn, v. 1, p. 320.

Scott was so clearly a legitimate and indispensable part of his large and attractive personality that Wordsworth, in becoming more intimate with him, was almost forced to admire his political principles. Sir George and Lady Beaumont were ornaments of their class, and in every way worthy of Wordsworth's affection. It is no wonder if association with them modified his views on the whole subject of class distinctions." [1] That suggests that Wordsworth's observation of the rich had been imperfect in 1798. " His sympathies," Harper wrote, " became less general. His admiration went out more and more to the privileged classes, to persons of distinction, to notable events in history. The poor and humble still figured in his poetry, but in smaller proportion, in a less true proportion, considering the part they play in life. . . . He opposed the abolition of the Test and Corporation Acts. . . . While professing to believe that freedom of the Press was the only safeguard of liberty, he declared that he was *therefore* in favour of vigorous restrictions. . . . He desired that a medical education should be kept beyond the reach of a poor student. . . . The fear of what might happen to the Church and to the prosperity of the wealthy classes if the people gained knowledge afflicted him, and he declared that ' Mechanics ' Institutes make discontented spirits and insubordinate and presumptuous workmen. . . . To the number of those to whom England owes the great advance in religious toleration and political freedom, and especially the precious though limited progress towards lifting the lower half of her population above barbarity and hunger . . . we cannot add the name of Wordsworth, or rather of that later Wordsworth who survived his better self. . . . He was haunted with visions of what might befall England should the Reform Bill pass. . . . His sonnets against the abolition of capital punishment were a clog upon a course of sound and greatly needed legislation." [2]

To Harper, we observe, there appeared to be two Wordsworths, the outlook of the second being a retrogression from that of the first—Wordsworth's " better self." But Jeffrey did not recognise this dual personality. To him there appeared to be a weakness in Wordsworth's thinking from the start. The discontent of the early Wordsworth which, in Harper's view, marked out the poet as a Christian patriot seemed to Jeffrey " splenetic and

[1] *Wordsworth*, v. 2, p. 130.
[2] *Ibid.*, v. 2, pp. 132, 325, 336, 377, 378, 423.

idle." By "splenetic" he meant, I imagine, based on emotion rather than on reason, and liable, accordingly, to vanish when the emotion, the movement in the spleen, disappeared. By "idle" he meant, I think, unlikely to produce any practical result. Is not this pretty much what happened? One may submit, therefore, that the two adjectives Harper dismissed as "gratuitous" are key-words in the indictment.

We recollect next Jeffrey's assertion to Carlyle that he had no higher mission in life than to be innocently happy. It has been suggested on an earlier page that the fact that his "prevailing state" throughout all the busy years of his life was one of "gaiety" indicates that Jeffrey tried to live up to his own philosophy. We recall his likening of the man who would mend a nation's ills to one who would cure a defect in the eye—that is, to a physician. It appeared as futile, I think, to Jeffrey for men to be "perpetually brooding" over the ills of society as it would be for a doctor to brood perpetually over an outbreak of typhoid. These words "perpetually brooding" seem to me to be also, therefore, key-words in the criticism.

Brooding was in Jeffrey's opinion worse than futile. Among the influences he regarded as having affected the Lakers was, we have observed, the "distempered sensibility" of Rousseau. The influence of Rousseau, we noted in an earlier chapter, appeared to him "unquestionably pernicious" in that it helped to cause a revolution. We have seen what he thought of revolution. To have it pointed out to him that his criticism of ways of thinking that might conceivably lead to revolution brought him into agreement in this respect with Canning, Frere, and the *Anti-Jacobin*, and to find it suggested that this agreement was somehow graceless on his part would, I imagine, have disconcerted him not at all.

II

It is evident that Jeffrey was so affected by the powerful personality of Wordsworth that even when reviewing a poem by Southey he could not refrain from discussing the work of Southey's fellow-Laker. At the same time his describing the two men as "Lakers" shows that they appeared to him to possess qualities in common.

He had found in *Thalaba*—I think it may be taken for granted that the longer narrative poems of Southey are not now very

widely known—a tale of an Arabian hero whose father and
seven others of whose family had been murdered by one of a
band of sorcerers dwelling in certain submarine caverns, the
reason for their deed being a prophecy that a member of this
family would destroy them ; whom one of the sorcerers attempted
to kill but was blasted by a simoom ; to whom a spirit conjured
up by a magic ring taken from the dead sorcerer's finger revealed
the identity of his father's slayer ; who was instructed by letters
marked upon a locust when to set out upon his mission of
vengeance ; who encountered, when on his journey, among other
creatures, two fallen angels, a maiden whose father made for
her companions out of snow, an enchanted image which was
the maiden's guardian, a sledge drawn by dogs which eventually
talked, and a car propelled by living wings ; and who, in the
end, destroyed caverns, sorcerers, and himself with them, but
was thereupon withdrawn to Paradise. The poem occupied
twelve books. We are now, I think, prepared for Jeffrey's
reaction. "Tales of this sort," he remarked, "may amuse
children, and interest, for a moment, by the prodigies they
exhibit . . . but the interest expires with the novelty. . . .
The pleasure afforded . . . is very much akin to that which
may be derived from the exhibition of a harlequin farce." He
perceived here, in other words, that juvenility of outlook which
seemed to him an essential Lakish characteristic. We note the
illustration from the theatre. "Those," he wrote, "who can
prefer this eternal sorcery to the just and modest representation
of human actions and passions, will probably take more delight
in walking among the holly griffins and yew sphinxes of the
city gardener, than in ranging among the groves and lawns
which have been laid out by a hand that feared to violate nature,
as much as it aspired to embellish her." [1] Once more the
charge of artificiality. There is similar criticism in his article
on the equally fantastic *Kehama*. Southey's taste in description
was "remarkably childish." His landscapes were "full of
coloured light, and gems, and metallic splendour," and reminded
his reviewer "of the old-fashioned grottos and shell-work of the
last generation, or the gilded caverns and full-lighted trans-
parencies of the opera-house." Again the illustration from the
theatre. The delineations of characters and emotions were
"marked with the same infantine character." All the poet's

[1] *Ed. Rev.*, No. 1, pp. 75-6.

interesting personages lisped " like sucklings," and his unamiable ones were monsters such as " nurses imagine to frighten naughty boys into obedience." There was little passion in his poetry beyond the affection of relatives and that sort of love which may be indulged by dutiful children under the inspection of their parents. This might be made sweet and interesting. Southey often made his readers feel how beautifully it might be represented. But the tone was too weak and too uniform. " Men," Jeffrey wrote, " are never brought forward to contend with men, in the management of great affairs ; or to display those social or lofty qualities by which they are enabled, in real life, to attach or to command their fellows." This might have been tolerable had the poet adopted the tone and addressed the audience suited to his subjects. But, Jeffrey asserted, he had " come with his whistle, and his gilded book of fairy tales, into the assemblies of bearded men, and audibly undervalued all other instruments and studies." [1] Jeffrey made it clear that he did not confine this criticism to Southey. Among " the most remarkable " of the Lakers' qualities he numbered, in the article on *Madoc*, " an affectation of infantine innocence and simplicity." [2]

He found in Southey also—we have just seen a hint of this— the characteristic Lakish " exaggeration of thought." The poet seemed anxious to present everything, great or small, under the most imposing aspect. If there was any room for a description it was sure to be thrust in and extended to a vast length, and if a striking sentiment or event was to be brought forward, so much care was taken to ensure it a favourable introduction as to give " rather a distressing impression " of the labour the author had bestowed on his composition, and of the value he attached to even the meanest of his ingredients. There was nothing so charming in poetry, Jeffrey asserted, as that appearance of ease which made the result perhaps of long study appear like the spontaneous effusion of an inspired mind, and raised the reader, " as it were, into the society of a higher order of beings." But the charm was destroyed the moment readers were allowed to peep behind the scenes and see the machinery by which the effect was produced. This, Jeffrey said, was well understood by the older writers : almost all their beauties seemed to have been produced by accident. " It is this miserable trick,"

[1] *Ed. Rev.*, No. 34, pp. 433-4.   [2] *Ibid.*, No. 13, p. 3.

Jeffrey wrote, " of overrating the importance of all our conceptions, that has made our recent literature so intolerably diffuse and voluminous." [1]

He found in Southey, too, the pseudo-simplicity of language he had found in Wordsworth ; and quoted from *Thalaba* in illustration.[2] In reviewing *Madoc*, he drew attention to what he called " this pretty good-night of a brother to a sister." The following is part of it :

> " Not yet at rest, my Sister ! quoth the Prince, . . .
> To bed, Goervyl ! Dearest, what hast thou
> To keep thee wakeful here, at this late hour, . . .
> . . . . Goodnight, Goervyl,
> Dear sister mine, . . . my own dear mother's child ! " [3]

The speaker was the twelfth-century " wild Welch chieftain " we have noticed Jeffrey select, in another article, as one of his illustrations of the incongruity in characterisation that seemed to him widespread in the literature of his time. Brothers did not, I imagine, commonly bid their sisters goodnight in that fashion in nineteenth-century Edinburgh.

Jeffrey's impatience with Southey made him sometimes distinctly unfair. Describing, for instance, in *Kehama*, a supernatural being called a " Glendoveer " Southey wrote :

> " Angelic power and dignity and grace
> Were in his glorious pennons ; . . .
> . . . . The permeating light
> Shed through their substance thin a varying hue ;
> . . . . now like the juice that flows
> From Douro's generous vine. . . .
> Through the broad membrane branched a pliant bone,
> Spreading like fibres from their parent stem,
> Its veins like interwoven silver shone . . .
> He furled his azure wings, which round him fold
> Graceful as robes of Grecian chief of old." [4]

In his synopsis of the poem Jeffrey changed the atmosphere considerably. " The wings of the Glendoveer," he wrote, " . . . were leathery, it seems, like the bat's, without feathers, very transparent, coloured like good port wine, divided into

---

[1] *Ed. Rev.*, No. 34, pp. 435-6.   [2] *Ibid.*, No. 1, pp. 68-9, 79.
[3] *Ibid.*, No. 13, pp. 15, 16 ; *Madoc*, Part II, Section III.
[4] Section VII, St. 5-8.

compartments by fibres of pliant bone of a silver hue, and folding up, when his flying was over, into the form of a very becoming drapery." [1] Of a miraculous car which carried the main characters into the Hindoo hell—called Padalon—Southey wrote that

> " Poised on a single wheel, it moved along,
>   Instinct with motion ; by what wondrous skill
>   Compact, no human tongue could tell." [2]

Jeffrey described the vehicle as " poised upon a single wheel like a wheelbarrow." [3]

Yet in spite of this criticism Jeffrey, like Macaulay afterwards, found much to admire in Southey's poetry. It would not be doing justice to the author's genius, he asserted in the first of his articles on Southey, if he did not add that *Thalaba* contained passages " of very singular beauty and force." [4] The " strange affectations " to be found in the Lakers' writings, he declared in the article on *Madoc*, if not unprecedented, were " never seen at least before in compositions of so much genius." [5] Southey's forte, he said later in the same review, was in the description of external nature : Southey had observed it with a poet's eye and had put into his description " so strong and so delicate an expression of associated emotions, as infallibly to awaken in the mind of his readers the sentiment with which the scene had affected his own." [6] Of a passage in *Kehama*, " The language," Jeffrey wrote, " (and this is no light praise) is like the finest parts of Mr Wordsworth's." [7] He considered *Roderick* the best of Southey's longer poems,[8] a not surprising choice considering the more human and credible character of the narrative. His review of *Roderick* was the only article on Southey that he reprinted. While he remarked that Southey was not a poet " of the highest order " and while he criticised the work in places, he accorded it at the same time high praise. He gave particular commendation—deservedly, as it seems to me—to the tenth section. " The meeting of Roderick and Florinda," he wrote, " was a touchstone for a poet who had ventured on

---

[1] *Ed. Rev.*, No. 34, pp. 442-3. [2] Section XXII, St. 14.
[3] *Ed. Rev.*, No. 34, p. 449. [4] *Ibid.*, No. 1, pp. 79-80.
[5] *Ibid.*, No, 13, p. 3. [6] *Ibid.*, p. 21. [7] *Ibid.*, No. 34, p. 458.
[8] *Cont.*, v. 2, pp. 404-5. Coleridge also considered *Roderick* the best of the longer poems of Southey (*Biog. Lit.*, p. 29).

such a subject ; and Mr Southey, we must say, has come out of the test, of standard weight and purity." [1] We have seen that he confessed in the *Contributions* that he had sometimes written petulantly of Southey. He was not conscious, he added nevertheless, that he had ever been unfair to Southey's poetry. If he had noted Southey's faults too arrogantly, he thought he had never failed to give cordial praise to Southey's beauties— " and generally dwelt much more largely on the latter than the former." The review of *Roderick* might be taken as conveying his " matured opinion " of Southey's merits, and would be felt, he trusted, to have done " no scanty or unwilling justice " to the writer's " great and peculiar powers." [2] Jeffrey closed his criticism, we observe, as he had begun it forty-one years earlier, by insisting that, whether or not Southey travelled on right roads, he was a poet with gifts.

[1] *Cont.*, v. 2, p. 420.   [2] *Ibid.*, v. 2, pp. 404-5.

N

CHAPTER XII

THE BATTLE CONTINUED

Appreciation of Lakers. The Lakish attitude. Attitude to Jeffrey of critics of Wordsworth. Review of Wordsworth's poems of 1807. Unnatural composition. Review of *The Excursion*. *The White Doe*. Refusal to retract. *Christabel*. Attitude to Coleridge and Shelley. Characteristics of early nineteenth-century poetry.

I

It is beginning to appear that Jeffrey's criticism of Wordsworth sprang, not from a complete inability to perceive the power there was in Wordsworth's writings, but, in part at any rate, from a recognition of that power. We saw that as early as 1802, long before admiration of Wordsworth had been made safely orthodox by the authority of a multitude of literary histories, at a time when all Wordsworth had published of importance was his share of *Lyrical Ballads*, Jeffrey explained that it was the amount of poetical talent apparent in the Lakers' works that had caused him to discuss these at such length. We saw that he remarked in 1805 that the Lakers' affectations were unprecedented in compositions " of so much genius," and that in 1811 he asserted that it was no light praise of a passage in Southey to say that its language resembled the best parts of Wordsworth's. He spoke in 1808, in the first of his articles on Crabbe, of the Lakers' " good intentions and extraordinary talents." [1] " Southey, and Wordsworth, and Coleridge, and Miss Baillie," he wrote in 1811, " have all of them copied the manner of our old poets ; and, along with this indication of good taste, have given great proofs of original genius." " We have said enough elsewhere," he remarked a little later in this article, " of the faults of those authors ; and shall only add, at present, that, notwithstanding all these faults, there is a fertility and a force, a warmth of feeling and an exaltation of imagination about them, which classes them, in our estimation, with a much higher order of poets than the followers of Dryden and Addison "
—yet another statement to be placed against the " chains of the

[1] *Cont.*, v. 2, p. 277.

eighteenth century " idea—" and justifies an anxiety for their fame, in all the admirers of Milton and Shakespeare." [1] We have only to imagine such a statement, made of contemporary work, appearing in a modern review to realise the greatness of that praise. " We have the greatest respect," he wrote in 1812, " for the genius of Mr Wordsworth." [2] " Undoubtedly," he wrote in 1816, " the finer passages of Wordsworth and Southey have in them wherewithal to lend an impulse to the utmost ambition of rival genius." [3] We observed in an earlier chapter that it appeared to a contributor to *Blackwood's* in 1817 that Jeffrey had given Wordsworth loftier commendation than had any other critic of the time.[4] In *Biographia Literaria*, published in 1817, Coleridge stated that he had heard Jeffrey—" the commander-in-chief of this unmanly warfare " he called him here—" make a boast of his private admiration of Wordsworth's genius. I have heard him declare," Coleridge wrote, " that whoever came into his room would probably find the *Lyrical Ballads* lying open on his table, and that (speaking exclusively of those written by Mr Wordsworth himself) he could nearly repeat the whole of them by heart." [5] Crabb Robinson recorded that Jeffrey told him in 1835 that he had always been an admirer of Wordsworth.[6] Haydon asked Jeffrey in 1846 to head a subscription list for Wordsworth. Jeffrey replied that he did not think he had any right to be at the head of the list. But he said he would go on it with pleasure, and added that he loved Wordsworth's genius more than he was afraid the poet believed.[7]

Robinson stated that, on the occasion just mentioned, he had been unable to repress the " unseemly remark " that Jeffrey had had a singular way of showing his admiration. Stephen accounted for Jeffrey's virulence towards the Lake poets very easily. It was explicable, he said, by the fact that " the *Edinburgh* wanted a butt." [8] Coleridge had, in *Biographia Literaria*, given a similar explanation. Reviews, Coleridge said, to be saleable, had to be " personal, sharp, and pointed." With their pens out of their hands critics were honourable men. To " write down " authors whose genius they admitted in private was " all in their vocation." [9]

---

[1] *Cont.*, v. 2, pp. 48-9. [2] *Ed. Rev.*, No. 38, p. 374. [3] *Cont.*, v. 2, p. 436.
[4] *Ante*, p. 27. [5] p. 236. [6] *Diary*, 1872 ed., v. 2, p. 158.
[7] *Life of Haydon*, 1853 ed., v. 3, p. 332. [8] *Hours in a Library*, v. 2, p. 258.
[9] p. 236.

It is interesting to compare the description in *Biographia Literaria* of the conversation in which Jeffrey spoke to Coleridge of his admiration for Wordsworth with the description Coleridge gave of the same conversation to Crabb Robinson seven years earlier. " Towards me, Coleridge added," ran part of Robinson's entry, " Jeffrey was even flattering. He was like a schoolboy, who, having tried his man and been thrashed, becomes contentedly a fag." [1] Jeffrey also described this interview, after encountering the reference to it in *Biographia Literaria*. He said that he had complimented Coleridge on that occasion " with perfect sincerity " ; but added that it had " rather appeared " to him " that Mr C. liked to receive compliments " [2]—which suggests that his critical faculties had not, even in Coleridge's presence, been in such complete abeyance as Coleridge imagined. Experienced barristers are not as a rule, one may fancy, so easily subdued. Nothing written about the Lakers by Jeffrey in the *Edinburgh* after 1810 suggests the thrashed and beaten schoolboy Coleridge described. Jeffrey, Robinson recorded that Coleridge told him also, had said that Wordsworth " had been attacked in the *Review* simply because the errors of men of genius ought to be exposed." [3] No doubt this statement seemed to Coleridge merely casual. By the time he came to write *Biographia Literaria* he had probably forgotten all about it. But we can now see that it was consistent with Jeffrey's whole way of thinking. The reason it furnishes for the criticism of Wordsworth is some distance from the purely mercenary motive Coleridge suggested.

We are reminded once more of Jeffrey's reference to the Lakish habit of dealing with those whose opinions differed from their own by animadverting upon the critic's character. We observe too, in this connection, that Coleridge spoke of Jeffrey's opposition to Wordsworth's ideas as " unmanly warfare." We are reminded of Jeffrey's observation also by certain passages in Wordsworth. " It is an awful truth," Wordsworth wrote for instance to Lady Beaumont in 1807, " that there neither is, nor can be, any genuine enjoyment of poetry among nineteen out of twenty of those persons who live, or wish to live, in the broad light of the world—among those who either are, or are striving to make themselves, people of consideration in society. This is a truth, and an awful one, because to be incapable of a feeling of poetry, in my sense of the word, is to be without love

[1] V. 1, p. 159.   [2] *Ed. Rev.*, No. 56, p. 510.   [3] *Diary*, v. 1, p. 159.

of human nature and reverence for God." [1] We recollect
Jeffrey's assertion that the Lakers thought it barely possible
for anyone to have a just notion of poetry, warmth of affection,
or large views as to the principles of happiness and virtue unless
he lived a life closely akin to that they had chosen for themselves.
It is plain from the context that the poetry Wordsworth had
particularly in mind was his own. " I hope," Wordsworth
wrote to Archdeacon Wrangham, speaking of *The White Doe*,
" it will be acceptable to the intelligent, for whom alone it is
written." [2] We observe the reflection ready in advance upon
the brain-power of any who should come short in appreciation. We read in the preface of 1815 of " the insults which the
ignorant, the incapable, and the presumptuous " had " heaped
upon " his writings.[3] In the *Essay Supplementary to the Preface*
we learn of " critics too petulant to be passive to a genuine poet,
and too feeble to grapple with him ; men, who take upon them
to report of the course which *he* holds whom they are utterly
unable to accompany." [4]   " Casually, and very rarely only,"
he wrote again, " do I see any periodical literature . . . but
I am not wholly unacquainted with the spirit in which my
most active and persevering adversaries have maintained their
hostility ; nor with the impudent falsehoods and base artifices
to which they have had recourse." [5]   Even Wordsworth's fellow
Lakers were not qualified to penetrate to the innermost shrine.
Crabb Robinson reported : " The approbation he has met
with from some superior persons compensates for the loss of
popularity, though no man has completely understood him,
not excepting Coleridge, who is not happy enough to enter into
his feelings. ' I am myself,' said Wordsworth, ' one of the
happiest of men ; and no man who does not partake of that
happiness, who lives a life of constant bustle, and whose felicity
depends on the opinions of others, can possibly comprehend the
best of my poems.' " [6]   It is not surprising after this to find
Jeffrey pushed out of all consideration, as a man too obtuse
for his ideas to be of any significance whatever. We noticed
in an earlier chapter Wordsworth's reference to the *Edinburgh*
editor's " incapacity," and his threat to deal with his reviewer

[1] *Memoirs of Wordsworth*, Ch. Wordsworth, v. 1, p. 332.
[2] *Ibid.*, v. 2, p. 57.   [3] *Poetical Works* (Oxford ed.), p. 957.
[4] *Ibid.*, p. 945.   [5] *Wordsworth*, Harper, v. 2, pp. 252-3.
[6] *Diary*, v. 1, p. 199.   Quoted by Harper, v. 2, p. 201.

by the intellectual argument of a kick in the " breech." In
his *Letter to James Gray* Wordsworth compared Jeffrey to
Buonaparte and Robespierre. " It is," he wrote, " a descent,
which I fear you will scarcely pardon, to compare these redoubt-
able enemies of mankind with the anonymous conductor of a
perishable publication. But the moving spirit is the same in
them all ; and, as far as difference of circumstances, and disparity
of powers, will allow, manifests itself in the same way ; by
professions of reverence for truth, and concern for duty—carried
to the giddiest heights of ostentation, while practice seems to
have no other reliance than on the omnipotence of falsehood." [1]
It is probable that Jeffrey was in Wordsworth's mind also when,
in a footnote to the *Essay Supplementary to the Preface*, he spoke
of Adam Smith as " the worst critic, David Hume not excepted,
that Scotland, a soil to which this sort of weed seems natural,
has produced." [2]

This tradition, I think it is fair to say, has lingered among
writers about Wordsworth. Harper, for instance, speaking of
those who mean by Wordsworth the " Daddy Wordsworth "
of Fitzgerald, a man absorbed in the contemplation of flowers
and animals, satisfied to put into verse the accepted philosophy
of his age, and incapable of affecting or being affected by the
political issues of his time, asserted : " To think thus of
Wordsworth is, of course, ignorant and presumptuous, but it is
common." [3] The first two adjectives, it will be observed from
one of the quotations in the preceding paragraph, are Wordsworthian ; the third suggests that a goodly proportion of us
require this castigation. The particular variety of intelligence
demanded by Wordsworth for comprehension of his *White Doe*
does not appear to be widespread : Harper remarked that this
poem has " rarely been understood." [4] " The great ' Intima-
tions ' ode," we read in Harper again, " is a stumbling-block
to prosaic and a temptation to over-speculative minds."
Wordsworth, we are told a sentence or so later, made, in
connection with this work, " an unnecessary and almost
humiliating concession to pragmatical and timid readers." [5]
Experts as well as ordinary men are liable to be caned in this
school. " There is certainly," Miss Edith Batho declared in

[1] *Prose Works*, ed. Grosart, 1876, v. 2, pp. 18-9.
[2] *Poetical Works* (Oxford ed.), p. 948.
[3] *Wordsworth*, v. 1, p. viii.   [4] *Ibid.*, v. 2, p. 153.   [5] *Ibid.*, v. 2, p. 121.

The Later Wordsworth (1933), "much that is wrong, because inaccurate or based on misunderstanding, in the popular and even the critical beliefs about Wordsworth." [1]

The complementary Lakish claim to "exclusive taste, judgment and morality"—this is implied, of course, in most of the above quotations—the idea that Wordsworth was not only a great writer, in the sense in which other men have been called great writers, but that he was a creature born and reared under such special auspices that he was scarcely to be numbered with the rest of humanity at all—may, I think, be equally readily illustrated. "I believe," Wordsworth wrote in the earlier version of *The Prelude*

> "That Nature, oftentimes, when she would frame
> A favor'd Being, from his earliest dawn
> Of infancy doth open up the clouds,
> As at the touch of lightning, seeking him
> With gentlest visitation . . .
> . . . and so she dealt with me." [2]

From his first dawn of childhood, he declared, the Wisdom and Spirit of the Universe intertwined for him the passions that build up the human soul—

> "Not with the mean and vulgar works of man,
> But with high objects, with enduring things." [3]

Even when he spoke, as he did upon occasion, of the value to be discovered in ordinary people, he did not fail to draw attention, simultaneously, to his own superior powers of insight. The roads, he remarked, were his schools, in which he read daily with delight the passions of mankind,

> "There saw into the depth of human souls,
> Souls that appear to have no depth at all
> To vulgar eyes."

We observe that in the later version "vulgar" was modified to "careless." [4] "Powers there are," he wrote in the *Address to Kilchurn Castle*

> "That touch each other to the quick in modes
> Which the gross world no sense hath to perceive,
> No soul to dream of." [5]

---

[1] p. 342.   [2] *Prelude* (Text of 1805), ed. Selincourt, 1933, p. 11.
[3] *Poetical Works*, p. 638.
[4] *Prelude*, ed. Selincourt, p. 222.   *Poetical Works*, p. 742.
[5] *Poetical Works*, p. 290.

That puts a goodly number of ordinary people in their places.
He declared in *The Prelude* that his lot was doubly fortunate in
that he first looked at mankind " through objects that were
great or fair "—" And thus," he continued,

> " Was founded a sure safeguard and defence
> Against the weight of meanness, selfish cares,
> Coarse manners, vulgar passions, that beat in
> On all sides from the ordinary world
> In which we traffic." [1]

Here, as before, we find Wordsworth's interpreters following
him. All who know *The Prelude* will recollect Wordsworth's
description, in the twelfth book, of the occasion when, a young
child, he became separated, when travelling among the
mountains, from a servant. He reached a spot where a murderer
had once been hung in gibbet irons. Fleeing from this place,
he reascended the bare common, and saw a naked pool beneath
the hills, Penrith Beacon on the summit, and, nearer him, a
girl with a pitcher on her head, forcing herself, her garments
streaming, with difficult steps against the wind. Words, he
said, could not describe the " visionary dreariness " that seemed
to him to invest the scene. " Visionary dreariness ! " Professor
Herford exclaimed in commenting on this truly vivid passage,
" The phrase suffices to assure us that the child *not yet six*, alone
in that wild and haunted place . . . already felt *the imaginative
awe as in the presence of infinity* which solitude and solitary things
habitually evoked in the man." [2]   (The italics are mine.)   " To
compare small things with great," wrote F. W. H. Myers,
" —or rather, to compare great things with things vastly greater
—the essential spirit of the *Lines near Tintern Abbey* was for
practical purposes as new to mankind as the essential spirit
of the *Sermon on the Mount.*" [3]   " Wordsworth's theory," a
nineteenth-century American critic asserted, of the connection
between the soul of man and the soul indwelling in visible
Nature " was almost as much a discovery in the realm of poetry
as Newton's demonstration of the law of gravitation was a
discovery in the realm of science." [4]   Harper made claims for
Wordsworth that are, in their own way, nearly as great.

[1] *Poetical Works*, pp. 703-4.   [2] *Wordsworth*, p. 6.
[3] *Wordsworth*, Eng. Men of Letters, p. 131.
[4] *Recollections of Eminent Men*, E. P. Whipple, Boston, 1886, p. 306.

" Wordsworth's poetry," he stated, " . . . has been enjoyed by men to whom no other kind of imaginative writing appeals." " Lucy Gray," he wrote, " will perhaps be remembered when all other English poetry of the century has been forgotten." [1] " For him," Professor Bradley declared of Wordsworth, " the ideal was realised, and Utopia a country which he saw every day, and which, he thought, every man might see who did not strive, nor cry, nor rebel, but opened his heart in love and thankfulness to sweet influences as universal and perpetual as the air. The spirit of his poetry was also that of his life—a life full of strong but peaceful affections ; of a communion with nature in keen but calm and meditative joy ; of perfect devotion to the mission with which he held himself charged ; and of a natural piety gradually assuming a more distinctively religious tone." [2] " He had, in fact," said Myers, " a reverence for human beings as such which enabled him to face even their frailties without alienation ; and there was something in his own happy exemption from such falls which touched him into regarding men less fortunate rather with pity than disdain." [3] " The Prelude," wrote Professor H. W. Garrod, " is, in fact, the history of a consciousness highly abnormal, and it is only in proportion as we realise this, that we can understand either Wordsworth himself or his poetry. . . . I mean that in fact Wordsworth saw things that other people do not see, and that he saw with quite unique clearness and frequency things which they see at most rarely and dimly. . . . We shall never understand poets unless we believe what they tell us. . . . The operations of genius are, in all examples of it, mysterious ; and it is possible that most of our mistakes about it proceed from our failure to realize the degree to which this (which we all admit in words) is true ; from a failure in us to assent effectively to the truism that inspired men belong to a different order from that of ordinary men." [4] It is obvious that in that last quotation we have reached the antithesis of Jeffreyanism.

By the time we have read all these statements " This will never do ! " begins to appear like profane swearing in church. And it may be that, as we so regard it, we begin to experience a subtle sense of satisfaction in the thought that we, at anyrate,

---

[1] *Wordsworth*, v. 1, p. 10 ; v. 2, p. 152.
[2] *Oxford Lectures on Poetry*, p. 107.   [3] *Wordsworth*, p. 150.
[4] *Wordsworth*, pp. 35, 95, 97-8, 136.

are not among the Jeffreys ; that we are not too petulant to be passive to a genuine poet ; that we are not to be numbered with the ignorant and the presumptuous who have been so rash as to criticise Wordsworth ; that our eyes are not those vulgar or careless ones that are blind to the depth of human souls ; that we are undoubtedly among the intelligent for whom *The White Doe* was written ; that whomever Wordsworth meant by the senseless and soulless " gross world " he certainly did not mean us. Perhaps that is how Wordsworthians are made.

It is plain that in the Jeffreyan position—in which are to be found only critics who claim to be no more than " experienced . . . readers whose business it is to pioneer for the lazier sort " —" exponents," Jeffrey called them in another place, " of the silent, practical judgment of the public " [1]—men regarding themselves as differentiated from their fellows only by particular training and perhaps, originally, by the possession of particular tastes, and believing that their judgments must be tested at the bar of general common sense—we are in much more ordinary company. We have recognised, too, that Jeffrey's attitude and methods have not won for him universal honour. " Jeffrey," Gates wrote, " pleads for common sense and the commonplace ; he is the type of what Lamb calls ' the Caledonian intellect ' " —another suggestion that his outlook was Scottish—" which rejects scornfully ideas that cannot be adequately expressed in good plain terms, and grasped ' by twelve men on a jury.' " [2] Carlyle who, as we observed, also noted that Jeffrey was always " essentially . . . as if speaking to a jury " added that " the thing of which he could not convince fifteen clear-headed men, was to him a no-thing, good only to be flung over the lists, and left lying without notice farther. This," Carlyle commented, " seemed to me a very sad result of law ! For ' the highest cannot be spoken of in words,' as Goethe truly says, as in fact all truly deep men say or know." [3] It must be recognised, besides, that whatever else may be said of the statements regarding Wordsworth that have been quoted, they constitute, coming from the sources that they do, indubitable testimony, if this were necessary, to the poet's possession of enormous literary strength. The court whose decisions Jeffrey held were final has, in this respect, passed an unequivocal verdict.

We remember, however, that in the Jeffreyan position we

[1] *Ed. Rev.*, No. 34, p. 429.　　[2] *Sel.*, p. xxi.　　[3] *Rem.*, v. 2, p. 41.

must be reasoners, not merely learners. If, as Jeffrey maintained, no two men have precisely the same personal limitations, every one of us should be able to see some things no other human being can see. According to Jeffrey's theory, we recollect also, it is by the accumulation of morsels of individual experience that common sense grows, and keeps on growing. It follows that when, in any society, this process is checked, something of value is lost. A scrutiny of the encyclopedical assertions that have been quoted may awaken questionings. Why should Gates, it may be asked for example, have identified the Jeffreyan common sense, product, in Jeffrey's view, of thousands of centuries of human evolution, with the commonplace? " Commonplace " is a word employed in everyday speech : common sense is immediately aware of the criticism implied by the use of it. That surely indicates that the two are not identical. Why should those of us who are ordinary citizens of the type of which juries are generally composed be expected to agree tamely and at once with the assumption that only ideas of a limited nature expressible in " plain terms " must be considered to be comprehensible by people of our sort ? The law of our country relies upon juries for its maintenance, and entrusts to juries decisions, sometimes involving life and death, that it is reluctant to place in the hands of any individual, however eminent. Many ordinary people have discovered, I imagine, not from Goethe or Carlyle but from life itself, that there are experiences that cannot be expressed completely in words. But common sense might suggest that when we have passed into the region in which verbal expression is impotent we have passed out of that of authorship altogether. It is not easy to see how one distinguishes between Carlyle's " truly deep men " and the " clear-headed men " to desire to convince whom stamps an author or speaker apparently as inferior. One begins to wonder if the " truly deep " are simply those who agree with Carlyle. Common sense tells us not to expect to be convinced always by syllogisms. Conviction may be sometimes emotional. But common sense may suggest that the proper purpose of authorship is to convince clear-headed men somehow—not merely to bully them. We recollect Jeffrey's description of Carlyle's attitude to " ordinary people "—as one of " sheer vanity and presumption."

What evidence is there in common experience, we may ask

next, moving backward a space, for Wordsworth's "awful truth" that it is almost impossible for genuine enjoyment of poetry to exist among people living in the broad light of the world or striving to make themselves persons of consideration in society? Wordsworth amplified his statement by speaking of routs, dinners, visits, discussions about politics and so forth. It is obvious that people who permit themselves to become too much absorbed in such matters must shut out of their lives much that is of value besides poetry. But surely large numbers of sensible men and women have shown themselves able to keep these activities in their places and to find time for appreciation of the arts. So far as the wider proposition is concerned, may it not be said that everyone who has published a book on poetry, or written an article on poetry, or delivered a lecture on poetry, or even sat an examination on poetry—including the poetry of Wordsworth—has been striving to make himself, in his own way, a person of consideration in society? Such people are not generally regarded as debarred from enjoyment of the poets. Why did Wordsworth send to his printers those enormous masses of verse? Surely it was in part in order to push himself into the broad light of the world and to make himself a person of consideration in society. Is a feeling for poetry, in sober reality, a sufficient touchstone of a man's love of his fellows and of reverence for the Almighty? Common sense might, I think, suggest tests of these things that are both more practical and considerably more exacting. Jeffrey, we have seen, certainly did not agree with Wordsworth in this respect. "She overrates the importance of literature," he asserted of De Staël, "either in determining the character or affecting the happiness of mankind." [1] We have to remember, when judging that statement, that it was made by a man a large part of whose own reputation was bound up with literature. Might it not be said that Wordsworth was influenced here by personal associations —by the fact that he was a poet? Are these among the statements we are expected to believe simply because Wordsworth made them? If not, how do we discriminate? [2] Wordsworth's assertion that no one had completely understood him may not appear to every juryman one of the wisest coming from a man

[1] *Cont.*, v. 1, p. 566.
[2] Garrod did not hold that everything Wordsworth said was to be accepted as absolute truth. See his *Wordsworth* passim.

the first purpose of whose craft was to transfer ideas from his
own mind to those of others. The writers who have stated
that *The White Doe* has rarely been understood, and that there
is much still even in the twentieth-century critical beliefs about
Wordsworth that is based on misunderstanding, may not appear
to everyone to be paying the greatest of compliments to an
author whose works have been so widely and so minutely studied.
Was Wordsworth's disparagement of those whose felicity depends
on the opinion of others entirely consistent with his outbursts
of fury against any who presumed to criticise him? What
evidence is there, apart from his own assertion, that Wordsworth
was one of the happiest of men? We grant at once that he
enjoyed the intense delights of a great artist. But is it clear
that he was free to a greater extent than others have been from
the artist's pains? "He was," Harper affirmed, "subject to
great physical and mental depression; composition exhausted
him; the physical act of writing made him ill; if left long to
himself, he doubted his own powers." On his return from
Germany—"He betrayed," Harper wrote, "undue concern
about the success of *Lyrical Ballads*, amounting almost to
petulance." Harper noted that he was at that time "distressed
for want of money." [1] Alluding to a morning in October 1800,
spent by Wordsworth and Dorothy in making additions to the
Preface, "As was generally the case," Harper remarked,
"excessive labour made William very ill, and he went to bed." [2]
Thomas Wedgwood wrote to his brother Josiah in 1802:
"Coleridge is astonished at my pertinacious regularity and
abstemiousness; says if Wordsworth had a quarter as much
control over himself he would be in perfect health instead
of great hypochondriacism." [3] Harper, commenting on
Wordsworth's reply in 1803 to Sir George Beaumont, who had
offered him a piece of land, stated, "The letter is a singular
exhibition of nervous hesitation, and makes one suspect that
Coleridge was, indeed, not far wrong in thinking his friend a
hypochondriac." [4] These statements may not, in the eyes of
all jurymen, bear out Wordsworth's description of himself as a

[1] *Wordsworth*, v. 1, p. 390.
[2] *Ibid.*, v. 1, p. 410. Cf. *Journals of Dorothy Wordsworth*, ed. Knight, 1934,
pp. 9, 13, 52, 54, 56, 58, 60, 73, 82, 83, 85, 86, 88, 103, 110, 119, 122, 124
130.
[3] *Wordsworth*, Harper, v. 2, p. 43.   [4] *Ibid.*, v. 2, pp. 69-70.

man possessing a sure safeguard and defence against the cares
that beat in from the ordinary world, or Bradley's picture of
him as one who saw Utopia every day, or Myers's reference to
that exemption from human frailties which entitled him to
look with pity upon less favoured fellow-mortals. The passage
in which Wordsworth spoke of his passions being entwined,
from his earliest days, not with man's " mean and vulgar works "
but with high objects and enduring things followed immediately,
in *The Prelude*, the description of his youthful adventure with
the shepherd's boat " by the shores of Patterdale." [1] The
experience was possibly associated in his mind, therefore, with
such thoughts. Common sense may not think it too obvious
to point out that, even at the moment when those ideas were
being inspired in him, Wordsworth was considerably indebted
to one of man's " mean and vulgar works," the boat, work of
some ordinary craftsman, without which it would have been
impossible for him to have had his adventure at all—and to
the shoes then protecting his feet, and to the clothes that weather-
fended his body, and to the food that ordinary people prepared
for him, without all of which he might have found finely-
associated passions a scanty defence against the winds and rains
beating down from those " high " and " enduring things " the
mountains. Common sense might suggest that Herford's
description of Wordsworth's mental processes at a time when
he was " not yet six " might be tested, not in a university
lecture-hall, but in an infant-room, in which youngsters are
learning their first lessons—or in the presence of a child of five
playing on one's hearth-rug. Is it easy for an ordinary man
to believe that any process going on inside those infant heads
—or even inside the head of an infant Wordsworth—is properly
describable by a phrase like " imaginative awe as in the
presence of infinity " ? Does the fact that, when a grown man,
Wordsworth, in re-creating the incident, used the words
" visionary dreariness," really tell us much about the kind of
mind that was his when he was five ? What evidence is there
for the statement that the essential spirit of *Tintern Abbey*, great
poem though that is universally judged to be, is comparable
for a moment with the essential spirit of the Sermon on the
Mount ? There are still scattered over the face of the world,
after nineteen centuries, countless testimonies in stone and lime

[1] *Poetical Works*, p. 637 ; *Prelude*, Selincourt, p. 11.

to the force of that Sermon's inspiration. Countless multitudes have, during these centuries, lived lives of sacrifice, and many have laid down their lives for the principles enunciated in that Sermon, or for what they have conceived to be those principles. How many people have been stirred to comparable action by the principles enunciated in *Tintern Abbey*? How many of us have met a single person who enjoyed Wordsworth's poetry and no other form of imaginative writing besides? How much evidence is there for the suggestion that *Lucy Gray* will outlast all the other English poetry of the nineteenth century?

We may notice at this point some sentences in a letter written by Jeffrey to John Wilson in 1816. " As to Wordsworth," he wrote, " I shall only say, that while I cannot at all agree, nor is it necessary, in your estimate of his poetical talents, I love and honour the feelings by which I think your judgment has been misled, and by which I most readily admit that your conduct should be governed. I assure you I am not the least hurt or offended at hearing his poetry extolled, or my remarks upon it arraigned as unjust or erroneous ; only I hope you will not set them down as sure proof of moral depravity, and utter want of all good affections. I should be sorry that any good man should think this of me as an individual ; as to the opinion that may be formed of my critical qualifications, it is impossible for anyone to be more indifferent than myself. I am conscious of being quite sincere in all the opinions I express, but I am the furthest in the world from thinking them infallible, or even having any considerable assurance of their appearing right to persons of good judgment." [1]

We observe once more the protest against the Lakish manner of reply, and the recognition of personal fallibility. We have there, I think, the Jeffreyan attitude at its best.

It may be well to note also, before we proceed farther on the ground we are now treading, that among those incidental tributes to Jeffrey's acuteness which we have seen to be not uncommon, some have come from men who have had in mind his dealings even with Wordsworth. " Jeffrey too," Stephen conceded for instance in a private letter, " said a true thing or two even about Wordsworth. Want of clearness *is* a fault in poetry as in everything else." [2] The author of the article on

---

[1] *Memoir of Wilson*, pp. 150-1.
[2] *Life and Letters of Leslie Stephen*, Maitland, p. 314.

Wordsworth in the eleventh edition of the *Encyclopædia Britannica*, remarking that " This will never do ! " has become " a byword of critical cocksureness," added, " But *The Excursion* has not ' done,' and even Wordsworthians who laugh at Jeffrey are in the habit of repeating the substance of his criticism."   Mr Herbert Read in his *Wordsworth* (1930) affirmed that " Jeffrey was an intelligent critic, though rather a priggish one." [1] (One may wonder if the second adjective came from a recollection of Saintsbury's essay.)   " Jeffrey," Harper asserted, " had a high appreciation of good literature, ancient and modern, a high sense of the importance of poetry, and a sincere desire to protect the public from false teaching. . . . To suppose that his adverse opinion of Wordsworth's poetry was determined solely, or even chiefly, by the fact that he had a strong taste for the ' classics,' or, in other words, that he was so hampered by literary prejudices as to be unable to accept a novel artistic doctrine, is to do injustice to his intellectual alertness." [2] " Jeffrey's famous article on *The Excursion*," Harper wrote also, " . . . . is by no means a criticism to be lightly set aside.   He had the instinct of a good football player, who always knows who is running with the ball." [3]

II

Jeffrey wrote four articles specifically on works by Wordsworth —the first, in 1807, on the *Poems* in two volumes ; the second, in 1814, on *The Excursion* ; the third, in 1815, on *The White Doe* ; and the fourth, in 1822, on the *Tour on the Continent.*[4] We have seen that he made frequent reference also to Wordsworth and to the Lakers in general when he was dealing with other writers.   We may take into consideration here a longish digression on Wordsworth that appeared in his article of 1808 on Crabbe.

The review of 1807 began with another of Jeffrey's recognitions of Wordsworth's ability.   The *Lyrical Ballads*, he remarked, had been " unquestionably popular " ; and, he had " no hesitation in saying, deservedly popular."   Despite " occasional vulgarity, affectation, and silliness," they were " undoubtedly characterised by a strong spirit of originality, of pathos, and natural feeling."

---

[1] p. 229.   [2] *Wordsworth*, v. 2, p. 135.   [3] *Ibid.*, v. 2, p. 240.
[4] *Ed. Rev.*, No. 21, Art. 14 ; *Ed. Rev.*, No. 47, Art. 1, *Cont*, v. 2, p. 504 ; *Ed. Rev.*, No. 50, Art. 4, *Cont.* v. 2, p. 540 ; *Ed. Rev.*, No. 74, Art. 8.

They were, moreover, " recommended to all good minds by the clear impression which they bore of the amiable dispositions and virtuous principles of the author." Here followed what is now very familiar doctrine. By the help of their good qualities these poems had been able, Jeffrey said, " not only to recommend themselves to the indulgence of many judicious readers, but even to beget among a pretty numerous class of persons, a sort of admiration of the very defects by which they were attended." " Childishness, conceit, and affectation," Jeffrey continued, were not in themselves very attractive, though novelty might give them a temporary currency. He would have had " no fear," however, of their prevailing " to any dangerous extent " had they not been graced in this instance with " more seductive accompaniments." " It was precisely," Jeffrey stated, " because the perverseness and bad taste of this new school was combined with a great deal of genius and of laudable feeling, that we were afraid of their spreading and gaining ground among us, and that we entered into the discussion with a degree of zeal and animosity which some might think unreasonable towards authors, to whom so much merit has been conceded." This, it will be observed, is exactly the attitude we have attributed to him. There had been occasions on which he had wondered if " a sense of public duty " had not carried him too far in reprobation of errors that seemed to be atoned for by no common excellences. But on others the " disgusting absurdities " into which the Lakers led their " feebler admirers " had made him regret he had not shown " still more formidable and decided hostility." Thus influenced by contrary emotions he had opened the new volumes with, he said, " greater anxiety " than either Wordsworth or Wordsworth's admirers would probably give him credit for. The effect, however, had been to free him from all doubt as to the justice of his previous censures, and to bring the matter to a test which he could not help hoping might be convincing to the poet himself. " It belongs," he wrote, " to the public, and not to us, to decide upon their merit." We note the customary position. But he was so convinced of the inferiority of the volumes before him, and of the reason for it, that he was " willing for once to waive " his " right of appealing to posterity " —a phrase which brings ourselves, nevertheless, into these discussions—" and to take the judgment of the present generation of readers, and even of Mr Wordsworth's former admirers, as conclusive on this occasion." If these volumes turned out to be nearly as popular as the *Lyrical Ballads* had been, then, he said, he would admit that Wordsworth had come much nearer the truth in his judgment of what constituted the charm of poetry than he had himself imagined, and would institute a more serious and respectful inquiry into the poet's principles of composition than he had hitherto thought necessary. But if the work were generally rejected there was room to hope that the author would be " persuaded to abandon a plan of writing " which defrauded his " talents of their natural reward." [1]

From here he passed to another of his criticisms of Wordsworth's language, with the customary caveat that he had not in mind any hackneyed poetic vocabulary. " Whatever," he wrote, " might have been the original character of these unlucky phrases, they are now associated with nothing but ideas of schoolboy imbecility and vulgar affectation." From the pleasure arising from beauty of diction, he declared however, readers of Wordsworth were " in a great measure cut off." The new poets were, he maintained, " just as great borrowers as the old " ; the only difference between them was that the Lakers had borrowed from " a scantier *gradus ad Parnassum*," namely " vulgar ballads and plebeian nurseries." Wordsworth had insisted also upon linking his loftiest and most passionate conceptions with what seemed to Jeffrey utterly unworthy associations. This might be the effect of " affectation and conceit alone," or it might have arisen " in some measure, from the self-illusion of a mind of extraordinary sensibility, habituated to solitary meditation." Even geniuses ought, in other words, to keep themselves in the main stream of common sense. To such a mind the sight of a friend's spade, or a sparrow's nest, or a man gathering leeches might suggest a train of powerful impressions, but to most minds such associations would " always appear forced, strained, and unnatural." [2]

At this point in his review Jeffrey tucked up his sleeves, as it were, and commenced to swing his bludgeon. The ode *To the Daisy*—that beginning " In youth, from rock to rock I went "—was, he declared, " very flat, feeble, and affected ; and in a diction as artificial, and as much encumbered with heavy expletives, as the theme of an unpractised schoolboy." Quoting some lines from *The Redbreast chasing the Butterfly*—

[1] *Ed. Rev.*, No. 21, pp. 214-6.   [2] *Ibid.*, No. 21, pp. 217-8.

" This, it must be confessed," he commented, " is ' Silly Sooth'
in good earnest." The lines

> " Could Father Adam open his eyes,
>   And see this sight beneath the skies,
>   He'd wish to close them again "—

were " downright raving." The stanza in *The Small Celandine*—

> " Thou art not beyond the moon,
>   But a thing ' beneath our shoon ' ;
>   Let, as old Magellan did,
>   Others roam about the sea ;
>   Build who will a pyramid ;
>   Praise it is enough for me,
>   If there be but three or four
>   Who will love my little flower "

was a " piece of babyish absurdity." The *Character of the Happy
Warrior* made the bludgeon pause in air for a moment : these
were " more manly lines." *The Horn of Egremont Castle*, too,
" without being very good " was " very tolerable." In the
Ode to Duty, however, the " lofty vein " was " very unsuccessfully
attempted." The lines—

> " Thou dost preserve the stars from wrong ;
>   And the most ancient heavens through thee are fresh and strong "

appeared to Jeffrey " utterly without meaning ; at least," he
added, " we have no sort of conception in what sense *Duty* can
be said to keep the old skies *fresh*, and the stars from wrong."
Beggars was " a very paragon of silliness and affectation." " If,"
he exclaimed after quoting part of *Alice Fell*, " the printing of
such trash as this be not felt as an insult on the public taste,
we are afraid it cannot be insulted." After summarising
Resolution and Independence and quoting from part of it, " We
defy," Jeffrey burst out, " the bitterest enemy of Mr Wordsworth
to produce anything at all parallel to this from any collection
of English poetry, or even from the specimens of his friend
Mr Southey." The bludgeon-strokes became more rapid.
Rob Roy was " very dull " ; than the address *To the Sons of Burns*
" never was any thing . . . more miserable " ; *Yarrow Unvisited*
was " a very tedious, affected performance " ; *To the Cuckoo*
was " a rapturous mystical ode . . . in which the author,

striving after force and originality," produced " nothing but absurdity." After quoting, from *The Blind Highland Boy*, the couplet in which the child is described as pushing off from the shore in

" A Household Tub, like one of those
Which women use to wash their clothes."—

" This," the reviewer ejaculated, " it will be admitted, is carrying the matter as far as it will well go ; nor is there any thing,— down to the wiping of shoes, or the evisceration of chickens,— which may not be introduced in poetry, if this is tolerated." [1]

On the next page we find the bludgeon again momentarily out of action. Jeffrey had encountered " some really sweet and amiable verses on a French lady, separated from her own children, fondling the baby of a neighbouring cottager ; "—an expression, in other words, of ordinary human feelings. On the following page, however, we find Jeffrey confronted by *The Immortality Ode*. " This," ran his comment, " is, beyond all doubt, the most illegible and unintelligible part of the publication. We can pretend to give no analysis or explanation of it ;—our readers must make what they can of the following extracts." He quoted forty-six lines.

The demerits of Wordsworth's " system," the reviewer continued, could not be fairly appreciated till it was shown that the author of the bad verses that had been extracted could write good verses when he pleased, and that, in point of fact, he did always write good verses when he was led by accident to transgress the laws of the school he desired to establish " on the ruin of all existing authority." It did not require much labour to find a decided contrast to some of the passages that had been cited. He quoted extensively, in illustration, from the *Song at the Feast of Brougham Castle* in which, he said, Wordsworth's putting his poem into the mouth of an ancient minstrel had led him almost irresistibly to throw aside his " babyish incidents and fantastical sensibilities." Wordsworth's imitation of Milton had helped him also to escape from the trammels of his " system." The consequence was that his sonnets were as much superior to the greater part of his other poems as Milton's were to his. Jeffrey quoted in full three of them—" Once did she hold the gorgeous East," " Milton ! thou shouldst be living," and " I grieved for Buonaparté."

[1] *Ed. Rev.*, No. 21, pp. 218-25.

When he looked at these, Jeffrey asserted, and many still finer passages, it was impossible not to feel a mixture of indignation and compassion at the strange infatuation that had bound up the poet from the fair exercise of his talents. " Nor," he wrote, " can any thing give us a more melancholy view of the debasing effects of this miserable theory, than that it has given ordinary men a right to wonder at the folly and presumption of a man gifted like Mr Wordsworth." [1]

" If," Harper wrote of this article, " one had grown up with a certain moderate attachment to Wordsworth's poetry and a general feeling of respect for his name, a perusal of this review would probably convert the attachment into ardour and the respect into affection ; it is so unfair, so gross, so atrocious." A juryman of strong common sense might refuse to permit his affections to be thus swayed by what are, after all, irrelevant considerations. But few, I think, would be inclined to disagree with Harper's last three adjectives : not one of them seems to me to be exaggerated. " The means invoked," said Harper, " were altogether disproportionate to any purely æsthetic offence." Again I think most of us would agree.

" The only conceivable excuse for Jeffrey's onslaught," Harper wrote, " is that he sincerely regarded Wordsworth as a menace to society." [2] This idea appeared, I have no doubt, fantastic to Harper ; he merely mentioned, but did not discuss it. It may appear fantastic, at first glance, to many of the jury also. We observe, nevertheless, how completely it explains not only Jeffrey's simultaneous admiration of Wordsworth's talents and character, and hostility to the poet's methods, but also his very phrasing. Had not Wordsworth's " system " had " seductive accompaniments " his reviewer would have had " no fear." It was because the perversity of the new school was combined with much " genius and . . . laudable feeling " that he was " afraid " of its gaining ground. It was a " sense of public duty " that had inspired his attack. In the review of Burns, written two years later, he spoke of the Lake School as one " against which we have thought it our duty to neglect no opportunity of testifying." [3] We recall his description of the tactics he regarded as permissible in one desiring to discredit a political opponent ; there may be significance in the fact

---

[1] *Ed. Rev.*, No. 21, pp. 226-31.   [2] *Wordsworth*, v. 2, pp. 139-40.
[3] *Cont.*, v. 2, p. 175.

that he referred to the Lakers as a "party in the poetical commonwealth." [1] Time has shown, of course, the faultiness of the procedure. This is one of the articles that have, in the long run, the boomerang quality spoken of in an earlier chapter. Jeffrey did not reprint this review ; but Wordsworthians desirous of genuinely investigating his criticism were bound to seek it out, to find in it evidence for regarding that criticism as the truncheon-wielding business Vaughan described, and to be affected in the way spoken of by Harper. If, by continuing to recognise the public as the final arbiter, and by making emphatic acknowledgement of the greatness of Wordsworth's gifts, Jeffrey guarded himself against the charge of Lakishness, as he understood the term, he gave us an opportunity of commenting that, at anyrate, the tendency to indulge in abuse of those who see the world from angles different from one's own was a weakness that was not confined to the Lakers. We observe at the same time that we are criticising Jeffrey from his own standpoint. He forgot here his own teaching ; in the violence of protest he ceased to steer by the ancient observations by which he affirmed that, when the way ahead is obscure, men should always be guided. In a book which the common sense of many centuries has regarded as a storehouse of the kind of wisdom to which Jeffrey alluded—which was in Jeffrey's country thus regarded so decidedly that it was long spoken of there as " The Book "—there is a strong saying about the man who calls his brother a fool.

At the same time none of this, as has just been suggested, has any bearing on the problem that is now unfolding itself to us. The question whether or not there was something in Wordsworth's poetry that constituted a menace to society is not at all affected by the fact that, in 1807, Wordsworth was the victim of an ill-considered attack.

III

The article on Crabbe made it clear that Jeffrey found in Wordsworth what appeared to him the typical early nineteenth-century artificiality of character-delineation. We noticed his assertion that Crabbe had exhibited the common people of England pretty much as they were. " Mr Wordsworth and his associates," he wrote, contrasting these with Crabbe,

[1] *Ante*, p. 144.

" . . . introduce us to beings whose existence was not previously suspected by the acutest observers of nature ; and excite an interest for them . . . more by an eloquent and refined analysis of their own capricious feelings, than by any obvious or intelligible ground of sympathy in their situation." [1] Again we note the suggestion that the Lakers were less interested in their characters, including the poor, than they were in themselves. " Thus," Jeffrey continued, " instead of employing the plain vulgar character, which may be read by all the world, these writers make use of a sort of cypher, which can only be learned with pains and study ; and, dressing up all their persons in a kind of grotesque masquerade habit, they have given birth to a species of composition more fantastic and unnatural than a pastoral or an opera "—once more the illustration from the theatre. Into this " unnatural composition " the Lakers had introduced so much eloquence and beauty that they had persuaded some that their conception of character was just, and that all preceding writers had been in an error with regard to this element of poetry. Many people, finding it impossible to understand the new writers, had given up the attempt in despair. " Many, however," Jeffrey wrote, " did understand a part ; and, in their raised imaginations, fancied that they admired the whole : while others, who only guessed at a passage here and there, laboured, by their encomiums, to have it thought that there was nothing which passed their comprehension." [2] We note the suggestion that the Lakers appealed, in part, to intellectual snobbishness. In some of his poems, Jeffrey continued in illustration, Wordsworth had delineated a village schoolmaster. The portrait had, however, none of the features that marked such a character " in common apprehension." Wordsworth's schoolmaster was, instead, " a sort of half crazy, sentimental person, overrun with fine feelings, constitutional merriment, and a most humorous melancholy." Portraying, in *The Thorn*, a frail damsel, the poet had contrived " in more than three hundred " lines [3] to tell his readers nothing whatever of the unfortunate fair one except her name, and that she went to the top of a hill in a red cloak, and cried " O misery ! " All he related of a rustic child was the fact that the boy amused himself with shouting to owls and hearing them answer. To make

---

[1] *Cont.*, v. 2, p. 278.   [2] *Ed. Rev.*, No. 23, p. 134.
[3] 253 lines in 1798 version.

amends for this brevity the method of mimicry was accurately described, and for the sake of this one accomplishment, we were told, the author had frequently stood mute and gazed on the child's grave for half-an-hour together. The idea that inspired the piece " Strange fits of passion " appeared to Jeffrey fantastic. " We leave it," he wrote, " to any reader of common candour and discernment to say, whether these representations of character and sentiment are drawn from that eternal and universal standard of truth and nature, which every one is knowing enough to recognise, and no one great enough to depart from with impunity." We note the explicit statement in the latter part of that sentence. As an illustration of the " narrowness of the plan " upon which Wordsworth wrote, Jeffrey drew attention to the long note the poet had appended to *The Thorn* describing in detail the " annuitant captain " who was supposed to tell the story. Jeffrey doubted if Wordsworth had a single reader who had known a person " of this very peculiar description " or who could form any conjecture of the turn of thinking this combination of attributes would produce. He found nothing in the language of the poem he could imagine as characteristic of its supposed narrator. The style was simply Lakish.[1]

We observe Jeffrey's challenge. He appeals to our candour. He asks us not to hide behind a smoke-screen of vague " encomiums." The test he proposes is plain. If we have actually met a schoolmaster like Wordsworth's Matthew, or if Matthew appears to us a character whom we can readily imagine ourselves meeting in real life, if we have actually known a woman, suspected of murdering her illegitimate child, whose method of expressing her sense of her frailty was to sit regularly in all kinds of weather throughout a period of twenty years " high on a mountain's highest ridge " repeating the words " Oh woe is me ! Oh misery ! " or if we can conceive of this as a likely proceeding in the real world, if we can think in this way also of the action described in the closing portion of " There was a boy," if the language of the sea-captain in *The Thorn* rings completely true to us, then our verdict must go to Wordsworth. But if Matthew appears to us in any degree an artificial or operatic character, if Martha seated in her scarlet cloak beside the aged thorn on the hill-top and Wordsworth standing gazing for half-an-hour on end at the boy's grave

[1] *Cont.*, v. 2, pp. 278-81.

appear to us in any degree stagy or tableau figures, if the language of real sea-faring men appears to us to be different, as a rule, from that in which *The Thorn* is written, then, to whatever extent these ideas are ours, we are in agreement with Jeffrey. He made only the one demand of us—that we be prepared to depone on our honour as responsible citizens that we have been honestly convinced.

IV

The notorious " This will never do ! " with which the article on *The Excursion* opened was an expression of despair. Wordsworth's earlier poems, Jeffrey said, were intended to recommend his " system." This poem, he thought however, had to be recommended by the system, and could succeed only where the system had been established. The new work had " less boldness of originality " than had marked Wordsworth's previous productions. There were to be found in it imitations of Cowper and Milton, " engrafted on the natural drawl of the Lakers—and all diluted into harmony by that profuse and irrepressible wordiness which deluges all the blank verse of this school of poetry." It filled " four hundred and twenty good quarto pages, without note, vignette, or any sort of extraneous assistance." Yet it was described in its preface as only " *a part of the second part* of a *long* and laborious work "—the italics are Jeffrey's—which was to consist of three parts. Jeffrey had no means of judging what were Wordsworth's ideas of length. But he could not help suspecting that they would be alarming to most readers. Apparently the whole was to contain a history of the author's mind. These four hundred and twenty pages gave an account of a youthful ramble which occupied " precisely the period of three days ! [1] So that," Jeffrey remarked, " by the use of a very powerful *calculus*, some estimate may be formed of the probable extent of the entire biography."

Jurors able to declare, in the manner just spoken of, that having read, pondered over, and digested the nine books of *The Excursion* they have not felt it to be a line too long are, of course, in a position to condemn Jeffrey for asserting that

[1] Readers of the sort mentioned in the next paragraph will be in a position to state whether or not that " precisely " is precisely correct. See *Excursion*, I, 970 ; II, 85-6 ; IV, 1317-24 ; IX, 768-96.

the work would " never do " on this account. Harper testified here on Jeffrey's side. " On this subject," he remarked, " Jeffrey simply had the frankness to say what everybody must think." [1] " The famous sentence," Thompson wrote also, " which opens the review of Wordsworth's *The Excursion* . . . finds echo in many hearts which have suffered from that bleating masterpiece." [2] We shall see, at the same time, that Jeffrey's attitude to the poem was by no means one entirely of condemnation.

The case of Wordsworth, he continued in his opening passage, was " now manifestly hopeless." Wordsworth's earlier eccentricities had, he said, appeared to him to be merely the effect of certain " experiments on public taste . . . poetical paradoxes,—maintained experimentally, in order to display talent, and court notoriety." The poet had now, however, been engaged for twenty years on work of this kind ; there was, therefore, too much " capital . . . sunk in the concern " for it to be possible for him to abandon it. Jeffrey could not but feel that he was by this time " a sincere convert to his own system." Long habits of seclusion and an excessive ambition of originality could alone account for the disproportion that seemed to exist between Wordsworth's taste and his genius. The " collision of equal minds " appeared necessary, Jeffrey remarked, to correct the tendency to extravagance and puerility into which genius was apt, when unrestrained, to be betrayed by self-indulgence and self-admiration. Again the familiar doctrine.

" Moral and religious enthusiasm," Jeffrey declared also, " though undoubtedly poetical emotions, are at the same time but dangerous inspirers of poetry ; nothing being so apt to run into interminable dulness or mellifluous extravagance, without giving the unfortunate author the slightest intimation of his danger." Harper commented that Wordsworth, on coming to this sentence, would probably cease to trouble himself about what might follow.[3] Zeal for the efficacy of his preaching, Jeffrey said, the writer was inclined to mistake for inspiration ; the glowing phrases supplied by a subject of this sort gave an illusion of originality and impressiveness ; commonplace notions were sanctified by the sublime ends for which they were employed ; in the end the speaker entertained " no doubt "

---

[1] *Wordsworth*, v. 2, p. 241.   [2] *A Scottish Man of Feeling*, p. 351.
[3] *Wordsworth*, v. 2, p. 243.

that he was " the chosen organ of divine truth and persuasion." [1]
These remarks may not appear pointless to everyone.

Jeffrey's synopsis of the work was full of complaints of
cloudiness. "The Ninth [Book]," he wrote for instance,
". . . is chiefly occupied with a mystical discourse of the
Pedlar ; who maintains, that the whole universe is animated
by an active principle, the noblest seat of which is in the human
soul ; and moreover, that the final end of old age is to train and
enable us

> ' To hear the mighty stream of *Tendency*
> Uttering, for elevation of our thought,
> A clear sonorous voice, inaudible
> To the vast multitude whose doom it is
> To run the giddy round of vain delight '—

with other matters as luminous and emphatic."

We note the conception of the " multitude." Jurors must
decide whether or not they find these matters luminous.

A page later Jeffrey quoted from the fourth book another
of the passages he found irritatingly obscure :

> " But, by the storms *of circumstance* unshaken,
> And subject neither to eclipse nor wane,
> Duty exists ;—immutably survive,
> For our support, the measures and the forms,
> Which an abstract Intelligence supplies ;
> Whose kingdom is, where Time and Space are not :
> Of other converse, which mind, soul, and heart,
> Do, with united urgency, require,
> What more, that may not perish ? "

Again we may apply our test.

Sometimes, Jeffrey said, the " silliness " of the incidents was
" enhanced by a paltry attempt at effect and emphasis."
" ' List ! ' " he mentioned for instance, " cries the old Pedlar,
suddenly breaking off in the middle of one of his daintiest
ravings—

> ' List !—I heard
> From yon huge breast of rock, *a solemn bleat !*
> Sent forth as if it were the Mountain's voice !
> As if the visible Mountain made the cry !

[1] *Cont.*, v. 2, pp. 504-10.

Again ! '—The effect upon the soul was such
As he express'd ; for, from the Mountain's heart
The solemn bleat appear'd to come ! There was
No other—and the region all around
Stood silent, empty of all shape of life.
—*It was a Lamb*—left somewhere to itself ! "

We note that, in later versions of the work, the " solemn bleat "
was transformed to a " solemn voice." [1]

At the same time, as has been said, Jeffrey found much in
The Excursion to admire. As might have been expected, he
seized for praise upon the work's less abstract passages. Of the
story of Margaret in the first book he declared that those who
got over its wordiness and the triteness of its incidents would
not "fail to be struck with the author's knowledge of the
human heart," and the power the poet possessed " of stirring
up its deepest and gentlest sympathies." The account, in the
third book, of the Solitary's marriage and early happiness was
" written with great sweetness." The agony of mind into which
the Solitary was thrown after the loss of his wife and children
was " described with a powerful eloquence." There was
" something peculiarly grand and terrible " in the imagery of
the lines—

" By pain of heart, now check'd, and now impell'd,
The Intellectual Power, through words and things,
Went sounding on,—a dim and perilous way ! "

The story of Ellen in the sixth book was " told with great
sweetness, pathos, and indulgence." It was characteristic of
Jeffrey to notice Wordsworth's " lively and impressive appeal
on the injury done to the health, happiness, and morality of
the lower orders, by the unceasing and premature labours of
our crowded manufactories " ; as well as the poet's " very
animated exhortation to the more general diffusion of education

---

[1] *Cont.*, v. 2, pp. 515-23. Nichol Smith has remarked that a comparison
of the final form of *The Excursion* with Jeffrey's citations will show that the
poet did not ignore the critic (*Jeffrey's Lit. Crit.*, p. 121). The nature and
extent of Wordsworth's indebtedness to Jeffrey would, it seems to me however,
be difficult to establish. Wordsworth revised the whole of *The Excursion*,
as he did other poems, very freely. The " solemn bleats " in the above passage
were not changed to voices until 1845 (*Poetical Works of Wordsworth*, ed.
Knight, v. 5, p. 159).

among the lower orders," and his " glowing and eloquent
assertion of their capacity for all virtues and all enjoyments."
We notice a variation of opinion in Wordsworth here.   Besides
more extended passages of interest or beauty there were, Jeffrey
asserted, " scattered up and down the book, and in the midst
of its most repulsive portions, a very great number of single
lines and images, that sparkle like gems in the desert, and startle
us by an intimation of the great poetic powers that lie buried
in the rubbish that has been heaped around them."   He found
" morsels of . . . majestic beauty," as when Wordsworth,
" assuming the weightier diction of Cowper," wrote—

> " Earth is sick,
> And Heav'n is weary of the hollow words
> Which States and Kingdoms utter when they speak
> Of Truth and Justice."

When he looked at such things he felt half inclined, Jeffrey
said, to rescind his earlier severe sentence.   But when he took
into consideration the work as a whole he could not revoke it.
The perversion of Wordsworth's " great powers " was now far
more visible than their original dignity.   While he collected
the fragments it was impossible not to mourn over the ruins
from which he was condemned to pick them.   Anyone who
doubted Wordsworth's perversity should ask why the poet made
his chief character a pedlar.   Did Wordsworth really imagine
that his doctrines were likely to gain in authority " by being
put into the mouth of a person accustomed to higgle about
tape " ?   Was there a word put into the Wanderer's mouth
that was characteristic of a pedlar ?   A man who tried to sell
flannel and pocket-handkerchiefs in this lofty diction would,
Jeffrey maintained, scare away every customer.   Or he would
pass either for a madman or for a gentleman who had assumed
the character in a frolic.[1]

The article on *The White Doe* began with a sentence which
is second in notoriety only to " This will never do ! "   " This,
we think," Jeffrey wrote, " has the merit of being the very
worst poem we ever saw imprinted in a quarto volume." [2]
The review re-emphasised Wordsworth's perversity, which was
demonstrated this time, in Jeffrey's opinion, by the poet's
concentration of interest upon the doe instead of on the human

[1] *Cont.*, v. 2, pp. 513, 527-39.   [2] *Ibid.*, v. 2, p. 540.

characters and situations. Thompson commented on that opening sentence that he was not " inclined to dispute the judgement." " The captious," he added, " should note the critic's qualification." [1] The review contains, at the same time, as its opening suggests, a considerable amount of renewed bludgeon-work. It may be felt that Jeffrey deserves a knock in return. It may appear to some that this may be administered to some extent by extracting two sentences from his article of 1822 on *The Tour on the Continent*. " The Lake School of Poetry, we think," Jeffrey wrote in that review, " is now pretty nearly extinct. Coleridge, who had by far the most original genius among its founders, has long ceased to labour for the fraternity, and gave their reputation a most unkind cut at parting, by the publication of his *Christabell*,—which they had all been lauding, while it remained unprinted, as the crowning glory of their sect." [2]

We noted earlier that Jeffrey confessed in a footnote in the *Contributions* that he had often spoken too bitterly and confidently of Wordsworth's faults. If, he went on, he were to deal with Wordsworth now, while his judgment might not be " substantially different," he hoped he would " repress the greater part of these *vivacités* of expression : And indeed," he continued, " so strong has been my feeling in this way, that, considering how much I have always loved many of the attributes of his Genius " —he acknowledged Wordsworth's gifts, we observe, from first to last—" and how entirely I respect his Character, it did at first occur to me whether it was quite fitting that, in my old age and his, I should include in this publication any of those critiques which may have formerly given pain or offence, to him or his admirers." He felt, however, that to omit all notice of these might be regarded as a " retraction " which he was " as far as possible from intending." He had, accordingly, reprinted his article on *The Excursion*, in which he believed he had pointed out, " not penuriously or grudgingly," beauties in Wordsworth as well as faults. But, as an example of his censures, he had reprinted also the review of *The White Doe*. He had done this to bring

[1] *A Scottish Man of Feeling*, p. 351. Cf. Wordsworth's remark to Sir Humphry Davy, quoted by Moore (*Memoirs*, v. 3, p. 163) : " Do you know the reason why I published the *White Doe* in quarto ? . . . To show the world my own opinion of it."

[2] *Ed. Rev.*, No. 74, pp. 449-50.

matters "fairly to issue." Between himself and people—he
had been told there were such—who not only admired *The
White Doe, Peter Bell, The Thorn*, and the *Sonnets upon the Punishment of Death*, but regarded these as Wordsworth's " best and
most characteristic productions," there could be " no . . .
ambiguity, or means of reconcilement."

" It was not till the middle of the century and the time of
Matthew Arnold," it has been asserted in a modern history of
literature, " that literary criticism caught up the Romantic
Movement. . . . It must, however, be said in Jeffrey's favour
that he learned enough to admit his errors when, at a later date,
he published a selection of his critical articles." [1] The compliment in that second sentence, we perceive however, if it can be
called a compliment, was undeserved. While Jeffrey expressed
regret for the way in which his criticisms had been worded,
thus confessing that he had passed outside the ancient guide-
marks, he stated explicitly—yet another quotation will
demonstrate the emphasis he laid upon this—" I still retain, in
substance, the opinions which I should now like to have seen
more gently expressed." [2]

Only in one portion of the footnote does Jeffrey seem to
me to have retracted, in the softness of age, anything essential
in his criticism. Looking back on Wordsworth's many years of
blameless living, seeing nowhere in the world any sign of harm
brought about by Wordsworth's teaching, remembering how
much in the poet and in his poetry critical honesty had compelled
him to admire, and realising how close both Wordsworth and
himself now were to the moment when books of poetry have
to be returned to their shelves for the last time, he was moved
to declare, as was noted in an earlier chapter, that in his dealings
with Wordsworth he had visited what were, even on his own
view, merely faults in taste or the effects of an excusable self-
partiality with an asperity that should be reserved for objects

[1] *A History of Eng. Lit.*, ed. John Buchan, 1935, p. 462 (from section
written by Dr E. A. Baker.)

[2] *Cont.*, v. 2, pp. 504-5. Cf. Crabb Robinson's *Diary*, v. 2, p. 200 (entry
for 1837) : " Empson related that Jeffrey had lately told him that so many
people had thought highly of Wordsworth, that he was resolved to re-peruse
his poems, and see if he had anything to retract. Empson, I believe, did
not end his anecdote ; he had before said to me that Jeffrey, having done
so, found nothing to retract, except, perhaps, a contemptuous and flippant
phrase or two."

of moral reprobation.[1] We have seen, however, that in his
first article on the Lakers he referred to their " moral character "
and that, in his days of strength, he discussed this, in one way
or another, over and over again.

V

We have just observed Jeffrey grant genius also to the third
member of the Lake School, Coleridge—though in a context that
was by no means flattering. He wrote no complete article on
any publication by Coleridge : we saw that the review of
Biographia Literaria has been shown to be a joint production by
himself and Hazlitt.[2] We gather from the footnote he appended
to that article that it was the archaisms in the diction of *The
Ancient Mariner*—there were more of these, it will be recollected,
in the original than in the final version of this work—that first
induced him to class Coleridge with the other Lakers. He
stated there also that he had thought Coleridge's *Love*—which
expresses, we note, ordinarily comprehensible human emotion
—the best of the *Lyrical Ballads,* and that this poem had always
seemed to him " extremely beautiful." [3] He was not so entirely
unappreciative of *Christabel* as the passage quoted from him a
moment ago might lead us to imagine. " I do not know," he
wrote to Moore in 1816, " exactly what to say of *Christabell,*
though with all its perversity and affectation I read it with
some pleasure. I do not mean the pleasure of scoffing and
ridicule. Indeed I scarcely ever read poetry in that humour,

---

[1] There may be a morsel of retraction also in the fact that the passage
in *The Excursion* Jeffrey's comment upon which Coleridge suggested was
unchristian was omitted from the citations in the reprint of the article. It
will be evident that a criticism of the soundness of his moral judgment was
one likely above all others to pierce home to Jeffrey. (*Cont.,* v. 2, p. 519 ;
Ed. Rev., No. 47, pp. 12-13 ; *Biog. Lit.,* p. 206).

[2] *Ante,* p. 70 ; *Jeffrey's Lit. Crit.,* Nichol Smith, p. 214.

[3] *Ed. Rev.,* No. 56, pp. 507-12. It has been held that, as Harper put it,
" There has never been any justification for the term ' the Lake School of
Poets.' " (*Wordsworth,* v. 2, p. 134). Jeffrey's answer was that if he " found
two or three . . . gentlemen living together—publishing in the same volume,
and adopting the same peculiar style and manner " he conceived himself
" entitled to hold them up as aiming, *de facto,* at the formation of a new
school," especially if he gave his " reasons and proofs at large for that
opinion." (*Ed. Rev.,* No. 56, p. 509). There may be significance in the fact
that Jeffrey's term has stuck in public memory to such an extent that Harper
felt it still necessary in 1916 to discuss the matter.

and usually find something to love and admire in works which I could never have courage or conscience to praise." [1] These sentences bear out Jeffrey's conception of himself as one more ready to criticise severely in public, from a sense of duty, than in private ; but they read oddly, when we consider the modern reputation of the poem. In an article published in 1812 he referred to Coleridge, in passing, as " that powerful and mis-directed genius." [2] His article on Mackintosh of 1835 contained a more detailed discussion of Coleridge. Coleridge, as Jeffrey saw him, had his share of Lakish childishness : it seemed absurd to Jeffrey that the scheme of a " Pantisocracy " should have been assented to by a " full-grown man." He found in Coleridge the characteristic Lakish cloudiness, and what appeared to him the characteristic Lakish error in ways of thinking and living. *Table Talk* rendered back, he wrote, " the image of a moody mind, incapable of mastering its own imaginings, and constantly seduced by them, or by misdirected ambition, to attempt impracticable things :—naturally attracted by dim paradoxes rather than lucid truths, and preferring, for the most part, the obscure and neglected parts of learning to those that are useful and clear—marching, in short, at all times, under the exclusive guidance of the Pillar of Smoke "—the illustration was not the happiest that might have been chosen—" and, like the body of its original followers, wandering all his days in the desert, without ever coming in sight of the promised land. Consulting little at any time," Jeffrey continued, " with any thing but his own prejudices and fancies, he seems, in his later days, to have withdrawn altogether from the correction of equal minds ; and to have nourished the assurance of his own infallibility, by delivering mystical oracles from his cloudy shrine, all day long, to a small set of disciples, to whom neither question nor interruption was allowed. The result of this . . . was . . . a daily increasing ignorance of the course of opinions and affairs in the world, and a proportional confidence in his own dogmas and dreams, which might have been shaken, at least, if not entirely subverted, by a closer contact with the general mass of intelligence." [3]

In a review, published in 1828, of Atherstone's *Fall of Nineveh*, Jeffrey, discussing the poetry of his own day, alluded

---

[1] *Memoirs*, Moore, v. 2, pp. 100-1.   [2] *Cont.*, v. 3, p. 623.
[3] *Cont.*, v. 3, pp. 662-9.

to another great poet of the time, Shelley, in words very similar
to those he had used earlier of Coleridge. " Three poets of
great promise," he wrote, " have . . . been lost, ' in the morn
and liquid dew of their youth '—in Kirke White, in Keats, and
in Pollok ; and a powerful, though more uncertain genius
extinguished, less prematurely, in Shelley." [1] There are two
passages in his letters—both written after he had retired from
the editorship of the *Review*—in which he described himself as
reading, not very strenuously, Shelley's poetry.[2] In all his
published work I have noticed only one other reference—it is
a mere mention of the poet's name—to Shelley. This is in the
so-called " prophecy," which falls due to be discussed later.

VI

Another sentence from the review of Atherstone was quoted
in an earlier chapter—that in which Jeffrey spoke of his age as
having a hundred times more poetry and more true taste for
poetry than the age that had immediately preceded it. Nichol
Smith drew attention to this portion of the article, characterising
it as a re-statement of Jeffrey's views on the eighteenth century.[3]
To me what follows is also interesting as summing up, near the
close of Jeffrey's career as a reviewer, in a way which, I think,
makes his line of thought still more evident, part of his criticism
of the writing of his own period.

In this, as in earlier articles, Jeffrey gave credit to Cowper
for shaking off the " numbing spell " that had come over poetry
after the Age of the Augustans—" for," he remarked, " Burns
was not generally known till long after." Cowper, Jeffrey
considered, was entitled to " the praise of absolute and entire
originality." Whatever he added to English poetry was drawn
directly from his own genius, or from his own stores of observation.
" He was a copyist of no style—a restorer of no style." This,
Jefffrey declared however, could not be said of the poets who
followed him ; and, he added, " the mere statement of the
fact, seems to us sufficiently to explain the present state of our
poetry—its strength and its weakness—its good taste and its
deficient power—its resemblance to works that can never die—
and its own obvious liability to the accidents of mortality."
His own period had, said Jeffrey, " advanced beyond the

---

[1] *Ed. Rev.*, No. 95, p. 48.   [2] *Life*, Cockburn, v. 1, p. 369 ; v. 2, p. 280.
[3] *Jeffrey's Lit. Crit.*, p. 30.

preceding age, simply by going back to one still older." It had "reformed merely by restoring; and innovated by a systematic recurrence to the models of antiquity." Scott had gone back to the romances of chivalry, and the Lakers to the early ballads, and both, and all who had since adventured in poetry, had "drawn, without measure or disguise" from the writers of the sixteenth and seventeenth centuries. To Jeffrey, in other words, one of the main weaknesses of the Romantic Revival lay simply in the fact that it was a revival.

It was, he went on, impossible to value more highly than he did the benefits of this restoration. It was a great thing to have made the public familiar once more with the mighty geniuses to whom contemporary authors had drawn attention. If the poets of his own day had to be copyists there was nothing so worthy of copying. The result had been that, even in the least inspired writers, there could be found some trace of the qualities of the Elizabethans. Nevertheless, in authors of whatever power, copying remained copying. "We have still a feeling," Jeffrey wrote, "that we are glorying but in second-hand finery and counterfeit inspiration." The models the men of the early nineteenth century had chosen might show their taste. The works they produced might show their skill in imitation. But these did not show them to have inherited the genius of their masters. They were not even evidence of their possession of sufficient genius to have enabled them to come up, without the assistance of models, to the level of their own imitations. Copiers, moreover, were lacking in that immediate contact with reality which, as we have seen, appeared always to Jeffrey a characteristic of the highest art. "The heroes of our modern poetry," he wrote, ". . . are little better, as we take it, than the heroes of the modern theatres "—the now very familiar parallel—" attired, no doubt, in the exact costume of the persons they represent, and wielding their gorgeous antique arms with an exact imitation of heroic movements and deportment—nay, even evincing in their tones and gestures, a full sense of inward nobleness and dignity—and yet palpably unfit to engage in any feat of actual prowess, and incapable, in their own persons, even of conceiving what they have been so well taught to personate." Contemporary poetry contained "little invention, little direct or overwhelming passion, and little natural simplicity." It was full of descriptions—" descriptions not only of actions and external objects, but of characters, and emotions, and the signs and accompaniments of emotion—and all given at full length, ostentatious, elaborate, and highly finished, even in their counterfeit carelessness and disorder." He did not, Jeffrey said, go so far as the mathematician who saw no beauty in poetry because it proved nothing. But he did think it not quite unreasonable " to insist on knowing a little what it is about." The " great want " of the poetry of his day was " the want of solid subject, and of persons who can be supposed to have existed." The consequence was that, while the short pieces of the time were frequently very delightful, in longer works, where a story had to be told, and interest sustained through a considerable train of incidents and variety of characters, the age's " want of vigour and originality " was " but too apt to become apparent." [1]

It is interesting to place beside this some sentences from Professor Allardyce Nicoll's *British Drama*. There, speaking of certain nineteenth-century plays, Nicoll wrote : " Majestic conceptions are in them and a rich rush of gorgeous poetry, but they betray the same weakness visible in all the poetic plays of the Romantic period ; they give nothing new to the theatre. Fundamentally they are but imitations of the grandeur of earlier dramatic activity." And again, speaking of the nineteenth-century poets, " These poets," Nicoll said, " . . . could not have brought to the playhouse anything save old themes treated in a finer way. Romance coloured their lives, and they knew not how to delve below into the sorrows of ordinary existence. What the theatre wanted was the impulse that comes from reality." [2] Jeffrey, we observe, writing in the midst of the period, and looking at its poetry in general, made precisely the same criticism. It is interesting to observe also, as a fact suggesting that the common sense of ordinary men had discerned the same weakness, that in the popular caricatures of the nineteenth century both poets and actors were commonly delineated as beings differentiated from the rest of mankind by bizarre hats, clothes of peculiar cut, and eccentric manes of hair.

[1] *Ed. Rev.*, No. 95, pp. 49-52.   [2] p. 328.

CHAPTER XIII

REALITY OR THEATRE

Extension of Jeffrey's case. Wordsworth's rescue of language. Early experiences of Wordsworth. " Nature." *The Immortality Ode. Resolution and Independence.* Recondite allusion. The test.

I

To idealise, as one is sometimes tempted to do, the subject of one's study would be to be false to the Jeffreyan doctrine that one should always face facts. Certain of the statements quoted from Jeffrey in the preceding chapter may be useful in checking any such tendency : some of them are of such a kind that they are now not worth controverting. In reply, for instance, to his affirmation of 1807 that from the pleasure arising from diction readers of Wordsworth are " in a great measure cut off," one need do no more than point, in *Tintern Abbey*, published in 1798, to " The still, sad music of humanity," or to the lines in *The Solitary Reaper*, published in the work he was discussing, about the Cuckoo-bird " Breaking the silence of the seas Among the farthest Hebrides," or, in the same poem, to " old, unhappy, far-off things, And battles long ago "—phrases that have haunted the minds of multitudes of readers since the day on which their author penned them. Jeffrey's praise, elsewhere, of Wordsworth's language does not completely wipe out that extravagant statement. In reply to his suggestion that the poems in the 1807 volumes would not be popular or be widely studied one has merely to point out that these volumes contained—besides *The Solitary Reaper—To the Cuckoo*, the *Ode to Duty*, the *Immortality Ode*, and *Resolution and Independence*, than which it is doubtful if there are now any better-known poems in the English language. By his assertion of 1822 that the Lake School was " now pretty nearly extinct," Jeffrey evidently meant simply that its members were no longer writing anything of value. This statement makes it clear at the same time that while, as has been emphasised, Jeffrey perceived that there was genius in the Lakers' works, he had no prevision of how great would be the Lakers' ultimate triumph. He never envisaged the arrival of a day when the period in which he lived might be named, as Herford named it in his study of its literature—without, I imagine, anyone ever seriously challenging the title—" The Age of Wordsworth."

But this leads us back to our problem. Hume pointed out in one of his essays that the authority of even the most despotic of leaders is based upon opinion : there must be something in a leader to which his followers respond.[1] When an age is given the name of a single man surely what is meant is that he both reflected and helped to mould that age's most characteristic thought. At the moment when these words are being written much of what man has regarded for centuries as emblematic of civilisation is being systematically reduced to rubble, and millions of people are systematically torturing one another. Humanity has evidently been somehow or other misled. There appear to be two possibilities. Either Herford in describing this as " The Age of Wordsworth," and Harper in saying that Jeffrey discerned who was " running with the ball," and Jeffrey in imagining that he perceived in the trends of thought reflected by Wordsworth something his instincts told him it was his duty to oppose by every means in his power, were all of them mistaken, and the world was actually following leaders still completely unrecognised ; or Jeffrey, Herford, and Harper were in the right. The suggestion that Jeffrey may have discovered " menace " there, and what has happened since, may appear to some to be a coincidence that warrants further examination.

The possession by leaders of " good intentions and extra-ordinary talents," and the fact that their characters and achievements may be such as to compel our admiration, are, we observe, as irrelevant to this question as that they may have been on occasion improperly attacked : we have seen the Jeffreyan argument to be that great merit, joined with error, conscious or unconscious, increases the danger.

Jeffrey's case was obviously impeded by the conditions under which it was framed. Those who have replied to him have been assisted by all that has been discovered, pondered over, and written about the leaders of the Romantic Revival in the interval between his day and theirs : their position is very different from that of the critic whose sole material for judgment consisted of the works of his contemporaries so far as these were published at the date of each particular article. It may

[1] *Essays*, World's Classics, p. 29.

be felt, therefore, that the Jeffreyan case cannot be fully appreciated unless it also is extended in the light of later knowledge.

We recall Jeffrey's remark to Horner that he always professed to write for babes and sucklings and took no merit but for making things level to the meanest capacities. " If you ever admit such a disquisition again," he wrote to his successor in the editorship of the *Review*, Macvey Napier, in connection with an article the latter had accepted from Sir William Hamilton, " order your operator to instance and illustrate all his propositions by cases or examples. . . . This is a sure test of sheer nonsense, and moreover an infinite resource for the explication of obscure truth, if there be any such thing." [1] This is a reminder of the method by which we must continue to proceed. There must be no over-ingenuity of argument. Examination must be restricted to the elements generally recognised as essential in the greatest works of the greatest nineteenth-century writers, and to characteristic criticisms of these writers. The jury must judge, as always, how far the thing is done fairly.

Jeffrey's criticism appeared to be centring itself, in the last passage from him we noted, upon the idea of theatricality. We may ask in the first place, then, if there is discernible in the thinking and writing of Wordsworth, the leading writer, by general agreement, of his time, and in the claims that have been made for him, an essential, not merely an occasional, theatricality. This is still, of course, a minor query, but it may lead to the major question, whether or not there was danger there.

We may return, to begin with, to one of the first points Jeffrey discussed in his criticism of the Lake School—their experiments with language. For these, as for so much else, Wordsworth has, in later times, been granted abundant recognition. Legouis, for instance, has written of " all con-temporary English poetry " as " shamed " by the example of Wordsworth " into casting aside the factitious adornments long soiled by conventional usage, rescued by him from the mere verbal imitation from which it was pining away." [2] " Wordsworth's theory of poetic diction," Harper wrote, " has

[1] *Corr. of Macvey Napier*, p. 70.
[2] *Early Life of Wordsworth*, 1921, pp. 9-10. Legouis was discussing the effect upon language of Wordsworth's " directness of vision."

given a fresh texture to nearly all English poetry for the last hundred years." [1] We recollect, however, Jeffrey's observation to a writer who, he thought, was claiming too much for eighteenth-century prose, that " soft, graceful, and idiomatic English " was at least as old as Chaucer, that the Bible was full of it, and that it was one of " the many languages spoken by Shakespeare." Most people must recall at once, in this connection, phrases like " He was a verray parfit gentil knight," " Yea, though I walk through the valley of the shadow of death," and " Goodnight, sweet prince, And flights of angels sing thee to thy rest "—than which Wordsworth never wrote anything more simply beautiful. In other words, Wordsworth had, in this respect, nothing really new to give to English literature. Ordinary men know that language constantly changes, and that change is most rapid in its most artificial forms : slang can become completely out of date in a decade. It is not easy for common sense to believe that this process was once suspended, that an artificial diction which reached its highest pitch of effectiveness in the work of Pope—who died in 1744—and which was later " soiled by conventional usage," retained undiminished sway over English poetry for a unique half-century in history in order that Wordsworth might gain the credit of ridding the world of it. " Lute, harp, and lyre, muse, muses, and inspirations, Pegasus, Parnassus, and Hippocrene, were all an abomination to him. In fancy I can almost hear him now, exclaiming, ' Harp ? Lyre ? Pen and ink, boy, you mean ! Muse, boy, Muse ? Your Nurse's daughter you mean ! Pierian spring ? Oh, aye ! the cloister-pump, I suppose ! ' " [2] These words come from Coleridge's description of his schoolmaster, James Bowyer. They refer to a time when Coleridge and Wordsworth were schoolboys. " There is," Jeffrey wrote to a cousin in 1792, when he was not yet nineteen, " a charm in simplicity and naturality of expression, for which neither excellent sense, nor egregious sentiment, nor splendid diction, can compensate. But this simplicity, in this vile, conceited, and puerile age, it is infinitely difficult to acquire ; and all our best writers since Shakspere, except the gentle Addison, and sometimes Sterne, have given up the attempt in despair, and trusted to gaudier vehicles for the conveyance of their respective reputations to the ears of

[1] *Wordsworth*, v. 1, p. 425.   [2] *Biog. Lit.*, p. 4.

posterity, and the mansion of fame ; which practice, you will
allow, is greatly to the prejudice of those who are taught to
consider them as the models of fine writing.   However, I intend
in a year or two to correct the depravity of taste, and to revive
the simple and the sublime in all their purity, and in all their
majesty.   This, you will perceive, is private and confidential." [1]
We may not agree with all the youthful Jeffrey's facts ; but it
is clear which side he was on.   " Must eternal changes," burst
out a reviewer in the *Monthly* in 1793, discussing Wordsworth's
Descriptive Sketches, " be rung on uplands and lowlands, and
nodding forests, and brooding clouds, and cells, and dells, and
dingles ? "   And again—" How often," he wrote, " shall we in
vain advise those, who are so delighted with their own thoughts
that they cannot forbear from putting them into rhyme, to
examine those thoughts till they themselves understand them ? " [2]
We seem to have encountered here an ordinary man who was
very weary, before Wordsworth began to study this question,
of " mere verbal imitation."   For criticising Wordsworth, he
paid, of course, the usual penalty.   " The ruthless critic,"
Harper wrote, " who hastily penned those flippant remarks
about Wordsworth's poetic diction deflected the current of
English literature." [3]   It seems unlikely, however, that Bowyer,
young Jeffrey, and the anonymous writer in the *Monthly* were
the only three people in Great Britain who were thinking in
this way before 1798.   We have seen that it appeared to Jeffrey,
writing in 1803, that Cowper had already freed English poetry
from the thraldom of Augustan phraseology.[4]   If in 1798 it
required further rescuing surely the task was complete when
Coleridge wrote that lovely stanza in *The Ancient Mariner* about
the hidden brook in the leafy month of June.   " In the delineation
of such objects," Jeffrey commented in 1806 upon some lines
describing the blind inmates of an institution, " we are perfectly
satisfied, that the school of Southey and Coleridge is right, and
that the whole effect of the representation must depend on the
humble simplicity of the statement." [5]   We observe that he
left out the extremist Wordsworth.   A poet so great as
Wordsworth was could hardly have failed to exercise an influence
upon language.   It may appear to some, nevertheless, that

---

[1] *Life*, Cockburn, v. 2, p. 9.   [2] *Wordsworth*, Harper, v. 1, pp. 223-4.
[3] *Wordsworth*, v. 1, p. 225.   [4] *Ante*, p. 74 ; *Cont.*, v. 1, p. 412.
[5] *Ed. Rev.*, No. 15, p. 157.

when he wrote his famous " advertisement " to the first edition of *Lyrical Ballads* he was hammering, not at a locked and iron-studded portal, but merely at a painted door-flat. I think Jeffrey would have maintained that it was to a considerable extent by theatricality that Wordsworth gained subsequent recognition as the chief leader of the new movement : the poet's early efforts seemed to him, we remember, to have been designed to " court notoriety." Every actor knows the value of contrast. There could hardly have been a more violent contrast than between the polished conventionalities of Augustan diction and

" Oh ! what's the matter ? what's the matter ?
What is't that ails young Harry Gill ? "

The " advertisement " to the *Lyrical Ballads* and the later lengthy prefaces might be regarded as theatrical posters the purpose of which was to ensure that no reader should overlook their author's originality. Wordsworth's declaration in 1799 that *The Ancient Mariner* had " on the whole, been an injury to the volume " [1] might be considered as having sprung in part from a desire that he, and he alone, should on so important an occasion occupy the position of centre-stage. This may appear to some a grotesquely business-like conception of the attitude of a great poet to his art. But Wordsworth wrote to his friend Mathews in 1794 : " I have another poem . . . ready for the press, though I certainly should not publish it unless I hoped to derive from it some pecuniary recompense." [2] " I published those poems," he wrote to Cottle, referring to the *Lyrical Ballads*, " for money, and money alone." [3] These statements express, no doubt, only one of his moods. But they show that, like a prudent actor-manager, he was sensible of the importance of the box-office. Jeffrey's insistence that the simple diction of the Lakers was really artificial was a charge of theatricality in another form. To Jeffrey this was not a reflection of the conversation of country people as it is heard in cottage, byre, and cattle-market ; it resembled rather the over-ingenuous speech of the stage-peasants who form a background to the hero of a musical play.

It is true that for some time after the publication of *Lyrical Ballads* poetic diction of the Augustan type remained a resource for versifiers desirous of obtaining a decorative effect by short

---

[1] *Wordsworth*, Harper, v. 1, p. 380.   [2] *Ibid.*, v. 1, p. 244.
[3] *Ibid.*, v. 1, p. 382.

cuts. In a poem, for instance, published in 1816, we read, in
a description of a church organ, that " the tubed engine feels
the inspiring blast " ; in another, published in 1822, a barometer
was spoken of as a " well-wrought Scale, Whose sentient tube
instructs to time A purpose to a fickle clime " ; and in another,
also published in 1822, we are told, in connection with an
eclipse, that " High on her speculative tower Stood Science
waiting for the hour When Sol was destined to endure *That*
darkening of his radiant face." All three poems were written,
as Lowell long ago pointed out, by William Wordsworth.[1] This
may suggest that his protest of 1798 was dramatic.

Jeffrey never saw *The Prelude*. He had no opportunity,
accordingly, of investigating the processes by which " Nature "
was pictured there as having moulded the poet's mind. We
may glance next, therefore, from the Jeffreyan viewpoint, at
some passages in this work that have been regarded as important.
One of these is that in which Wordsworth spoke of himself as
wandering at night, as a child, on the heights near the Vale of
Esthwaite, " scudding away from snare to snare." " I heard
among the solitary hills," Wordsworth wrote,

> " Low breathings coming after me, and sounds
> Of undistinguishable motion, steps
> Almost as silent as the turf they trod "—

and this demonstrated how he

> " grew up
> Fostered alike by beauty and by fear." [2]

Professor W. P. Ker emphasised the difference between
" Wordsworth's love of Nature " and " mere critical observation
of the ' beauties ' of Nature." " It is through life," Ker wrote,
" that Nature is revealed to him . . . and the old panic terror
found him, about his tenth year, in night raids on the fells."
Ker cited in illustration the lines about the breathings and so
forth that have just been quoted.[3] I think that Jeffrey would
have agreed at once that Wordsworth must, even as a child,
have been singularly sensitive to his environment. But I think
he might have held that there may be dramatisation also here,
that there is an explanation of the experience that is more
consonant with common sense than that it was occasioned by

---

[1] *English Critical Essays*, 19th Cent., ed. Jones, 1922, pp. 592-3.
[2] Book I, ll. 301-25.   [3] *Chambers's Cyclopædia of Eng. Lit.*, v. 3, p. 11.

contact with some supernatural " Nature," and that Wordsworth
has, by the accuracy of his detail, himself suggested it.   Wordsworth had, upon his own confession, just before that momentary
" terror " had been stamped upon his memory, filched a woodcock
from a snare set by someone else.   This hearing of " low
breathings " and the rest might, therefore, before the episode
became transformed with the passing of time by the stage-light
of his imagination, have been simply the effect, in a child's
mind, of fear of a possibly irate pursuer.

We noticed in our last chapter the equally famous experience
on Ullswater when the future poet, rowing out into the lake,
saw rising, from behind a craggy steep on the horizon, a huge
peak which, as he moved farther from the shore, with " measured
motion like a living thing " strode after him.   " After I had seen
That spectacle," he wrote,

> " for many days, my brain
> Worked with a dim and undetermined sense
> Of unknown modes of being." [1]

We observe that the initial impression was again that of something
pursuing.   And again, I think Jeffrey might have pointed out,
the circumstances were such as to disturb the conscience of a
sensitive child.   Wordsworth had stolen the boat.

We turn next to an even more famous passage in *The Prelude*,
that describing the morning on which, an undergraduate on
vacation, on his way home from a dance in the country,
Wordsworth realised that he was destined to be a poet.   Harper
spoke of this as " the supreme religious moment " of Wordsworth's
life.[2]   That lonely young figure standing in the dawn, his heart
stirred to a passionate love of Nature's beauty that was to remain
with him all his life, is certainly very fine theatre.   The scene
is none the less convincing on that account ; and the language
is worthy of the occasion.   The moment when a great poet
awakens to a consciousness of his vocation is beyond all question
an important one in history.   " I made no vows," Wordsworth
wrote,

> " but vows
> Were then made for me ; bond unknown to me
> Was given, that I should be, else sinning greatly,
> A dedicated Spirit." [3]

---

[1] *Prelude*, Book I, ll. 357-400.   [2] *Wordsworth*, v. i, p. 74.
[3] *Prelude*, Book IV, ll. 297-338.

The passage reminds us of that in which Milton expressed his hope that " by labour and intense study " he might " perhaps leave something so written to aftertimes, as they should not willingly let it die," and of Milton's declaration that it was his duty to employ his talents, if grace were given him to use them, as ever in his " great Task-master's eye." [1] As we examine the lines, however, we perceive a difference between the attitude of Wordsworth and that of Milton. Wordsworth, it would seem, had not the task, as Milton and no doubt many millions of lesser men have felt that they had, of striving with humility to make themselves worthy of being employed in some way in God's service. He did not require to make vows. " Nature " had the work in hand. We recall Jeffrey's affirmation that the collision of equal minds seemed necessary to correct the extravagance into which genius was liable to be betrayed by self-admiration. What should we think of a man's asserting seriously, in an ordinary room, in a company of level-headed contemporaries, that, as he stood one day in the light of the rising sun, supernatural powers singled him out from the rest of mankind and undertook the guidance of his future activities —and that from that moment he became " a dedicated Spirit " ? I imagine that to a Jeffrey at anyrate such a speech would appear suited, whatever the gifts of the speaker, not to the world of actual men, but to a darkened theatre, and a figure standing dignified and alone on a stage, declaiming in rich tones—not in real dawnlight, but in the light of an appropriately coloured spot.

Between four and five years after this dedication there appeared the first fruits of it, Wordsworth's *Evening Walk* and *Descriptive Sketches*. Harper remarked that in the first of these there were to be found echoes from Shakespeare, Milton, Spenser, Tasso, Rosset, Thomson, Beattie, Young, Burns, Greenwood, Clark, Collins, and Dr John Brown.[2] The second he described as characterised by " astonishing verbal dependence upon poetic tradition." [3] The supernatural powers aforesaid were evidently unable to relieve Wordsworth from the labour of learning his trade in precisely the way in which ordinary apprentices in other trades learn theirs, by copying the work of journeymen.

[1] *Reason of Church Government.   On His Having Arrived at the Age of Twenty-three.*

[2] *Wordsworth*, v. 1, pp. 189-90.   [3] *Ibid.*, v. 1, p. 194.

In 1793 came the famous walk along the Wye Valley, and, in 1798, the description of it in *Lyrical Ballads*. If Jeffrey had not read *The Prelude* he had read *Tintern Abbey*. He quoted, slightly inaccurately, three and a half lines from it in his review of Alison's *Taste*, and remarked that he was quoting from memory.[1] This confirms his assertion to Coleridge that he had much of *Lyrical Ballads* by heart. But nowhere in his dealings with Wordsworth did he mention this poem by name. There is a passage, in his first criticism of the Lakers, which appears to me to have been directly inspired by *Tintern Abbey*. It is that, already noted, in which he declared that among the devices employed by these poets to give the appearance of animation to a very ordinary conception the most usual was to wrap it up in mysterious and unintelligible language which flowed past with so much solemnity that it was difficult to believe it conveyed nothing of value. There is no poem in *Lyrical Ballads*, it seems to me, to which this remark could more directly refer. The charge, we observe, is again one of theatricality. This is undoubtedly cavalier treatment of a work that has been described as of " flawless and noble beauty," [2] as " the crown and coping stone of the *Lyrical Ballads*," [3] as one of the two " summits " [4]—the other being the *Immortality Ode*— of Wordsworth's poetry, and as the " *locus classicus* or consecrated formulary of the Wordsworthian faith." [5] We are not permitted, we recollect however, to answer Jeffrey by simple " encomiums." However naive the exercise may appear in connection with a work so long famous and so generally studied, we have to demonstrate, if we are to reply to Jeffrey adequately, that we ourselves understand the poem, and are convinced that the magnificence of its lines is fully justified.

Undoubtedly there is much in *Tintern Abbey* that even the most ordinary of us can appreciate. Most of us know how a landscape can tug at the heart. Jeffrey knew that. We remember how, when he was in London in 1832, he longed for a glimpse of the Scottish Highlands. Most of us can understand too how, amid " the din of towns " memories of beauty can pass into the mind " with tranquil restoration." We recall Jeffrey's writing from London to Cockburn that had it not been for his love of beautiful nature and poetry, his heart would

---

[1] *Ed. Rev.*, No. 35, p. 29.   [2] *Wordsworth*, Herford, p. 106.
[3] *Wordsworth*, Garrod, pp. 107-8.   [4] *Nineteenth Cent. Lit.*, Saintsbury, p. 54.
[5] *Wordsworth*, Myers, p. 33.

have died within him. We are not departing from the Jeffreyan
position if we agree also, though the point may be disputable,
that storing the mind with such pictures may have no slight
influence on the " best portion of a good man's life " : Jeffrey
said something not unlike this when he affirmed that one of the
uses of a faculty of taste was to assist in the cultivation of a finer
morality. We may understand Wordsworth's description of the
phases through which his mind passed in his appreciation of
natural beauty. Greatly, however, though all this is expressed
—more greatly than Jeffrey ever acknowledged—there is nothing
in these ideas to justify the poem's being described as containing
the " consecrated formulary " of a new " faith." But *Tintern
Abbey* contains more than these ideas. It purports—albeit with,
at one point, a brief saving clause not quite to be expected in a
work the discovery in which has been compared to that of
Newton—to show us a way of access to a

> " blessed mood,
> In which the burthen of the mystery,
> In which the heavy and the weary weight
> Of all this unintelligible world,
> Is lightened. . . .
> While with an eye made quiet by the power
> Of harmony, and the deep power of joy
> We see into the life of things."

It purports to introduce us to something which " never did
betray The heart that loved her " ; to something which has
power

> " Through all the years of this our life, to lead
>   From joy to joy " ;

to something which can

> " so inform
> The mind that is within us, so impress
> With quietness and beauty, and so feed
> With lofty thoughts, that neither evil tongues,
> Rash judgments, nor the sneers of selfish men,
> Nor greetings where no kindness is, nor all
> The dreary intercourse of daily life,
> Shall e'er prevail against us, or disturb
> Our cheerful faith, that all which we behold
> Is full of blessings."

However difficult it may be to get to know this something, the effects of acquaintanceship with it are indicated so plainly as to be comprehensible by even the most obtuse of us. If there is no theatricality in these lines, if their impressiveness springs from the greatness of the thought in them and not merely, as Jeffrey held, from the deceptive solemnity of the phrasing, then surely—especially in this mid-twentieth century, in which the weight of the unintelligible world has for millions become inexpressibly heavier—there is here something that even the most ordinary of jurymen might cry out to understand.

It seems immediately clear that the " Nature " that accomplishes these things is not Nature as we ordinarily understand the word. Mr Aldous Huxley has, nevertheless, discussed the matter from this angle. In a tropical jungle, he remarked in one of his essays, Wordsworth would not have been so serenely certain of the " Presences of Nature " he was in the habit of worshipping on the shores of Rydal.[1] But surely it is not necessary to travel to the equator in order to discern this. It is not easy to imagine a Westmoreland farmer at a time, say, when his fields were being flooded, and he was living in hourly dread of bankruptcy, declaring seriously that Nature, as we normally think of it, was lightening for him the weary weight of the unintelligible world ; or a Cumberland shepherd, discovering that flukes were sucking at the livers of his sheep, declaring that he was being led, by this phenomenon, to a cheerful faith that all which he beheld was full of blessings. Yet Stephen also spoke of Nature in this sense in connection with Wordsworth. " He seems at times," Stephen wrote, " to have overlooked that dark side of nature which is recognised in theological doctrines of corruption, or in the scientific theories about the fierce struggle for existence."[2] " Seems . . . to have overlooked " ! This, so far as *Tintern Abbey* is concerned, is surely putting the matter mildly. Might it not be said that if this is the " Nature " here delineated, Wordsworth was reducing something that is bewilderingly and terrifyingly complex to a depth of fictitious innocuousness as low as that of the most naively-drawn of stage-peasants that ever appeared in a children's pantomime ?

Whether or not this is fair criticism of Wordsworth, there

[1] *Do What You Will*, pp. 113-4.
[2] *Hours in a Library*, v. 2, pp. 285-6.

does appear to be a simplification of Nature's complexity in some of his interpreters' expositions of his teaching. " He believed," Harper wrote of the adventure with the stolen woodcock, " and probably for this reason treasured up this incident and gave it prominence, that the soul of the universe, uttering its august precepts through the clean air and the unsullied earth, speaks an intelligible language to the heart of man ; because law and duty are the same for man and star and flower." [1] What precisely, an ordinary juryman might ask, recollecting Jeffrey's insistence upon illustrations, are these precepts uttered in intelligible language through the air and the earth ? What, in plain words, is this law that is the same for man, star, and flower ? Does it apply also to birds ? If the woodcock seized by Wordsworth could have contributed to the discussion might it not have argued that the only law or duty that appeared to it deducible from the episode was that one must learn to look after oneself, and strive to acquire sufficient cunning to outwit one's fellow-creatures ; and the only precept that, if one cannot do this, there is every likelihood of one's ending one's days in torture ?

Wordsworth did, it is true, make " Nature " enunciate on occasion precepts of the kind to which Harper possibly refers. We recall the close of *Hart-Leap Well.*

" One lesson, Shepherd, let us two divide,
　　Taught both by what she [Nature] shows, and what conceals ;
　　Never to blend our pleasure or our pride
　　With sorrow of the meanest thing that feels."

Does Nature, however, as common sense recognises it, really teach this lesson ? We may place beside Wordsworth's poetry an extract from Dorothy's diary. " Wm. and Mary," runs an entry for 14th December 1801, " walked to Ambleside in the morning to buy mouse-traps." [2] Does not that tiny sentence raise the whole dark and obvious difficulty—that we can none of us live in comfort without killing ? The precepts of Wordsworth, " Nature's " great interpreter, do not appear always consistent in this respect. It is odd to find the author of the sentiment just quoted making his " Wanderer " in *The Excursion*

[1] *Wordsworth*, v. 1, p. 42.
[2] *Wordsworth*, Harper, v. 2, p. 16 ; *Journals of Dorothy Wordsworth*, ed. Knight, 1934, p. 71.

Q

strive to correct the despondency of the " Solitary " by such advice as the following :—

> " Take courage, and withdraw yourself from ways
> That run not parallel to nature's course.
> . . . . with all your might
> Chase the wild goat ; and if the bold red deer
> Fly to those harbours, driven by hound and horn
> Loud echoing, add your speed to the pursuit ;
> So, wearied to your hut shall you return,
> And sink at evening into sound repose." [1]

In one of the poems Jeffrey mentioned in 1807, *The Redbreast chasing the Butterfly*, we find Wordsworth definitely confronted by our problem. What are we to say to the Nature that has so fashioned this most attractive of little birds that it cannot live except by obliterating its fellow-mortals ? We await eagerly the words of the Sage who taught that " Nature " led " from joy to joy." He speaks to the bird.

> " What ailed thee, Robin, that thou couldst pursue
> A beautiful creature,
> That is gentle by nature ?
> . . . .
> The cheerer Thou of our in-door sadness,
> He is the friend of our summer gladness :
> What hinders, then, that ye should be
> Playmates in the sunny weather,
> And fly about in the air together !
> His beautiful wings in crimson are drest,
> A crimson as bright as thine own :
> Wouldst thou be happy in thy nest,
> O pious Bird ! whom man loves best,
> Love him, or leave him alone ! "

What hinders ? Is not the answer obvious ? Is it not simply Nature—which so fashioned the robin's stomach that it hungered for butterflies ? Are we really here being confronted by profound contributions to thought ? Jeffrey, we remember, called this poem " Silly Sooth."

We had better call upon another witness. And, as we are mere ordinary jurymen striving to grasp this, it may be well to call upon a witness who addressed himself professedly to elementary students. " Wordsworth," Stopford Brooke wrote,

[1] Book IV, ll. 489-504.

" conceived, as poet, that nature was alive. It had, he imagined, one living soul which, entering into flower, stream, or mountain, gave them each a soul of their own." The words " as poet " and " imagined " may appear, at first glance, to concede Jeffrey's whole case. They may seem to suggest that in the eyes of a subsequent generation Wordsworth's " discovery " did actually belong to the realm of fantasy. This, however, is perhaps going too fast. We may agree that through all things there moves force, something we may think of as soul. " Between this Spirit in nature," Brooke continued, " and the mind of man there was a prearranged harmony which enabled nature to communicate its own thoughts to man, and man to reflect upon them, until an absolute union between them was established." It may be agreed that there exists harmony between man and Nature in the sense that man is ineradicably a part of it. We observe in this connection another entry in Dorothy's diary. " I broiled Coleridge a mutton chop," she wrote against the date 1st September 1800, " which he ate in bed." [1] There is nothing to indicate that Coleridge's fellow-Laker did not enjoy an occasional mutton-chop also : there survives the testimony of a butcher's boy that he was " very partial to legs—' lived on legs, you may almost say.' " [2] This undoubtedly reveals a union between Wordsworth and the other creatures of Nature ; it shows that his stomach belonged to the same order as that of the robin he addressed in that poetical " Naughty, naughty ! " But it does not show him to have been in harmony with the " Nature " of *Hart-Leap Well*. " This," continued Brooke, " was, in fact, the theory of the Florentine Neo-Platonists of the Renaissance." I am afraid that, as Jeffreyans, we cannot permit our attention to be distracted by this flutter of academic lace. We are not concerned with what some Italians may have thought in the fifteenth century ; we are trying to find out what Wordsworth discovered at the end of the eighteenth. " They did not care for nature," Brooke went on in partial explanation of his statement, " but when Wordsworth either reconceived or adopted this idea, it made him the first who loved nature with a personal love, for she, being living, and personal, and not only his reflection, was made capable of being loved as a man loves a friend. He could brood on her character,

[1] *Wordsworth*, Harper, v. 1, p. 406 ; *Journals*, ed. Knight, p. 48.
[2] *Wordsworthiana*, ed. Knight, 1889, p. 86.

her ways, her words, her life, as he did on those of his wife or
sister." [1] We agree at once that the " Nature " Wordsworth
delineated was not his own reflection ; we have just suggested
that we cannot picture that " Nature " as being " very partial
to legs." But what we are asking is whether that " Nature "
really existed at all or was merely a theatrical figment. Surely
to most of us a wife or a sister appears different from a Nature
that obliges us to kill in order that we may survive—from
whom, it is true, we may derive great blessings if we are able to
co-operate with her, but who, if we do not co-operate, whether
from our own fault or because we are helpless and cannot, is
implacably merciless. We must look for further help.

" It is not easy," Ker wrote, " to determine or explain what
Wordsworth meant by Nature." We may agree with that.
" Or rather," Ker went on, " it is easy to explain prosaically
in such a way as to leave the result unprofitable." Again we
may wonder if we are being asked to look at something that is
visible only in stage-lighting. " The essence," said Ker, " of
Wordsworth's theory is poetical, not distinctly philosophical,
though it touches on philosophy. Where it is most philosophical,
it is a belief in imagination, sometimes called the Imaginative
Will, as a power of interpreting the world—not altering reality,
nor remoulding the scheme of things, but reading it truly.
It is this faculty that gets beyond ordinary trivial, partial,
disconnected perceptions, and finds the solemn life of the
universe astir in every moment of experience." [2] The phrase
" Imaginative Will " is certainly Wordsworthian : it occurs in
The Excursion.[3] But what we are looking for is some sort of
evidence that Wordsworth did not alter reality, but read it
truly. What is meant by the assertion that the Imaginative
Will can do this ? Does it mean that we can deprive the jungle
tigress of her terror by calling her Poor Puss and announcing
with determination that she will do us no harm ? A man
choking in a snowstorm is certainly finding the life of the universe
astir in every moment of the experience. Can we say to him
that if he were possessed of the Wordsworthian Imaginative
Will he would be able, without altering reality or remoulding
the scheme of things, to realise that all the sensations that were
his were no more than trivial, partial, disconnected perceptions,

[1] Eng. Lit., p. 154.   [2] Chambers's Cyclopædia of Eng. Lit., v. 3, p. 14.
[3] Book IV, l. 1128.

and that all around him, interpreted truly, was full of blessings ?
We had better call another witness.

   After his sojourn in France, said Mr Herbert Read,
Wordsworth evolved a theory of art and a theory of life which,
because of the inclusiveness of its scope, the grandiosity of its
conception, and the exaltation of its expression, " has been
subject to a good deal of misapprehension." This, we observe,
is the old Wordsworthian charge against a goodly number of us.
By now, however, we are perhaps becoming hardened to it.
" The mind," Read wrote, " with him is always the creative
masculine principle, Nature is always the feminine or reproductive
principle." The distinction, Read asserted, " drawn between
the life of Nature and the life of Man is perhaps the most important
point to remember in considering Wordsworth's poetry. . . .
The romantic poet projects into Nature his own feelings and
sentiments. . . . For Wordsworth, however, Nature had her
own life, which was independent of ours, though a part of the
same Godhead." [1] It is not easy for an ordinary man to see
Tintern Abbey illuminated by this explanation. To substitute the
words " feminine or reproductive principle " for " Nature "
every time it is mentioned in the poem leads to results that are
odd, and somewhat different, it seems to me, from what
Wordsworth intended. We note that Read, like Brooke,
emphasised the point that to Wordsworth " Nature " was not
a reflection of his own, or of human feelings. Might it not
appear, however, to an ordinary juryman, that in speaking of
it as a " nurse," a " guide," and a " guardian " of his heart
Wordsworth was giving to it definite human qualities ?

   " Ought not he," Harper remarked, " to have remained
content, to whom had been vouchsafed high intercourse with
something so divine as the voice which spoke to him near
Tintern Abbey ? " [2] This suggests something which is perhaps
more intelligible to an ordinary reader—that what Wordsworth
was describing was a vision of an omnipresent God. Harper,
after quoting the central passage of the poem, spoke of " this
pantheism, for it is nothing less." [3] Myers, however—whom
we notice, by the way, observing, in words with which we may
again agree, that " to define with exactness . . . what was this
new element imported by our poet into man's view of Nature

[1] *Wordsworth*, pp. 171, 182, 183-4.   [2] *Wordsworth*, v. 2, p. 149.
[3] *Ibid.*, p. 148.

is far from easy,"—asserted of Wordsworth's worship of
" Nature " : " Such worship, I repeat, is not what we commonly
imply either by paganism or by pantheism." [1] It might appear
to an ordinary man that to identify not merely Nature but,
as it may have seemed to us, certain limited aspects of it with
God is not very far from paganism. But here Wordsworth
himself may be called as a witness on the other side. Read
has drawn attention to an unknown Unitarian lady's having
angered the poet in this connection. " She talks," Wordsworth
wrote to Mrs Clarkson, " of my being a worshipper of nature,
a passionate expression uttered incautiously in the poem upon
the Wye has led her into this mistake." It is interesting to
notice that there could be incautious expressions in this poem
of " flawless and noble beauty." " She condemns me," said
Wordsworth, " for not distinguishing between Nature as the
work of God, and God himself. But where does she find this
doctrine inculcated ? " " But the only help," Read commented,
" Wordsworth gives the Unitarian lady is an admonition to use
her intelligence, and be humble-minded. He does not tell her
what his conception of the Supreme Being actually is." [2] The
stock riposte !

What, again, is an ordinary juryman to make of the following
sentence in Harper ? " The perfect sonnet *To Sleep*—'A flock
of sheep that leisurely pass by '—shows the conquest he has
achieved over his unquiet soul, and how nature no longer haunts
him like a passion, but has become a ' Dear mother of fresh
thoughts and joyous health.' " [3] Does this particular sonnet
demonstrate that " Nature " is something in which Wordsworth
has found to exist a source of quiet ? Does not the poet say
very definitely that he has not been quietened at all, that he
has lain awake for three nights and is afraid of being sleepless
for a fourth, and that thinking of things we often associate with
Nature, of sheep, the sound of rain, bees, waterfalls, and so
forth has been powerless to calm him into slumber ? Was it
really " Nature " that Wordsworth called the " Dear mother of
fresh thoughts " ? Was it not sleep ? Are the two the same
thing ? Does " Nature " to a Wordsworthian mean anything
he pleases ?

When, in the rarefied atmosphere of a theatre, an actor of

[1] *Wordsworth*, Myers, pp. 124-5, 130.   [2] *Wordsworth*, Read, pp. 176-7.
[3] *Wordsworth*, Harper, v. 2, p. 106.

commanding presence delivers in richly-sounding tones lines
that are noble and vague, members of the audience may attach
to these musical phrases thoughts of their own, and imagine
these thoughts were present in the original. No doubt each
of the writers just quoted would be, or would have been, able
to defend his opinions powerfully. But the fact, nevertheless,
that we encounter so many different explanations of Wordsworth's
teaching, and that everyone seems so ready to call everyone
else stupid for not accepting his particular explanation, may
suggest that some such process has taken place here.

II

Yet the Wordsworthian doctrine came from so great a poet,
and has interested so many able minds, and promises so rich
benefits to those who accept it, that patient and unbiassed
jurymen may be even yet unwilling to abandon this enquiry.
There remains another way in which the matter may be regarded.
An electrician constructing a radio set may be unable to explain
clearly to the uninitiated the forces he is bringing into play.
But he is soon able to furnish unmistakable evidence that he is
in contact with these forces. Can something similar be said of
Wordsworth ? We may be unable to grasp his teaching. But
the results he described as accruing from it are, as has been said,
certainly definite. Did Wordsworth, we may ask then, himself
turn to " Nature " for help in his every time of distress and
find that she never failed him—that she led him unerringly
" from joy to joy," made him vastly stronger in spirit than is
the average man against life's vexations, and gave him the
undisturbable " faith " of which he spoke ? The pictures we
have seen drawn of him by Myers and Bradley suggest that all
these things were true. So does Wordsworth's description of
himself as one of the happiest of men. We have noted, however,
that " Nature " did not strengthen him to any superhuman
degree against the depreciation of hostile criticism, or prevent
him from becoming exhausted by the labour of composition,
or from worrying about money, or from appearing to Coleridge
to be a hypochondriac. Can it be that Wordsworth, in theatrical
parlance, " put on an act," and that Myers and Bradley were
deceived by it ?

De Quincey mentioned a period in Wordsworth's life when,
being momentarily without an income, he was faced by the

possibility that he might have to earn his living in the way in which ordinary men have to do it—by ordinary work. " He had all but resolved," De Quincey even asserted, " . . . to take pupils." " In this crisis of his fate," De Quincey wrote, " it was that Wordsworth, for once, and once only,"—Coleridge's, Dorothy's, and Harper's statements hardly bear this out— " became a martyr to some nervous affection." There is no record, however, of " Nature's " having helped him in this " crisis." The " remedy, or palliation," De Quincey tells us, which Wordsworth's friends adopted was to play with him every night at cards. De Quincey evidently found this difficult to believe ; yet, he wrote, " so it was ; for my information could not be questioned : it came from Miss Wordsworth." [1] Wordsworth graduated in 1791. In 1794—Calvert's legacy did not come till 1795—he must have been still pressed for money. But he had had in the interval numerous opportunities of deriving consolation from " Nature." In 1791 he had been in Wales, and in 1791 and 1792 in France ; in 1793 he had gone on walking tours, including that which took him along the Wye valley, and in part of 1794 he was among his native mountains and lakes. By now, therefore, we expect to encounter the man to whom " Nature " was " all in all." Yet in this year he wrote to Mathews from Keswick : " I begin to wish much to be in Town. Cataracts and mountains are good occasional society, but they will not do for constant companions." [2] " It is a denial," Read commented, " of the central doctrine of the *Prelude*, and one of those minute fissures of reality that make us doubt the autobiographical validity of that idealistic structure." [3] It is hardly, at anyrate, a remark we would have expected from the Wordsworth delineated in *Tintern Abbey*.

" Nature," it must be admitted, had not in Wordsworth's case too many serious occasions for giving him the mighty solace of which he declared her capable. Endowed with genius of an order seldom granted to man, given an education of the best kind England could bestow, afforded opportunities, from the age of twenty, of foreign travel, set free, at twenty-five, to do the work for which he was specially talented, he was surely exceptionally fortunate. In 1805, however, there did come a

---

[1] *Reminiscences of Eng. Lake Poets*, Everyman, pp. 144-5.
[2] *Wordsworth*, Harper, v. 1, p. 246.
[3] *Wordsworth*, Read, p. 121.

time when he was in real need of comfort—when his sailor
brother was drowned. " The shock of John's death," Harper
wrote, " with the exchange of sympathy which followed, roused
William to a salutary quickening of contact with his fellow-men.
This he has acknowledged in his *Elegiac Stanzas suggested by a
Picture of Peele Castle.*" [1] This poem contains, it will be recalled,
one of Wordsworth's most famous phrases. Mention of this
reminds us of a passage in which Myers linked this poem with
Tintern Abbey. " Unless," Myers wrote, " the words which
describe the intense and sympathetic gaze with which he
contemplates Nature convince us of the reality of ' the light
which never was on sea or land,'—of the ' Presence which disturbs
him with the joy of elevated thoughts,' . . . there is no argument
by which he can prove to us that he is offering a new insight to
mankind." [2] Can the two poems, we may ask however, be
linked together quite so easily ? Was Wordsworth's attitude to
" Nature," in this time of deep grief, quite so " sympathetic "
as it was in 1798, when he had no serious need of her consolation ?
May we look at *Peele Castle* for a moment with this question in
mind ?

Wordsworth informs us, we recollect, that he had once stayed
near this castle for four summer weeks. During all this time
the air had been calm, and the sea quiet. He could have
fancied, he wrote—and surely, in the circumstances, there is
pathos in the words—

> " that the mighty Deep
> Was even the gentlest of all gentle Things."

Had he been a painter, he said, he would have painted the
scene so, and added

> " the gleam,
> The light that never was, on sea or land,
> The consecration, and the Poet's dream."

These lines are generally thought of as describing what De
Quincey called " a light radiating from some far spiritual
world " [3]—the magic that dwells in all great art. It is interesting
at the same time to look at them in their context. " Such,"
Wordsworth wrote,

---

[1] *Wordsworth,* Harper, v. 2, p. 84.   [2] *Wordsworth,* Myers, p. 129.
[3] *Rem. of Eng. Lake Poets,* p. 104.

" in the fond illusion of my heart,
Such Picture would I at that time have made :
And seen the soul of truth in every part,
A steadfast peace that might not be betrayed.

So once it would have been,—'tis so no more ;
I have submitted to a new control :
A power is gone, which nothing can restore ;
A deep distress hath humanised my Soul."

" Fond illusion ! " Surely these are strange words to
associate with that " light " the " reality " of which Myers
suggested it was Wordsworth's aim constantly to convince us.[1]
Was it merely by accident that Wordsworth used here the
same verb " betray " which he used in *Tintern Abbey* ? Was
he not realising now that Nature could betray—realising the
cruelty that may lurk behind even her most perfect beauty ?
Never, he declared, could he now behold a smiling sea, and
be what he had been. The spirit of Beaumont's picture was
" wise and . . . well chosen " : he loved to see the look with
which the castle braved lightning, wind, and waves. Is this
trusting Nature to lead us on from joy to joy ? Is it not rather
defying and wrestling with her ? " Farewell," he went on,

" farewell the heart that lives alone,
Housed in a dream, at distance from the Kind !
Such happiness, wherever it be known,
Is to be pitied ; for 'tis surely blind."

Might it not appear to an ordinary juryman that these words are
a renunciation of the whole teaching of *Tintern Abbey* ? Are
they not a confession that, when sorrow comes which really
withers, theatrical illusions afford no solace, cataracts and
mountains become suddenly void of consolation, and we yearn
instinctively all of us, poet and member of the vulgar world
alike, as all the generations since Adam before us have yearned,
for the comforting of human friends ? Wordsworth, one might
venture to suggest also, was not merely brought down from his
stage position and " humanised " by this experience ; he was
now more of a man than he had been in the days when he

[1] Cf. Irving Babbitt : " ' The light that never was . . . ' of which
Wordsworth speaks, is likewise as appears very plainly from the context,
Arcadian." *Rousseau and Romanticism*, p. 303.

rejoiced in the existence of a " nurse." We recall the closing
stanza.

> " But welcome fortitude, and patient cheer,
> And frequent sights of what is to be borne !
> Such sights, or worse, as are before me here.—
> Not without hope we suffer and we mourn."

Harper connected the death of Wordsworth's brother also
with *The Ode to Duty*.[1] There are few people nowadays, I
imagine, who would do other than violently disagree with
Jeffrey's hasty and adverse criticism of this poem. We may
look for a moment, however, at his declaration that he had no
sort of conception in what sense Duty could be said to keep the
old skies fresh and the stars from wrong. Harper commented
that it was " not intelligence or taste " that Jeffrey lacked " so
much as goodwill." [2] The editor of one of the foremost reviews
of his time could hardly have missed, it is true, the obvious
parallel. But has Harper said all that may be said on the
matter ? Was not Wordsworth back here at his old game of
transforming Nature by stage-lighting into an innocent and
kindly rustic schoolmaster ? Is duty, in the helpful, human,
moral sense of the word, in reality at all the same thing as
Nature's " duty " ? Were not the waves carrying out their
duty, in precisely the same way as the stars do, on that night in
February 1805 when they poured into the stricken *Abergavenny*
and choked the life out of poor John Wordsworth ? [3]

By one regarding Wordsworth as Jeffrey saw him, as a being
made of the same clay as other men, an attempt might be made
to explain *Tintern Abbey* psychologically. It was not, we
recollect, only poverty that troubled Wordsworth in his earlier
years. There had occurred, when he was abroad, something
his silence about which all the rest of his life suggests he looked
upon as a blunder. Legouis states that, on his return from the
continent, he was afraid to face his guardians, and begged his
sister to do his talking for him.[4] He was evidently on the
look-out for someone on whom to lean at that time. Dorothy
referred, in a letter written to Jane Pollard in 1793, to the

---

[1] *Wordsworth*, v. 2, p. 83. [2] *Ibid.*, v. 2, p. 140.

[3] " It is not quite clear that the law of duty in the breast of man is the
same law that preserves ' the stars from wrong.' " *Rousseau and Romanticism*,
Babbitt, p. 286.

[4] *William Wordsworth and Annette Vallon*, p. 28.

" prejudices " of her uncles against her brother.[1] By 1795,
however, with the coming of Calvert's legacy, Wordsworth's
situation had changed. Those nine hundred sovereigns might
seem to a mundane juryman, considering Wordsworth's circumstances, to have had a considerable measure of healing-power
in them. We remember the shout of joy at being " now free,
Free as a bird " with which *The Prelude* opens, the elation that
runs through the lines in which he commemorated his walk
from Bristol to Racedown with " Long months of ease and
undisturbed delight . . . in prospect." He was going to live
with his beloved and worshipping sister. Soon he was to be
encouraged by contact with a great fellow-poet. Selincourt
has remarked that Wordsworth's " escape from the slough of
despond was due, as far as it was due to external influence, to
Dorothy and to Coleridge." [2]

But Wordsworth was not merely an ordinary young man
whom good fortune and the sympathy of friends had lifted out
of an imbroglio. He was a poet, and a poet with ambition.
And he had, by some means or other, to rehabilitate himself
in his own eyes. What swifter and more effective way was
there of doing this than by becoming a teacher of mankind and
the herald of a new gospel ? The fact that to certain of his
senior relatives it might have appeared that he had not, up to
that time, shown himself outstandingly qualified to instruct
others in the management of their lives might be no deterrent
but rather the reverse : he would show them ! The material
for a message was ready to his hand. He had been brought
up among scenery of great natural beauty. He loved that
beauty with a passionate intensity. He had become, now at
twenty-eight, conscious that he had a gift of words worthy of
any message. So to him " Nature " became suddenly all in
all. Garrod has pointed out a difference between Wordsworth's
attitude to Dorothy in *The Prelude* and that in *Tintern Abbey*.
In *The Prelude*, he observes, it was from Dorothy we are informed
that the author learned to tame a soul " too reckless of mild
grace "—too prone to seek beauty with terror in it. In *Tintern
Abbey*, Garrod reminds us however, it is Wordsworth who has
advanced the farther : Dorothy's feet are on the path that he
has already trod.[3] In the mood of *Tintern Abbey*, in other words,

---

[1] *Wordsworth*, Harper, v. 1, p. 202. [2] *Prelude*, ed. Selincourt (1933), p. 320.
[3] *Wordsworth*, Garrod, p. 103 ; *Prelude*, Book XIV, ll. 244-50.

the prophet must occupy stage-centre. Life had, for some years, been for him a disquieting experience ; but now peace had come to him and a sense that the world was full of blessings. The new gospel made it necessary that to the mystical influence of " Nature "—not at all to the warm human-kindliness of Calvert, Coleridge, and Dorothy—the credit for this should be given. No doubt the uncles had cast reflections upon his character : now, however, he had found in " Nature " an " anchor " for his purest thoughts, and, so secured, he could face them—and the rest of life—without fear. He had felt the need of someone—had not Dorothy performed the office ?—to shield him from " evil tongues, rash judgments " and the " sneers of selfish men "—possibly the uncles again. Now, however, he was independent of human aid ; " Nature " was now his " guardian " against all such—a guardian that " never did betray The heart that loved her." One wonders if it ever occurred to Wordsworth that a cynical and hostile uncle might have commented that Nature would appear to have already betrayed him in France.

III

There is no need, after this lengthy discussion of *Tintern Abbey* and the doctrines involved in it, to spend time in developing Jeffrey's criticism of the equally famous *Immortality Ode* as " illegible and unintelligible." The subsequent reputation of the poem rules the first adjective completely out of court. The second cannot, however, be dismissed so easily. Wordsworth himself told Aubrey de Vere that he held the belief in the Ode " with a poetic, not a religious, faith." [1] Some of Coleridge's criticisms of the poem—his blunt question, for example, regarding one passage in it, " What does all this mean ? " and his perceiving there " an approximation to . . . mental bombast "—might have been written by Jeffrey for the *Edinburgh*.[2] Arnold found " the great *Ode* not wholly free from something declamatory." [3] There remains the attitude of critics like Saintsbury. " Its theory," Saintsbury wrote, " has been scorned or impugned by some ; parts of it have even been called nonsense by critics of weight. But, sound or unsound, sense or nonsense, it is

[1] *Essays, chiefly on Poetry*, Aubrey de Vere, 1887, v. i, p. 258.
[2] *Biog. Lit.*, pp. 221-2.
[3] *Essays in Criticism* (Second Series), " Wordsworth."

poetry, and magnificent poetry, from the first line to the last—
poetry than which there is none better in any language, poetry
such as there is not perhaps more than a small volume-full in
all languages." [1] I think that Jeffrey would have said that
when a work containing what thinking and able men can
describe as nonsense, and professing, at the same time, by the
tone in which it is composed, to contain deep and serious truth,
is regarded by responsible criticism, on the sole ground that it
excites by its power, as having reached the highest summit of
art, there is here a profoundly significant phenomenon in history.

We counted Jeffrey's outburst of 1807 in connection with
Resolution and Independence among the criticisms that now injure
the reviewer more than they ever did the poet. Even Jeffrey's
more reasoned adjuration to Wordsworth, in a later article, to
contrast his " fantastical personages of . . . sententious leechgatherers " with Burns's " authentic rustics " may appear, at
first glance, impertinent in every sense of the word : there
are, I imagine, few lovers of poetry to-day who fail to appreciate
the impressiveness of that solitary wanderer on the moor
preserving, in the utmost decrepitude of age and in deepest
poverty, courage, and self-respect, and the dignity of a gentleman.
The poem might be said to be a complete and triumphant answer
to the assertion of the early and inexperienced Jeffrey that the
poor cannot interest us, in poetry, by any sentiments peculiar
to their condition. As for authenticity, might it not be said
that the leech-gatherer, with his courteous Scottish speech, his
lofty utterance, his gravity, and his firmness of mind, might
have been Burns's own father had fate made these William
Burnes's circumstances ? " He found ready access," Harper
wrote of Wordsworth, " by innate sympathy, to the emotional
range of the humble and uneducated, no less than to that of
the most privileged persons or the most extraordinary." [2]
Wordsworth claimed, we remember, that he " saw into the
depth of human souls." Jeffrey spoke of Wordsworth's
" knowledge of the human heart." *Resolution and Independence*
might be adduced as a piece of evidence in favour of all three
statements.

It cannot be alleged, in partial extenuation of his criticism,
that Jeffrey had gone completely berserk in that article of 1807 :
a page or so later, we have seen, he spoke of the sweetness of

[1] *Nineteenth Cent. Lit.*, p. 54.   [2] *Wordsworth*, v. 1, p. 18.

Wordsworth's *Emigrant Mother*. One reading the article alone, without other knowledge of Jeffrey, might readily be inclined to fall back upon the theory of Vaughan, that these are merely chance strokes. I think, however, that we are now in a position to understand his attitude. The point seems to me sufficiently important to warrant amplification.

We may commence by turning away, for a moment, from Wordsworth's delineations of rustics to some of his rustic neighbours' delineations, recorded by an observer, of the poet himself. "He would come round the garden," said one who, as gardener's lad, saw the poet daily for some years, "but never ' say nowt.' Sometimes, but this was seldom, he would say, ' Oh ! you're planting peas ? ' . . . but only as a master would ask a question of a servant." "He was a kind mon," the ex-gardener's boy remarked nevertheless, "there's no two words about that : if any one was sick i' the plaace, he wad be off to see til 'em." "He wozn't a man," declared another, "as said a deal to common folk. But he talked a deal to hissen. . . . We woz noan of us very fond on 'im." "He was distant, ye may saäy," remarked another, "varra distant." "Had he any particular friends among the shepherds ? " asked the investigator. "Na, na," was the reply, "not as ever I kent or heard of ; but he wozn't a mountaineer, was moastly down below upo' the road." "He niver cared for children," said the ex-butcher's boy, ". . . ya may be certain of that, for didn't I have to pass him four times in t'week, up to the door wi' meat ? And he niver oncst said owt. Ye're well aware if he'd been fond of children he 'ud 'a spoke." "He was fond of children like enough," we read again, "but children was niver vara fond o' him. . . . I'm not so sure he was fond of other foak's bairns, but he was very fond of his own, wi'out a doubt." "Wudsworth was no dog fancier ; and as for cats, he couldn't abide them." [1]

Is not the picture vivid ? One is driven to wonder if Wordsworth ever really saw as far into the depth of human souls as he imagined he did. There are fine pictures of peasants in Wordsworth ; but how often do we perceive, in his poetry, signs of an awareness that, when he was among his rustics, he

---

[1] *Reminiscences of Wordsworth among the Peasantry of Westmoreland,* by H. D. Rawnsley in *Wordsworthiana,* ed. Knight, 1889, pp. 89, 90-1, 92, 101, 103, 86, 113, 114.

was being judged as well as judging—that he was surrounded
all the time by those not unkindly but still shrewdly-appraising
eyes ?   I do not fancy anyone would hold that Wordsworth
saw farther into human souls than did Shakespeare, whom
Jeffrey placed at the head of all poets.   Yet Shakespeare never
claimed that he possessed this X-ray vision.   We remember
how Lear was baffled by the character of his own daughter,
Regan : we recall the old man's cry, " Is there any cause in
nature that makes these hard hearts ? "   Many of us may feel
with Bradley that this was an expression of Shakespeare's
bewilderment as well.   " Is not his [Shakespeare's] mind . . .
expressed," Bradley exclaimed again, " . . . in the scornful
rebuke of those who take upon them the mystery of things as
if they were God's spies ? " [1]   Surely we all feel that to
Shakespeare as to Hamlet man was infinite in faculty, and
therefore infinitely incalculable.   " Hamlet," Aldous Huxley
makes a character remark in one of his novels, " inhabited a
world whose best psychologist was Polonius.   If he had known
as little as Polonius, he would have been happy.   But he knew
too much . . . Polonius and the others assumed as axiomatic
that man was a penny whistle with only half a dozen stops.
Hamlet knew that, potentially at least, he was a whole symphony
orchestra." [2]   Perhaps it is shocking to compare our modern
scientific psychologists with Polonius.   Possibly it is still more
shocking to suggest that there was something of Polonius in
Wordsworth.   But we remember, at the same time, Polonius's
reference to the class of men to which he belonged—" We of
wisdom and of reach."   We recall his boast to Claudius—

> " Hath there been such a time,—I'd fain know that,—
>   That I have positively said, ' 'Tis so,'
>   When it prov'd otherwise ? "

and his declaration, in eloquent blank verse,

> " If circumstances lead me, I will find
>   Where truth is hid, though it were hid indeed
>   Within the centre."

Are these remarks entirely unWordsworthian ?

   We may turn next to Dorothy's account of the prototype of
the leech-gatherer.   " An old man almost double. . . . His face

---

[1] *Shakespearean Tragedy*, pp. 264, 274.   [2] *Eyeless in Gaza*, p. 144.

was interesting. He had dark eyes and a long nose. John, who afterwards met him . . . took him for a Jew. He was of Scotch parents, but had been born in the army. He had had a wife, and ' she was a good woman, and it pleased God to bless us with ten children.' All these were dead but one, of whom he had not heard for many years, a sailor. . . . He lived by begging, and was making his way to Carlisle, where he should buy a few godly books to sell. He said leeches were very scarce. . . . Leeches were formerly 2s. 6d. per 100 ; they are now 30s. He had been hurt in driving a cart, his leg broken, his body driven over, his skull fractured." [1]

Is there not very much here that is not in the poetry ? The portrait awakens question after question. Was there nothing more than simple fortitude behind that interesting face ? Was there a reason for that exotic cast of features despite the alleged Scottish parentage ? Had the repeated death-strokes that had destroyed those nine children and their mother left no scars upon that soul ? Why the estrangement from the one remaining son ? Did no warping of the mind accompany the torture of that twisted body ? Is there any significance in that business-like account of the rising price and growing scarcity of leeches and the projected substitution for commerce in them of a trade in " godly books " ? Is there a possibility, especially when we consider that it is probably with a half-Jew, half-Scotsman, that we are dealing, that the conversation which so impressed his hearers was a line of sales-talk ? The man was a professional beggar. Did he coax something out of William and Dorothy ?

We cannot object to Wordsworth's selecting and altering in order to construct his poem ; he was an artist, not a photographer. We ourselves have been merely conjecturing. But was it not lucky that this chance-encountered stranger, with all these potentialities, did not, as he appears in *Resolution and Independence*, disturb by so much as a single ejaculation the harmony of the lesson ? Mendicant and poverty-stricken rusticity, well-disciplined as " Nature," faithfully performed its office of illustrating the Wordsworthian philosophy. The poet's supernatural guardians, we are given to understand, were at their usual post of duty on this occasion as well. It was, we remember, perhaps " by peculiar grace, A leading from above, a something given " that Wordsworth met the leech-gatherer.

[1] *Journals of Dorothy Wordsworth*, ed. Knight, pp. 50-1.

R

One would wish to have respect for the lesson Wordsworth taught, for the character he drew, and for the power with which he told his story. But surely we are being led to a somewhat easy solution of the problem of human suffering, surely it is being made easy for us to see the world " full of blessings," if it is suggested that the unfortunate exist in order to provide lessons for those who are better off than themselves. And surely it becomes easy to imagine that we can plumb the depths of human character when we shut out from consideration all that may conflict with our theories.

Wordsworth spoke of his *Prelude* as having " the same kind of relation " to his *Recluse* " as the ante-chapel has to the body of a gothic church," and likened his minor pieces to " the little cells, oratories, and sepulchral recesses, ordinarily included in those edifices." [1] This architectural simile, I think Jeffrey might have commented, described exactly the " system " he criticised. The poet, he remarked in his summary of *Resolution and Independence* in 1807, was " so wrapped up in his own moody fancies " that he did not seem at first to be able to attend to the leech-gatherer's answer.[2] It was in the next number but one of the *Review* that he asserted that the Lakers drew attention to themselves rather than to the situation of their characters. These characters, he said in the same article, had " an idiosyncrasy, upon which all common occurrences " operated " in a peculiar manner." [3] It was Wordsworth's " fantastical personages of . . . sententious leechgatherers "—in the plural— that he asked the poet to contrast with the " authentic rustics " of Burns. He thought of the leech-gatherer, that is, not in isolation, but as a member of a class. It was this uniformity of characterisation that caused him to speak of Wordsworth's dramatis personæ as all dressed in a kind of " masquerade habit " and made him compare the species of composition in which they appeared to an opera.[4] To Jeffrey, in other words,

---

[1] Preface to *The Excursion*. [2] *Ed. Rev.*, No. 21, p. 223. [3] *Ibid.*, No. 23, p. 134.

[4] Cf. Gates, speaking of *Resolution and Independence* : " Wordsworth has no right, Jeffrey insists, to treat the peasant merely as the symbol of his own peculiar mood."—*Three Studies*, p. 24 : and Babbitt : " At a given moment in this poem the leech-gatherer undergoes a strange transformation ; he loses all verisimilitude as a leech-gatherer and becomes a romantic symbol, a mere projection, that is, of the poet's own broodings. To push this symbolizing of mood beyond a certain point is incipient hallucination." *Rousseau and Romanticism*, p. 296.

this was not an orderliness of life but simply of melodrama—
that sort of orderliness which allows no character to say or do
anything which does not contribute to the unfolding of the
plot, or which might detract from the impressiveness of the
moment when, the performance completed, and all the mock
difficulties of the evening triumphantly surmounted, the hero
and actor-manager acknowledges majestically the plaudits of an
admiring audience.

On Jeffrey's comment on one of the passages in *The Excursion*
that seemed to him unnecessarily obscure—that commencing
" But by the storms of circumstance unshaken "—Harper
remarked, " If the editor of *The Edinburgh Review* really did not,
as he asserted, form the slightest guess as to the meaning of
the . . . passage . . . this shows how slow Englishmen—and
even Scotsmen—were to acquaint themselves with the terms
and conceptions of Kant." [1] I share the scepticism expressed
in the first part of Harper's sentence. I think Jeffrey could have
worked out the meaning of the passage, and found the key
to it in philosophical Edinburgh, had he been willing to take
the trouble. But I think that he was speaking, as always, for
the ordinary reader. " If poetry is intended for general delight,"
he said to Southey on one occasion, " ought not its language
to be generally intelligible ? " [2] He was insisting that thoughts
should be impressive in themselves. He was refusing to allow
to them the theatrical pseudo-impressiveness that comes from
mere recondite allusion.

The later-nineteenth-century tendency to picture Jeffrey
as a stage villain because of his criticism of one of the age's
literary heroes might be regarded as another indication of the
period's leaning towards theatricality. But Jeffrey was not the
only reader of his time to express opinions of the kind we have
been noticing. It was suggested in an earlier chapter that
there was a similarity between the outlook of Jeffrey and that of
Keats. " It may be said," Keats wrote in one of his letters,
" . . . that Wordsworth, etc., should have their due from us.
But, for the sake of a few fine imaginative or domestic passages,
are we to be bullied into a certain philosophy engendered in
the whims of an egotist ? Every man has his speculations, but
every man does not brood and peacock over them till he makes
a false coinage and deceives himself." That passage contains,

[1] *Wordsworth*, v. 2, p. 242.   [2] *Cont.*, v. 2, p. 434.

we observe, precisely the Jeffreyan charge of theatricality. " We hate poetry," Keats wrote, " that has a palpable design upon us, and, if we do not agree, seems to put its hand into its breeches pocket." [1] There we have the Jeffreyan protest against the characteristic Lakish attitude. " I have read fifty articles," Lockhart wrote in 1851, " on Wordsworth's philosophy. Hang me if I don't suspect 'tis all an airy sham—beyond what lies on the very surface. . . . It seems to be assumed that William Wordsworth made some wonderful discovery, which Homer, Dante etc., etc., lived and died without having had even a glimpse of. I beg to doubt. . . . I suspect there is more of artifice than of art in all that has been relied on for proof of this modern originality." [2] Carlyle, speaking of the scenery around St Mary's Loch, remarked that it was nowhere without " solidly characteristic features . . . presented to you in naturâ, not as in a Drury Lane with stage-lights and for a purpose." [3] Carlyle may have had certain contemporary dealings with nature in mind when he wrote that. At anyrate, he made his opinion of the Wordsworthian philosophy clear enough. " To my private self," he wrote, " his divine reflections and unfathomabilities seemed stinted, scanty, palish and uncertain ; perhaps in part a feeble reflex (derived at second hand through Coleridge) of the immense German fund of such." [4] " I am altered very much about Wordsworth," Haydon wrote, " from finding him too hard, too elevated, to attend to the voice of humanity. No, give me Byron with all his spite, hatred, depravity, dandyism, vanity, frankness, passion, and idleness, rather than Wordsworth with all his heartless communion with woods and grass." [5] Lowell, speaking of " the ancients and our own Elizabethans," remarked, " If they had not discovered the picturesque, as we understand it, they found surprisingly fine scenery in man and his destiny, and would have seen something ludicrous, it may be suspected, in the spectacle of a grown man running to hide his head in the apron of the Mighty Mother whenever he had an ache in his finger or got a bruise in the tussle for existence." [6] Legouis referring, in the next century, to the sonnet, " It is a beauteous evening," remarked, " There

[1] *Life and Letters*, Houghton, pp. 60-1.
[2] *Life and Letters*, Lang, v. 2, p. 280.   [3] *Reminiscences*, v. 1, pp. 134-5.
[4] *Ibid.*, v. 2, p. 331.   [5] *B. R. Haydon and His Friends*, Paston, p. 143.
[6] *Eng. Crit. Essays*, 19th cent., ed. Jones, 1922, p. 607.

is certainly nothing in this pious effusion, full of biblical and religious evocations, to betray the presence of a natural daughter of the poet. . . . To us who are better informed, this almost sacerdotal blessing offers a striking example of the way in which Wordsworth was apt to solemnise the most mundane passages of his life." [1] The resemblances between these statements and Jeffrey's criticisms are sufficiently obvious.

For us at the Jeffreyan viewpoint the test must be the usual one. If a juryman sincerely feels that the Wordsworth who is the hero of all Wordsworth's poetry, and who is held up as a prophet and example to us all, was a faithful reflection of the real Wordsworth, if he is sincerely convinced that Wordsworth did actually discover a new way, missed by all who had lived before him, of mastering life's difficulties, a new way of access to influences by means of which all around us may, in sober truth, be transformed into blessings and we may see " Utopia . . . every day," and if he is persuaded accordingly, as in such a case he must undoubtedly be, that all those triumphant thunderings were fully justified, then to him Jeffrey is simply a critic who was completely in the wrong. But if any juryman has a suspicion that the hero of Wordsworth's poetry resembled in some degree those theatrical heroes described in the article on *Nineveh*, wielding resplendent weapons with an exact imitation of heroic gesture, evincing in speech and deportment a full sense of inward nobleness and dignity, and yet never engaging in any feat of actual prowess, if he wonders if the hero-Wordsworth's victories over sorrows were to be accounted for, despite the imposing background music with which they were accompanied, not so much by the greatness and strength of the philosophy as by the fact that the enemy was seldom outstandingly formidable, if he suspects, in other words, that Wordsworth may have been as histrionic, in his own way, as was Byron—then this is a juryman whom Jeffrey, I think, would have claimed to be approaching agreement with himself.

[1] *Wordsworth and Annette Vallon*, pp. 68-9.

CHAPTER XIV

THE MENACE

The boundary-line. Difference between Elizabethan and nineteenth-century romanticism. Effects of the later romanticism. Lakish ideas in the modern world. Further aspects of the Jeffreyan attitude. Common sense and common people.

I

THE puzzle Saintsbury found in Jeffrey was, we saw in our second chapter, to discover the boundary-line between the ancient and the modern elements in his criticism—between, that is, classicism and romanticism. I think we are now close to an answer. We may look at this point at two passages in Gates. " As long," Gates wrote, " as Romanticism seemed chiefly decorative, as in Scott or Keats, Jeffrey could tolerate it or even delight in it. But the moment it began, whether in Byron or Wordsworth, to take itself seriously, and to struggle to express new moral and spiritual ideals, Jeffrey protested. Just here lies the key to what some critics have found a rather perplexing problem,—the reasons for the varying degrees of Jeffrey's sympathy with the poets of his day." And again, " So long . . . as the fire and the heat of Romanticism spent themselves merely in giving imaginative splendour to style, Jeffrey could tolerate the movement, and could even regard it with favour, as a return to that power and fervour and wild beauty that he had taught himself to admire in Elizabethan poetry. But the moment the new energy was suffered to penetrate life itself and to convert the conventional world of dead fact, through the vitalizing power of passion, into a genuinely new poetic material, then Jeffrey stood aghast at what seemed to him a return to chaos. Byron with his fiery bursts of selfish passion, Wordsworth with his steadily glowing consciousness of the infinite, and Shelley with his ' white heat of transcendentalism,' were all alike for Jeffrey portentously dangerous forces and unhealthy phenomena." [1] I do not find myself in complete agreement. I think that Jeffrey perceived when romanticism in Scott and Keats became more than what Gates called

[1] *Three Studies*, pp. 25, 27.

" decorative," and that he expressed disapproval then immediately. The difference to which Gates pointed, between something which Jeffrey could admire, and something he felt obliged to do battle with, does not appear to me precisely describable as a difference between a romanticism that was chiefly an embellishment and a romanticism that went deeper : the distinction seems to me subtler. I know no evidence for the assertion that Jeffrey " taught himself to admire " the beauty of Elizabethan poetry. We have seen that when he was only eighteen, in discussing a literary point, the name of Shakespeare came first to his pen. We have observed with what enthusiasm he wrote of the Elizabethans in the *Review*. " There, now," he exclaimed in a letter written when he was sixty-six, " you see what it is to set me off upon Shakespeare ! " [1] But I think, nevertheless, that Gates provided us here with a valuable guide-post. We observe that Gates, like Harper, suggested that Jeffrey saw peril in the new ideas. To Gates, of course, who was writing, as Harper was, in a seemingly secure environment, words like " portentously dangerous " appeared employable, in this connection, only in a Pickwickian sense.

We compared, in our last chapter, certain of the ideas of Wordsworth with those of Shakespeare. If we carry this comparison a little farther, and consider the difference between the outlook and artistic practice of the Elizabethans, as Jeffrey saw them, and those of the authors of his own day, the road on which we are travelling may become still plainer. We noticed, to recommence with another simple illustration, Jeffrey's assertion that the older writers made no attempt to draw attention to their skill by laying bare the machinery of composition. Where do we find Shakespeare bemusing himself by lengthy theorisings about poetic diction? " There are few persons, of good sense," Wordsworth wrote in his preface of 1802, " who would not allow that the dramatic parts of composition are defective, in proportion as they deviate from the real language of nature, and are coloured by a diction of the Poet's own." " Each time the wonder grows," a twentieth-century critic commented on this sentence, " what ' sleepy drench' could make Wordsworth come to this "—and he quoted, among other things, Claudio's " To lie in cold obstruction, and to rot," and Macbeth's " The multitudinous seas

[1] *Life*, Cockburn, v. 2, pp. 310-12.

in carnadine." [1]   Yet this same Shakespeare could, without writing dissertations on the function, in poetry, of simple language, " leave us," as Bradley put it, " on the topmost peaks of poetry " with a phrase like " Undo this button." [2]   Shakespeare, in other words, like most ordinary people, left his work to speak for itself.   Nowhere in Shakespeare do we find rustics of an order so special that their passions are necessarily " incorporated with the beautiful and permanent forms of nature."   His rustics' associations of ideas are as various as those of any other class of men : the gravedigger in *Hamlet*, throwing up the skull of his old friend Yorick, was moved only to remembrance of a flagon of Rhenish which that joker once poured over his head. Where in Shakespeare do we encounter Nature the " nurse " ? Surely no man ever perceived more keenly than Shakespeare did the loveliness of the natural world.   But that perception did not blind him to the existence of biting winds which, when they blow upon our bodies, feelingly persuade us what we are ; to that of frosts, keen piercing as man's ingratitude ; to that of tempests which could, like servile ministers, beat without mercy on the white head of a helpless old man.   Shakespeare nowhere teaches that beatific wisdom may be acquired merely by sitting passive and absorbing impulses from vernal woods : he knew that a man might peak, like John-a-dreams, unpregnant of his cause, and thereby bring himself and all around him to ruin.   Shakespeare classed together the lunatic, the lover, and the poet as being " of imagination all compact " : but he did not suggest that the devils the madman saw were actually there, and that it was only because ordinary men had inferior vision that they could not see them as well.   The lover saw Helen's beauty in a brow of Egypt ; but his sweetheart's brow remained sunburnt.   The poet gave to airy nothing a local habitation and a name ; but Shakespeare did not suggest that the airy nothings poets saw were in truth high realities which the grosser world had to take on trust.   He left us to think of his fairies, his ghosts, his witches, his Ariel, his Caliban, as symbols, if we care so to regard them, of the beauty of flowers and of woodland, of mysteries of life and death, of powers of evil ranging the world, of forces available for man's controlling, of brute mind in contact with culture—or in any other way we please.   Nowhere

---

[1] *The Decline and Fall of the Romantic Ideal*, F. L. Lucas, p. 181.
[2] *Shakespearean Tragedy*, p. 293.

does he give us the impression that he stands over us like a schoolmaster, in possession of keys to life's enigmas unknown to us, with his hand ready to spring to his breeches pocket for our chastisement if our solutions to the Universe's problems differ from his. Shakespeare had, in other words, sufficient respect for us to allow to us thoughts of our own. Where upon earth is to be found lordlier company than his great men—Brutus, the noblest Roman of them all ; Hamlet, the expectancy and rose of the fair state ; Othello, the valiant Moor ; Macbeth, saviour of his country and the idol of its army ; Lear, who was in youth every inch a king, and who retained in his countenance, even in broken old age, that which men call authority ? Surely it may be said of these portrayals that the conventional world of dead fact was there converted, through the vitalizing power of passion, into genuinely new poetic material. If that which permits us to penetrate to the core of experiences remote from our own, into the depths of minds more richly adorned than ours can ever be, be true romanticism, then surely romanticism is here, not merely a decoration, but part of the web of the fabric. But where can it be said that Shakespeare revealed to us " new moral and spiritual ideals," undreamed of by mankind during all its centuries of existence till he hit upon them ? That high idealism is useless unless accompanied by practical knowledge of men, that thinking too precisely on the event may paralyse action and bring about disaster, that the noblest are sometimes at the mercy of the unscrupulous and that jealousy is cruel as the grave, that sin leads to sin and the way of sin to death, that years may come and understanding lag behind —do not all these ring true with the age-old common sense of humanity ? Who of the great men of Shakespeare would have claimed he could show us the key to life's mysteries and the true road to happiness with the confidence of the stage-Wordsworth ? Are they not all, at bottom, like the poor rest of us, simply mariners steering the ships of their destinies with, in their case, a splendour of dignity—that they never lose—but without sufficient skill, at times, in the darkness, and no more able to control or even foresee the paths of tempests than any one else ? Are they not, in other words, as Jeffrey put it, " all drawn with the full lineaments and just proportions of real men ? "

When we return to the nineteenth century we perceive at once the change of atmosphere. It was not only in Wordsworth,

we remember, that Jeffrey found theatricality. "According to
Fichte," Carlyle wrote for instance, introducing us to beings
of an order evidently different from that to which Shakespeare
and his characters belonged, "there is a 'Divine Idea' pervading
the visible Universe ; which visible Universe is indeed but its
symbol and sensible manifestation. . . . Literary Men are the
appointed interpreters of this Divine Idea ; a perpetual priest-
hood, we might say, standing forth, generation after generation,
as the dispensers and living types of God's everlasting wisdom,
to show it in their writings and actions, in such particular form
as their own particular times require it in." Later in the same
essay, speaking of certain literary men—"These men," Carlyle
wrote, ". . . have penetrated into the mystery of Nature ;
after long trial they have been initiated ; and to unwearied
endeavour, Art has at last yielded her secret ; and thus can the
Spirit of our Age, embodied in fair imaginations, look forth on
us, earnest and full of meaning, from their works. As the first
indispensable condition of good poets, they are wise and good
men : much they have seen and suffered, and they have
conquered all this, and made it all their own ; they have known
life in its heights and depths, and mastered it in both, and can
teach others what it is, and how to lead it rightly." Critics
were not expected, of course, to rise to these levels. But they
too had their rôles in this neatly-ordered drama. "Criticism,"
Carlyle asserted, "stands like an interpreter between the
inspired and the uninspired ; between the prophet and those
who hear the melody of his words, and catch some glimpse of
their material meaning, but understand not their deeper import."
The opinions of ordinary people like ourselves were, we observe,
nowhere taken into the reckoning. "To apprehend this beauty
of poetry," Carlyle wrote, "in its full and purest brightness,
is not easy, but difficult ; thousands on thousands eagerly read
poems, and attain not the smallest taste of it." To some of the
"vulgar world" he threw, at the same time, a crumb of comfort
—large enough, perhaps, to keep the book-market alive. "Yet,"
Carlyle added, "to all uncorrupted hearts, some effulgences of
this heavenly glory are here and there revealed ; and to
apprehend it clearly and wholly, to acquire and maintain a
sense and heart that sees and worships it, is the last perfection
of all humane culture." [1]

[1] *Critical and Miscellaneous Essays*, 1888, v. 1, pp. 44, 50, 39, 42.

Common sense tells us that true greatness should be honoured. We have seen that part of Jeffrey's teaching was that great writers should have their meed of authority. But it may be reasonable for us, who are trying to keep ourselves at the Jeffreyan viewpoint, to ask, as Jeffrey instructed us, for " examples " of the men Carlyle meant. Wordsworth, it may be imagined, would have numbered himself among them. We saw a few pages back, however, what Carlyle thought of Wordsworth. He could hardly have included Coleridge among the literary men of whom he spoke : he asserted of Coleridge that his " express contributions to poetry, philosophy, or any specific province of human literature or enlightenment had been small and sadly intermittent." [1] He could scarcely have included Southey. He expressed respect for Southey, said even that " one could not help loving such a man " ; yet he " rather felt " as if Southey were " a shrillish thin kind of man, the feminine element perhaps considerably predominating and limiting." [2] He could not have included Shelley, Lamb, or Austen ; we saw in our first chapter what he thought of them. He could hardly have included Scott : he declared of Scott that he had " turned the history of his country into an opera " [3]—significant word. He could hardly have included Dickens. He said of Dickens that he had written nothing which would be " found of much use in solving the problems of life " ; though he did concede that Dickens was " worth something ; worth a penny to read of an evening before going to bed." [4] When we look back to Carlyle's essay to see to whom precisely he referred we discover that it was to certain German poets whose works were probably sufficiently unfamiliar to most of his readers for distance to lend enchantment to the view. Is it unreasonable to suspect theatricality here ?

Jeffrey accepted Carlyle's essay for the *Edinburgh*. But he made his personal opinion plain on these matters. " I fairly tell you," he wrote to Carlyle, " that I think your taste vicious in some points, and your opinions of your German idols erroneous." And he refused positively to permit himself to be numbered even among his friend's lesser heroes. " I wish," he wrote to Carlyle in 1828, referring to some " magnificent

---

[1] *Coleridge*, H. D. Traill, p. 198.   [2] *Reminiscences*, v. 2, p. 311.
[3] *Carlyle to Threescore-and-Ten*, Wilson, p. 52.
[4] *Carlyle at his Zenith*, Wilson, p. 126.

compliments " the latter had been paying him, " I were worthy of them—or rather I wish you would like me without supposing that I am. But you mystics will not be contented with kindness of heart and reasonable notions in anybody—but you must have gifts and tasks and duties—and relations with the universe, and strugglings to utter forth the truth—God help you and your vain-glorious jargon, which makes angels smile I take it, and sensible men laugh outright." [1]

We have noted that while Jeffrey spoke with deep admiration both of the character and of the works of Scott, he spoke also —and we have suggested he was speaking seriously—of the " perversion " of Scott's genius, and of Scott's being " corrupted " by romanticism. I do not think Jeffrey would have desired us to dwell long on this point when a man like Scott was concerned. In support of the suggestion that Jeffrey's instincts told him there was danger here we may quote simply the testimony of Scott's own son-in-law. " An imagination such as his," Lockhart wrote, " concentrating its day-dreams on things of this order, soon shaped out a world of its own—to which it would fain accommodate the real one. . . . Fancy rebuilt and most prodigally embellished the whole system of the social existence of the middle ages. . . . He desired to plant a lasting root. . . . By this idea all his reveries—all his aspirations—all his plans and efforts, were overshadowed and controlled. . . . He wished to revive the interior life of the castles he had emulated. . . . The author of such a series of romances as his must have, to all intents and purposes, lived more than half his life in worlds purely fantastic. . . . He appears to have studiously escaped from whatever could have interfered with his own enjoyment— to have revelled in the fair results, and waved the wand of obliterating magic over all besides ; and persisted so long, that . . . he became the dupe of his own delusions. . . . The indulgence cost him very dear." [2]

We recall Jeffrey's assertion that the effect of Byron's writings was to shake our confidence in virtue to the foundation. The test of Byron's " new moral and spiritual ideals " must, for a Jeffreyan juryman, be, as always, simple. He must ask himself honestly if he would be glad to see a son of his own adopt all the sentiments, perform all the actions, and undergo all the

---

[1] *Carlyle to French Rev.*, pp. 28, 74.
[2] *Life of Scott*, v. 7, pp. 401-7.

experiences of Byron. Byron's description of his sufferings has been itself sometimes called theatrical. We noticed, however, Arnold's opinion that he who stops at the theatrical preludings does not know Byron. If it appear to a juryman that a theatrical " make-up," donned by the poet in the first instance largely out of a romantic desire to see himself as the hero of his own fantastic compositions, infiltrated gradually into the being of the man—penetrated, in Gates's phrase, " life itself "—so that, before the play was finished, he found it impossible to remove it, and to prevent what had been in the beginning a mock-tragedy from becoming a real one—that juryman may feel that it is in sober truth " portentously dangerous " to play-act in real life.

We saw that Jeffrey read *Christabel* " with some pleasure," but that he was affected, in his public criticism, by what appeared to him the extravagance of its admirers. We may gain an idea of the kind of appreciation he might have thought extravagant if we glance for a moment at a piece of romantic criticism of the work. Watts-Dunton, referring to the line

" The night-birds all that hour were still,"

commented, " This is the very highest reach of poetic wonder. . . . It required a poet steeped in the true poetic wonder of pre-Augustanism—it required Coleridge, whose genius was that very

> ' Lady of the Lake,
> Sole-sitting by the shores of Old Romance '—

to feel the most tremendous and awe-inspiring picture, perhaps, in all poetry called up to his imagination—

> ' The night-birds all that hour were still.'

The nearer in temper any other line approaches this, the nearer does it approach the ideal of poetic wonder." [1] Many of us may have found pleasure in *Christabel*—more pleasure than Jeffrey allowed himself to feel—as an exquisite fragment of magic and moonshine. But I wonder how many of us can say with complete honesty that our pulses really missed a beat when we came to the line about the night-birds. The employment,

[1] *Chambers's Cyclopædia of Eng. Lit.*, v. 3, pp. 7-8.

in connection with such a work, of epithets like " tremendous "
and " awe-inspiring " may wrench some of us out of fairyland
and force us to compare Coleridge's unsubstantial personages
with people of flesh and blood—compel us to ask, for instance,
how it came about that Christabel could pray in a wood at
midnight in a chilly April, and later ascend long, probably
stone, stairs without her shoes on, and that Geraldine could lie
unconscious in the same wood in the same chilly weather for
longer, if her words are to be believed, than she was able to tell,
with her neck, arms, and feet bare, without the beauty of either
being marred by the slightest blueness of nose, or the poetic
atmosphere being disturbed by so much as a sneeze. Are
jurymen possessed of ordinary common sense really expected
to be moved to the depths of their beings by the experiences
of creatures whose troubles, they know, can be dispelled at
any moment by the same easy magic as has rendered them
immune from the effects of draughts? Jurors of the mid-
twentieth century, who have had reason to be aware of the
terrors that stalk the actual world, may understand how it
came about that Jeffrey, who believed that a sense of proportion
was among humanity's most precious possessions, was driven into
violent rebellion.

This, it might be said, is criticism of Watts-Dunton, not
of Coleridge, who asked for no more from his readers than a
" willing suspension of disbelief." It is not difficult, however,
to see Coleridge as Jeffrey saw him, as a man seduced by his
own imaginings. He declared oracularly, for example, in the
prospectus to his Watchman, that " Knowledge is Power " ; [1]
but apparently it did not occur to him that it was his own
business at that moment to acquire sufficient practical knowledge
to give that periodical a reasonable chance of success. When
thirty years old he sent to Southey a scheme of a " Bibliotheca
Britannica " so grandiose that even that industrious and
methodical student described it as too gigantic and quite beyond
his powers—as if Coleridge imagined that he could charm from
himself the circumscriptions of time and his temperament as
easily as he charmed away pneumonia from the characters in
Christabel.[2] At the age of thirty-nine he had still so little sense
of responsibility that he was willing to impose on Southey,

[1] Biog. Lit., p. 81.
[2] Coleridge, Traill, p. 102 ; Letters of Southey, World's Classics, pp. 69-72.

" himself heavily burdened, those duties which every man of feeling and honour proudly and even jealously guards as his own "—the duty, that is, of providing for his wife and children.[1] In 1816, at the age of forty-three, he entered the house in which he was from that time looked after like a child himself. Yet we find him proclaiming, in 1831, in *Table Talk* : " Alas ! I look in vain for some wise and vigorous man to sound the word Duty in the ears of this generation." [2] Does not this suggest a man who got fact and fancy mixed in his thinking ?

There is evidence that this lack of grip upon actuality was infectious. Traill tells us of one of Coleridge's disciples, Joseph Henry Green, surgeon and fellow of the Royal Society, who, conceiving it his duty to systematise, develop, and establish his master's philosophical doctrines, retired from his profession, studied " theology, ethics, politics and political history, ethnology, language, æsthetics, psychology, physics, and the allied sciences, biology, logic, mathematics, pathology . . . in at least their basial principles and metaphysics," set himself to improve his knowledge of Greek, reached the age of sixty and decided he must now learn Hebrew, took up Sanskrit still later, found himself, when nearing seventy, obliged to abandon his project in its most ambitious form, and died at seventy-two with his work still unpublished.[3]

Gates, we noted, included Shelley's transcendentalism among the phenomena Jeffrey considered unhealthy. Jeffrey's neglect of Shelley might be regarded as a negative form of judgment : his allusion to Shelley's genius as " powerful " but " uncertain " is definite if brief criticism. Mary Shelley, Arnold has told us, asking counsel from a friend about the school she should choose for her son, was advised to send the boy somewhere where he would be taught to think for himself. " Teach him to think for himself ? " replied Mrs Shelley. " Oh, my God, teach him rather to think like other people." " Undoubtedly," Arnold commented, " the brilliant and attaching rebel who in thinking for himself had of old our sympathy so passionately with him, when we come to read his full biography makes us often and often inclined to cry out : ' My God ! he had far better have thought like other people.' " [4] No one will surely describe these as superficial pleas for conventionality. Are they not

---

[1] *Coleridge*, Traill, p. 140.   [2] V. 1, p. 263.   [3] *Coleridge*, pp. 180-6.
[4] *Essays in Criticism* (Second Series), " Shelley."

rather expressions of one of Jeffrey's fundamental ideas ? We
recall the circumstances of Shelley's expulsion from college—he
had settled while yet in his teens the non-existence of God—his
youthful impulsive marriage, his belief that he could, at nineteen,
settle the Irish question, his sending out his plans for reforming
the world in boxes floating on rivers, his asking Harriet to join
Mary and himself in Switzerland. Shelley, Arnold declared,
had " a superhuman power of self-deception." Surely these
are the acts of a man who turned his face away from reality
and saw himself as the hero of a play. A charitable juryman
might suggest that we should merely smile at these things as
eccentricities of generous youth. But to Mary Shelley they
were not a joke. The death of Harriet was not a joke. We
recognise that this Jeffreyan view would not be approved by all
modern critics. " He even proposes," Herford wrote, replying
to Irving Babbitt who, many years after Jeffrey, criticised both
Shelley and romanticism in general, " to make conduct the court
of final adjudication upon the worth of the ideas. ' By their
fruits ye shall know them.' The history of theological controversy
abundantly illustrates the hazards incident to this procedure."
And again, " One is almost ashamed to have to reiterate,"
Herford asserted, " a century after his death, that deeper in
him [Shelley] than the merely centrifugal revolt, and in all his
greatest achievements transforming and spiritualizing it, was
the passionate self-subjection to a higher law, sometimes to be
called Beauty, sometimes Love. Everyone can feel this in his
verse." [1] These sentences appear to me to illustrate the profound
importance of the questions we are now discussing. Everyone
knows that the moment we commence upon problems of ethics
we enter a sea that is thick with quicksands. But it may appear
to some jurymen that we are all of us afloat on that sea whether
we recognise the fact or not—living in a world in which acts
and ways of thinking have, in the long run, moral consequences
as certainly as they have physical consequences—and that it is
theatricality, turning life into a play again, to imagine that
we have it in our power to refuse to enter it. We grant at once
that as the test by fruits is that which bears hardest on us all
it is a test we are all strongly tempted to avoid. But surely
this does not invalidate it. To say that a " higher law " is
discoverable in Shelley's poetry may appear to some to be like

[1] *Ess. and St. by Members of Eng. Assn.*, v. 8, pp. 110, 130-1.

saying that even if sailing directions send ships to the bottom it is a sufficient defence of them that the manner of their wording afforded indisputable evidence of genius, and that they teemed with lofty and moving aspirations. It might be argued that our reasoning is being affected here by a trope—that there may be controversy about the results as well as about the principles—that what appears to one man to be shipwreck in this metaphorical sea may appear to another entry into a desirable haven. We remember, however, Jeffrey's insistence that when we trust fearlessly to common sense we discover that uncertainty in such matters is actually very limited. Dowden wrote of Harriet, " There is no doubt she wandered from the ways of upright living." [1] Does common sense allow that this may be said with impunity of Harriet simply because she wrote no beautiful poetry, but that it must not be breathed against her husband simply because he did ? Jeffrey, we remember, granted genius no such " dispensing power." Dowden's volumes, Arnold said, give us " data for picturing anew the Shelley who delights " ; but they picture also, he added, " a Shelley who, to speak plainly, disgusts." When we find a responsible critic impelled to describe thus the conduct of a man whom in many respects he admired, whom it was his strong inclination to defend, are we not approaching a point where uncertainty must cease ? If there be serious weakness in a man's way of thinking can this fail to be reflected, in some shape or another, in his writing ?

Is there no significance in these repeated tragedies in the lives of these greatly gifted men ? Surely we can say, without losing anything of proper respect for the great, wherein they were worthy, and without losing anything of our own proper humility, " O ! the pity of it." Shakespeare teaches us to say this over and over again. Can we afford, for the sake of the world we live in, to say anything else ?

It has been suggested earlier that one of the reasons for Jeffrey's being attracted by the poetry of Keats was that he perceived instinctively that Keats's viewpoint was nearer to his own than were those of many of their contemporaries. But he warned Keats also against allowing his imagination to master him—against permitting himself to be " rapt into an extra-mundane Elysium."

[1] *Life of Shelley*, v. 2, p. 65.

S

II

It might be argued at this point that we have been doing here precisely what we accused Wordsworth of doing—selecting examples to suit our theories.   The Lakers whom Jeffrey attacked most constantly were Southey and Wordsworth.   Both poets lived lives which, judged by common sense standards, were surely highly successful.   " What makes the life of Southey eminent and singular," Dowden wrote, " is its unity of purpose, its persistent devotion to a chosen object, its simplicity, purity, loyalty, fortitude, kindliness, truth." [1]   There is no sign there of " new moral and spiritual ideals."   If Southey filled his poetry with romanticism, he kept his feet, in everyday life, upon " the beaten highway," to quote another of Jeffrey's phrases, " of morality." [2]

May not the same be said of his fellow-Laker ?   May it not be said of Wordsworth that in those many days of his during which he was a quiet master of the art of living his actions were governed, not by any original ethical code, but simply by adherence to ancient and normal virtues—temperance, perseverance, patience, plainness of living, recognition of the value of household laws—and by adherence to modes of procedure consonant with ordinary common sense ?   If he asserted in his poetry that one impulse from a vernal wood could teach us more of man, of moral evil and of good than could all the sages, he did not allow this thought to prevent him from studying many books, or from producing many printed pages of his own.   If he romanticised rustics he never committed the social *faux-pas* of identifying himself with them.   If he theorised about the value for poetry of peasant-diction, this did not prevent his utilising for his own poetry all the resources of an educated man's vocabulary.   When troubles assailed him he did not merely sit a solitary communicant with woods and grass : he accepted comfort also from human friends.   When, as a married man with a family, he found his responsibilities increasing, whether or not he looked for " Nature's " guidance on the subject, he did not omit to supplement that guidance by the very practical step of applying for the patronage of Lord Lonsdale.[3]

---

[1] *Southey (Eng. Men of Letters)*, p. 82.   [2] *Cont.*, v. 2, p. 583.
[3] *Wordsworth*, Harper, v. 2, pp. 205-6.

This may suggest a very easy solution of the problem with which we have been concerning ourselves. All it seems necessary to do is to confine romanticism to the theatre, to the lecture-room, and to volumes of poetry, and, like sensible actor-managers, become practical men the moment the curtain drops, the class is dismissed, or the poetry-book is replaced on its shelf. This, it might be said, is simply what in ordinary sensible circles has been done. " Perhaps," Morley wrote, speaking of the poets of the romantic school, " the fact that their active force is spent, and that men find in them now only a charm and no longer a gospel, explains the difference between the admiration which some of us permit ourselves to feel for them, and the impatient dislike which they stirred in our fathers. Then they were a danger, because they were a force, misleading amiable and highminded people into blind paths. Now," Morley added however, " this is at an end." [1]

We note again both the thought that it was possible to per-ceive peril in the romantic movement, and the sense of security that marked the period that followed Jeffrey's. Some jurymen may feel that romanticism was persisting—in the belief that modes of thought which had had terror in them, and which had been supported by the utmost genius, could, within so short a period of time, be regarded as dead things, harmless, completely controllable, bottled, preserved in alcohol, labelled, and arranged neatly on shelves for examination by students. Are there still trends of thought in the world to-day, we may ask, that correspond to the trends Jeffrey opposed ? Is there anything, for instance, corresponding to that experiment with language which was one of the first things in which Jeffrey felt there were seeds of danger ? I think there is. I think that there exist in the modern world enormous quantities of verse which, while not a result of the Wordsworthian experiment—that phenomenon was itself, it seems to me, a reflection of a trend of thought—is in the direct line of descent from that experiment. It is verse that has broken away from poetry's ancient traditions—verse composed definitely and deliberately in diction adapted from " the language of conversation in the middle and lower classes of society." We do not require to go to libraries in search of it : we can hear it any day we wish, attached to music, poured out hour after hour from our radio sets. It is not verse that

[1] *Critical Miscellanies*, 1871, p. 265.

aspired to be poetry and failed because of its makers' unskilfulness. In its aim it is as a rule successful : were it not considered to be so it would not have reached our radio sets. It is not verse with the naïveté of our old ballads, a naïveté that had itself a long tradition behind it. It is produced by clever, sophisticated, and often, I imagine, well educated men who compose it for precisely the purpose for which Wordsworth said he composed the *Lyrical Ballads,* for " money, and money alone." There is no need to be superior in one's attitude to compositions which, it is evident, give pleasure to large numbers of one's fellow-beings and occasionally even, if one permits oneself to be honest, to oneself. The subjects and emotions with which they deal are precisely those—Jeffrey, we remember, remarked that this was true of all minor verse—that are dealt with in the loftiest poetry. The immediacy of their contact with the world in which they are produced makes their diction often far more closely akin, it appears to me, to the real language of ordinary people than

> " That evermore his teeth they chatter,
>   Chatter, chatter, chatter still "

and so forth—which seems to me to fall below the level of sensible adult conversation in any class of human society I have known. To some jurymen, nevertheless, it may appear that in the transition from Romeo's

> " O ! she doth teach the torches to burn bright.
>   It seems she hangs upon the cheek of night
>   Like a rich jewel in an Ethiop's ear "—

lines steeped in poetic tradition yet written for a general audience and for bread and butter by a man sprung from the people—to " Yessir ! She's got what it takes ! She's my ba-a-aby ! "— or whatever be the latest equivalent—something important has been lost. It may appear to some that in the enormous spread of education in the modern world education in culture has not kept pace with other forms of education, and that part of the evidence for this is to be found in the fact that multitudes of people, more highly skilled in certain directions than any previous generation in history, have come to find apparently complete satisfaction for their emotional requirements in traditionless verse of the kind we are discussing. It may appear to some that a considerable proportion of mankind have tended in consequence to lose background, to lose awareness of the nobility and grace of which humanity at its best is capable, and to cease accordingly to be able to place in long perspective noisy and obtrusive claims to their attention and respect.

Next, we may turn still again to the Wordsworth " Nature " doctrine. Myers quoted " almost at random " the following account from Dorothy's diary of the doings of a single day : " November 24, 1801. Read Chaucer. We walked by Gell's cottage. As we were going along we were stopped at once, at the distance, perhaps, of fifty yards from our favourite birch-tree ; it was yielding to the gust of wind, with all its tender twigs ; the sun shone upon it, and it glanced in the wind like a flying sunshiny shower. It was a tree in shape, with stem and branches ; but it was like a spirit of water. After our return William read Spenser to us, and then walked to John's Grove. Went to meet W." [1] Myers spoke of this as part of the description of " a life seldom paralleled in its intimate dependence on external nature." Once, Moore has told us, he was beginning to expatiate to his friend Byron upon the beauty of a sunset in Venice when his companion suddenly clapped a hand over his mouth and exclaimed with a laugh, " Come, damn it Tom, *don't* be poetical." [2] " Doesn't this subdue you, Carlyle ? " said Edward Irving one evening as the two friends looked at the river at Aberfeldy. " Subdue me ? " was the reply. " I should hope not ! I have quite other things to front with defiance, in this world, than a gush of bog-water tumbling over crags as here ! " [3] The first impression one derives from these anecdotes may be that Byron and Carlyle had descended, temporarily at anyrate, from the lofty plane habitually occupied by the artistic Dorothy to one much nearer that inhabited by the ordinary rest of us. We have seen, however, that Jeffrey regarded the Wordsworthian way of living as by no means an ideal one. We have wondered if it gave Wordsworth all the qualities he claimed it did. We may now ask if it gave to Dorothy a mind kept serene by " the deep power of joy," " an eye made quiet by the power of harmony," and all the rest of it. We recall De Quincey's description of her eyes, " wild and

---

[1] *Wordsworth*, p. 57. Cf. *Journals*, ed. Knight, pp. 65-6.
[2] *Life of Byron*, p. 412.　　　[3] *Carlyle till Marriage*, Wilson, p. 304.

startling, and hurried in their motion." De Quincey spoke
too of a struggle between " the irrepressible instincts of her
temperament" and her " obedience to the decorum of her sex
and age," which " gave to her whole demeanour, and to her
conversation, an air of embarrassment, and even of self-conflict,
that was almost distressing to witness. Even her very utterance
and enunciation," De Quincey said, " often suffered, in point
of clearness and steadiness, from the agitation of her excessive
organic sensibility." [1] Read, referring to this passage, commented bluntly, " She was, of course, neurotic." [2] Some may
feel, on viewing these facts, that there is soundness in the ordinary
man's instinct that tells him there is something " unhealthy "—
we are back, we observe, at one of Gates's words—in perpetual
cosseting of the emotions. It may be felt that this brings the
Wordsworthian doctrine into line with other cults that have
been widely accepted in modern times without very much of
" that scrupulous estimate of the grounds of decision " which
Jeffrey held should " precede the formation of all firm and wise
opinions."

We recall next Jeffrey's objection to Wordsworth's use, in
The Excursion, of the esoteric diction of Kant, his suggestion to
Southey that writing intended for the general public should
be generally intelligible, his criticism that the most usual
contrivance employed by the Lakers to give the appearance of
force to a very ordinary conception was to wrap it in mysterious
language, his assertion that learning was often used as a bully
instead of as a fair auxiliary, and his remark that inferior persons
wore their lace on their coats while gentlemen kept their gold
in their pockets. We are dealing here with strength and weakness
interwoven. Everyone knows that technical language is an
essential tool for departmental uses. Can we say, however,
with complete honesty, that the tool is never, in modern times,
brought improperly out of the factory for the purposes for which
Jeffrey accused the Lakers of employing it ? In a book which
lies beside me at the moment it is observed that in the *International
Catalogue of Scientific Literature* for the year 1914 the titles alone
of original articles in the various departments of physical science
occupy seventeen closely printed volumes.[3] Jeffrey, we recollect,

[1] *Reminiscences,* p. 97.
[2] *Wordsworth,* Read, p. 126.
[3] *Famous Plays of* 1934 (Gollancz), p. 150, footnote.

held that undue preoccupation with scholarship tended to keep men schoolboys. In a world in which writing accumulates at such a rate, and in which so many problems clamour for solution, to plume oneself on the simple fact that one happens to know the meaning of a few words unfamiliar to the generality, or that one happens to have read a book that a neighbour may not have encountered, is a practice that must surely appear increasingly childish to common sense. The matter has also a more serious aspect. This reliance for impressiveness upon recondite terms and allusions is an attempt to evade instead of a welcoming of the assistance of our brothers' judgments ; it dazzles ordinary men out of the habit of judging for themselves, and smooths the way in consequence for imposture.

" I wish," Wordsworth told Sir George Beaumont, on one occasion, " either to be considered as a teacher, or as nothing." [1] Jeffrey, there is little doubt, would have linked this statement with the Lakers' " assumption of exclusive taste, judgment and morality." Wordsworth, it might be said, expressed there what has become the modern passion. Surely there has never been an age in history more filled with instruction than the twentieth century : from every side—from posters on hoardings, from cinema screens, from wireless sets, from periodicals, from exhibitions, from art-galleries, from museums, from lecture-rooms, from concert-halls—instruction beats upon the ordinary man. Again we are dealing with interwoven strength and weakness. Much of this instruction is undeniably efficient and helpful—just as Wordsworth's was—especially when regarded from a departmental viewpoint. But the fruits of modern civilisation, judged as a whole, surely appear to common sense a poor harvest from this omnipresent didacticism.

This may suggest a weakness in the instructors. It may appear that these tend to build up Wordsworthian " systems " by the Wordsworthian method of ignoring everything which they do not feel concerns themselves—that they tend to see men and women, not as creatures infinite in faculty, but as beings interested or not interested in their particular activities. The system may induce in the instructors a Wordsworthian illusion of mastery—till reality crashes through.

Departmentalism may tend to produce a sense of proprietor-ship, a propensity, when it is literature that is in question, to

[1] *Memoirs of Wordsworth*, Christopher Wordsworth, v. 1, p. 342.

insist that the works of the masters must be studied only according to the methods laid down by the instructors, an itch to surround these works with the barriers of abstruse and intimidating commentary Jeffrey criticised so strongly, an inclination to erect around them notices warning against trespass by the uninitiated : we recall Pinkerton's objection to the Scottish peasants' enjoying, in modern spelling, the works of their nation's old poets. Thus men and women may be kept all their lives dependent upon—in Jeffrey's words—" the maxims of tutors, and the oracles of literary patrons."

Departmentalism may lead to the particular focus of attention of which Jeffrey spoke—to regarding errors in prosody as more important than errors in thought, the thrill as more important than the message, and labelling ideas as more important than searching for those that are good and opposing those that are bad—to a " sensibility," as we have seen Jeffrey put it, " to small faults, and an incapacity of great merits—a disposition to exaggerate the value of knowledge that is not to be used, and to underrate the importance of powers which have ceased to exist." All these modern processes, I think Jeffrey would have argued, in that they are based upon people's constructing fantasy-worlds in which they live, are fundamentally romantic.

We have, in these latter days, heard a man, inhabiting a realm of thought obviously fantastic to the eyes of common sense, declare that he was inspired, that his intuitions proceeded from a plane higher than that upon which ordinary intellects operate, that it was the duty of ordinary people simply to believe what he told them, and that it was his mission in life to proclaim a new order. These, it will be observed, are exactly the claims that were made for Wordsworth. The scholarship of a great and highly-educated nation found itself without a weapon with which to prevent that man's gaining mastery over its every expression of opinion. There, I think Jeffrey would have said, is the logical conclusion to the trends of thought he did his best to check in his day.

We have now, I think, an answer to the question we propounded to ourselves at the beginning of this chapter. Jeffrey could take delight in romanticism that dealt with the really strange. He could find pleasure in imaginary worlds so long as it was recognised that these were imaginary—though he suggested that to construct such worlds was a dangerous exercise.

But when he found men beginning to break contact with humanity's age-old culture and wisdom, ceasing to check their impressions with humility by those of wide common sense, endeavouring to intimidate common sense instead of seeking its help, fashioning out of their morsels of individual experience theatrical dream-worlds in which they were comfortable and supreme, and persuading themselves and others into imagining that these dream-worlds were real—then his instincts were aroused to a sense of danger as are those of a watch-dog.

III

Jeffrey's endeavour to see literature—and life—as a whole could not but make him appear easy meat for the departmentalists. Gates, for example, while joining with Macaulay in admiration of his versatility, remarked, " That his air of bravado and of unquestionable mastery was something of a trick, we now know very well." [1] The *Quarterly* article of 1852 made a similar point. " As," said the *Quarterly*, " he was utterly above the paltry dishonesty of affecting research, his confessions in the *Review* of superficial preparation are full and frequent. He apologises for the imperfection of criticisms because he writes from imperfect recollections ; for the inaccuracy of passages translated from the French because he was too indolent to correct the blunders ; and for not giving extracts from a book, because he had unhappily mislaid his copy. There is something engaging in this scorn of false pretension, and it pervaded every portion of Jeffrey's character." [2] There is considerable disagreement, it will be observed, between the two statements : the man who was " utterly above the paltry dishonesty of affecting research " could hardly be described as a trickster. The *Quarterly* reviewer, it will be noted, gave some evidence for his statements. He did not, however, give references. The passage in which Jeffrey spoke of having lost a book occurs at the end of his review of *A Sicilian Story*. He had noticed, Jeffrey remarked there, an advertisement of a new edition of Cornwall's *Dramatic Scenes*, and would have submitted to his readers some extracts from this work, which he desired to recommend, had he not mislaid his copy.[3] I have not, in the mass of Jeffrey's reviewing, noticed the other passages alluded to by the *Quarterly*. Similar remarks are to be found, however,

[1] *Selections*, p. x. [2] No. 181, pp. 153-4. [3] *Ed. Rev.*, No. 65, p. 155.

elsewhere in his writings. In discussing, for instance, the
Memoirs of Alfieri, he said that he had not been able to procure
a complete copy of Alfieri's works, and had read only part of
those that were in his possession ; [1] in reviewing Campbell's
Specimens he stated that he did not profess to be acquainted
with the works of Peele, and that he had, before reading
Campbell's account of Hall and Chamberlayn, been unfamiliar
with these writers ; [2] in criticising a group of twelve " Secondary
Scotch Novels " he remarked, on coming to *Reginald Dalton*, that
he did not propose to say anything of this work as he had
" really . . . not yet read it fairly through." [3]

It seems to me, nevertheless, that even the *Quarterly's* sentences
give an imperfect picture of the facts. It was suggested in an
earlier chapter that the extent of Jeffrey's knowledge might be
underestimated. In dealing with the works that appeared
between 1802 and 1829, the years during which he was a reviewer
—it is for his criticism of these that he is chiefly important—
Jeffrey had not at his disposal any of the " tempting summaries,
abstracts, and tables " which, he said, were tending in his own
day to make what looked like acquirement of knowledge
deceptively easy and swift. He studied these works at first
hand throughout a period of twenty-seven years : I do not
think that many specialists in literature have been able to spend
more time upon the productions of this era. I do not think
that any modern should permit himself to speak patronisingly,
as an expert dealing with a non-expert, of Jeffrey's knowledge
of early nineteenth-century literature before he is prepared to
sign an affidavit that he has himself studied with care the twelve
books of *Thalaba*, the forty-five sections of *Madoc*, the twenty-four
sections of *Kehama*, the twenty-five sections of *Roderick*, the four
books of *Endymion*, all the chief works of Byron, Scott, and
Wordsworth, including the nine books of *The Excursion*, the two
books of Crabbe's *Village*, the three parts of *The Parish Register*,
the twenty-four letters of *The Borough*, Crabbe's twenty-one
Tales, the twenty-two books of the *Tales of the Hall*, and all the
other volumes on a multitude of subjects—the list of works has
been little more than commenced—that Jeffrey discussed in
such detail and with such an amplitude of what has since been
recognised to be well-selected quotation. The remark in the

---

[1] *Cont.*, v. 1, p. 391.   [2] *Ibid.*, v. 2, pp. 19, 23.
[3] *Ibid.*, v. 3, p. 142.

article on Cornwall's poetry occurs in the last paragraph of a
detailed discussion, spread over eleven pages, of the poems
contained in the volume—not *Dramatic Scenes*—with which
Jeffrey was dealing.   It is not, therefore, evidence of inadequate
preparation for the actual review.   In asserting that the kind
of statement to which he referred illustrated Jeffrey's scorn of
pretension, the writer in the *Quarterly* expressed, I think, part
but not all of the truth.   The similar statements that have been
mentioned here were reprinted, it will be observed from the
references, in Jeffrey's *Contributions*—the volumes containing
" the work by which," as Nichol Smith said, " on full deliberation,
he was willing to be judged." [1]   This suggests that we are in
touch with principles.   All criticism must be affected by human
limitations—limitations of memory, of attention, of judgment,
of knowledge, of experience, of time.   To see one's own limitations
with clear eyes, deliberately to direct the jury's attention to
them, is not, it seems to me, to apologise, but simply to lay one's
findings fairly before the court.   When a man pretends, his
criticism is valueless ; when the pretence is unrecognised, his
criticism is misleading and may be dangerous.   But, Jeffrey
considered, having acknowledged the conditions within which
he was judging, it was the critic's duty to give his verdict with
complete fearlessness.

   An illustration of Jeffrey's attitude is to be found in his
review of *Wilhelm Meister*.   It was in this article that Stephen
perceived " a kind of indecency," it will be recollected, on
account of its treatment of " a contemporary classic."   Jeffrey
was completely aware of the reputation of *Meister*.   He defined
his own critical position with the utmost care.   *Meister*, he said,
was allowed by the general consent of Germany to be the
greatest work of their greatest writer.   He had received it
accordingly with respect, and had perused it with great attention.
He had read it, he explained, only in translation.   But the
translation was by a professed admirer, and by one who was
plainly, moreover, both a person of talents and a master of
English.   Jeffrey professed to judge of the work only according
to his " own principles of judgment and habits of feeling,"
and " meaning nothing less than to dictate " to the Germans
what they should think of their favourite authors, proposed
only to let them know " in all plainness and modesty " what he,

------

[1] *Jeffrey's Lit. Crit.*, p. v.

and he believed most of his fellow-countrymen, thought of it.[1]
Where he could honestly appreciate he did not curb his praise.
He had encountered in *Meister*, he stated, what he did "not
hesitate to pronounce the most able, eloquent, and profound
exposition of the character of Hamlet, as conceived by our
great dramatist, that has ever been given to the world." [2] His
general verdict on the work was, however, without ambiguity.
"To us," he asserted, "it certainly appears, after the most
deliberate consideration, to be eminently absurd, puerile,
incongruous, vulgar, and affected." [1] "It is all kept in the
air," ran another of his findings, "like a piece of machinery
at the minor theatres, and never allowed to touch the solid
ground." [3] Jeffrey found the characteristic Lakish weaknesses,
in other words, strongly represented in this German masterpiece.
Carlyle dealing, two years later, in his essay on German literature,
with the allegation that *Meister* and *Faust* were full of errors
in taste, and with Jeffrey's article undoubtedly in mind, growled
that "the objection would have more force, did it seem to
originate from a more mature consideration of the subject." [4]
Carlyle's line of criticism is one that is always justifiable. He
certainly knew more about German literature than Jeffrey did.
Jeffrey accepted Carlyle's essay for the *Review*. But he reprinted
also his own article in the *Contributions*. It seems like a challenge.
"This," Jeffrey seems to be saying, "is how, reading in the
circumstances I have described, this masterpiece appeared to
me ; and I am not to be browbeaten out of this honest opinion
by any show of authoritativeness." In case anyone who, like
myself, has not read the one thousand and thirty pages of
Carlyle's translation, much less the work in the original German,
should be tempted, nevertheless, to permit Jeffrey's judgment
of it to become fixed too speedily in his mind as what cannot
be other than a mere perverse expression of singularity, it may
be wise to note here the comment of a modern scholar on
Jeffrey's description of the work as "absurd," and the rest.
"With the translation," Thompson wrote, "I am unfamiliar,
and I dislike kicking an author with four adjectives when he
has been laid flat by one, yet I think that the adjectives are
judiciously selected." [5]

[1] *Cont.*, v. 1, p. 263.   [2] *Ibid.*, v. 1, p. 284.
[3] *Ibid.*, v. 1, p. 264.   [4] *Crit. and Mis. Essays*, v. 1, p. 30.
[5] *A Scottish Man of Feeling*, pp. 350-1.

IV

The common sense on which Jeffrey laid so much emphasis might be variously regarded. It might be pointed out, for example, that common sense was a term general in eighteenth-century philosophy. We recall, however, how Jeffrey spoke of those whose pastime it was to pick " rotten bones out of the earth." " He was interested in the past," Nichol Smith wrote of Jeffrey, " only in so far as he saw its bearings on the present." [1] The danger in date-stamping ideas lies in the insinuation that the ideas are dead. To pursue a historical enquiry would be obviously to quit the Jeffreyan position.

It might be said that Jeffrey appears to have been advocating, to employ a phrase he used himself in discussing the work of Reid, " an appeal from the decisions of the learned to the voice of the multitude." [2] We saw, however, that where literature was concerned Jeffrey recognised the importance of trained readers. Common sense tells us immediately that the opinion of the specialist must have weight in his department. A motor-mechanic is not entitled to pass judgment on a doctor of medicine's method of diagnosing the ailments of his body ; a doctor of medicine may be unqualified to pass judgment on a skilled mechanic's method of diagnosing the ailments of an internal combustion engine. But it does not follow that common sense has been superseded. Each may still judge the other's work by its fruits.

But, it may be said, the verdicts of the multitude are notoriously fickle. Every schoolboy recalls in this connection Shakespeare's picture of the crowd that was swayed by Mark Antony in *Julius Caesar*. Is this illustration, however, entirely convincing ? Antony based his whole procedure on the assumption that the existence, in ordinary people, of certain stable qualities was a fact that could be completely relied upon. We recall the instincts to which he appealed in his famous speech—generosity to the dead, pity, faithfulness to friends, placing the good of the herd before self, gratitude, sympathy with grief, family affection, and also—because Shakespeare knew that human characters are never unmixedly good—greed and delight in destruction. Antony expected his audience to respond immediately to that appeal : he was not disappointed.

[1] *Jeffrey's Lit. Crit.*, pp. xix-xx.   [2] *Cont.*, v. 2, p. 603.

The virtues he mobilised on his side are all common sense virtues. It was not common sense his hearers lacked, but ability to exercise it.

The moral qualities of literature on which Jeffrey laid particular stress are precisely those on which ordinary men are best qualified to pass judgment. Every man is obliged, by the mere fact that he has to live with other men, to be a student of ethics.

Jeffrey, it might be said, suggested that the moral instincts of ordinary men are likely to be sounder than those of specialists. Is there not something, however, to be said for this? Which was higher ethically, Mark Antony's audience, whose moral sympathies were so readily aroused, or the expert in mob oratory who played remorselessly on those sympathies for his own ends, who was pitiless in his removal of his opponents, and who schemed, once the situation was under his control, " how to cut off some charge in legacies " ? The more general the body of men to whom an appeal for honest judgment is made, the more likely are individual associations to cancel themselves out. The expert, within his own department, is always in danger of being affected by particular considerations. The moment he moves out of it he also becomes an ordinary man. We can judge him therefore from both angles. Which, we may ask, does common sense tell us instinctively is on the higher moral plane, the chemist in his laboratory disclaiming, because he is a " pure " scientist, all responsibility for the use that may be made of anything he discovers, or the same man in private life, unwilling to leave so much as a popgun lying about unsupervised if he has a suspicion that his children may harm themselves or their companions by means of it ; the historian in his library, discussing chicane and brutality as interesting moves in statecraft, or the same man as we may imagine him in his everyday environment, despising liars and reluctant to injure a single fellow-being ; the poet in his study, in complete control of a fictitious world of his own creation and romanticising himself into a god, or the same man in his family circle, knowing that they know as well as he does his human weaknesses ; the critic who maintains that the duty of literature is to provide us with thrills and to hold up the mirror to nature in any way it pleases, or the same man restraining his tiny son from using phrases picked up, it may be innocently, in the street, because he knows that words can have in them a potency of the devil and that dwelling on certain aspects of things can attract to it evil and unhappiness as a magnet attracts iron filings ?

Common sense, it might be argued, has varied from age to age. To be sure it has. So has every other human standard of judgment. Does not the fact that in writings composed in distant lands by men dead for centuries we may find expressed ideas of right and wrong with which our instincts immediately agree show that there is a constant element here as well ?

It might be said that this doctrine, that we should judge by common sense, makes matters too easy—that the doctrine has the same pseudo-simplicity as, it was suggested, characterised the " Nature " doctrine of Wordsworth. We recollect, however, that Jeffrey never claimed that common sense was an infallible guide. He merely said that it afforded the nearest approximation to a just standard of good and evil that the nature of our faculties would allow—just as, to extend his own analogy, while no one would claim that our eyes never deceive us, no one supplies us with any better guide by which to walk.

It is not easy to pierce down to our individual common sense. In order to reach it we have to strip from our minds layer after layer of vanity, of cowardice, of indolence, of self-interest, of self-illusion : and, when we have stripped away these layers, the light that streams up from common sense is often so fierce, so pitiless to our defects and to the defects of the things we have worshipped, that we hasten to put the sheltering layers back again.

Do not part of our illusions about art, for instance, arise from a species of self-interest—from the fact that all the men who discuss art in books are themselves interested, perhaps because their knowledge of it gives them a sense of distinction, or it may be even mainly financially, in exalting it ? Can we say when we look at the matter with ruthless honesty that the achievements even of the geniuses—this is not a contradiction of the idea that men may lose background—are as important to us as the deep daily faithfulness to duty of the ordinary people who wrestle with the seas and the earth to provide us with food, and under the earth to provide us with fuel, to whom we entrust our bodies when we travel with reliance so implicit that we seldom even think of it, who patrol the streets around our houses when we are asleep and beat out the flames should our homes go on fire, who run to pick us up should we be knocked down in the road and who nurse us by day and by night when we are sick, who come to us in lifeboats when we are shipwrecked and who, when our country is in danger, form bulwarks around it with their breasts—without the protection of whom we would all soon die? To Jeffrey it did not appear that they were. " For my part," he declared to Carlyle, " the more I see of philosophers and men of genius the more I am inclined to hold that the ordinary run of sensible, kind people, who fill the world, are after all the best specimens of humanity, and that the others are, like our cultivated flowers, but splendid monsters, and cases of showy disease." [1]

[1] *Carlyle to French Rev.*, Wilson, p. 204.

CHAPTER XV

THE SCALE OF VALUES

The Jeffreyan prophecy.   Campbell and Rogers.   Enviable superiority.
Serious assertions.   A less-noticed Jeffreyan prophecy.

I

WE may glance at this stage in our journey, from the Jeffreyan viewpoint, at the passage that made Stephen doubt Jeffrey's sanity. " It seems almost incredible now," Stephen remarked, " that any sane critic should pick out the poems of Rogers and Campbell as the sole enduring relics from the age of Wordsworth, Shelley, Keats, Coleridge, and Byron." [1] " Every schoolboy," J. H. Millar wrote, " in these days of ' general knowledge ' . . . can gibe at the prediction that the fame of Rogers and Campbell would outlive that of Shelley and Byron." [2] The passage appeared in the *Review* for October 1829, in an article on two volumes of poems by Mrs Hemans.

" We have seen too much," Jeffrey wrote, " of the perishable nature of modern literary fame, to venture to predict to Mrs Hemans that hers will be immortal, or even of very long duration. Since the beginning of our critical career we have seen a vast deal of beautiful poetry pass into oblivion, in spite of our feeble efforts to recall or retain it in remembrance. The tuneful quartos of Southey are already little better than lumber : —and the rich melodies of Keats and Shelley,—and the fantastical emphasis of Wordsworth,—and the plebeian pathos of Crabbe, are melting fast from the field of our vision. The novels of Scott have put out his poetry. Even the splendid strains of Moore are fading into distance and dimness, except where they have been married to immortal music ; and the blazing star of Byron himself is receding from its place of pride. . . . The two who have the longest withstood this rapid withering of the laurel, and with the least marks of decay on their branches, are Rogers and Campbell ; neither of them, it may be remarked, voluminous writers, and both distinguished rather for the fine

---

[1] *Hours in a Library*, v. 2, p. 255.   [2] *Lit. Hist. of Scotland*, p. 488.

taste and consummate elegance of their writings, than for that
fiery passion, and disdainful vehemence, which seemed for a
time to be so much more in favour with the public." [1]

As Jeffreyans, we must read words as they appear to us.
The first obvious point we notice here is that the only verb in
the extract which is in the future tense, the tense of prediction,
is that which applies to Mrs Hemans herself; all the others are
either in the present tense or in the past. In other words the
passage, read in its plain sense, contains simply an account of
the public attitude to poetry as it was in October 1829. It was
natural for Jeffrey to take stock as it were in that month. He
had just closed his career as conductor of the *Edinburgh*. The
previous number was the last he edited. [2]

We notice, in the second place, that Jeffrey did not express
satisfaction with what appeared to him to have happened. On
the contrary, he stated explicitly that this vast deal of beautiful
poetry had passed or was passing into forgetfulness in spite of
his own efforts to keep it remembered.

Stephen made a point of the fact that the passage was
" republished in 1843, by which time the true proportions of
the great reputations of the period were becoming more obvious
to an ordinary observer." We have seen, however, that Jeffrey
did not consider himself entitled to make essential changes in a
professed reprint, and that he remarked, in connection with
Scott's novels, that readers might be interested to have a record
of contemporary impressions. I do not think that, even if public
opinion had changed by 1843, this would have caused Jeffrey
to conceal how matters had appeared to him in 1829.

We observe, in the third place, that Jeffrey did not in 1843,
any more than in 1829, indicate approval of what had seemed
to him the state of public taste in the earlier year. Not only
did he republish in his *Contributions* all the praises of the poets
mentioned in the " Hemans " passage that have been quoted
here from these volumes, but also, in added footnotes, he referred,
as we have seen, to Southey's " great and peculiar powers " ;
asserted that a poet of great power and promise had been lost
by the premature death of Keats and asked readers to reconsider
the merits of this poet ; said that he had always loved many
of the attributes of Wordsworth's genius ; suggested that Crabbe
had had insufficient justice done to him ; and declared that

[1] *Cont.*, v. 2, pp. 567-8.   [2] *Life*, Cockburn, v. 1, p. 285.

there was much in Scott's poetry which the age should not allow to be forgotten.

The question seems to resolve itself, then, into this—whether or not Jeffrey was completely incapable in 1829 of giving a description of the contemporary public taste for poetry. It was suggested on an earlier page that, so far as Keats was concerned, Jeffrey was stating what was, in 1829, simply a fact, and that even in 1843 his added testimony to Keats's powers was by no means superfluous. As a single juryman, living more than a century later, I should hesitate to place my view of such matters beside that of the foremost editor of the day. A few notes from my reading may not, at the same time, be entirely irrelevant.

In 1813, by which year a large part of what is now regarded as Wordsworth's greatest poetry had been published, Byron, stating that he was basing the order more upon what he believed to be popular opinion than upon any decided opinion of his own, placed Scott at the head of the poets of the day, Rogers second, Moore and Campbell in the third rank, and Southey, Wordsworth, and Coleridge only in the fourth, immediately above " the many." [1] " With regard to poetry in general," he wrote to Murray in 1817, " I am convinced, the more I think of it, that he [Moore] and *all* of us—Scott, Southey, Wordsworth, Moore, Campbell, I,—are all in the wrong, one as much as another ; that we are upon a wrong revolutionary poetical system, or systems, not worth a damn in itself, and from which none but Rogers and Crabbe are free ; and that the present and next generations will finally be of this opinion." [2] In 1824, a writer in *Blackwood's* declared that Byron's characters, being all similar, had been rejected by the public at last, that Scott had long retired, that Moore's, Southey's, and Campbell's latest poems had been all bad, that Coleridge was dumb " at least on paper," that Rogers had taken to punning, Crabbe to his parsonage, and Wilson to his work as a professor. " Few," he went on, " write poetry, (except Will Wordsworth, who keeps weaving away with his old indefatigable serenity), and nobody at all reads it." The writer admired Wordsworth, nevertheless ; and he was no admirer of the *Edinburgh*. But his opinion resembled Jeffrey's and Byron's in one respect. " Is there a chance," he wrote, " that going back to write about human

[1] *Life of Byron*, Moore, p. 206.   [2] *Ibid.*, p. 367.

affairs, about the actions and passions . . . of actual conceivable people, not thieves, or pirates, or Peter Bells, or heaven-scaling and hell-taming Qui-his, would succeed ? We hope there is, though, perdy, we are not over sanguine." [1] " Campbell," a writer in *Blackwood's* asserted in 1825, " will always be a classic —and elegantly bound and richly lettered, he will, as far as we can see, lie on the drawing-room tables of the ingenuous and polite, until the extinction of civility in this empire." [2] " Had that man," it was declared of Wordsworth in the *Noctes* for September 1825, " been a great poet, he would have produced a deep and lasting impression on the mind of England ; whereas his verses are becoming less and less known every day, and he is, in good truth, already one of the illustrious obscure . . . Crabbe, with all his defects, stands immeasurably above Wordsworth as the Poet of the Poor. . . . Had that man in youth become the member of any profession . . . he would soon have learned in the tussle to rate his powers more truly. How such a man as Jeffrey, with his endless volubility of ingenious argumentation, would have squabashed him before a jury ! " [3] Arnold recollected hearing Macaulay say after Wordsworth's death in 1850, when subscriptions were being asked for a memorial, that ten years earlier more money could have been raised in Cambridge than was then raised throughout the whole country. Arnold thought Macaulay might have exaggerated ; but it appeared to him that there was a decrease in Wordsworth's reputation after 1840. [4] We saw that Lockhart was wondering in 1851 if Wordsworth's philosophy was not an airy sham. " She saw the rise of Wordsworth's fame," the *Daily News* said of Miss Berry in 1852, " . . . and she lived to see its decline. . . . She saw the beginning and the end of Moore's popularity ; and the rise and establishment of Campbell's." [5] " There had been a period of a few years, in my youth," Harriet Martineau wrote in her *Autobiography*, " when I worshipped Wordsworth. . . . I found more disappointment than pleasure when I turned again to his works. . . . His fame seems to have now settled in its proper level. Those who understand mankind are aware that he did not understand them." [6]

---

[1] V. 15, pp. 675-6.　　[2] V. 17, p. 102.　　[3] *Noctes*, v. 1, pp. 34-6.

[4] *Essays in Criticism* (Second Series), " Wordsworth."

[5] *Autobiography*, Harriet Martineau, v. 1, p. 439. The article was written by Harriet Martineau (v. 1, p. 370).　　[6] *Ibid.*, v. 2, pp. 238-9.

It may appear from these quotations that the question of what proportion of reputation ought properly to be allotted to each of the early-nineteenth-century poets was an open one in 1829, and still undecided even in 1843. Some of us may wonder if the reputations even of completely established writers can ever be regarded as having arrived at " true " and thereafter, in consequence, unalterable proportions. Many little-anticipated changes have occurred in the world since the nineteenth century. At anyrate it may seem fair to submit that a suggestion that Jeffrey's account of public opinion in 1829 showed him to be scarcely sane should be accompanied by some evidence.

II

Jeffrey wrote two articles on Campbell's poetry,[1] and one on the poetry of Rogers.[2] He reprinted all three articles in the *Contributions*.

He found faults in the works of both poets. We saw that he perceived in Campbell's Pennsylvanian farmer the typical early-nineteenth-century artificiality in characterisation ; Campbell's writing appeared to him at times over-elaborate ; Campbell's best work, he said, was to be found in the shorter pieces in the composition of which the poet might be presumed to have felt least anxiety.[3] Rogers's " outline," he considered, was " often rather timidly drawn," and there was " an occasional want of force and brilliancy in the colouring." [4]

Jeffrey did, at the same time, estimate Campbell's and Rogers's poetry more highly than subsequent generations have done, and he did expect their appeal to posterity to be greater than it has turned out to be. There is no longer space for detailed comment. A few quotations will show why he found their works attractive. The leading ideas will now be readily recognised.

" We rejoice once more," he wrote in opening his review of *Gertrude of Wyoming*, " to see a polished and pathetic poem— in the old style of English pathos and poetry. . . . If the true tone of nature be not everywhere maintained, it gives place,

---

[1] *Gertrude of Wyoming* (*Ed. Rev.*, No. 27, Art. 1 ; *Cont.*, v. 2, p. 176) ; *Theodric* (*Ed. Rev.*, No. 82, Art. 1 ; *Cont.*, v. 2, p. 199).

[2] *Human Life* (*Ed. Rev.*, No. 62, Art. 4 ; *Cont.*, v. 2, p. 391).

[3] *Cont.*, v. 2, pp. 193-8.   [4] *Ibid.*, v. 2, p. 394.

at least, to art only, and not to affectation. . . . Considering
the habits of the age in which we live . . . and the fashion,
which, though not immutable, has for some time run steadily
in an opposite direction, we should not be much surprised if a
poem, whose chief merit consisted in its pathos, and in the
softness and exquisite tenderness of its representations of domestic
life and romantic seclusion, should meet with less encouragement
than it deserves . . . but Mr Campbell's name has power, we
are persuaded, to insure a very partial and a very general
attention to whatever it accompanies, and, we would fain hope,
influence enough to reclaim the public taste to a juster standard
of excellence." [1]   In the second of his reviews of Campbell,
introducing a quotation from the poet's " noble ode to the
Memory of the Spanish Patriots who died in resisting the late
atrocious invasion "—" Brave men who at the Trocadero fell,"
—" Mr Campbell," he wrote, ". . . has held on his course
through good and through bad report, unseduced, unterrified ;
and is now found in his duty, testifying as fearlessly against the
invaders of Spain, in the volume before us, as he did against the
spoilers of Poland in the very first of his publications.   It is a
proud thing indeed for England, for poetry, and for mankind,
that all the illustrious poets of the present day—Byron, Moore,
Rogers, Campbell—are distinguished by their zeal for freedom,
and their scorn for courtly adulation ; while those who have
deserted that manly and holy cause have, from that hour, felt
their inspiration withdrawn, their harp-strings broken, and the
fire quenched in their censers ! " [2]   The implication in Jeffrey's
last sentence is undoubtedly questionable.   But if the ideas he
stressed here have been regarded as irrelevant for departmental
literary criticism, they are ideas for which the common sense of
our nation still expects its citizens to hazard their lives.

" The true character and poetical effect of the work," Jeffrey
wrote of Rogers's *Human Life*, " seems, in this instance, to depend
much more on its moral expression, than on any of its merely
literary qualities."   " The life," he wrote, " which it endeavours
to set before us, is . . . not the life of warlike paladins, or
desperate lovers, or sublime ruffians—or piping shepherds or
sentimental savages, or bloody bigots or preaching pedlars—
or conquerors, poets, or any other species of madmen—but the
ordinary, practical, and amiable life of social, intelligent, and

[1] *Cont.*, v. 2, pp. 176-80.   [2] *Ibid.*, v. 2, p. 209.

affectionate men in the upper ranks of society [1]—such, in short, as multitudes may be seen living every day in this country—for the picture is entirely English—and though not perhaps in the choice of every one, yet open to the judgment, and familiar to the sympathies, of all. . . . Its marking peculiarity . . . is, that it is free from the least alloy of acrimony or harsh judgment. . . . This . . . we believe, is the tone of true wisdom and true virtue—and that to which all good natures draw nearer, as they approach the close of life, and come to act less, and to know and to meditate more, on the varying and crowded scene of human existence." When, Jeffrey continued, youth's inordinate hopes, which provoke their own disappointment, have been sobered by experience, when the rivalries of riper years have been abandoned, and we have seen friends and enemies lowered into the grave, when derision once thought pungent has come to seem flat, when we think how often we have mourned and been comforted, how often our opinions have changed and we have come to be ashamed of things of which we once were proud, we are led in imagination " to retrace the whole of our career, and that of our contemporaries, with feelings of far greater humility and indulgence than those by which it had been actually accompanied :—to think all vain but affection and honour—the simplest and cheapest pleasures the truest and most precious—and generosity of sentiment the only mental superiority which ought either to be wished for or admired." [2] There we have, writ plain, the Jeffreyan scale of values.

III

We referred in an earlier chapter to the volume long spoken of in Scotland as " the Book." It may be interesting and not irrelevant to glance at this volume for a moment from the Jeffreyan angle. There is probably no book in the world that has been more subjected to annotation than the Bible has been. Yet, despite all that is sometimes said of modern neglect of it, there is probably no book in the world that is, by ordinary people, more widely and constantly read. The barriers of commentary have been unavailing here. Surely one reason for this is simply that much in that Book—not everything, because

---

[1] The words " in the upper ranks of society " were added in the reprinted version of the review (*Ed. Rev.*, No. 62, p. 325 ; *Cont.*, v. 2, p. 392).

[2] *Cont.*, v. 2, pp. 391-3.

human thought does change—rings perennially true to man's fundamental ethical instincts—that it is the most widely-recognised repository in, at anyrate, the western world of those rules of the kind spoken of by Jeffrey, rules evolved from experience beside which the experience of a generation is as a few grains of sand on a seashore, by which he held it was wisest for men to direct their conduct in every circumstance of life. This idea does not, of course, preclude the possibility of that Guidance under which it is implied in the Book that it was written.

We recall the first of the commandments in the Book : " Thou shalt have no other gods before me." Men may think of God in many ways. But however they think of Him, He must surely be always an Embodiment of the highest good they know, a Personification of those moral impressions which Jeffrey held were present in the minds of us all. Viewed from this angle, the commandment becomes an explicit instruction that in every sphere of human activity—no exception is made for " pure " criticism, " pure " science, or " pure " anything else—moral considerations should be paramount. And Jeffrey's primary critical doctrine becomes simply a repetition, in his own sphere, of that instruction. We recall how that commandment is worded in the second part of the Book. " Thou shalt love the Lord thy God with all thy heart, and with all thy soul, and with all thy mind." There is no room left for departmental activity there. " This," we are told, " is the first and great commandment. And the second is like unto it, Thou shalt love thy neighbour as thyself." There is no division there between poets, experts, and the vulgar world. " On these two commandments," declares the Book, " hang all the law and the prophets." We recall the second commandment in the earlier version. " Thou shalt not make unto thee any graven image. . . . Thou shalt not bow down thyself to them, nor serve them : for I the Lord thy God am a jealous God, visiting the iniquity of the fathers upon the children unto the third and fourth generation." Perhaps this has been our modern error, that we have placed human genius before Him. " Woe unto them," says the Book, " that call evil good, and good evil. . . . Woe unto them that are wise in their own eyes." That may have an application to mortals who presume to devise " new moral and spiritual ideals " out of their own infinitesimal experience. Language, however beautiful, that gives no more than the supreme poetic thrill, erudition that leads to no results in action, are of no account in the Book's scale of values. " Though I speak," it says, " with the tongues of men and of angels, and have not charity, I am become as sounding brass, or a tinkling cymbal. And though I . . . understand all mysteries, and all knowledge . . . and have not charity, I am nothing." " Prove all things," says the Book : " hold fast that which is good." That is addressed to us all : it puts responsibility on every individual of us. It might be said also to define the supreme task of scholarship. " Be not ye called Rabbi : " says the Book, " for one is your Master . . . and all ye are brethren." That suggests that we should learn from one another. " Whosoever will save his life," says the Book, " shall lose it." That may be a warning to a scholarship tempted to win reputation by the easy road of authoritativeness. The Book's test of teaching is that which has been noted. " Beware of false prophets," it says. " Ye shall know them by their fruits." Something is bearing fruit in this twentieth century. There is no ambiguity in the Book's teaching in such matters. Ignoring its instructions it describes as sin. " The wages of sin," it says, " is death." If these words have any meaning, they contain a pretty serious assertion.

We may be still dealing with coincidences. But the coincidences are becoming numerous.

It does not appear to me surprising that ideas basic in Jeffrey's teaching should be discoverable to be ideas basic also in the Bible. We recall his assertion that all the elements of which his opinions were composed had " a certain national cast." The ideas in that Book had been for long enwoven into Scottish thinking. Fundamental in Jeffrey's standards, it seems to me, were the standards of his Covenanting forefathers.

It might be argued that in discussing Jeffrey's teaching with an awareness in mind of what has happened in the world since his day we have been departing from our brief. It is evident that Jeffrey would have been the last person to wish us to dramatise him as a prophet. Yet I think that his prescience may, like his scholarship, be underestimated. We may look, at this point, at another of his glances into the future. It is to be found in the passage immediately following that in which he asserted that men were learning instead of reasoning, remembering instead of meditating, and the rest. " If these, however," Jeffrey wrote, " are the consequences of accumulated and diffused knowledge, it may well be questioned whether the human intellect will gain in point of dignity and energy by the only certain acquisitions to which we are entitled to look forward. For our own part, we will confess we have no such expectations. There will be improvements, we make no doubt, in all the mechanical and domestic arts ;—better methods of working metal, and preparing cloth ;—more commodious vehicles, and more efficient implements of war. Geography will be made more complete, and astronomy more precise ;—natural history will be enlarged and digested ;—and perhaps some little improvement suggested in the forms of administering law. But as to any general enlargment of the understanding, or more prevailing vigour of judgment, we will own, that the tendency seems to be all the other way ; and that we think strong sense, and extended views of human affairs, are more likely to be found, and to be listened to at this moment, than two or three hundred years hereafter. The truth is, we suspect, that the vast and enduring products of the virgin soil can no longer be reared in that factitious mould to which cultivation has since given existence ; and that its forced and deciduous progeny will go on degenerating, till some new deluge shall restore the vigour of the glebe by a temporary destruction of all its generations." [1]

That passage was written in 1813.[2] Jeffrey thought it important enought to reprint in the *Contributions*. A writer in *Blackwood's* in 1852, quoting the last sentence, referred to it as a very desperate conclusion.[3] I have little doubt that for many years after that sentence was written, it appeared, to such readers as chanced to notice it, to contain a statement as theatrical as any that was ever made by the most romantic of nineteenth-century romanticists. I wonder if there was made, in the whole of the nineteenth century, a statement that was in cold fact less theatrical.

It was remarked in the introduction to this study that Jeffrey perceived as clearly perhaps as any of his successors in criticism the perilous nature of the ground on which his generation were setting their feet. That sentence is part of the evidence.

It may appear to some of the jury that Jeffrey's perception of that danger and his application of those principles in his

[1] *Cont.*, v. 1, pp. 101-2.   [2] See *Ante*, p. 76.   [3] V. 72, p. 279.

criticism are as important for an assessment of his sanity as the fact that his emphasis upon the principles caused him to over-estimate the technical strength of Rogers and Campbell.

Jeffrey's teaching, and the infinitely greater teaching of which we have suggested it was a morsel were not, of course, merely negative. If both doctrines contained a warning they contained also a hope.

CHAPTER XVI

SUMMING-UP AND CONCLUSION

Stephen. Saintsbury. Gates. Hughes. Thompson. Beatty. Elsner. Jeffrey's influence in criticism. Nichol Smith. Obstacles to Jeffrey's fame. Charge against Jeffrey. His philosophy in practice. Farewell.

I

It follows from our reasoning in this study that if the conclusions regarding Jeffrey arrived at by others were totally unlike those arrived at here, the latter should be suspect, as being outside the orbit of common sense.

It will be clear, at the same time, that I have found it impossible to agree with the suggestion that Jeffrey was simply an " ass." For the conception of him as a mere " follower of the fashion " I have discovered no evidence.[1] And his criticism does not appear to me at all properly describable as a mere continuation of pseudo-classical thought : the ideas he held in common with the writers of the Augustan period he held in common also, it seems to me, with men in numerous other ages including, I should like to think, our own.

It will be evident that I have found Saintsbury's criticisms of Jeffrey stimulating, and that I am in agreement with Saintsbury in thinking that Jeffrey's work has been undervalued. To test properly, however, the accuracy of Saintsbury's labelling of Jeffrey as " Gallic " would require, first, a scrutiny of the psychology of the entire French nation, and second, an examination of Saintsbury's conception of that psychology : the fate of Joseph Henry Green is a warning against one's undertaking tasks of that order the moment they are suggested. Saintsbury certainly furnished, as we have seen, a list of the qualities in Jeffrey he regarded as French. The list flattered neither Jeffrey nor Frenchmen. I agree that Jeffrey possessed qualities

[1] Two portions of Stephen's evidence remain. He described Jeffrey as putting up, " because admiration was respectable," with " Rogers's flattest ' correctness,' " and ": Southey's most ponderous epic poetry." We have noticed Jeffrey's criticism of Rogers's " outline." He spoke of Southey's " interminable redundancy " (*Ed. Rev.*, No. 13, p. 4). As to epic poetry in general, " The greater part of polite readers," he wrote, " would now no more think of sitting down to a whole Epic, than to a whole ox." (*Ed. Rev.*, No. 42, p. 299).

resembling in some measure those spoken of by Saintsbury. But Saintsbury's way of enumerating them made his description, it seems to me, not so much a portrait of Jeffrey and his thinking as a caricature of them.

The frequency with which I have mentioned Gates's contribution to the study of Jeffrey will show that I have found his ideas also stimulating. " Neither in Johnson nor anywhere else before Jeffrey," Gates asserted, " do we find a critic constantly attempting to detect and define the moral atmosphere that pervades the whole work of an author, and to determine the relation between this moral atmosphere and the author's personality as man and as author." [1] The first part of that sentence contains a bold statement. But in his use of the word " atmosphere " Gates made, I think, an essential point : in striving to detect the moral tendencies of works Jeffrey was not dealing with the sentiments to be found on the surface of writing. " To have perceived the value of this ethical criticism," Gates wrote, " to have practised it skilfully, and to have fostered a taste for it, these are true claims to distinction ; and Jeffrey's services in these directions have been too often forgotten." [1] It will be plain that I think this just. As has been hinted, however, it seems to me that Gates's criticism of Jeffrey was strongly influenced by the sense of security that characterised the men of the later nineteenth century, and by the disposition, which accompanied that sense of security, to see all history as a story with a happy ending in their own fortunate time. " Beyond the pseudo-classical point of view," Gates wrote for example, " Jeffrey had passed, just as certainly as he had never reached the Romantic point of view." [2] It appears to be taken for granted in that sentence that the journey to romanticism was a travelling up the hill of progress. But Jeffrey maintained throughout the whole of his critical career that that path led downward. His arguments of a lifetime were brushed aside by a single metaphor. We perceive the same tendency in the assumption that the men of the late nineteenth century had arrived at an " interpretation " of the romantic age which Jeffrey was incapable of discovering. " He was," Gates claimed for Jeffrey, "among the earliest English critics to see the importance for the study of literature of the historical point of view and to take into close account, in the study of an author

---

[1] *Selections*, p. xxvi. [2] *Three Studies*, pp. 18-19.

or of a whole literature, the social environment ; " and Gates
drew attention to passages in which Jeffrey employed this
method.[1] " Despite, however," Gates wrote, " his clear perception of the principles on which the use of the historical method
rests, Jeffrey is never to be trusted to make intelligent and
effective use of the method, or to be faithful to the point of view
it presupposes." [2] Gates was certainly entitled both to discuss
Jeffrey's criticism from any angle he pleased, and to speak of
the historical method in criticism as superior to Jeffrey's if that
was his opinion. But there is a difference between this and
describing Jeffrey as " never to be trusted " to be faithful to a
viewpoint that was not his own. Jeffrey's occasional resort to
the historical method may be further evidence of his acuteness ;
but he employed this method only incidentally. " More and
more, since Jeffrey's day," Gates wrote, " criticism has concerned
itself with the scientific explanation and the interpretation of
literature ; less and less has it posed as the ultimate science
of right thinking and right doing in literary art." We may
agree that this is true. But the point is surely that the latter is
what Jeffrey thought criticism should aim at being : it is not
an ignoble conception. " This change," Gates continued, " has
been brought about partly by the Romantic movement with
its fostering of individualism in art, and partly through the
development of historical conceptions in all departments of
thought. Both these forces were in full play during Jeffrey's life,
and of neither did he at all measure the scope or significance." [3]
May it not be held that Jeffrey did in fact measure the significance
of these forces very carefully—by instruments which critics of
the later school threw—rashly, Jeffrey would have argued—out
of their workshop into the lumber-room ? " The greater breadth
of view of later critics," Gates wrote again, " and their surer
appreciation of ethical values should not be allowed to deprive
Jeffrey of his honor as a pioneer in ethical criticism." [4] And
again—" The ethical critic of to-day pushes his analysis far beyond
the point where Jeffrey stopped. Compare with this essay of
Jeffrey's Mr John Morley's essay on *Byron* in his *Critical*

---

[1] *Three Studies*, p. 33 ; *Selections*, p. xxvii. Gates mentioned the articles
on Ford's *Dramatic Works* (*Ed. Rev.*, No. 36, Art. 1 ; *Cont.*, v. 2, p. 38), on
de Staël's *De la Littérature* (*Ed. Rev.*, No. 41, Art. 1 ; *Cont.*, v. 1, p. 79), and
on *Wilhelm Meister* (*Ed. Rev.*, No. 84, Art. 7 ; *Cont.*, v. 1, p. 257).

[2] *Selections*, p. xxviii.   [3] *Three Studies*, p. 38.   [4] *Selections*, pp. xxvi-xxvii.

Miscellanies, vol. 1." [1] The optimistic assertion quoted from that essay in an earlier chapter [2] may suggest one reason why Gates felt his mind in harmony with Morley's. It was hardly to be expected that Morley's essay would be a duplication of Jeffrey's. We remember, however, Jeffrey's warning that when we are striving to cure the ills of one part of the body we may, without knowing it, be paralysing another. It is not easy to perceive in the world of to-day convincing evidence of the steadily-strengthening grip upon ethical values to which Gates referred.

Speaking of Jeffrey's " dogged persecution of Wordsworth "— " It is," Merritt Hughes wrote, " all honest, clear-eyed criticism ; and it all springs from a conviction that Wordsworth was confounding life's plainest distinctions in the mystical mist with which he had surrounded himself for years in the solitude of the Cumberland hills." [3] This, it will be evident, is precisely how the matter has appeared to me. We noted in an earlier chapter Hughes's suggestion that the principle inspiring Jeffrey's criticism might be called " Platonism." " Jeffrey," Hughes wrote, " stands alone as the one man who accepted the final deliverance against poets in the *Republic* in just the way that it was intended to be understood. He never said anything about it, and he may not have been aware that he was a disciple, but his influence and originality as a critic were both due to his loyal faith to Plato's creed. . . . Platonism of this kind is a liberal creed, although it has had a reputation for bigotry in England ever since Gosson invoked it amiss and called down Sidney's classic answer to its Puritan misapplication. From Sidney to Jeffrey it remained in abeyance." [4] In remarking that it " might not be impossible " to prove a Platonic " influence " on Jeffrey, Hughes, I think, strained the evidence. Jeffrey's references to Plato are few and far between.[5] But the parallel is interesting.

---

[1] *Selections,* p. 199.   [2] *Ante,* p. 275.
[3] *Mod. Lang. Rev.,* v. 16 (1921), p. 247   [4] *Ibid.,* v. 16, pp. 244-5.
[5] In Cockburn's selection from Jeffrey's correspondence—the first letter is dated 1789, and the last 1850—I have noticed only three references to Plato (*Life,* v. 2, pp. 29, 295, 335). None of these suggests to me discipleship. I have noticed three allusions to Plato in the *Contributions.* Two (v. 1, pp. 112, 113) are merely passing references. In the third, discussing *The Greater Hippias,* Jeffrey wrote : " There are . . . many marks of that singular incapacity to distinguish between what is absolutely puerile . . . and what is plausible . . . which may be reckoned among the characteristics of ' the divine philosopher.' " (v. 1, pp. 15-16).

" There is no mistake in the *Republic*," Hughes wrote, " about
the cost of its point of view. If truth is not beauty, nor beauty
truth, and you choose truth, you cannot avoid the consequence
that some beauty must be sacrificed, and it is likely to prove
to be the very purest sort of beauty that you must give up, the
sort, that is, which is produced by art whose chief interest is
in its own perfection." " Jeffrey," Hughes remarked however,
" was never quite clear about this point." [1] " The trouble
with Jeffrey," he said, " was that he never thought strenuously
through the problem of the conflict between the ethical requirements of the lives of the people for whom he wrote and the
purpose of the artist struggling to make that union of imagery
and truth which Doctor Johnson said constitutes poetry. The
conflict is one of the differences between the insight of poetry
and the dimness of the ethical level of every day, where conventions, sophistries, and sentimentality are the only guides that
even the best of us can often find." [2] In these last sentences,
it will be observed, Hughes moved completely away from the
Jeffreyan viewpoint. The answer suggested to Hughes is the
same as that suggested to Gates's affirmation that Jeffrey pleaded
for common sense and the commonplace. The fact that
everyone knows the meanings of the words " conventions,
sophistries, and sentimentality " shows that the everyday vision
of ordinary people perceives these to be inefficient guides.
Jeffrey refused to believe that any individual poet, however
eminent, had insight deeper than that of mankind's general
common sense. It does not appear to me that Jeffrey's thinking
was so imperfect as Hughes suggests. It seems to me that
Hughes himself indicated quite accurately the kind of writing
Jeffrey opposed : it was writing that confounded " life's plainest
distinctions." I agree that Jeffrey did not solve the problem
of the conflict between moral standards of judgment and those
of artistic effectiveness. Neither, I think, has anyone else. It
is a problem the answer to which cannot but tend to change
in different ages and in varying circumstances. But it was a
problem from which Jeffrey never ran away. He carried his
own attempt at a solution to its logical conclusion. A man
may have examined scientifically a hundred philosophies and
himself possess none ; Jeffrey had arrived at a philosophy and
he adhered to it consistently at, as Hughes suggested, whatever

[1] *Mod. Lang. Rev.*, v. 16, p. 247. [2] *Ibid.*, p. 248.

cost. Therein lay, I think, his unusualness—I would not go so far as to say originality—as a critic.

" All that is needed," Thompson wrote, " to understand the point of view of Jeffrey is to understand the Scottish tradition which he inherited from Mackenzie." [1] " All " appears to me a large word in that context. It seems to me that Thompson gave too much prominence to the writer around whom he built his study of eighteenth-century Scotland. But it will be evident, at the same time, that his conclusion comes close to my own. It seems to me that if an " explanation " of this kind has to be given for the shape taken by Jeffrey's thought, mine must be the obvious one suggested by Chasles, by Cockburn, and by Jeffrey himself. A man so devoid of pretence as he was, brought up and spending practically all his days in Scotland, could hardly have failed to be Scottish. It is not suggested that Jeffrey was a nationalist in any narrow sense of the word : he spoke of the Restoration as breaking down the barriers of " our " literary independence, and reducing " us " to the position of a province,[2] ignoring the fact that in 1660 the governments of England and Scotland were not yet united ; he described what Scotsmen now prefer to call the British army as the " English forces " ; [3] he spoke, in his article on the fall of Buonaparte, of " our exultation at the glory of England " ; [3] he referred to the *Review* itself as an " English journal." [4] It is not suggested that Jeffrey was a " typical Scot " : " types " are as purely-theoretical as are purely-personal and purely-universal associations. There was no trace in him of that love of self-dramatisation which was spoken of in an earlier chapter as a Scottish characteristic ; he had none of the author of *Waverley's* interest in Scotland's romantic past. What is suggested is that Jeffrey was right in thinking that all the elements of which his opinions were composed had a national cast, and that a recognition of this does help towards understanding him. His love of argument, the strong ethical trend in him, his delight in poetry of the sort that gives pleasure to ordinary people, were, I think, Scottish. His emphasis on the value of " kind affections " was characteristic of the race whose best-known poet declared that

---

[1] *A Scottish Man of Feeling*, p. 348.
[2] *Cont.*, v. 2, p. 42.
[3] *Ibid.*, v. 3, p. 189.
[4] *Ibid.*, v. 3, p. 228.

" To make a happy fire-side clime
To weans and wife—
That's the true pathos and sublime
Of human life."

The energy and ambition that carried him to simultaneous success in two exacting professions, the caution that caused him to shrink from expecting too much of life and made him suspicious of all extravagance, and the abrupt leap into rashness when the circumstances appeared to justify it that marked his first marriage—the same rashness is evident sometimes in his criticism—were Scottish. So also were the independence of outlook that enabled him to free reviewing from the tyranny of booksellers, and caused him to write in his criticisms what he sincerely thought, irrespective of what anyone might say of them, his love of natural beauty, and especially of the beauty of his own country, and the pressure upon fact that prevented that love from luring him into any recognition of Nature-myth, and prevented the romanticism of his day from dazzling him out of seeing the world as it actually is. Chasles, we remember,

---

[1] Mention may be made here of the essay by Elsner alluded to, *Ante*, p. 17, and of an interesting article on " Lord Jeffrey and Wordsworth," by Joseph M. Beatty, Jr., in the publications of the Modern Language Assn. of America (vol. XXXVIII, 1923, pp. 221-35). Beatty asserted that " Jeffrey was a great reviewer." " In the twentieth century," he said, " age of science and disillusion—not essentially unlike the eighteenth in its intellectual questionings—we no longer condemn Jeffrey without a hearing as a profaner of the temples of the gods." " In an age of sentimental Germanized emotionalism," Beatty wrote, " he [Jeffrey] believed in the reasonableness of intellectual activity." Beatty pointed out, as has been observed here in footnotes, that there is an occasional similarity in outlook between Jeffrey and Irving Babbitt. He made it clear that his paper was " not a brief for rationalistic commonsense " ; it was " simply a statement of Jeffrey's case." I do not find myself in complete agreement with the description of the twentieth century as an age of science and disillusion. The period seems to me characterised still also by sentimental emotionalism. Therein lies one of its greatest dangers. Jeffrey's position does not seem to me precisely describable as one of rationalistic commonsense ; we have seen that he held that humanity's safest guides were " moral impressions." The last statement quoted from Beatty indicates that he occupied the orthodox position on the tower of academic impartiality. But what if we are confronted by modes of thought the outcome of which may be to sweep away critic, tower, academy, and all !

Hughes described Elsner's thesis as devoting " its space to a brilliant analysis of the sources of neo-classic and romantic thought woven into the *Edinburgh* criticism." (Hughes alluded to it as the work of " Herr Reisner."

discussing the *Edinburgh Review*, spoke of the genius of Scottish criticism as eager to control its rival England and to claim the right of legitimate examination. I do not imagine that Scotland was conscious of this. I think, nevertheless, that Chasles indicated a fact. In Jeffrey we have, it seems to me, for the first time— the word, I think, may be risked upon this occasion—the full fearless impact of the Scottish critical genius upon English literature. We observed that Cockburn described the period of Jeffrey's youth as the last purely Scotch age Scotland was destined to see. The Scottish genius did not die. Like its relative, the Scottish language, it has a toughness in it. But I do not think that that impact has ever been so clearly perceptible in criticism again.[1]

It is orthodox in studies of this nature to attempt to estimate the significance of the subject's achievement. Something of this has already been touched upon. We noticed the greatness of Jeffrey's reputation in his own day. We have observed that his work has attracted attention in certain quarters, down to modern times. We have seen what Gates said of his ethical

But he gave the place and date of publication as Berlin, 1908. As these appear on Dr Elsner's thesis, I take it that this is the study that is meant.) Elsner's essay — bibliography and list of Jeffrey's articles, etc. apart — occupies about eighty-five pages. His method was to arrange statements by Jeffrey under headings like "Aufgabe der Kritik," "Grundfragen der Poesie," "Besondere Bemerkungen über den Stil," etc., and to compare and contrast these with statements by other authors whose writings Jeffrey may have read. It does not follow, however, when two men have expressed similar ideas, that the thought of the second was necessarily derived from that of the first. Both may have been simply drawing from the general stock of thinking in the world. The English language played some tricks upon Elsner. He remarked : "Ueber die Rhythmik hat Jeffrey nur wenige Angaben hinterlassen, was durch einen Ausspruch wie : For our part we prefer the prose to the poetry (E.R. xxxIII, 8) leicht erklärich wird." (p. 59). What Jeffrey said will be found *Ante* p. 126. "Wilson," Elsner wrote, "dessen Isle of Palms . . . und City of the Plague . . . von Jeffrey doch günstig rezensiert worden waren, lässt den Shepherd sagen : I hae a great affection and respect for Mr Jeffrey, but why should a real man o' letters like him ? " (p. 86). What the Shepherd said was, ". . . why should a real man o' letters like him . . . suffer ony o' his yelpin curs to bite the heels o' the Shepherd ? " (*Noct. Amb.*, v. 1, pp. 265-6). I cannot but admire, at the same time, the thoroughness with which this young scholar of twenty-five performed the task he had set himself. I have to add that, as my knowledge of German is very small, my acquaintance with Elsner's work has been made possible by a translation furnished by a generous friend, supplemented by struggles with a dictionary.

criticism, and what Hughes said of his originality. We recalled a moment ago what Jeffrey did for the trade of reviewing. Gates remarked that the Reviews that succeeded the *Edinburgh* followed its plan and copied its methods of organisation.[1] (I do not think that Jeffrey would have expected much credit on that score : both were fairly obvious.) Jeffrey claimed in the preface to his *Contributions* that the *Edinburgh* raised the standard and increased the influence of all such occasional writings not only in Britain but also over the greater part of Europe and the free states of America. He stated also that the *Review* " enlarged the capacity, and improved the relish of the growing multitudes to whom such writings were addressed, for ' the stronger meats ' which were then first provided for their digestion." [2] The literary taste that made his citations an anthology of the best passages in contemporary literature, and the provocative gusto and fertility of argument with which he dealt with the literary productions of his day must have induced readers, even when his judgments were adverse, to discuss these productions, and must have assisted, accordingly, in making the works known. " The opinions expressed in the early numbers of the *Edinburgh Review*," Nichol Smith wrote, " have permeated English criticism to an extent not commonly recognized." [3] Even if only the excerpts quoted here from Jeffrey are taken into consideration, they bear out, I think, to a considerable extent, the truth of that statement.

We recollect at the same time Nichol Smith's assertion that Jeffrey was interested in the past only in so far as he saw its bearings on the present. I do not think that had Jeffrey been able to join us in this discussion he would have been impressed by purely historical claims for himself. It seems to me that— looking with his habitual ruthlessness at the exiguous space given to him in modern histories of literature, facing the fact that all that is popularly remembered, out of the many pages filled with keen discussion that he laid before his contemporaries, is, as was remarked on the first page of this study, " This will never do ! " and that that exclamation is generally quoted merely in order to show the greatness of his chief opponent's triumph—he would have said frankly that his influence upon subsequent thought appeared negligible.

This may be accounted for in part by circumstances and

[1] *Three Studies*, pp. 58-9. [2] *Cont.*, v. i, p. xi. [3] *Jeffrey's Lit. Crit.*, p. xxiv.

by Jeffrey's manner of writing. " It may be doubted," Nichol Smith wrote, " if any selection smaller than his own can give an adequate impression of his powers." That statement represents the fact as I have felt it to be. " His work," said Nichol Smith, " . . . is cumulative in effect." [1] That has been also my impression. In an endeavour to interpret his case against his age I have, as has been seen, felt myself obliged to go beyond even the *Contributions*. Had the clues to his thinking been clearly visible in any one essay, or in any small group of essays, this study need not have been written. We agreed that his habit of addressing " the grand jury of public opinion " demanded an effort on the part of his readers which many, in an age accustomed to concise authoritative instruction, might be unwilling to make. The great genius of the men whose ideas he opposed was against Jeffrey. Against him was the bludgeoning method he occasionally employed, and which he helped to make fashionable. Against him also was the change to the scientific and interpretative methods of criticism mentioned by Gates, a change that caused the portion of his criticism on which he laid greatest stress to be regarded as priggish or out-of-date.

But there may be still some of the jury who may find it an interesting exercise to observe the reactions of the man who might be called our first great reviewer to the eminent works of literature that appeared in his day. There may be some who may perceive, as we have noted others have perceived before them, an acuteness in his criticisms that makes these still valuable. Further—Jeffrey, I feel certain, would have considered this most important of all—the portion of common sense which he thought might support his leading ideas may be still in existence in the world. It was suggested earlier that it might seem that romanticism of the nineteenth-century sort could be confined to theatres, to lecture-rooms, and to volumes of poetry. It may appear to some of the jury that this has been proved to be impossible so long as overmuch respect is paid to it even there—that the world has been allowed to slip out of the control of common sense and into that of the romanticists. It may appear to some that, wonderful though the work of the experts has been within the departments, and sometimes very precious to mankind, there is romanticism in

[1] *Jeffrey's Lit. Crit.*, pp. v-vi.

the idea that fashions of thought derived from sciences that are the hothouse growth of a few generations' specialised activity are fit to supersede rules for living derived from the experience of five thousand centuries. Some, recalling a sentence in the Book, may think it sensible for ordinary people, finding themselves in a ditch, to investigate for themselves how it has come about that they have arrived there, and how they may get out of it, instead of waiting tamely to be instructed by others who, despite the guides' badges they have worn, have landed in the ditch beside them. It may appear to some that fear of possible pronouncements that he has gone " astray " and committed " blunders " [1]—which everyone commits—should not be permitted to deter any man from attempting to add to humanity's store of knowledge the particular morsel of imperfect truth that has been revealed to him. Some may be inclined to suggest that the pronouncement that a man went astray should be accompanied by a clear indication of the ditch into which he fell. Some may feel that their instincts are informing them with increasing strength as history unrolls itself that all human achievement is in sober truth as nothing beside the cultivation of charity, that, as Jeffrey put it, generosity of sentiment is the only mental superiority that ought to be admired, that the supremely valid test of every culture, national or individual, is the conduct it produces. Some may agree with the suggestion made in an earlier chapter that the only real safeguard of truth —and scholarship—is the presence in the world of multitudes of jurymen by whom that of which they have not been properly convinced is regarded fearlessly as a " no-thing." It may appear to some that the doctrine that criticism of ideas should be confined to " scientific explanation and . . . interpretation " and never allowed to lapse into moral judgment is based on a romantic illusion that there are beings in the world who can remain permanently observers, unaffected by the forces they are utilising or studying. Ordinary people, evangelists at street-corners trying to make their voices heard above the traffic—simple-minded and little-heeded folk, yet in closer touch, perhaps, because they are unprotected and unsubsidised, with the world as it is than are some of our more imposing instructors

---

[1] " Judged even by present standards, Jeffrey was a notably effective critic ; he made blunders not a few, but he was acute, entertaining, and suggestive, even when he went astray." Gates, *Three Studies*, p. 5.

—have long told us passionately that the principles men and women believe in and act upon involve matters of life and death to them.

It would be un-Jeffreyan to suggest that a wide reintroduction of the emphasis he regarded as supremely important would carry us out of storms into regions of perpetual calm. Yet a twist of a steering wheel may have sometimes important effects.

II

Two criticisms of Jeffrey remain. The first is contained in Millar's *Literary History*. " Defenders," Millar wrote, " may not be wanting for Jeffrey's political opinions, but few, probably, will absolve him of all blame for the needlessly flippant tone which his *Review* habitually adopted in discussing questions of religion." [1] This, it is evident, is a judgment which, substantiated, would cut across a certain amount of our thinking. It is, I imagine, an echo of a charge that was first made against the *Edinburgh* by *Blackwood's* about 1818. It was mentioned in Mrs Gordon's *Memoir* of John Wilson. Wilson's daughter made no attempt to defend the *Magazine*, beyond remarking that the original provocation came from the Whig side, though not from the *Edinburgh* or from Jeffrey. Instead she printed a letter of protest, written by the Rev. Robert Morehead, which she described as " admirable," and another, which she described as " manly and honourable," from Jeffrey himself. " I say, then," Jeffrey wrote to Wilson, " that it is *false* that it is one of the principal objects, or any object at all, of the *Edinburgh Review* to discredit religion, or promote the cause of infidelity. I who have conducted the work for nearly fifteen years should know something of its objects, and I declare to you, upon my honour, that nothing with that tendency has ever been inserted without its being followed with sincere regret both on my part and on that of all who have any permanent connexion with the work. That expressions of a light and indecorous nature have sometimes escaped us in the hurry of composition, and that in exposing the excesses of bigotry and intolerance, a tone of too great levity has been sometimes employed, I am most ready with all humility to acknowledge ; but that anything was ever bespoken or written by the regular supporters of the

[1] *Lit. Hist. of Scotland*, pp. 486-7.

work, or admitted, except by inadvertence, with a view to
discredit the truth of religion, I most positively deny, and that
it is no part of its object to do so, I think must be felt by every
one of its candid readers." [1] These do not strike me as the
words of a man who was willing to see religious matters taken
lightly. "The Christian revelation," Jeffrey wrote in the
Review, "is no doubt the most precious of all Heaven's gifts
to the benighted world." [2] He described Bishop Heber, for whose
character we have observed him express so great admiration,
as a man "looking on all men as the children of one God, on
all Christians as the redeemed of one Saviour, and on all Christian
teachers as fellow-labourers, bound to help and encourage each
other in their arduous and anxious task." [3] Describing in 1844
a walk with his grandchild, "Our talk to-day," he wrote, "was
of the difference between plants and animals, and of the half-life
and volition that were indicated by the former ; and of the
goodness of God, in making flowers so beautiful to the eye, and
us capable of receiving pleasure from their beauty, which the
other animals are not" [4]—which is much simpler than the
Wordsworth-doctrine, but may be as near the truth. *Blackwood's*
in November 1818, while not departing from the general
accusation, spoke of the editor of the *Edinburgh* as "safe in his
genius and his virtue." [5] In the preface to his *Contributions*,
alluding to some heavy imputations that had been publicly
made against him—and with this one I imagine in mind—
"As," Jeffrey wrote, "they never gave me a moment's anxiety
at the time, so I am now contented to refer, for their refutation,
to the tenor of all I have ever written,"—a considerable number
of our extracts are, I think, relevant—"and the testimony of
all to whom I have been personally known." [6] The matter
may, I think, be left there—with the single additional suggestion
that, when criticisms of this kind are repeated, an indication
should be given of the precise evidence upon which they are
based.

The last point may come from ourselves. We have criticised
the philosophies of other men by their fruits. What, it is
legitimate to ask then, were the fruits of Jeffrey's? We have
already the beginnings of an answer. There was, first of all,

---

[1] *Memoir of John Wilson*, p. 213.
[2] *Cont.*, v. 1, p. 725.
[3] *Ibid.*, v. 3, p. 438.
[4] *Life*, Cockburn, v. 2, p. 388.
[5] V. 4, p. 230.
[6] *Cont.*, v. 1, p. xx.

his worldly success, success won by fair and honest exertion. Secondly, there was that gaiety which, as Cockburn testified, neither drudgery nor lack of optimism could extinguish. Cockburn first came to know Jeffrey as they walked home together from a class conducted by Dugald Stewart. " I remember," Cockburn wrote, " being struck with his manner, and delighted by his vivacity and kindness. From that time we were never for a moment estranged." [1] " No one," Cockburn wrote of his friend, " could take a walk . . . with him, without having all his rational and generous tastes confirmed, and a steadier conviction than before, of the dependence of happiness on kindness and duty." [2] We observe the characteristic Jeffreyan doctrine. The first impression made by Jeffrey on Carlyle was that he was " by much the most lovable of all the literary men " Carlyle had seen.[3] Lady Holland spoke of his " candour and sweetness of disposition." [4] Hunt said that Jeffrey " left a charm " on the name of Craigcrook.[5] Thomas Constable referred in his memoir of his father to the " unfailing consideration and the liberal kindliness that were Mr Jeffrey's eminent characteristics." [6] " The flow of his kindness," Macaulay wrote, " is quite inexhaustible " ; and again, speaking of Jeffrey's wife and daughter, they " absolutely idolise him," Macaulay declared, " and I do not wonder at it." Macaulay observed at the same time : " I could not help suspecting him of being very hypochondriac ; for all his late letters to me "— this was written in 1828—" have been filled with lamentations about his various maladies. His wife told me . . . that I must not absolutely rely on all his accounts of his own diseases " [7]— which prevents our being tempted to regard him as too much exempt from ordinary human weaknesses. " He is a person," Hazlitt wrote of Jeffrey, " that no one knows without esteeming." [8] " I can truly say," Brougham declared of Jeffrey in 1841, " that there never in all my life crossed my mind one single unkind feeling respecting him, or indeed any feeling but that of the warmest affection and the most unmingled admiration of his character, believing and knowing him to be as excellent and

[1] *Life*, v. 1, pp. 119-20.   [2] *Ibid.*, v. 1, p. 363.
[3] *Life of Carlyle*, Froude, v. 1, p. 396.
[4] *Memoir of Sydney Smith*, v. 1, p. 83.
[5] *Correspondence of Leigh Hunt*, 1862, v. 2, p. 223.   [6] V. 2, p. 215.
[7] *Life of Macaulay*, Trevelyan, v. 1, pp. 152-3.   [8] *Spirit of the Age*, p. 300.

amiable as he is great in the ordinary, and, as I think, the far less important sense of the word." [1]　We note the Jeffreyan scale of values. " Never," Hugh Miller wrote, " was there a man more thoroughly beloved by his friends." [2]　" No one ever came into close contact with him," said the *Quarterly* in 1852, " either as a private gentleman, as barrister, or as editor, without being impressed with a sense of the real kindliness of his spirit and intentions." [3]

Speaking of his work as an editor, " He directed," Cockburn wrote, " and controlled the elements he presided over with a master's judgment. There was not one of his associates who could have even held these elements together for a single year." He acquired this power, Cockburn said, " by his capacity of discussing almost any subject, in a conciliatory spirit, with almost any author ; by the wisdom with which his authority was exercised ; by the infusion of his personal kindness into his official intercourse ; and his liberal and gentlemanlike demeanour." [4]　We may see there a fruit of his doctrine that men should learn to mix with their fellows. " There is no subject," Hazlitt declared of him, " on which he is not *au fait* : no company in which he is not ready to scatter his pearls for sport." [5]　Cockburn's prose, when he was describing Jeffrey's conversation, turned almost into poetry. " A large man," he wrote, " could scarcely have thrown off Jeffrey's conversational flowers without exposing himself to ridicule. But the liveliness of the deep thoughts, and the flow of the bright expressions, that animated his talk, seemed so natural and appropriate to the figure that uttered them, that they were heard with something of the delight with which the slenderness of the trembling throat, and the quivering of the wings, make us enjoy the strength and clearness of the notes of a little bird." [6]　In Carlyle's *Reminiscences* there is a passage, similarly written, describing an evening at Craigenputtock on which Jeffrey fell to mimicking various kinds of public speakers, and did it, Carlyle said, " with such a felicity, flowing readiness, ingenuity and perfection of imitation as I never saw equalled, and had not given him credit for before. Our cosy little drawing-room," Carlyle exclaimed, " bright-shining, hidden in the lowly wilderness, how beautiful it looked

[1] *Corr. of Macvey Napier*, p. 356.　　[2] *Essays, Historical and Critical*, p. 77.
[3] No. 181, p. 126.　　[4] *Life*, v. 1, p. 302.　　[5] *Spirit of the Age*, p. 298.
[6] *Life*, v. 1, p. 364.

to us, become suddenly as it were a Temple of the Muses."
The performance was rounded off with " the abstruse costive
specimen, which . . . ended in total downbreak, amid peals
of the heartiest laughter from us all." [1]   Wilson dates the incident
1828.[2]   As a critic Jeffrey's reputation was by this time European
and American as well as British.   Eight years before he had
been Lord Rector of the University of Glasgow.   His status in
the legal profession was such that in the next year he was to be
elected Dean of the Faculty of Advocates ;   in 1830 he was to
be appointed Lord Advocate, and in 1834 to be elevated to
the Bench.   He had raised himself to this position out of poverty
as great as was then Carlyle's, and had, in accomplishing this,
solved problems of precisely the kind that Carlyle was then
wrestling with.   At the moment he was still editor of the
Edinburgh, one of its chief writers, and a barrister in the full
tide of practice.   It was in this year, as we have just noticed,
that Macaulay found him complaining, in his letters, of his
diseases : he was probably overworked.[3]   But despite all this
he had remained " light, light "—light enough, that is, and
self-sacrificing enough to journey out into the " wilderness "
in order to try, by such performances, to inject as much pleasure
as he could into the lives of two lonely friends, both of whom
were his juniors by more than twenty years.   " The great
business of Man," Carlyle wrote of Jeffrey in 1830, " he—
intellectually—considers as a worldling does :   *To be happy*.   I
have heard him say :   ' If Folly were the happiest, I would be
a fool.'   Yet his daily Life belies this doctrine, and says :—' Tho'
Goodness were the most wretched, I would be good.' "   " This,"
D. A. Wilson commented, " is delicious.   One can see the
God-like Ariel, as he says this in the drawing-room, looking
through the corner of his eye to see how Carlyle is taking it." [4]
I think that Wilson was in the right of it.   Carlyle did not allow
for the spice of mischief there was in Jeffrey, mischief that had
helped to keep him sane.   But if Carlyle did not perceive all
that might be said for the Jeffreyan attitude to life's problems
he did, as we have seen, perceive much in Jeffrey that he could
admire.   " Yet on the whole," he asserted in the passage in
which he spoke of Jeffrey as too light, " he is about *the best man*
I ever saw . . . I have seen gleams on the face and eyes of the

[1] V. 2, p. 37.   [2] *Carlyle to French Rev.*, p. 69.
[3] See also *Ante*, p. 100.   [4] *Carlyle to French Rev.*, p. 181.

man that let you look into a higher country. God bless him ! " [1]

Wilson remarked that Jeffrey never responded, as John Wilson had done, to Carlyle's curiosity about persons, thus giving the younger man " a practical lesson in the gospel of silence." About some of the attacks in *Blackwood's* Jeffrey said to Carlyle, " I should hate above all things to have any going back upon such matters " [2]—another morsel of instruction in the art of living. " He had," Moncreiff declared, " no jealousies and no antipathies, and neither open spite nor covert detraction could find endurance at his hands, whoever the author and whoever the object of them." [3]

" It is really worth while," Jeffrey said to Horner on one occasion, " to try to make people happy." " He could be absurd enough," Harriet Martineau wrote, " in his devotion to a clever woman ; and he could be highly culpable in drawing out the vanity of a vain one, and then comically making game of it ; "—the mischief again—" but," she went on, " his better nature was always within call ; and his generosity was unimpeachable in every other respect—as far as I knew him. His bounties to needy men of letters,—bounties which did not stop to make ill-timed enquiries about desert,—were so munificent, that the world, which always knew him to be generous, would be amazed at the extent of the munificence : and it was done with so much of not only delicacy but respect,—in such a hearty love of literature, that I quite understand how easy it would be to accept money from him." [4] The remark to Horner was made in a letter in which he asked if his friend could do something for three girls, daughters of " the learned Dr —— of St Andrews," who had gone to London to try their fortunes as dressmakers.[5] There was a similar request in a letter written in 1805, nearly two years earlier, to his brother John. " Her husband speculated," Jeffrey wrote of the woman in this instance, " and was ruined. For the last year they have been penniless ; and the poor girl has subsisted the whole family, in a great measure, by the labour of her own innocent hands ; has maintained an heroic cheerfulness and equality of temper ; and agreed, without murmuring, to accompany her imprudent husband to a strange country, at a distance from all her friends. There is more magnanimity in this than in speaking blank verse and swallowing

---

[1] *Carlyle to French Rev.* p. 182. [2] *Ibid.*, p. 113. [3] *Lord Jeffrey and Craigcrook*, p. 27.
[4] *Autobiography*, v. 1, pp. 315-6. [5] *Life*, Cockburn, v. 2, p. 121.

laudanum." [1] The old doctrine of placing the most important things first ! In 1818, having heard that Hazlitt was in financial trouble, Jeffrey wrote to him saying that a man of genius could not be permitted to suffer in this way. He took " the liberty," therefore, of sending £100 to be repaid in reviews. If a further hundred pounds was required this was " heartily " at Hazlitt's service.[2] In the same year, learning that Moore was in difficulties, Jeffrey asked the poet if it would be " impertinent " in him to say that he had £500 at Moore's service, and as much more that he could advance upon reasonable security of repayment in seven years. No living soul should know of his " presumption " but Moore himself.[3] In 1819 he offered to send Moore " £300, or £500 " through Rogers. He asked that Moore should not be " burdened with the knowledge " of who was his benefactor.[4] In 1826 Moore wrote to Jeffrey to say that he was at his " wit's end " for money and asked if £100 could be advanced to him to be worked out by writing. Jeffrey sent the money instantly, remarking that this was the very thing he had been going to write the poet about, as he had never required the help of a " fine, light hand " like Moore's more than at that moment.[5] In 1830 Jeffrey offered Carlyle an annuity " with a generosity," Froude commented, " the merit of which was only exceeded by the delicacy with which the offer was made." The whole matter, Jeffrey said, would be a secret between them : he would not tell even his wife of it.[6] Wilson, referring to the death of Carlyle's sister, Margaret, in the same year, wrote that Carlyle " poured out his feelings to Jeffrey in a week or two . . . and was comforted as by a father." [7] In September 1830 the dying Hazlitt asked Jeffrey to send him a hundred pounds. As soon as possible after reaching home, Wilson tells us, Jeffrey sent off fifty pounds for Hazlitt's immediate needs, " leaving half the letters waiting him unread to be in time at his banker's." [8] Wilson, speaking of Jeffrey in London in 1833, remarked that, handicapped though he was from sickness, he was soon thanking Carlyle for putting him on seeing Leigh Hunt, whom he visited, came to like, and helped

---

[1] *Life*, Cockburn, v. 2, p. 98.   [2] *Constable and his Lit. Corr.*, v. 2, p. 219.
[3] *Memoirs*, Moore, v. 2, pp. 138-9.   [4] *Life*, Cockburn, v. 1, pp. 257-9.
[5] *Memoirs*, Moore, v. 5, p. 45.
[6] *Life of Carlyle*, Froude, v. 2, pp. 63-4. ; *Carlyle to French Rev.*, p. 138.
[7] *Carlyle to French Rev.*, p. 154.   [8] *Ibid.*, p. 180.

to extricate from debt. "Wherever he passed," Wilson commented, "the 'dainty little spirit' seemed to sweeten the air, like another St Ives, reputed the only lawyer saint in the Church. Let him be called our Protestant lawyer saint—he can bear the comparison." [1]

Of his old age—"He mellowed so sweetly," Cockburn wrote, "that there was no period of his life when he attracted more respect and affection than during its last five years." [2] Mrs Oliphant remarked in her *Literary History of England* that when she had "put forth into the world, in all the inexperience of extreme youth, a modest little novel, this great critic and prince in literature took the trouble to write to the unknown novice, of whose very name he was ignorant, a letter full of the most delicate criticism and fatherly commendation. This," she added, "was only a few weeks before his death, and the hand was already tremulous with weakness which bade the newcomer welcome." [3] On the 4th and 6th of January 1850, Cockburn tells us, "he sent two letters of advice and encouragement, one to Mr Alexander Maclagan of Edinburgh, and one to Mr John Crawford of Alloa, each of whom had presented him with a volume of his poems." [4] He died on the 26th.

"Dear fellow!" Macaulay wrote on hearing of Jeffrey's death, "I loved him as much as it is easy to love a man who belongs to an older generation. And how good, and kind, and generous he was to me!" [5] Dr John Brown wrote to a friend in 1850, "Jeffrey's death would affect you a good deal; me it did a great deal—foolishly. I was under a sort of spell when I met that bright old man." And to another friend at the same time he alluded to Jeffrey as "that divine old man." [6] "A beautiful little man," was Carlyle's valediction to him in the *Reminiscences*—the words were penned in 1867—". . . and a bright island to me and to mine in the sea of things, of whom it is now again mournful and painful to take farewell." [7]

I think it may be said of the man of whom these things were written that he scored a pass-mark in the examination set to him by life.

---

[1] *Carlyle to French Rev.*, p. 314.   [2] *Life.*, v. 1, p. 394.   [3] V. 2, pp. 67-8.
[4] *Life*, v. 1, p. 406.
[5] *Life of Macaulay*, Trevelyan, v. 2, p. 277. Macaulay dedicated his collected essays to Jeffrey.
[6] *Letters of Dr John Brown* (Nelson), pp. 108, 110.   [7] V. 2, p. 66.

III

Jeffrey confessed to the Carlyles on one occasion that if his trade was law his heart was in letters.[1]   On the evening of the day preceding that on which he died he dictated a letter, the last he composed, to the Empsons.   He described how, during portions of the three previous nights, he had lain in a curious state between dreaming and waking, seeing visions of part of a proof-sheet, newspapers, and books.   " I read the ideal copies," he said, " with a good deal of pain and difficulty, owing to the smallness of the type, but with great interest, and, I believe, often for more than an hour at a time ;   forming a judgment of their merits with great freedom and acuteness, and often saying to myself, ' this is very cleverly put, but there is a fallacy in it, for so and so.' " [2]

Jeffrey, we have seen, commenced criticism when he was little more than a child.   He remained a critic, we observe, to the very end.

[1] *Carlyle to French Rev.*, p. 128.   [2] *Life*, Cockburn, v. 1, pp. 407-8.

INDEX

X

RHETORIC AND ENGLISH COMPOSITION

by Sir HERBERT GRIERSON

Some opinions of the first edition

' . . . all that writers could desire. Sir Herbert Grierson, offering a selection of his lectures as Professor of Rhetoric and English Literature at Edinburgh, covers delightfully, with unobtrusive erudition and indisputable judgment, the whole art of persuasion, spoken and written, in the true tradition.'—*Time and Tide.*

' Rhetoric is commonly regarded as a dry subject, like grammar : in Sir Herbert's hands it becomes a fascinating study, full of sympathetic insight, and enlivened every now and then by those shrewd thrusts and homely instances which we have learned to expect from him whatever he writes about.'—*The Scotsman.*

Third Impression.   Crown 8vo.   Price 6s. net

A STUDY OF WORDSWORTH

by J. C. SMITH

Some opinions of the first edition

' But how strange and wonderful a genius he really was, this little book, quite short and yet completely satisfying, makes clear to us. It is the best study of Wordsworth that I have ever read, unpretentious yet most discerning, by a scholar and a man of taste, who has an easy mastery of his subject and a true understanding of what poetry is.'—*The Observer.*

' Well worth reading. It is what such a monograph should be, unpretentious and thorough.'—*The Sunday Times.*

' A young student could not do better than read his Wordsworth with this book as " guide, philosopher and friend." '—*The Scotsman.*

Third Edition.   Crown 8vo.   Price 5s. net

OLIVER AND BOYD, TWEEDDALE COURT, EDINBURGH

STUDIES IN LITERARY MODES

by A. MELVILLE CLARK, M.A., D.Phil.

Studies in Literary Modes is written for those cultured readers who are interested not only in books but in the philosophy of literature and its kinds.

The topics include the following : the problem of supplying historical fiction with convincing details of setting, speech and sentiment ; the art and the morality of the satirist ; a plea for rhetoric against Plato ; the relation of poetry to verse ; the various movements from the Renaissance onwards against rhyme ; Greek and Latin rhyme ; difficulty and ease in poetry and in artistic creation generally ; and the suitability or unsuitability of rhyme for different poetic purposes.

'In this handsome volume Dr Melville Clark has brought together eight critical studies of unusual distinction.'— *The Scotsman.*

'Dr Clark's essays may be described as "bookish" in the best sense of the word. They are the work of a writer with a wide range of scholarship in several languages, and are heavily laden with quotations which are always apt and sometimes illuminating. He wears his learning lightly and is never dull or ponderous. There must be few readers whose culture would not be widened and enriched by the study of these genial and learned discourses.'—*English.*

Demy 8vo.   Price 15s. net

OLIVER AND BOYD, TWEEDDALE COURT, EDINBURGH